A BIG JEWISH BOOK

ALSO BY JEROME ROTHENBERG

New Young German Poets (1959)

White Sun Black Sun (1960)

The Seven Hells of the Jigoku Zoshi (1962)

Sightings I–IX (1964)

American playing version of Hochhuth's *The Deputy* (1965)

The Gorky Poems (1966)

Ritual: A Book of Primitive Rites & Events (1966)

Between: Poems 1960–1963 (1967)

The Flight of Quetzalcoatl (1967)

Conversations (1968)

Poems 1964–1967 (1968)

Gomringer by Rothenberg (1968)

Technicians of the Sacred (1968)

The 17 Horse Songs of Frank Mitchell, *Nos. X–XIII* (1969)

A Book of Testimony (1971)

Poems for the Game of Silence 1960–1970 (1971)

Shaking the Pumpkin (1972)

America a Prophecy (with George Quasha, 1973)

Esther K. Comes to America (1973)

The Cards (1974)

Poland/1931 (1974)

Revolution of the Word (1974)

Seneca Journal I: A Poem of Beavers (1975)

Seneca Journal: Midwinter (1975)

The Pirke and the Pearl (1975)

The Notebooks (1976)

Seneca Journal (1978)

A
BIG
JEWISH
BOOK

Poems & Other Visions of the Jews
from Tribal Times to Present

Edited by
JEROME ROTHENBERG

with
Harris Lenowitz

& with
Charles Doria

ANCHOR BOOKS
ANCHOR PRESS/DOUBLEDAY
GARDEN CITY, NEW YORK
1978

A BIG JEWISH BOOK was originally published in hardcover by
Anchor Press/Doubleday in 1978.

Anchor Books edition: 1978

ISBN: 0-385-02630-7
Copyright © 1978 by Jerome Rothenberg
All Rights Reserved
Printed in the United States of America

BOOK DESIGN BY BENTE HAMANN

GRATEFUL ACKNOWLEDGMENT IS MADE TO THE FOLLOWING FOR PERMISSION TO
REPRINT MATERIAL COPYRIGHT OR CONTROLLED BY THEM:

Barry Alpert for excerpt from interview with David Antin, which first appeared in *Vort 7.* Reprinted by permission.

Yehuda Amichai for "Travels of a Latter-Day Benjamin of Tudela" translated
by Ruth Nevo, which appeared in *Exile,* 1975. Reprinted by permission of
Acum Ltd. "National Thoughts" in *Poems,* translated from the Hebrew by
Assia Gutmann. Copyright © 1968 by Yehuda Amichai. Translation copyright
© 1968, 1969 by Assia Gutmann. Reprinted by permission of Harper & Row,
Publishers, Penguin Books Ltd. Original Hebrew version by permission of
Acum Ltd.

David Antin for "The Black Plague" section, "The Constellation," and Meditations 12;15." Reprinted by permission of the author.

Archaeological Museum, Istanbul, for "The Gezer Calendar Inscription" from
*Inscriptions Reveal: Documents from the Time of the Bible, the Mishna and
the Talmud.* Original in the Archaeological Museum, Istanbul.

Isaac Babel for "The Cemetery at Kozin" from *The Collected Stories,* copyright © 1955 by S. G. Phillips, Inc. Reprinted by permission of the publisher.

Asa Benveniste for "Green," which first appeared in *Tree: 5.* Reprinted by permission of the author.

Carol Bergé for "Double Memory," which first appeared in *Genesis/West.*
Reprinted by permission of the author.

Robert Bly for "Inner Trees" from *Yvan Goll, Poems,* copyright © 1968 by
Robert Bly. Published by Kayak Press. Reprinted by permission of Robert Bly.

William G. Braude, translator, for excerpts from *Pesikta Rabbati,* (Judaic
Series, No. 18). Reprinted by permission of Yale University Press.

Michael Brownstein, for translation of Max Jacob: "1914," which first appeared in *The World* magazine. Translation copyright © 1970 by Michael
Brownstein. Used by permission.

Martin Buber for excerpt from *I and Thou,* translated by Walter Kaufmann.

© 1968 by Allen Ginsberg. Reprinted by permission of City Lights Books. "Jaweh and Allah Battle." Reprinted by permission of the author.

Nahum N. Glatzer, editor, for "Beauty That Withers" and "Torah on Earth" from *Hammer on the Rock: A Midrash Reader,* copyright 1948, © 1962 by Schocken Books Inc. Copyright © renewed 1975 by Schocken Books, Inc. Reprinted by permission of the publisher.

Judah Goldin, editor, for excerpts from *The Fathers According to Rabbi Nathan,* copyright © 1955 by Yale University Press. Reprinted by permission of the publisher.

Erwin R. Goodenough for *Jewish Symbols in the Greco-Roman Period,* Bollingen Series XXXVII. Vol. 2, *The Archeological Evidence From the Diaspora,* copyright 1953 by Princeton University Press. Vol. 9, *Symbolism in the Dura Synagogue* (Text, i), copyright © 1964 by Princeton University Press. Short selections reprinted by permission of the publisher.

Robert Bartlett Haas for "An Elucidation" by Gertrude Stein, from *A Primer for the Gradual Understanding of Gertrude Stein,* copyright © 1971 by Robert Bartlett Haas. Reprinted by permission of Black Sparrow Press.

Richard Grossinger for "Talisman: Star Magic," which appeared in *Io,* issue no. 6, 1969, Ethnoastronomy. Reprinted by permission of Richard Grossinger.

Jack Hirschman for excerpts from "Baraita of Work of Creation," "On the Hebrew Letters" (section 9), which appeared in *Tree: 2,* Summer, 1971. Copyright © 1971 by Jack Hirschman. "Book of the Letter" from *The Path of the Names: Writings by Abraham ben Samuel Abulafia,* translation copyright © 1973 by Bruria Finkel and Jack Hirschman. Published by Tree Books. Excerpts from *The Book of Noah, Hymn: He Promises His Name,* translated by Jack Hirschman, published by Tree Books, 1976. "There Is a Beautiful Maiden Who Has No Eyes," which appeared in *Tree: 3,* Winter 1972. Copyright © 1972 by Jack Hirschman. All selections reprinted by permission of Jack Hirschman.

Irving Howe, editor, for "Poor People" by Rajzel Zychlinska, translated by Lucy S. Dawidowicz and Florence Victor, "Bowery Motifs, I" and "Bowery Motifs, II" by Aleph Katz, translated by James Wright, "Poem" and "Poem" by Peretz Markish, translated by Armand Schwerner, from *A Treasury of Yiddish Poetry,* copyright © 1969 by Irving Howe and Eliezer Greenberg. Reprinted by permission of Holt, Rinehart and Winston, Publishers.

David Ignatow for "The Stranger" from *Poems 1934–1969,* copyright © 1955 by David Ignatow. Reprinted by permission of Wesleyan University Press.

Isidore Isou, for "The Young Girl's Tears" from *La Poesie Lettrisie,* edited by Jean-Paul Curtay. Published by Edition Seghers, 1974.

Edmond Jabès for "The Book of the Absent," part two from *The Book of Questions,* translated by Rosmarie Waldrop. Copyright © 1973 by Rosmarie Waldrop. Reprinted by permission of Wesleyan University Press.

Alexandro Jodorowsky, for excerpt from *El Topo,* Douglas Books, N.Y.

Franz Kafka for passages from *Dearest Father: Stories and Other Writings,* copyright 1954 by Schocken Books Inc. (British edition: *Wedding Preparations in the Country,* translated by Ernst Kaiser and Eithne Wilkins); "Before the Law" from *The Penal Colony,* translated by Willa and Edwin Muir. Copyright 1948 by Schocken Books, Inc. Copyright © renewed 1975 by Schocken Books, Inc. (British edition: *The Penal Settlement*). Reprinted by permission of Schocken Books Inc. and Martin Secker & Warburg Limited.

Aryeh Kaplan for "Vision Event" from *Rabbi Nachman's Wisdom,* copyright © 1973 by Leonard M. Kaplan. Reprinted by permission of Rabbi Aryeh Kaplan.

Alan Kaprow for "Words: An Environment" from *Assemblages, Environment and Happenings,* copyright © 1966 by Alan Kaprow. Reprinted by permission of the author. Published by Harry Abrams.

Milton Kessler and Gerald E. Kadish for "Love Songs and Tomb Songs of Ancient Egypt," appeared in *Alcheringa 5, 1973.* Copyright © 1973 by the Editors and Trustees of Boston University. Reprinted by permission of Milton Kessler and Gerald E. Kadish.

Richard Kostelanetz for "The East Village" from *I Articulations* (Kulchur Fdn., 1974). Copyright © 1974 by Richard Kostelanetz. Reprinted by permission of the author.

Denise Levertov for "Illustrious Ancestors" from *The Jacob's Ladder,* copyright © 1958 by Denise Levertov Goodman. Reprinted by permission of New Directions Publishing Corp. and Laurence Pollinger, Limited.

Baruch Levine for Translation of Ugaritic Text 611: (14 lines) from *In the Presence of the Lord.* Published by Voorheen E. J. Brill, 1974. Reprinted by permission of the publisher.

Jackson Mac Low for "1st Light Poem: for Iris—10 June 1962," from *22 Light Poems,* copyright © 1968 by Jackson Mac Low. Published by Black Sparrow Press. Excerpt from an interview with Jackson Mac Low. Reprinted by permission of the author.

Osip Mandelstam for an extract from "The Stalin Epigram" in *Selected Poems,* English translation copyright © 1973 by Clarence Brown and W. S. Merwin. Reprinted by permission of Atheneum Publishers and Oxford University Press, London.

David Meltzer for "Tohu," first published in *Knots,* copyright © 1971 by David Meltzer. Published by Tree Books. "3rd Shell," which first appeared in *Hero/Lil,* copyright © 1973 by David Meltzer. Published by Black Sparrow Press. "The Golem Wheel," which first appeared in *The Dark Continent,* copyright © 1967 by David Meltzer. Published by Oyez. All selections reprinted by permission of David Meltzer.

Stephen Mitchell, translator, for "Job," which appeared in *Tree: 4.* Reprinted by permission of the translator.

Robert Mezey, translator, for "I Have a Garment" by Abraham Ibn Ezra and "We Were Not Like Dogs" by U. Z. Greenberg from *Poems from the Hebrew.* Copyright © 1973 by Robert Mezey. Reprinted by permission of T. Y. Crowell, U. Z. Greenberg, and Robert Mezey.

L. Nemoy for excerpts from *Karaite Anthology,* copyright 1952 by Yale University Press. Reprinted by permission of the publisher.

H. Odeberg for excerpts from *3 Enoch or Hebrew Book of Enoch.* Reprinted by permission of Cambridge University Press, 1928.

George Oppen for "Semite" and "Exodus" from *Collected Poems,* copyright © 1972, 1974 by George Oppen. Reprinted by permission of New Directions Publishing Corp.

Rochelle Owens, translator, for "Damn the One Damn" by Kalonymos ben Kalonymos. Reprinted and adapted by permission of Rochelle Owens; "The Voluminous Agony of Karl Marx" and Introductory poem "Din" from *I Am the Babe of Joseph Stalin's Daughter,* copyright © 1972 by Rochelle Owens.

Published by Kulchur Press. "Wild Man and the Temptation in the Forest" from *The Joe 82 Creation Poems,* copyright © 1974 by Rochelle Owens. Published by Black Sparrow Press. All selections reprinted by permission of Rochelle Owens.

Raphael Patai for excerpt from *The Hebrew Goddess,* copyright © 1967 by Raphael Patai; excerpts from *Man and Temple,* copyright © 1967 by Raphael Patai. Reprinted by permission of KTAV Publishing Company.

Edgar Pauk, translator, for "The Song of Lilith" by Rossana Ombres from *The Ballad of Noah's Daughter and Other Poems.* Reprinted by permission of the translator.

Robert Payne for extracts from *The Unknown Karl Marx,* copyright © 1971 by Robert Payne. Reprinted by permission of Bertha Klausner International Literary Agent, Inc.

Ezra Pound for "Canto 53" (four lines) from *The Cantos,* copyright 1940 by Ezra Pound. Reprinted by permission of New Directions Publishing Corp. and Faber & Faber, Ltd.

F. T. Prince for excerpt from *Drypoints of the Hasidim.* Reprinted by permission of the Menard Press, London.

George Quasha, editor, for "Apple-Lilith-Night" by Charles Stein from *An Active Anthology.* Copyright © 1974 by George Quasha. Reprinted by permission of Charles Stein.

Burton Raffel and A. Burago for "Nothing Can Be Done for This Night" from *Complete Poetry of Osip Emilevich Mandelstam,* copyright © 1973 by State University of New York Press. Reprinted by permission of State University of New York Press.

Carl Rakosi for "Drinking Song" and "Song" from *Ere-Voice,* copyright © 1971 by Callman Rawley. Reprinted by permission of New Directions Publishing Corp.

Charles Reznikoff for "How difficult for me is Hebrew . . . ," "What are you Doing . . . ," "Palestine Under the Romans," "The Moon Shines . . . ," "From Jehuda Halevi's Songs to Zion," "From the Apocalyptic Ezra" from *By the Waters of Manhattan,* copyright 1927, 1929, 1934, 1936, 1948, 1951, © 1959 by Charles Reznikoff. Reprinted by permission of New Directions Publishing Corp. and Laurence Pollinger, Limited.

Edouard Roditi for "The Conspiracy" from *Emperor of Midnight,* copyright © 1974 by Edouard Roditi. Reprinted by permission of Black Sparrow Press.

David Rosenberg for "Psalm 19," "The Universe Unfolds" in *Blues of the Sky.* Interpreted from the original Hebrew Book of Psalms, copyright © 1976 by David Rosenberg. Reprinted by permission of Harper & Row, Publishers, and Sanford J. Greenburger Associates, Inc.

Roy A. Rosenberg for excerpts from *The Anatomy of God,* copyright © 1973 by Roy A. Rosenberg. Used by permission of KTAV Publishing House, Inc.

Jerome Rothenberg for "Woman's Event" (1–6), "The Murder Inc. Sutra," "Isaac Luria's Hymn to Shekinah for the Feast of the Sabbath, Newly Set Rosh Hashonah 5733" from *Poland/1931,* copyright © 1970, 1974 by Jerome Rothenberg. Reprinted by permission of New Directions Publishing Corp.

Nelly Sachs for "Glowing Enigmas: These Millennia" from *The Seeker & Other Poems,* translated from the German by Ruth and Matthew Mead and Michael Hamburger. Copyright © 1970 by Farrar, Straus & Giroux, Inc.

"If the Prophets Broke In" from *O the Chimneys,* translated from the German by Ruth and Matthew Mead. Copyright © 1967 by Farrar, Straus & Giroux, Inc. Reprinted by permission of Farrar, Straus & Giroux, Inc., and Jonathan Cape, Ltd.

J. A. Sanders, editor, for excerpt from *The Dead Sea Psalms Scroll,* copyright © 1967 by Cornell University. Used by permission of Cornell University Press.

Zalman Schacter for excerpt from "Torah of the Void." Reprinted by permission of the author.

Gershom S. Scholem for "Charm Against Lilith" (Striga) from *Jewish Gnosticism, Merkabah Mysticism and Talmudic Tradition,* copyright © 1960 by Jewish Theological Seminary. Reprinted by permission. *Sabbatai Sevi: The Mystical Messiah,* Bollingen Series XCIII. Copyright © 1973 by Princeton University Press. Prose adaptation from *The Vision of Rabbi Abraham.* Reprinted by permission of Princeton University Press and Routledge & Kegan Paul. Excerpts from *On the Kabbalah and Its Symbolism,* copyright © 1965 by Schocken Books Inc. Reprinted by permission of the publisher. Excerpt from *Kabbalah,* copyright © 1974 by Keter Publishing House, Jerusalem, Ltd.

Howard Schwartz for "The Sacrifice" and "Rabbi Nachman's Dream" from *Midrashim: Collected Jewish Parables,* copyright © 1976 by Howard Schwartz. Published by Menard Press, London. Reprinted by permission of the author.

Armand Schwerner for "Tablet V" from *The Tablets I–XV,* copyright © 1968 by Armand Schwerner. Reprinted by permission of Grossman Publishers. "Prologue in Six Parts," sections II and III; and "Earth" from *Domesday Dictionary.* By permission of Armand Schwerner.

Idries Shah for excerpt from *The Secret Lore of Magic.* Published by arrangement with Citadel Press (a division of Lyle Stuart, Inc.).

Harvey Shapiro for "Time" from *This World,* copyright © 1969 by Harvey Shapiro. Reprinted by permission of Wesleyan University Press.

Isaac Bashevis Singer for "The Faithful" from *Satan in Goray,* copyright © 1955 by Isaac Bashevis Singer. Reprinted by permission of Farrar, Straus & Giroux, Inc., and Jonathan Cape, Ltd.

David Slabotsky for "The Mind of Genesis" from *The Mind of Genesis,* copyright © 1975 by David Slabotsky. Published by Valley Editions, Ottawa, Canada. Reprinted by permission of the author.

Herbert Spencer, editor, for selections from *Typographica* (new series, no. 16). Published by Lund Humphries, London. Reprinted by permission.

Shalom Spiegel for excerpt from *The Last Trial,* copyright © 1967 by Shalom Spiegel. Reprinted by permission of Pantheon Books, a division of Random House, Inc.

Gertrude Stein for excerpts from *Bee Time Vine and Other Pieces,* copyright 1953 by Alice B. Toklas. Reprinted by permission of Yale University Press.

Arlene Stone for "The Initiation" and "The Vigil" from *The Shule of Jehovah.* Published by Emmanuel Press. Reprinted by permission of the author.

James Strachey, translator and editor, for excerpt from *The Interpretation of Dreams* by Sigmund Freud. Published by Basic Books, Inc., by arrangement with George Allen & Unwin Ltd. and The Hogarth Press, Ltd.

The Sumac Press for "In the Mountain of the Song That Shows" by R. Jodorowsky, translated by Dan Gerber in *An Active Anthology,* edited by George Quasha. Reprinted by permission of the publisher.

Nathaniel Tarn for "Section: The Invisible Bride: VII" and "Section: The Kitchen (1): The Need for Writers" from *Lyrics for the Bride of God,* copyright © 1975 by Nathaniel Tarn. Reprinted by permission of New Directions Publishing Corp.

Joshua Trachtenberg for passage from *Jewish Magic and Superstition: A Study in Folk Tradition.* Copyright 1939 by Behrman's Jewish Book House, Inc. Reprinted by permission.

Tristan Tzara for "Angel" from *Oeuvres Complètes,* vol. I, translated by Pierre Joris. Copyright © 1975 by Flammarion. Reprinted by permission of Flammarion and Pierre Joris. "Tristan Tzara," translated by David Ball, reprinted from *The World.* Reprinted by permission of Flammarion and David Ball.

Rosmarie Waldrop, translator, for "The Disappearance" from *Elya* by Edmond Jabès. Published by Tree Books. Reprinted by permission of the translator.

Hannah Weiner for excerpt from "The Retreat," which appeared in *Clairvoyant Journal,* 1974. Reprinted by permission of the author.

Ruth Whitman, editor and translator, for "Cadenza and What We Can Learn from His Death" and "Good Night, World" from *The Selected Poems of Jacob Glatstein,* copyright © 1972 by Ruth Whitman. Published by October House. Reprinted by permission of Ruth Whitman.

Yigael Yadin for passim lines of poetry from *Bar-Kokhba,* copyright © 1971 by Yigael Yadin. Reprinted by permission of Random House, Inc., and George Weidenfeld & Nicholson, Ltd.

Karl Young for three selections from *Cried & Measured,* copyright © 1977 by Karl Young. Published by Tree Books. Reprinted by permission.

Louis Zukofsky for excerpts from *Bottom: On Shakespeare,* copyright © 1963 by Celia Zukofsky and Louis Zukofsky. Published by The Ark Press for the Humanities Research Center, University of Texas Press. Reprinted by permission of the author. Selections from *All: The Collected Short Poems, 1956–1964,* copyright © 1966 by Louis Zukofsky. Reprinted by permission of W. W. Norton & Company, Inc., and Jonathan Cape, Ltd.

Illustrations:

"Additional Meanings: 46 = Chaos" by Karen Shaw from the collection of Seth Kahn. Reproduced courtesy of Seth Kahn.

Plate 20 from *Aramaic Incantation Texts from Nippur* by J. A. Montgomery and Babylonian Cursive Script on the Incantation Bowl. Courtesy of the University Museum, University of Pennsylvania.

"Image on the Wall" by Wallace Berman, *Tree 5.* Reproduced by permission of Shirley Berman.

"Le Coeur à Gaz" and "Calligram" from *Oeuvres Complètes,* vol. I, 1975, by Tristan Tzara. Copyright © 1975 by Flammarion. Reproduced by permission of Flammarion.

Hebrew Amulet, courtesy of Hebrew Union College–Jewish Institute of Religion Library, Cincinnati.

Roger Welch and Herbert Lieberman for illustration and excerpt from "Ginivishov, Poland—1885," which appeared in *Big Deal ⚡3.* Reprinted by permission.

Illustration accompanying "Hidden Sacred Book of Moses" reproduced courtesy of Charles Doria.

Photos by Robert McElroy and "Words: An Environment" from *Assemblages, Environment and Happenings* by Allan Kaprow. Copyright © 1966 by Allan Kaprow. Published by Harry Abrams.

"Scroll of Esther as a Bear," reproduced from *Jewish Symbols in the Greco-Roman Period,* Bollingen Press, by permission Princeton University Press.

Judith Malina and Julian Beck for chart and excerpts from *Paradise Now: Collective Creation of the Living Theatre,* copyright © 1971 by Judith Malina and Julian Beck. Reprinted by permission of Random House, Inc., and the authors.

In memory of
Morris Rothenberg & Bernard S. Lenowitz
fathers & teachers

Rabbi Eliezer said
        "prayer 'fixed'?
        "his supplication bears no fruit

. . . .

the question next came up: what
        is FIXED?
Rabba & Rabbi Yosef answered
        "whatever blocks the will
        "to MAKE IT NEW

                        (Talmud)

Contents

THE VISIONS

THE WRITINGS

Pre-Face

1

There was a dream that came before the book, & I might as well tell it. I was in a house identified by someone as THE HOUSE OF JEWS, where there were many friends gathered, maybe everyone I knew. Whether they were Jews or not was unimportant: I was & because I was I had to lead them through it. But we were halted at the entrance to a room, not a room really, more like a great black hole in space. I was frightened & exhilarated, both at once, but like the others I held back before that darkness. The question came to be the room's name, as if to give the room a *name* would open it. I knew that, & I strained my eyes & body to get near the room, where I could feel, as though a voice was whispering to me, creation going on inside it. And I said that it was called CREATION.

I now recognize that dream as central to my life, an event & mystery that has dogged me from the start. I know that there are other mysteries—for others, or for myself at other times, more central—& that they may or may not be the same. But CREATION— *poesis* writ large—appeared to me first in that house, for I was aware then, & even more so now, that there are Jewish mysteries that one confronts in a place no less dangerous or real than that abyss of the Aztecs:

> . . . a difficult, a dangerous place, a deathly place: it is dark, it is light . . .

& with a sense too that this space must be bridged, this door opened as well—the door made just for you, says the guardian in Kafka's story. Yet Kafka, like so many of us, poses the other question also: "What have I in common with Jews? I have hardly anything in common with myself. . . ."

For myself it had suddenly seemed possible—this was in 1966 or '67 & I was finishing *Technicians of the Sacred*—to break into that other place, "my own . . . a world of Jewish mystics, thieves, & madmen." From that point on, it opened up in stages. Images, once general & without particular names, now had identified themselves. I let my mind—& the words of others, for I had learned as well to collage & assemble—work out its vision of "fantastic life," as Robert Duncan had called it for all poetry: an image in this instance of some supreme yiddish surrealist vaudeville I could set in motion. With those poems (*Poland/1931*) I made a small entry, American & eastern European; yet something had dropped away, so that it was now possible to be "in common with myself," to experience the mystery of naming, like the thrill & terror of my Jewish dream.

Still the event wasn't "mine" but part of a process of recovery in our time, of the "long forbidden voices" invoked by Whitman over a century ago, the "symposium of the whole" set forth in Duncan's "rites," now pulling all our impulses together:

> . . . The female, the proletariat, the foreign; the animal and vegetative; the unconscious and the unknown; the criminal and failure—all that has been outcast and vagabond must return to be admitted in the creation of what we consider we are. (R.D.)

And the Jew too among the "old excluded orders," not in the name of "the incomparable nation or race, the incomparable Jehovah in the shape of a man, the incomparable Book or Vision," but come into "the dream of everyone, everywhere." A primal people, then, as instance of those cultures of the old worlds, built through centuries of preparation, not to be repeated, whose universality arises, like all others, from its own locations, its particulars in space & time.

The work of many, poets & others, has gone into that process, both inventing & re-inventing—the Jewish side of which turns up for us in contemporaries like Celan, Hirschman, Jabès, Meltzer, Owens, Tarn, as well as others, friends or enemies, who struggle with that Jewish daemon, force us to renew, to make again, the statement of the great refusal. Jewish, human at the core.

2

The work, as set out here, includes both terms: the Jewish & the human. In that second, larger frame—of which the first is, for myself, a central & sufficient instance—the matters that touch on the "recovery" are, first, the idea of *poesis* as a primary human process; second, the primacy of the "oral tradition" in *poesis;* third, the re-invigoration of the bond between ourselves & other living beings; fourth, the exploration of a common ground for "history" & "dream-time" (myth); & fifth, the "re-invention of human liberty" (S. Diamond) in the shadow of the total state.[1] These are the keys to any "modernism" still worth its salt. And they are the keys also to the oldest poetry we know: that of the shaman-poets, "technicians of the sacred," whose visionary use of song & speech had its roots, by every mark we've learned to read, back into the Old Stone Age. And it was just this poetry, this language-of-vision in a culture that was commualistic, anarchic, & egalitarian, that the newer city-states tried to destroy, no less in Judaea—where the cry was "thou shalt not suffer a shaman to live"—than in other civilizations throughout the world.

The poet, if he knows his sources in the "sacred actions" of the early shamans, suffers anew the pain of their destruction. In place of a primitive "order of custom," he confronts the "stony law" & "cruel commands" Blake wrote of—"the hand of jealousy among the flaming hair." Still he confirms, with Gary Snyder, the presence of a

---

[1] By *poesis* I mean a language process, a "sacred action" (A. Breton) by which a human being creates & re-creates the circumstances & experiences of a *real* world, even where such circumstances may be rationalized otherwise as "contrary to fact." It is what happens, e.g., when the Cuna Indian shaman of Panama "enters"—as a landscape "peopled with fantastic monsters & dangerous animals"—the uterus of a woman suffering in childbirth & relates his journey & his struggle, providing her, as Lévi-Strauss tells it, "with a language by means of which unexpressed or otherwise inexpressible psychic states can be immediately expressed." This "power of the word," while often denied or reduced to posturings or lies in the "higher" civilizations, has continued as a tradition among poets & others who feel a need to "express the inexpressible" (see below, page 4)—a belief in what William Blake called "double vision" or, in Lévi-Strauss's paraphrasing of Rimbaud, that " 'metaphor' can change the world."

"Great Subculture . . . of illuminati" within the higher civilizations, an alternative tradition or series of traditions hidden sometimes at the heart of the established order, & a poetry grudgingly granted its "license" to resist. No minor channel, it is the poetic *mainstream* that he finds here: magic, myth, & dream; earth, nature, orgy, love; the female presence the Jewish poets named Shekinah.

In the Jewish instance—as my own "main main"—I can now see, no longer faintly, a tradition of *poesis* that goes from the interdicted shamans (= witches, sorcerers, etc., in the English Bible) to the prophets & apocalyptists (later "seers" who denied their sources in their shaman predecessors) & from there to the merkaba & kabbala mystics, on the right hand, & the gnostic heretics & nihilist messiahs, on the left.[2] But I don't equate it with mysticism *per se* ("which appears to love a mystery as much outside as it does in," writes Charles Olson), rather prize it in every breakthrough of "poetic mind"—that drive to *make it new* (E. Pound), to pit the old transformative ways of thought against the other, intervening drive toward an authoritative written text &, what confronts us once again, the reduction of particulars to what has become the monoculture. I would expect it, as much as anywhere else, in the secular poets of our own time, even or most particularly those who resemble what Gershom Scholem calls "nihilist mystics," for whom "all authority is rejected in the name of mystical experience or illumination" & who leap, like Rimbaud's seer-poet "into the unknown"—the "cauldron" Scholem names it, place of "promiscuity," etc., "in which the freedom of living things is born." Separated from mysticism, *poesis* persists as process, as preparation: it is evolving, contradictory, not fixed or rigid but "with an infinite capacity for taking on new forms." The poet meets the mystic where "their end, their aim"—wrote Moses Porges, 1794—"is liberation from spiritual & political oppression."

Now, all of this I would have stressed in any approach to the development of *poesis* in the "West"—an area I deliberately avoided

[2] This follows roughly the stages (torah, mishna, kabbala, magic & folklore, etc.) by which the "oral tradition" ("torah of the mouth") was narrowed & superseded by the written. But not without resistance; says the *Zohar:* "The Voice should never be separated from the Utterance, & he who separates them becomes dumb &, being bereft of speech, returns to dust." An ongoing concern here.

when I was compiling *Technicians of the Sacred*. Before coming to the idea of "a big Jewish book," I had in fact played with the possibility of a pan-European gathering. But that seemed too diffuse for present purposes, & I thought to speak instead from the Jewish instance, which, through diaspora, would still touch all bases, European & more than European—& from an idea too that the specific & even local circumstances (of which I was certainly a part) provided the most direct line for poetic vision. In its Jewish form, then, I could isolate a series of topics & conflicts, tensions, that were either unique or more developed there than elsewhere, or that were developed with concrete, often "dramatic" particulars that formed a hedge against "abstraction" & mere "objectivity." While most turn up in the texts & commentaries below, there are a few I would stress as those that hold me to the Jewish work:

• a sense of exile both as cosmic principle (exile of God from God, etc.) & as the Jewish fate, experienced as the alienation of group & individual, so that the myth (gnostic or orthodox) is never only symbol but history, experience, as well;

• from which there comes a distancing from nature & from God (infinite, ineffable), but countered in turn by a *poesis* older than the Jews, still based on namings, on an imaging of faces, bodies, powers, a working out of possibilities (but, principally, the female side of God—Shekinah—as Herself in exile) evaded by orthodoxy, now returning to astound us;

• or, projected into language, a sense (in Jabès's phrase) of being "exiled in the word"—a conflict, as I read it, with a text, a web of letters, which can capture, captivate, can force the mind toward abstract pattern or, conversely, toward the framing, raising, of an endless, truly Jewish "book of questions";

• &, finally, the Jews identified as mental rebels, who refuse consensus, thus become—even when bound to their own Law, or in the face of "holocaust," etc.—the model for the Great Refusal to the lie of Church & State.

And it's from such a model—however obscured by intervening degradations from *poesis,* impulse to conform, etc.—that I would understand Marina Tsvetayeva's dictum that "all poets are Jews."

3

If this keeps me attached to the "history of the Jews" & identified with it, I realize too that the terms in which I present it often go beyond what has seemed reasonable to those living within it. Like other peoples with a long history of life under the gun, Jews have tended in their self-presentation (whether to themselves or others) to create an image that would show them in the "best light" & with the least possibility of antagonizing their oppressors. By doing so we have often denied ourselves the assertion of a full & multi-sided humanity, choosing to present an image that was gentle, passive, sensitive, & virtuous, & that in its avoidance of complication tended to deny negative emotions or experiences & to avoid claims to ideas & personalities that our antagonists had staked out as their own. This was further assisted by the circumscriptions of Jewish orthodoxy, with its concept of the single immutable vision & text, & with its hostility to innovators & counter-culturists among its own people. For many Jewish poets & artists, working within a Jewish context came to mean the surrender of claims to the sinister & dangerous sides of existence or to participation in the fullest range of historical human experience. In the process many came to confuse the defensive or idealized image with the historical & to forget that the actual history of the Jews was as rich in powers & contradictions as that of the surrounding nations.

Once into this book, it also seemed to me that much that I had taken for granted about the Jewish past—& present—no longer held up. Since such discoveries influenced my further work, even as I made them, I think I should present some of them here—or present them (for economy) along with a series of statements on the sources & boundaries of this book.

As supreme wanderers—even before & after the forced disaspora —the Jews' historical & geographical range has been extraordinary. To map this in "a big Jewish book," I have included works from the ancient Jewish languages—Hebrew & Aramaic—& from those like Yiddish & Ladino developed in the course of exile, as well as from other languages (Greek, Spanish, Arabic, German, English, Persian, French, etc.) used by Jews in biblical & post-biblical times. But I have been impressed as well by the continuity of a specifically

Hebrew poetry which, far from being stifled in the aftermath of "Bible," has produced a series of new forms & visualizations, the diversity of which is in itself a matter of much wonder.[3]

Alongside this continuity, there are three turning points in the history of Jewish consciousness that I would stress here:

• a shift, early along, from both the older shamanism & the general pattern of ancient Near Eastern religion to the centralized & gradually dominant monotheism of the Priests & Prophets;

• a series of changes around the time of Jesus (but really from a century or two before to a century or two after), in which the Jews—as a *large* & mobile population,[4] scattered throughout the Mediterranean & maintaining an active poetic & religious tradition in both Hebrew & Greek—generated a number of conflicting movements: christian & gnostic on the one hand, rabbinic, messianic, & kabbalistic on the other;

• with the triumph of Church & Synagogue, the entry of Jewish consciousness into an extraordinary subterranean existence that would erupt later in a series of libertarian movements: within a Jewish frame, the 17th- & 18th-century Sabbateans & Frankists, 20th-century Zionists, etc., & outside it the critical role of Jews & ex-Jews in revolutionary politics (Marx, Trotsky, etc.) & avant garde poetics (Tzara, Kafka, Stein, etc.).

Work for this book has accordingly been drawn from both "sacred" & "secular" sources, with the link between them *my* stress on a poetic/visionary continuum & on the mystical & magical side of the Jewish tradition. And since poetry, in the consensus of my contemporaries, is more concerned with the "free play of the imag-

[3] A reconsideration of that continuity in a more chronological order than my own can be found in T. Carmi's anthology of Hebrew poetry (Penguin Books), itself in preparation at this writing.

[4] Recent estimates for the 1st century B.C. set the Jewish population as high as 8 million, thus 6–9% of the Roman Empire, 20% of the eastern provinces, 33% of Alexandria, etc. (Michael Grant, *The Jews in the Roman World,* page 60, plus relevant sections in Louis Finkelstein, *The Jews: Their History, Culture, & Religion.*) And prior to their later defeat & subjection, the Jews were also heavily into conversion—both full & partial—& "almost uniquely among the subjects′of Rome . . . were still producing an extensive literature of their own." (M. Grant.)

ination" than with doctrinal certainties *per se,* I've made no attempt to establish an "orthodox" line or to isolate any one strain as purer or more purely Jewish than any others. Instead my assumption has been that poetry, here as elsewhere, is an inherently impure activity of individuals creating reality from all conditions & influences at hand.

Concretely this non-doctrinal approach has called for attention to sources like the following, many not usually found in such a gathering:

• tribal & polytheistic remnants, like the battle of Yahveh & the Sea Serpent, the story of Lilith, the accounts of the Sons of God, even Ugaritic (Canaanite) narratives of Baal & Ashera, etc.;

• non-canonical & "heretical" texts, viewed as a subterranean continuation of the earlier traditions—but principally celestial spirit journeys & power dreams in the work of merkaba & apocalyptic visionaries; this includes both acknowedged apocrypha (4th Book of Ezra, Book of Enoch, etc.) & more heterodox texts like *Sefer ha-Hekhalot* (Book of Palaces), "The War of the Sons of Light against the Sons of Darkness" from the Dead Sea Scrolls, etc.;

• visionary poetry of early Jewish Christians & Gnostics, including New Testament works like the Book of Revelation, & gnostic ones like the "Round Dance of Jesus" in the Acts of Saint John or those of messianic figures like Simon Magus, etc.; also anti-christian writings like the *Toldot Yeshu* counter-gospel;

• kabbala, as the last great oral (thus: secret, whispered) tradition of ancient Judaism, leading from 2nd-century mystics like Simeon bar Yohai & Ishmael ben Elisha to the *Zohar* of Moses de Leon, the discourses & mystic hymns of Isaac Luria, the "abstract" graphics of Abulafia & Cordovero, the later messianic heresies of Sabbatai Zevi & Jacob Frank, etc.;

• the Jewish magical tradition, in all its manifestations, as a poetry of naming & invocation: ancient texts like the 3rd-century *Sefer ha-Razim* (Book of Mysteries), magical texts in the recognized kabbala & in "spurious" classical & medieval works like the "Book of Moses on the Secret Name," & later oral & folkloristic traditions in Hebrew, Yiddish, Arabic, etc.;

• the poetry of Jewish groups outside the European &/or rabbinical "mainstream": Essenes, Samaritans, Karaites, Falashas, Chinese Jews, etc.;

• previously downgraded figures like the medieval *paytanim,* liturgical poets whose poems (*piyutim*) have remained in prayer books but long been ignored or ridiculed in favor of the more literary & "classical" Hebrew poets of Spain, etc., though many of the latter are shown as well;

• Jewish poems whose forms are derived from other literary traditions, like the Hellenistic *Eisagoge* ("tragedy of Moses") by the tragic poet Ezekielos, or medieval Jewish narratives & epics;

• the work of later Jewish poets, even where it develops into an apparently "anti-Jewish" point of view. (Here the proliferation in our time & place of the Jewish side of *poesis* is itself a point worth making—not only as theme [ancestral poetry, etc.] but in the energy of a large number of poets [Stein, Zukofsky, Ginsberg, Mac Low, etc.] who have been central to the "real work of modern man: to uncover the inner structure & actual boundaries of the mind" [G. Snyder]).

While such sources show some of the ways in which I've tried to break new ground, most of the older matter in the book has in fact been drawn from the generally accepted literature (Bible, Mishna, Talmud, Zohar, etc.) & from poets for whom the problem of "identity" probably never arose. But even here my intention was to stress process over the mere re-statement of earlier ideas (the poem not as a " 'fit' but a unification of experience"—William Carlos Williams) & to return to a sense of the original moment, renewing the poetic event by all means of interpretation (translation) at my disposal. Thus, visionary & dream accounts in the prophetic books (Daniel, Ezekiel, etc.) have been retranslated to emphasize the immediate experience, or the very ancient Song of Deborah has been treated as an oral performance piece or re-enactment by a poet-singer who assumes a range of roles & voices. And, as much here as elsewhere, I have tried to show the many sides of Jewish experience, including instances (e.g., the gloating over Sisra's death in "Deborah," etc.) that went against my grain but revealed some part of the reality.

As in *Technicians of the Sacred,* I have also worked by analogy with contemporary forms of poetry & art, to isolate structures not usually included in the conventional anthologies or not thought of as poetry *per se.* The most striking of these are the many types of language happenings that form the "mantric" base of traditional Jewish mysticism & kabbala: "masoretic" visual poems; word-events used in the transformation of older texts &/or in the creation & discovery of the names of God; sound-poems arising from that process or in the wordless chanting of religious celebrants, etc. In addition, various ritual forms have been treated, where relevant, in the manner of intermedia events & happenings, & because of the book's range ("from tribal times to *present"*) have been presented alongside contemporary artists & poets like Kaprow, Mac Low, the Living Theatre, etc. Such inclusions have re-enforced my sense that both a contemporary critique of "civilization" & a concern with experimental, often non-ikonic forms of language have a particular resonance & an actual history within the Jewish context.

4

I have seen the work of this book as itself an act of *poesis:* the creation—from all conceivable sources & attempts at definition—of "a big Jewish book," a composition & collage that would project my vision of the Jewish mysteries. That intention has determined the structure of the book as a whole. In brief, then, my first decision as to structure was to stress idea over author, or, by a non-chronological arrangement, to play up the relationship between older work & very contemporary developments in poetry, particularly those practiced in the U.S. over the past few decades. (I would have done the same for any work with such a time-scale.) The model for the present gathering is in fact the "big Jewish book" par excellence, the *Bible:* an anthology (some, even in that instance, would say "collage") whose common name in Hebrew (*TaNaKh*) is an acronym based on its three traditional divisions: *Torah* (or "Law"), *Neviim* (or "Prophets"), & *Khtuvim* (or "Writings"). With this in mind I worked out a similar three-part structure into Ways, Visions, & Writings, & a movement from myth to history to language & poetics *per se.*

Thus, the opening, *Ways* (a designation derived from the equation by the Chinese Jews in K'ai-fêng of torah & tao—plus my own urge toward the plural), begins with a "Book of Powers" that explores both old & new attempts to name & describe the "unnameable" & "ineffable" god of the traditional religion, as well as the other beings & domiciles associated with that ancient reality concept; & it moves in its second part to a "Book of Worlds," or the attempts to give an image to the process of creation & the phenomena it generates. (These two "books" correspond to the "Work of the Chariot" & the "Work of Creation" of the merkaba mystics.)

The second major section, *Visions,* moves from "myth" to "history" & plays between visionary experience in its dream-time aspects & visionary experience as the attempt to locate or to re-locate ourselves in space & time. It is again divided into two "books": an older section or "Book of *Beards"* (the literal Hebrew word for Patriarchs or Elders), whose order of events, though not of composition, goes from mythic Adam to the first openings & losses in the time of Jesus; & a later section called "A Book of the Wars of Yahveh," in which the theme of exile (seen cosmically in "Powers" & "Worlds") takes on a desperate new meaning in the life of individual & nation, & in which the implied hero is the dangerous messiah-poet (Jesus is only the best-known instance) who asserts the possibilities of freedom in a world of "cruel commands" & spiritual withdrawals.

The final major division of the book, *Writings,* continues much of this imagery, etc., but here the focus is on the forms of both the written & spoken language in a culture presumably dominated by "the book" yet permeated as well by the idea of an oral tradition that underlies & brings the written word to life. To explore this even minimally a two-part division again seemed necessary, into a "Book of Extensions" (the recovery of forms of language & "language happenings" that our conventional poetics has long ignored) & a "Book of Writings," in which, for the only time in these pages, a chronological approach by author is used to reveal highlights of Jewish *poesis* from the time of the Gezer Calendar (10th century B.C.) to the work of contemporaries from the generations immediately preceding my own. The final "book" is further divided into four numbered sections: ancient, medieval, oral (& therefore not straight chronological), & "modern." The last of these concludes with American poets of the age of Zukofsky & Reznikoff, & European poets like Jabès & Celan, most of whom are a decade or two my seniors. (The presence of more recent contemporaries is felt as a kind of commentary-by-juxtaposition throughout the book.)

In addition I have used a variety of "commentaries" in a more extensive & often more personal way than in my previous gatherings. Thus four of the six "books"—all but "Wars of Yahveh" & "A Book of Writings"—have running commentaries of some sort, & the first three "books" also include a number of sections subtitled "from the notebooks," which are my own inside takes on the matters at hand. I have tried to be judicious in the use of all of these, eliminating or depersonalizing them as the poems or sections seemed to demand. And along with the "commentaries"—& the dates & languages included in the titling of each poem, plus the principal translators' names (or, in my case & those of Lenowitz & Doria, initials) at the conclusion of each translated text—I have appended a final section of notes on "sources, etc," not only to identify where the material comes from but to keep the process of commentary & collage going until the very end. I suppose, finally, that this tendency to uninterrupted discourse is itself a part of the Jewish "oral tradition": a tradition which, at its best, recognizes the double origins of *poesis* in song & speech, its survival to address a silent God & universe.

5

Regarding some of the restrictions or ground rules under which I've chosen to work, I have limited the anthology as such to poets who fall, by various definitions, within a Jewish grouping, though I've kept no such sense of boundary in translations, commentaries, notes, & pre-face. Obviously, too, there are omissions that could have been avoided in a more biographical, less mythic anthology, where I might have shown, for example, a large number of Yiddish & contemporary Hebrew poets & made an even greater representation of Jewish poets who participated in the proliferation of American poetry in my own generation.[5] And if I have inevitably played

[5] The reader might here consult Larry Fagin's poem "Our Crowd" (c. 1970), which is a listing of 52 poets' names as "works by N.Y. Jews," among them:

up "Jewish" themes in the book—though not always, I hope, the ones expected—I haven't done so invariably, since my understanding is that the poets so defined, particularly the recent ones, have been as free to range apart from the concerns of ethnicity, etc. as poets elsewhere.

While selection & commentary have been my own responsibility, I have been aided throughout by the advice & knowledge of Harris Lenowitz, without whom the work could neither have been undertaken nor completed. Principally Lenowitz has been my guide to Hebrew & Aramaic &, in a few necessary instances, Ugaritic. A formidable translator & a poet in his own right (*vide* the range of Semitic translations in *Origins,* the book of ancient Near Eastern cosmogonies he co-authored with Charles Doria), he has not only made major new translations on his own (Jacob Frank's "Sayings of the Lord," Gabirol's "Crown of Kingdom," etc.) but has joined me in a series of co-translations & discoveries that hopefully have brought us back to word-at-source. For myself that confrontation with the Hebrew language has been a deeply exhilarating experience—for the history of the Jews is also the history of a language; but beyond that, I have been moved by Lenowitz's own devotion to the traditions & mysteries it both hides & opens to us. His presence here is in no real sense secondary to my own.

I've been fortunate also to have benefited from Charles Doria's attention to the often neglected Greek & Hellenistic side of Jewish *poesis:* a process he has carried forward from his earlier work in

---

Tuli Kupferberg, Allen Ginsberg, Lewis Warsh, Jonathan Cott, Larry Fagin, Peter Orlovsky, Kenneth Koch, Allen Katzman, Norman Mailer, Joel Oppenheimer, Carol Bergé, Sandra Hochman, Chuck Stein, Lewis MacAdams, Kenward Elmslie, Ruth Krauss, Michael Benedikt, Denise Levertov, Ted Greenwald, & Edward Dahlberg. (L. Fagin, *Rhymes of a Jerk,* 1974.) Others not listed but occupying roughly the same terrain include David Antin, Eleanor Antin, Kathy Acker, Harvey Bialy, Edward Field, Ed Friedman, Michael Heller, David Ignatow, Richard Kostelanetz, Frank Kuenstler, Jackson Mac Low, Leonard Neufeld, Joachim Neugroschel, Toby Olson (by conversion), Rochelle Owens, George Quasha, Rochelle Ratner, Charles Reznikoff, Carol Rubenstein, Muriel Rukeyser, Armand Schwerner, Harvey Shapiro, Susan Sherman, Nathaniel Tarn, Robert Vas Dias, Louis Zukofsky, & the present author. While the surrounding poetic context for most is scarcely Jewish or "Jewish-dominated"—& the "jewishness" in some cases emphatically rejected as such— the source of energy suggested is, to say the least, astonishing.

Origins (some of it reprinted here), to present an important series of new works, several of which have never before appeared in English. Like Lenowitz, he has also advised me on commentaries & notes throughout the book, though we never collaborated on translations as such. In a similar way, still other poets—George Economou, Pierre Joris, Rochelle Owens, Armand Schwerner—have provided new translations for the book. And there are others who helped with suggestions & information—some of them strangers encountered on reading trips, etc., whose names I never even got to know. Of those who come to mind, I would like to acknowledge my special indebtedness to Barbara Kirshenblatt-Gimblett, who advised me on Yiddish folklore; to David Meltzer, who shared the work of *Tree* & of his own anthology of the kabbala, *The Secret Garden;* & to Barbara Einzig, who was my assistant & friend during a year spent at the University of Wisconsin—Milwaukee; & in different ways to Warren Bargad, Alan Corré, T. Carmi, Peter Glassgold, Edmond Jabès, Charlie Morrow, Harvey Richman, Edouard Roditi, Diane Rothenberg, Tony Rudolf, Howard Schwartz, Ian Tyson, & Karl Young. Finally, too, I owe a debt of a still different order to authors like Gershom Scholem & Raphael Patai, whose work has been germinal to my own & that of many other poets.

During an important year of research on the book, I was a fellow & a visiting professor at the Center for 20th Century Studies of the University of Wisconsin—Milwaukee, where I was greatly helped by the friendship & consideration of its director, Michel Benamou. Much of the necessary library time was spent there, but I was also able to use other collections & resources in the U.S. & abroad: the New York Public Library, Jewish Theological Seminary, & YIVO collections in New York; the Gaster Collection, etc. at the British Museum, the collection of the Bodleian Library at Oxford, & collections at the Hebrew Union College in Cincinnati, Spertus College in Chicago, & the Middle East Center of the University of Utah. I was also assisted, on the institutional side, by a grant from the John Simon Guggenheim Foundation &, on the personal side, by Bill Strachan, my friend & editor at Anchor Books. At the same time a translation grant from PEN International assisted Harris Lenowitz in his part of the project.

A FINAL NOTE. The end of our work on *A Big Jewish Book* was marred by the death, at his home in Seguin, Texas, of Harris Lenowitz's father. The event brought back to me the death of my own father, a gentle free-thinker & committed Jew, some 16 years before, & the death of his father, a Hasidic follower of the Rebbe of Radzymyn, some 40 years before that. I believe that in some sense— as much genetic as mystical—they are the fierce ghosts & messengers behind the present work. Much of that work they would have failed to understand or would have seen, each in his own way, as a reversal of their own works & lives. It is my hope that they would have also seen the continuities.

JEROME ROTHENBERG
SAN DIEGO
NOVEMBER 1976

The Baal Shem Tov used to go to a certain place in the woods & light a fire & pray when he was faced with an especially difficult task & it was done.

His successor followed his example & went to the same place but said: "The fire we can no longer light, but we can still say the prayer." And what he asked was done too.

Another generation passed, & Rabbi Moshe Leib of Sassov went to the woods & said: "The fire we can no longer light, the prayer we no longer know: all we know is the place in the woods, & that will have to be enough." And it was enough.

In the fourth generation, Rabbi Israel of Rishin stayed at home & said: "The fire we can no longer light, the prayer we no longer know, nor do we know the place. All we can do is tell the story."

And that, too, proved sufficient.

THE WAYS

Question. Is not the liturgical poet who first
writes that clay vessels in which leaven was
cooked must be broken before Passover, & then
states that they may be stored away in wooden
sheds, guilty of a contradiction?

Answer. It is poetic liberty to state together
two contradictory propositions.

—RABBI MEIR OF ROTHENBURG

I form the light & create darkness
I make peace & create evil
I Yahveh do all these things

—ISAIAH BEN AMOZ, THE SEER

A Book of Powers

(proem)   into the darkness of the jewish life   mysterious   un-
tamed   he enters   stars & jellies at the core   a substance I never
had the grasp of   light is lightless   there is something before
light   light is still to be created   journey deeper   light beneath
the skull   before my birth   my mind

(Latin, from Hebrew/Greek, c. 100 A.D.)

THE FIRST, THE LAST   "A Poem of Ezra"

He said to me: In the beginning of the world
Before the gates of heaven stood
Before the blasts of thunder sounded
Before the flashes of lightning blazed
Before the foundations of Paradise were set
Before the beauty of its flowers was seen
Before the powers of the earthquake were laid down
Before the innumerable hosts of angels came together
Before the heights of air were raised up
Before the spaces of the sky were named
Before the footstool of the Mountain was established
Before the present years were reckoned up
Before the evil planners were denounced
& those who gather in the jewels of faith were sealed—
Then I considered all of this & through me
& through no other all came into being—
So the end will come through me & through no other

(Hebrew, c. 3rd century A.D.)

From THE GREATER HEKHALOT   "A Cosmic Hymn"

A measure of holiness   a measure of power
A measure of fearfulness   a measure of terror
A measure of trembling   a measure of shaking
A measure of awe   a measure of consternation
Is the measure of the Garment of Zoharariel YaHVeH God of Israel
Who comes crowned in the throne of his own massiveness
& the robe engraved in every part within without is YaHVeH
    YaHVeH
& no creature that has eyes to look at it
Not the eyes of flesh & blood the eyes of many servants
& whoever looks upon it sees or glimpses it
Whirling gyrations grip his eyeballs
Eyeballs as his eyes flash cast out torches
& enkindle him & burn him
For the fire that emerges from the man who looks
Enkindles him & burns him
Why?
Because it is the garment of Zoharariel YaHVeH God of Israel
Who comes crowned to the throne of his own massiveness

J.R./H.L.

COMMENTARY

(1)   Toward the *Ein-Sof,* the "endless," "limitless," or this: the basic
proposition of the search: for what is out of reach, unknowable: the secret of the Jewish mysteries that strains the powers of a language. Here
the poetry is in the telling, *is* the telling: the account through language,
by whatever means, to approach the secret by its outer forms: as rays, as
emanations, as bodies, as images, as sounds, as words, as names. But
the process thus stated is doomed to fail, for the *Ein-Sof,* writes

Gershom Scholem (*Kabbalah*, page 89), is "not accessible even to the innermost thought of the contemplative," rather "a term or image signifying the domain of the hidden God that lies beyond any impulse toward creation." As one instance this leads to that (gnostic) dualism in which our world becomes, exists, in separation as the creation of a second force completely evil. Otherwise, as here, the limitless ("beyond all thought") is that to which all thought somehow returns as source. "Cause of all causes." Or again: "Root of all roots."

(2) from "the notebooks"   10/74   to be a holiness is like a wholeness   in a ring   the male & female   mouth that holds its tail   convulses   is what vision gathered in a trance   the dancers we watch in circles move the dance against the center   dreams within a sleep so imageless it rises to a scream   a name   becomes a name   becomes the name to name the secret places   "you are each born in my birth   each body passes through a bridge of bodies through a narrow space past rocks becomes a field of flowers   sounds   the blue lips of the sacred stag   you zvi   you zion"   (j.r.)

(3) Rabbi Simeon cited the following from the Book of Mystery. "The Divine Name has both a revealed & an undisclosed form. In its revealed form it is written Y-H-V-H, but in its undisclosed form it is written in other letters, this undisclosed form representing the most Recondite of all." (*Zohar:* Numbers 146b.)

Edmond Jabès (French, b. 1912)
From ELYA

Door II
(The Name)

With your screams you have composed his name. And every scream is one of the letters which names you.

To learn my name from the sign. To spell and fear, to cherish and flee it.

To learn reading my life in the Book of the Dead.
Anguish glows above the ashes.
On the log the flame takes its revenge against the forest.
To reach the sky where the fire spreads.
Day recovers its unity.
Morning by
morning,
night by
night.

. . . .

ROSMARIE WALDROP

Moses de Leon (Aramaic, c. 1240–1305)

From THE GREAT HOLY ASSEMBLY　　　　　　"The Names"

(First Set)

(1) In my distress I called upon the Lord
(2) The Lord answered me with generosity
(3) The Lord is with me. I shall not fear
(4) The Lord is with me among those who help me
(5) It is better to trust in the Lord
(6) It is better to trust in the Lord

(Second Set)

(1) The Lord is with me. I shall not fear: what can Adam do to me
(2) It is better to trust in the Lord than to trust in Adam
(3) It is better to trust in the Lord than to trust in princes

6　　THE WAYS

(1) In my distress I called upon the Lord
(2) The Lord answered me with generosity
(3) The Lord is with me. I shall not fear
(4) What can Adam do to me
(5) The Lord is with me among those who help me
(6) I will gaze upon those who despise me
(7) It is better to trust in the Lord
(8) Than to trust in Adam
(9) It is better to trust in the Lord than to trust in princes

(*Zohar*)

ROY A. ROSENBERG

COMMENTARY

(1) Naming as a primal language happening, later transferred to the written word as well. Writes Gershom Scholem: "Revelation is revelation of the name or names of God, which are perhaps the different modes of His active being. God's language has no grammar; it consists only of names." And Joseph Gikatilla (14th century): "The whole Torah is nothing but the great name of God."

(2) The "names" above as verses from tradition reassembled (in this case Psalm 118.5–.9): a process like African praise-namings, etc. Here the verses are taken as the celebration (by David as orphic poet) of the "nine formations of the Divine Beard," itself a sacred "name" of God. The third set is a reassembling of the first two.

  The namings below proceed by "lights" & other means.

From SEFER RAZIEL   "Hymn"

He promises His Name. They praise its power and beauty.
He promises through the treasures of snow.
They praise in flux of fire,
In lustrum clouds and flashing palaces.
He who rides the sky promises,
And their praise sweeps through the armies.
He promises the Mystery of the Flame.
They praise through voices of thunder
And quick flashing lightning.
Earth praises, abyss praises,
Waves of the seas praise.
Praise the pristine Name on the throne in each soul
In each creature
Infinitely.

JACK HIRSCHMAN

Naftali Bacharach (Hebrew, 17th century)

A POEM FOR THE SEFIROT AS A WHEEL OF LIGHT

(the image)

. . . .

(the rim)

& going 'round
the ten
sefirot
of
the ball

& orbit
of the world
of first space

. . . .

(the spokes)

1
crown

light from light
extreme light

2
wisdom

splendor from splendor
hidden light

3
understanding

sparkle from sparkle
sparking light

4
greatness

splendor from splendor
pure light

5
power

light from splendor
of light   pure

6
beauty

sparkle from light
light shining

7
victory

light from sparkle
light refined

8
majesty

splendor from sparkle
light bright

9
foundation

sparkle from splendor
purer light
pure   pure

10
kingdom

most precious precious
shining light is

J.R./H.L

COMMENTARY

(1) Medieval Jewish *poesis* plays off the image of ten *sefirot* (emanations) as the resonance of *Ein-Sof* (the limitless) into the world of our possible perception. Unified within God—goes one telling—or identical with him, they appear to the human mind as differentiated stages, mapped in a sacred language game by words descriptive of their source. Thus from the First Book of Chronicles (29.11) come the terms *gedula* (greatness), *gevura* (power), *tiferet* (beauty), *netsaḥ* (victory), *hod* (majesty), & *malkhut* (kingdom), to which are added the three upper *sefirot: keter* (crown), *hokhma* (wisdom), & *bina* (understanding), in the most common of the sefirotic namings. Synonyms for *sefirot* do in fact

include *shemot,* names, & *diburim,* sayings, but they are also known as lights, powers, crowns, qualities, garments, mirrors, shoots, sources, sapphires, & their configuration imaged as a tree, a man, a chariot, a series of concentric circles or reflected lights, even (thus Scholem): "a candle flickering in the midst of ten mirrors set one within the other, each a different color." (For an earlier formulation in which the *sefirot* = letters & numbers, see page 97, below.)

In the present instance the "wheel of light" is not a fixed or static image (from which the "limitless" could as well be excluded) but an image in motion & tied finally to the mystery of creation as worked through by the 16th-century kabbalist & poet Isaac Luria. Here the limitless that fills all space contracts itself to leave a point or vacuum behind in which the universe originates. The act of withdrawal is called *tsimtsum* ("contraction") & the point is called *tehiru,* the primordial space. A ray of light moving across this circular space fills it with the ten *sefirot,* which surround it like a wheel of light. Only a residue of *Ein-Sof* stays within it—like little drops of oil.

(2)   "At the outset the decision of the King made a tracing in the supernal effulgence, a lamp of scintillation, & there issued within the impenetrable recesses of the mysterious limitless a shapeless nucleus enclosed in a ring, neither white nor black nor red nor green nor any color at all. . . . The most mysterious Power enshrouded in the limitless then split, without splitting its void, remaining wholly unknowable until from the force of the strokes there shone forth a supernal & mysterious point. Beyond that point there is no knowable, & therefore it is called *Reshit* (beginning), the creative utterance which is the starting-point of all." (*Zohar:* Genesis 15a.)

(3)   "One can disintegrate the world by means of very strong light. For weak eyes the world becomes solid, for still weaker eyes it seems to develop fists, for eyes weaker still it becomes shamefaced and smashes anyone who dares to gaze upon it." (Franz Kafka, *Reflections on Sin, Suffering, Hope & the True Way.*)

Jackson Mac Low (b. 1922)

1ST LIGHT POEM: FOR IRIS—10 JUNE 1962

The light of a student-lamp
sapphire light
shimmer
the light of a smoking-lamp

Light from the Magellanic Clouds
the light of a Nernst lamp
the light of a naphtha-lamp
light from meteorites

Evanescent light
ether
the light of an electric lamp
extra light

Citrine light
kineographic light
the light of a Kitson lamp
kindly light

Ice light
irradiation
ignition
altar light

The light of a spotlight
a sunbeam
sunrise
solar light

Mustard-oil light
Maroon light
the light of a magnesium flare
light from a meteor

Evanescent light
ether
light from an electric lamp
an extra light

Light from a student-lamp
sapphire light
a shimmer
smoking-lamp light

Ordinary light
orgone lumination
light from a lamp burning olive oil
opal light

Actinism
atom-bomb light
the light of an alcohol lamp
the light of a lamp burning anda-oil

Allen Ginsberg (b. 1926)
From AETHER

GREAT CREATOR

WHOSE NAME I NOW

PRONOUNCE:

GREAT CREATOR OF THE UNIVERS, IF

THY WISDOM ACCORD IT

AND IF THIS NOT BE TOO

MUCH TO ASK

MAY I PUBLISH YOUR NAME?

I ASK IN THE LIMA

NIGHT

FEARFULLY WAITING

ANSWER,

hearing the buses out on
the street hissing,
Knowing the Terror
      of the World Afar—

LIMA, PERU
MAY 28, 1960

A PROLOGUE TO "THE VISION OF
THE CHARIOT"

(1)   The story of creation should not be expounded before two persons, nor the chapter on the Chariot before one person, unless he is a sage & already has an independent understanding of the matter.

(2)   Whoever ponders on four things, it were better for him if he had not come into the world: what is above, what is below, what was before time, & what will be hereafter.

(Talmud)

Ezekiel ben Buzi (Hebrew, fl. 590 B.C.)
THE VISION OF THE CHARIOT

> in the 30th year
> the fourth month
fifth day of the month
> when I was with the captives
> along the River Kvar
skies fell open
> I saw
> visions of ELOHIM
the fifth day of the month
> fifth year after
> Yoyakhin's capture
YaHVeH's word reached
> Priest Ezekiel Buzi's son
> was in Chaldea by the River Kvar

YaHVeH's hand was on him
                              & I looked
                  looked & saw a storm wind
came from the north
                         a large cloud
             fire feeding fire
so bright around
                           "electrum"
             in the center
at the fire's heart
                          an image
             FOUR
were living creatures
                          visioned
             in image of a man
each had four faces
                          had four wings
             straight footed
their soles were like a calf's foot
                          sparked into colors
             polished brass
a man's hands
                          under their wings
             on all four sides
& other faces
                          wings
             the wings were joined
like a woman to her sister
                          they didn't turn when
             moving
each moved before its face
                          had faces like
             a man
all four had lions' faces
                          on the right
             all four
bulls' faces from the left
                          & all four also had
             the faces of
an eagle

                        was how their faces were
                wings stretched upwards
two wings joined
                        man to man
                the other two were
covering their bodies
                        each moved out from his face
                direction of the wind
they moved & didn't
                        turn when moving
                these were like living creatures looked
like coals of fire
                        burning
                lamps
flashed swung around among
                        the living creatures
                brightness
of fire
                        lightning ran from it
                the living creatures turned
raced back & forth
                        like the sighting of a lightning flash
                I saw
& saw the living creatures saw one wheel
                        was on the earth
                the four sides of the wheel
between the living creatures
                        the wheels were worked
                were gold in color
jasper
                        all four looked alike
                were like a wheel inside
a wheel
                        moving from side to side
                on all four sides
they didn't turn when moving
                        rims were high
                & dreadful
rims full of eyes all over

18   THE WAYS

                        the living creatures moved
                the wheels moved
if the living creatures left the earth
                        the wheels did
                in the direction of the wind
they went
                        the wind would drive them
                wheels were lifted up with them
because the living creature's
                        wind
                was in its wheels
these went
                        those went
                these stopped
those stopped
                        these lifted from
                the earth
the wheels would lift with them
                        because the living creature's
                wind was
in its wheels
                        an image
                over the living creatures' heads
dome of the firmament
                        like ice
                a terror stretched above
their heads above them
                        under the dome
                their wings were straight
a woman to her sister
                        two were covering
                their bodies from each side
I heard the voice the wings
                        was like the voice of many waters
                Shaddai's voice
came with their movements
                        voice of thunder
                voice of armies
when they stood

                        voices of the wings grew softer
              voice over the sky dome
came above their heads
                        when they were standing
              quieting their wings
above the dome their heads
                        the sighting of
              a sapphire stone
in image of a chair
                        on the chair's image
              image sighting
of a man upon it
                        was above I saw
              "electrum"
sighting of a fire circle
                        upwards from his crotch
              & downwards
sighting of a fire
                        glowing circle
              sighting of a rainbow
in a cloud
                        some rainy day
              yes sighting of
the glowing circle
                        that I saw
              I fell upon my face
heard the voice of someone speaking

Date of the vision: July 593 B.C.
Babylonia.

J.R./H.L.

COMMENTARY

(1)   This, etc., from a stratum of Jewish image-making earlier than the sefirotic circles (see above, page 11), though the reader can likely sense their presence here & ready for transformation into such, like the geometrizing or abstraction of the basic form. The "vision of the chariot," for which the first chapter of Prophet Ezekiel was the traditional

biblical source, is the central image or *yantra* of Jewish mysticism from at least a century before the time of Jesus. As *ma'ase merkaba* (i.e., "the work of the chariot") it proliferated into attempts to "see" & "measure" the chariot, the throne, the wheels, the living creatures, the image of the man-god on the throne, the halls, the doors, the palaces, etc. The other great image-making areas of that time were apocalypse (visualizations, that is, of the end of our known world) & the so-called "work of creation": & these, along with talmudic exegeses, ritual & moral reinterpretations of the Bible, Hellenistic commentaries, poems & incantations, produce a work of such dimensions that the historian Michael Grant can conclude that Jewish *poesis* not only didn't end with the final transcriptions of the Bible but that "the Jews, almost uniquely among the subjects of Rome, had produced and were still producing an extensive literature of their own."

(2)   For all its highly touted image-breaking tendencies—from Abraham's iconoclasting the Chaldean statues onward—the Jewish enterprise develops a range of phanopoeia (image-making) as fantastic as any going in the ancient Near East. Such traditions, usually called esoteric, may better be viewed as the surfacing, or the maintenance as hidden oral lore (kabbala), of those other, by then subterranean, cultures against which the makers of the Torah wrote: "You shall destroy their images & cut down their groves," etc. (Exodus 34.13.) It is now possible to see in the survival of those images the practice of a poetry subversive to the literalized monotheism that would displace the fantastic life of the gods (in Hebrew: *elohim*) & the individualized visions emerging therefrom with rules of behavior at the service of the hierarchic state. Of this survival & its resultant paradoxes—not only among the Jews but all others undergoing an accelerated civilization—D. H. Lawrence wrote in his description of the still very Jewish Apocalypse of Saint John (see below, page 600): "The Apocalypse is, in its movement, one of the works of the old pagan civilization, and in it we have, not the modern process of progressive thought, but the old pagan process of rotary image-thought. Every image fulfills its own little circle of action and meaning, then is superseded by another image. . . . Every image is a picturegraph, and the connection between the images will be made more or less differently by every reader. . . . We must remember that the old human conscious process has to *see something happen,* every time. Everything is concrete, there are no abstractions. And everything *does* something." (D. H. Lawrence, *Apocalypse,* page 83.)

Thus, too, the *concrete* question of the measurement of God.

Ishmael ben Elisha (Hebrew, c. 2nd century A.D.)
From SHI'UR KOMA   "The Measure of the Body"

This is the measure of the stature spoken in the Book of the Measure

"Great is our lord *and much power*"

236,000 leagues   the height of the Creator be He blessed   The
measure of his league is 3 miles   and the mile is 10,000 cubits
and the cubit is 3 spans   and the span fills the whole world   and
there is another accounting besides this   a thousand thousand myriad myriad and six-hundred thousand myriad and nine thousand
myriad and sixty-two myriad   thirty-nine hundred leagues and thirteen leagues and a third of a league   and Rabbi Ishmael ben Elisha
the high priest noted that the measure in all is two thousand
myriad leagues of a myriad myriads   one thousand leagues
high   one thousand thousand myriad leagues broad   The measure
of his league is three miles   and the mile is ten thousand cubits
and the cubit is three spans   and the span fills the whole world
as it is said   "The skies with a span you set up"

So much according to Rabbi Ishmael

                                                          H.L.

COMMENTARY

(1)   "I have seen the measure of the height of the Lord, without di-
mension & without shape, which has no end." (Slavonic Book of Enoch
13.8.) To which—re "measure" as the hypostasis both of cosmos &
poesis—add Charles Olson, among other of our own contemporaries:
"*Experience* itself—and *Measurement*. Is there *anything* imaginably

else? / 'Everything issues from the Black Chrysanthemum, and nothing is anything but itself measured so.' . . . In other words *spontaneously*, from its *exire*—from its coming out, *everything*—which means, everything—is nothing but itself measured by the overwhelmingly important fact that everything *does* issue." (C. Olson, "Experience & Measurement," in *Olson: The Journal of the Charles Olson Archives,* number 3, page 59.)

(2)   *Shi'ur Koma,* or "measure of the body," is the culmination of the shaman-like journey of the merkaba mystic through heavens & cosmic palaces & into the presence of the "image of the man-god on the chair." From measurement of the height, the description goes on to various parts of the body, measuring & naming them. The version here is attributed to Ishmael ben Elisha, 2nd-century contemporary & companion of Rabbi Akiba. The procedure begins numerologically, by adding up the letters (numbers) in Psalm 147.5 "& much power" (*ve-rav koah*) = 236, then multiplying by 1,000 leagues, etc.

(3)   from "the notebooks"   9/75   descent *into* the chariot   their wording for the journey goes   I walk into my own blood   here are giant eyes above the lake   frozen another winter   wheels move past us animals with rubber skins rolled into balls   I take the measure of the sea
    the street   my arm   a number on the tape I still can't read   but wonder   if the mind is endless (endless) who is lost?   (j.r.)

Armand Schwerner (b. 1927)
TABLET V

is the man bigger than a fly's wing?	what pleasure!
is he much bigger than a fly's wing?	what pleasure!
is his hard penis ten times a fly's wing?	what pleasure!
is his red penis fifteen times a fly's wing?	what [pleasure]!
is his mighty penis fifty times a fly's wing?	what pleasure!
does his penis vibrate like a fly's wing?	what terrific pleasure!
is his arm four and one half times a strong penis?	.... a great arm
is his arm two-hundred-twenty-five times a fly's wing?	in the shape of petrified wood
is his body three times his great arm?	what pleasure!
is his body thirteen times his red penis?	what pleasure!
is his body three-hundred-thirty-six times a big fly's body?	what pleasure!
does he touch his body with pleasure?	what pleasure!
does she count fly's wings throughout the night?	what pleasure!
is her vulva tipped with spring color?	what terrific pleasure!
does he move behind in her?	let us have rain!
does she vibrate like the wheel on the axle?	let us have rain! what pleasure!
let us call a fly's half-wing *kra*	lay a *kra* on this bull's horn
let us call a fly's half-wing *kra*	lay another *kra* on this bull's horn
let us call a fly's half-wing *kra*	lay another *kra* on this bull's horn
let us call a fly's half-wing *kra*	lay another *kra* on this bull's horn
let us call a fly's half-wing *kra*	lay another *kra* on this bull's horn
let us call a fly's half-wing *kra*	hold the bull down quiet
let us call a fly's half-wing *kra*	lay another *kra* on this bull's horn
look, the bull's horn is more than six *kra!*	hold down the bull's head
let us call the man's red penis *pro*	lay a *pro* on this cow's vulva
let us call the man's red penis *pro*	lay another *pro* on this cow's vulva
let us call the man's red penis *pro*	lay another *pro* on this cow's vulva
look, the cow's vulva is five *kra*	what pleasure!
look, the cow's vulva is almost three *pro*	what terrific pleasure!

pro kra kra pro kra kra kra pro
the man's sacrificed hand is more than
  one *pro,*
the man's aching head is forty *kra* round
the man's sick groin is three *pro*
let's sacrifice this twig
let's sacrifice this great melon
let's sacrifice this shank
the hand is furious
the aching head screams
the sick groin is furious
+++++++++
++++++++
+++++++++++

kra what pleasure! *pro* what pleasure!

      this twig is more than one *pro*
this great melon is forty *kra* round
feel this lamb shank, three *pro*
what a pleasure!
what a pleasure!
what a terrific pleasure!
how will we frighten the strangers now?
how will they piss in their pants?
how will we frighten the strangers now?
+++++++++++
++++++++++++++++
++++++++ for water

A PROLOGUE TO "THE BOOK OF CONCEALMENT"

    & he said you can not see my face for no man can see my face & live

    & Yahveh said look there is a place beside me & you will stand upon a rock

    & it will happen when my presence passes by that I will put you in a cleft of the rock & will cover you with my hand while I pass by

    & I will take away my hand & you will see my hind parts but my face will not be seen

From THE BOOK OF CONCEALMENT

"The Forms / The Faces"

(1)
a skull

(2)
the crystal dew inside it

(3)
a skin of air

(4)
a wool beard

(5)
his force is written on his forehead

(6)
the eye stays open

(7)
whose nostrils breathe life
to the world below

(Zohar)

COMMENTARY

(1) "God is *the Master in the White mantle and the glowing Visage.* The White of His Eye forms four thousand worlds, and the Righteous of this world will each inherit four hundred worlds illumined by the White of the Eye. Millions of worlds have their basis and their support in His Head. The Dew that rises in the Head and falls from it will revive the dead in the future world. It is this Dew that is the Manna of the Righteous in the world to come. It is white, as the diamond is white, yet giving forth all the colors. Every day there is emitted from the Brain thirteen thousand myriads of worlds, which receive their subsistence from Him and whose weight is supported by Him. The Whiteness of the Head throws light in all directions. Because of the length of the Visage, the Ancient of Days is known as the *Great Face,* Which is composed of three natures or principles superimposed: male, female and son. In order to create the worlds which can exist only in God and through God, the *Great Face* has drawn a veil in front of Itself. And on this veil is graven the Divine Essence, Which is known as the *Little Face.* In front of this veil many other veils are placed at certain intervals, and seen through each of these veils the Divine Essence appears under a different form: as Mercy (the heart), as Strength (the arm), as Wisdom (the brain), etc., and these are known as the *Sephiroth.*" (*Zohar:* "The Great Holy Assembly," translated by Ariel Bension in *The Zohar in Moslem & Christian Spain,* 1932.)

(2) Naming becomes the speaking of a vision, in which speech & sight, language & vision, are in constant interplay. The word creates the vision, vision images the word—as language by outracing sight asserts a paradox & puts a face (or, rather, *faces*) on [H.L.: makes faces at] the limitless. And even for the Jews, as martyrs (witnesses) to the "One God," the mind mirrors an infinite series of such images. More characteristically the reduction is to three or four—as here, the Great Face, Small Face, & Shekinah, the Father, the Son, & the Mother, who are also the trinity of the early Jewish Christians; elsewhere a quaternity, in which the sacred name, the tetragrammaton, is read as Y the Father, H the Mother, V the Son, & H the Daughter, sometimes taken as a pair of androgynous figures. Thus, Raphael Patai's translation of a key passage from the *Zohar:* "The Supernal H (i.e. the Mother) became pregnant as a result of all the love and fondling—since the Y never leaves her—and she brought forth the V (the Son), whereupon she stood up and suckled him. And when the V emerged, his female mate (the Daughter, represented by the second H in the Tetragrammaton) emerged together with him." (*The Hebrew Goddess,* page 174.)

FOR THE BEARD OF THE GREAT FACE

A Vision & Poem

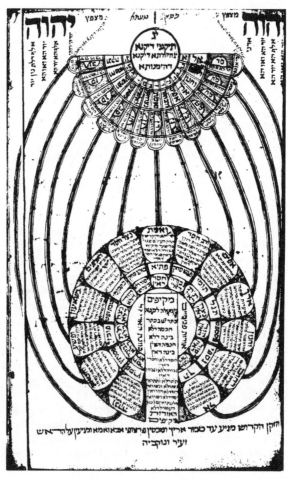

Gloss: The two lines at the bottom read: *The Holy Beard goes as far as the navel of the Great Face & covers the faces of the Father & the Mother & rests upon the head of the Small Face & the Female.*

COMMENTARY

(1)   As an extension of the *Shi'ur Koma* impulse (see above, page 23), the later Jewish image-making extends to the appearance of the Great Face (also called Ancient of Days, etc.) & the Small Face, but most complexly to their "beards." The Beard of the Great Face appears in thirteen configurations or segments describing "mercy," that of the Small Face in nine describing "power"—of which much else is said in "The Book of Concealment," "The Great Holy Assembly," & "The Lesser Holy Assembly" of the *Zohar*. Thus: "Rabbi Simeon bar Yoḥai began & said: Woe unto him who extendeth his hand unto that most glorious supernal beard of the Holy Ancient One, the most concealed of all. These are the praises for that beard: the beard which is concealed & most precious in all of its configurations: the beard which neither those above nor those below have known: the beard which is the praise of all praise: the beard which neither man nor prophet nor holy man has approached as to behold it: the beard whose long hairs hang down even to the navel, white as snow: the adornment of adornments, the concealment of concealments, the truth of all truths." (*Zohar,* "The Book of the Great Holy Assembly," 130b.)

   The visualization, above, maps out the thirteen measures of mercy in the Ancient One's beard. The beard is itself taken as another name of God.

(2)   from "the notebooks"   9/75   the faces   of the faces in our common world   an old man walks his dog across my line of vision   with a newspaper against a fence the wind holds tight   in place   all places down to earth   "I make a map for you" his maggid (angel) spoke   o praise the messenger   tra la   the figure in the diagram   geometrized what precious lines & circles   of whom the beard is anchor of the world   whose eyes involve his sun   I mean his *son*   reflected   shining cheeks of old men in the act of love   the secret   in the young girl's face   the daughter   mother   we call shekinah   blossoms   hovering above   alive   what other gods beside these *perfect* strangers?   (j.r.)

(3)   "All faces are His. Hence, He has no face. —Reb Alen" (From E. Jabès, *The Book of Questions.*)

Isaac Luria (Aramaic, 1534–72)

A POEM FOR THE SMALL FACE

sons of his palace
were shy
who witness rays from
the small face

these to be here
at this table
the king cuts
grooves from his ring in

be pleased with
this meeting
this center of powers
all wingd

to bring joy to it
now
is his hour of peace
without anger

draw near me
thou see my companions
be night without
judgment

those dogs
wild with *chutzpah*
keep out
may not enter

but send for
Ancient of Days
exchanging
the jewel in his forehead

his peace
as he sees it
releases the light from
the shells

& will flow with it
into each orifice
these will conceal
under domes

will be here
in praise of the evening
a poem for
the small face

J.R.

COMMENTARY

The Small Face is the "son" of the tetragrammaton (YHVH), who as the reflection, even the inversion, of the Ancient of Days, is known as the "impatient one" (= *ze'ir anpin* = "small face"), the angry face of the reality confronting us. Anyone who opens to suffering—who, like the schizophrenic, leaves his nerve endings raw, unguarded—will recognize that face as "evil," not in a moralizing sense but as part of a science (poetics would be a better term) of contraries, kept alive by poets & other visionaries in an age of literalized "belief." Viewed otherwise, as "the godhead in its endless growth & development" (G. Scholem), the Small Face is the bridegroom of the Shekinah, & their marriage is celebrated at the Sabbath. Like the gods of the earlier fertility religions, he is heaven & she is earth; or drawing from the going Jewish god-names, he is Yahveh & she is Elohim.

The "shells" (*klipot*) of the poem's ending (for which, see below, page 88) are the hard husks, the material, of our world, covering over those seeds or germs of light that are the remnants of *Ein-Sof*'s withdrawal in the act of *tsimtsum* (see above, page 12). In meditation, etc., participants worked with the Ancient of Days & the Small Face to release the light toward that "cleansing of the doors of perception" that William Blake named for us in his recovery & invention of an actual poetics. Then would come the sensual awakening & the inflow of light through the body's orifices: the union of God & his bride.

The occasion of Luria's "Poem for the Small Face" was the Sabbath celebration by his circle of mystics in the city of Safed. It marked the final meal of the Sabbath, as the "Poem for the Shekinah" that follows marked the opening, & its intent was to drive off distractions by the unreconstructed forces of "the other side," to allow a balance of powers within the world itself. Writes Scholem: "It is not a mere description of an exorcism, it *is* an exorcism." (*On the Kabbalah & Its Symbolism,* page 145.)

Isaac Luria (Aramaic, 1534–72)

A POEM FOR THE SHEKINAH ON THE FEAST OF THE SABBATH

I have sung
an old measure

would open
gates to

her field of apples
(each one a power)

set a new table
to feed her

& beautifully
candelabrum

drops its
light on us

Between right & left
the Bride

draws near in
holy jewels

clothes of the sabbath
whose lover

embraces her
down to foundation

gives pleasure
squeezes his strength out

in surcease of
sorrow

& makes new faces
be hers

& new souls
new breath

gives her joy
double measure

of lights & of
streams for her blessing

o Friends of the Bride
go forth

all's sealed
within her

shines out from
Ancient of Days

Toward the south
I placed

candelabrum
(o mystical)

room in
the north

for table
for bread

for pitchers of wine
for sweet myrtle

gives power to
lovers

new potencies
garlands

give her many
sweet foods to taste

many kinds of
fish

for fertility
birth

of new souls
new spirits

will follow the 32 paths
& 3 branches

the bride with
70 crowns

with her King who
hovers above her

crown above crown in
Holy of Holies

this lady all worlds are
formed in

of words for her
70 crowns

50 gates
the Shekinah

ringed by
6 loaves

of the sabbath
& bound

all sides to
Heavenly Refuge

the hostile
powers

have left us
demons you feared

sleep in chains

J.R.

COMMENTARY

(1) *"Shekhina* is the frequently used Talmudic term denoting the visible and audible manifestation of God's presence on earth. In its ultimate development as it appears in the late Midrash literature, the Shekhina concept stood for an independent, feminine divine entity prompted by her compassionate nature to argue with God in defense of man. She is thus, if not by character, then by function and position, a direct heir to such ancient Hebrew goddesses of Canaanite origin as Asherah and Anath." (Raphael Patai, *The Hebrew Goddess,* page 137.) She is identified with the tenth *sefira—Malkhut,* or Kingdom—& her counterpart among the *sefirot* of the left side is Lilith, "the night wailer" (see below, pages 62, 182). Her reappearance among us is an event of contemporary *poesis, not* religion—"She / in whom the Jew has his communion / . . . maiden to the eye." (R. Duncan.)

(2) THE PEOPLE'S ANSWER TO THE PROPHET JEREMIAH (circa 590 B.C.): then all the men all those who knew that their wives made offerings to other gods & the whole great crowd of women standing with them even all the people dwelling in the land of Egypt said as for the word that you have spoken to us in the name of Yahveh we shall not listen to you but we will certainly do everything we said we would we will burn incense to the Queen of Heaven & pour libations for her as we used to do our fathers & our kings & princes in the cities of Judah & in the streets of Jerusalem for then we had plenty of food & we all were well & saw no evil but since we ceased burning incense to the Queen of Heaven & pouring her libations we have wanted everything & have been consumed by sword & famine (Jeremiah 44.15–.19.)

Jack Hirschman (b. 1933)

THERE IS A BEAUTIFUL MAIDEN WHO HAS NO EYES WHO IS THE TRUE MESSIAH

And all the people saw the voices
  were rainbows in the sky
    between the thighs
      of both sexes
in the dream of the rabbi Christ.
                    What
                                does that mean?
said my finger
pointing the lips
of the beautiful maiden who has
no eyes to the page
already blinded by her presence.

  It means the nipple on the right
shall be kissed and taken
into the mouth and the nipple
on the left squeezed till
the heart begins beating again,
at which point it too shall be
taken into the mouth, while
the other is softly fondled.

She laughs, she has no mercy, she
cries, she has no pain.

She opens my sex like an amulet
with her tongue and fingers.
She swallows the holy letters and the dawn
                  we sprawl inside each other's
                            womb.

A child she is light
  with, and light
    is skin,
      I feel my belly
also with him.

Nine months ago
  in a moment.
    Who is come.
In the beginning, what.
  Atom.

COMMENTARY

"In the usage of the Kabbalah . . . the Shekhinah becomes an aspect of God, a quasi-independent feminine element within Him. . . . [The conception of] the exile of the Shekhinah goes back to the Talmud, 'In every exile into which the children of Israel went, the Shekhinah was with them.' In the Talmud this means only that God's presence was always with Israel in its exiles. In the Kabbalah, however, it is taken to mean that a part of God Himself is exiled from God. . . . The exile of Shekhinah . . . in other words . . . [is] the separation of the masculine and feminine principles in God." (G. Scholem, *On the Kabbalah & Its Symbolism*, 1965.)

Nathaniel Tarn (b. 1928)

From LYRICS FOR THE BRIDE OF GOD   "The Kitchen"

They said we don't know about a female aspect of God
it goes against the grain and has little to do with the tradition
our fathers rammed down our throats with castor oil
    but I was very much in love with her and could have eaten her
        shit
had she ever asked, but she never did in that time.

It was in several other countries and she often died in her prime.

    She was supposed to collect my particle of soul
    came by on that last visit to take it out of me by force
    because I wasn't ready to let go of it at any price
    and she recited the good authors, talked about Grete and Bea:
    how even the top performers had been reconciled in the end—

and who was I to object for the good of Israel /
                            I mean: we had *that* sort of pride?

II

—I'll stay alone from now on
won't collect any other soul until I have yours
that stage of my life is over and you can have my chastity too
since that's what you've been wanting in the first place
                it's all so simple
although you have a genius for complications sure enough

    (but I had wanted it some time before that
        and perhaps no longer wanted it now.)

III

I said I'd feel small without the particle mean and diminished
                    poor poor poor poor poor
sort of two-dimensional and unable to excite anybody
and lost without the light of my life quite put out
with no energy to go on to anything new or finish anything begun
                                        (reference: the Orphic myths)
        and also and more importantly I'd never be able to write again—

but she said how this was going to be a different world
                        without need of writers
        because everything would be perfect from now on
        we'd spend the whole time looking into her eyes
                        as she looked into her husband's
Jesus I said how dull but it was the wrong thing to say
        she was going on about a house she would build me
                        I could travel to and from

                        she was whispering all the time
        don't kill us   don't kill us   don't kill us

I suppose she meant the holy particles which united her and me
I felt guilty because I had led her to believe that we might make it
        and now she was going back without my particle
                        and would have nothing to do
        with her life except raise those children
                        she did not want and had never loved
        so how could one cry vengeance and say yes
                        one had yes fallen out of salvation /

she said it's all there for you whenever you want it
                                        you are everything still.

COMMENTARY

from "the notebooks"   9/75   a letter to Nathaniel Tarn   to honor *lyrics
for the bride of god*   at this point in the writing

. . . .

& seeing the old struggle there
—even in God the Androgyne   division
conflict of the sexes
later would tend to pull the world apart—
the mind evades it   almost
smug in the male imagination builds a house for her
or sets her up in it
the House of God
though if it's HIS house or if it's HER house who could say now?
as the other day a letter from our old friend Clayton came
"that the Shekinah is just another one of the 'masks' that male
   origin wears"   he wrote
—I wouldn't doubt it for a minute either
though   that adjustment made   the question will still remain
of domicile   of building up that greater world
that replication of the *shi'ur koma*
& the mind   the mind will ache from it forever
throbbing   call it   habitation
call it palace   "image of the world"   they said
& wrote about the heavens
seven by their count
now I have read the *hekhalot* the books of palaces
before Shekinah   GOD THE MOTHER   in her exile
sat outside the town & heard the trains call
like the voices of her angels
she who first experienced the *galut* poor old soul

(j.r.)

(Hebrew, medieval)

From THE REVELATION OF MOSES

"A Poem for the Seven Heavens"

one

Moses ascends the heaven of the first day   there where the waters
stand in line   a heaven full of windows   angels standing at each
window   Moses asks him what the windows are   he says   the
window of prayer   the window of request   the window of ap-
peal   the window of tears   the window of joy   the window of
fullness   the window of famine   the window of poverty   the
window of riches   the window of war   the window of peace   the
window of pregnancy   the window of birth   the window of the
treasures of the rain   the window of dew   the window of sin
the window of repentance   the window of smallness   the window
of largeness   the window of death   the window of life   the win-
dow of disease in man   the window of disease in beasts   the win-
dow of healing   the window of sickness   the window of health   &
MOSES SAW GREAT THINGS PAST FINDING OUT YES
MARVELOUS THINGS WITHOUT NUMBER

two

& then the second heaven heaven of the second day   he saw a
second angel   length of the angel was a thousand miles   had circa
half a million angels facing him   fire & water angels   faces upward turned toward the Shekinah   all sang hymns (said)   GREAT
IS THE LORD & GREATLY TO BE PRAISED etc   Metatron
said   these are the angels of the clouds   the wind   the rain
their faces turned toward the Shekinah   from the day that God
created them they haven't moved a breath

three

third heaven of the third day   Moses saw another angel   whose
length's a journey of 500 years   has 70,000 heads   each head
with 70,000 mouths   each mouth with 70,000 tongues   each
tongue with 70,000 kinds of speech   had 700 million angels facing
him   white fire angels   singing   praising Elohim (said)
THINE O LORD THE GREATNESS & THE POWER etc   Moses
asked him who are these   he said   these are the Erelim   the
lords of grass   trees   fruits   grains   go forth to obey HIS orders
    then return

four

Moses to the fourth heaven   saw the temple built   red fire columns   sides green fire   thresholds of white fire   the hooks &
planks a blinding fire   portals of carbuncle   halls made of spar-
kling gems   whose angels sang like David said   BLESS THE
LORD O YOU HIS ANGELS MIGHTY ONES IN STRENGTH
FULFILL HIS WORD etc   Moses asked him who they were &
Metatron said   these are the angels   lords of earth   sun   moon
    stars   planets   spheres   are Yahveh's singers   Moses saw
two stars   each large as the whole earth   one's name was Nogah
which is Venus & the other Ma'adim was Mars   one stood above
the sun   the other stood above the moon   & higher than all others
    Moses asked him   Metatron said   this one stands above the
sun in summer   cools the earth off from the sun's heat   while the
other's near the moon   warms the earth up against the cold of
moons

five

Moses to the fifth heaven   he saw armies of angels   half of fire
half of snow   the snow was resting on the fire did not put it out
for God made peace between them saying   PEACE IN HIS HIGH
PLACES   Moses asked   what are these doing   Metatron said
these are the Erelim called Ishim meaning men   as written   I
WILL CALL YOU *ISHIM*

six

Moses to the sixth heaven   saw an angel   whose length's a journey
of 500 years   was wholly ice   & thousands & ten thousands stood
beside him   angels   numberless   all singing   praising one who
spoke & formed the world   then Moses asked him who are these
he answered   these are holy watchers

seven

Moses to the seventh heaven   saw an angel wholly fire   & two
other angels   chains of fire red & black around them kept them
bound   length of each angel was 2000 miles   & Moses asked him
who are these   he answered   Wrath & Anger   whom God created
in the first six days to do his will   then Moses said   I am afraid   I
cannot look   & Metatron said   Moses   Yahveh's lover   far
from fear & trembling   then Moses calmed down then he felt at
peace

J.R.

COMMENTARY

(1) The visionary journey, first called an "ascent" but not long after
"going down" or "in": "descent *into* the chariot" that gave its name
(*merkaba* = "chariot" = "metaphor" by punning) to the process: therefore a trip into the mind of the initiate himself. And if we now think of all
that as *poesis*, as an ongoing creation through those techniques that
Eliade tells us were the great resources of the early shaman-poets ("technicians of the sacred"), the link to the subterranean tradition is here all
the clearer. The ecstasy & the journey do persist, then, & the impulse to
poesis survives the disappearance of the shamans.

   What is seen gives a name to the process of seeing & speaking: as
ma'ase merkaba ("work of the chariot," defined above) or as *hekhalot*
(books of palaces & halls encountered on the trip), in the vocabulary of
mystics from the first & second centuries. Seven is here the key number:
seven heavens that hold the seven palaces, with seven doors & halls, &
seven orders of angels as lesser gods, etc.: a mirror image of the seven

earths below &, starting from "the other side," the seven anti-worlds, of contraries, destructive of our own. But if the journey was possible in all directions, it is the sky-trip that is here the most illuminated, as if even the first shaman-poets, the ones at source, were specialists in the "descent to heaven"—like the Altai shamans climbing to the sky, to see the great god Ulgan on his throne, surrounded by guards & mystic animals, much like the *ḥayot* ("living creatures") in the vision of Ezekiel (above) & onward. The record that results is at once fantastic architecture & cosmology, a series of maps & blueprints, marked with threats & dangers, even—the more occulted & doubtful the tradition becomes (thus: Kafka, "Before the Law," below)—with presentiments of the trip deferred.

(2)   from "the notebooks"   9/75   not hell's brilliance   butterflies that sting   stung us into vision   but as here   illumination of the mind   is from the upper worlds   their hell mere ugliness   so that the pain of vision   terror   finds its place in heaven   though it blinds the eye

. . . .

(variation)

& I never knew heaven could be terrible as hell   or be as bright   (j.r.)

(3)   Metatron, also called the "boy" (*na'ar*) & "little Yahveh," is here the guide to Moses & represents the transformed figure of the human Enoch now become an angel (= *ben Elohim* = son of God, a god). Moses himself will undergo such transformation, along with the other patriarchs (see below, pages 199, 207) &, by extension, the practicing mystics themselves. In this role Metatron/Enoch closely resembles the mythical "first-shaman" of many other cultures, times & places.

From THE APOCALYPSE OF GORGORIOS

"The Temple"

---

was in heaven
       temple of the highest
length & width preserved
& built of emeralds
the light of emeralds inside the garden
that I saw
& columns
           vaults
                topazes
                      hyacinths in red & gold
& images the color of the sky
inlaid with pearls
the silent angels praising God
said
      praise
           the high god
                  who is highest
& animals in sky & earth
knew fear

. . . .

a white sea pearl was in it
shining brightly
if they opened the interior of this *zion*
would illuminate the ends of earth
its light be brighter than
the light of sky
was made of shining pearl & pure gold

a crown of green pearl
(emerald)
adorned with three white silver pieces
that would blind the eye

. . . .

& saw four angels
who were like a pearl (rose-colored)
& a pearl the color of the sky
set in pure gold
& fire
from their mouths a voice came out
(sang)
holy is the king
              his holy name
                      he lives in
& the ark's wood
like white pearl
a clash of images & colors
red
     green
         color of the sky
               of lilies
                    other colors
till I fell down on my face & cried
for the wonders that God shows
the foolish sons of men

. . . .

               (coda)

the angel to Gorgorios
        now something greater
   than anything in earth or sky
I heard
a sound of songs
& melodies the heart heard
praises   hymns
a light appeared like lightning
fragrance that revives the dead

I turned back   saw
a woman dressed in purple
that I couldn't look at
marveled
            praised God
                        then fled
(where was I?)
but the angel told me
"this is the Heavenly Jerusalem"
I saw
        above the door
                        the temple of the sanctuary
a sign in roman writing
made of lights   (it said)
THIS IS THE HEAVENLY JERUSALEM   FOR THE ONE WHO
GAVE HIMSELF FOR GOD'S WORD   FOR THOSE WHO DE-
SPISED THE GLORY OF THE EPHEMERAL WORLD   FOR
THOSE WHO RETIRED TO THE HILLS & CAVERNS   & FOR
THE HERMITS WHO SERVED GOD

J.R.

COMMENTARY

"Seven things were created before the world was created. They are: the
Torah, Gehinnom, the Garden of Eden, the Throne of Glory, the
Temple, Repentance, & the Name of the Messiah." (*Pirke de Rabbi
Eliezer,* 3.) Thus Torah, among the other powers, exists as the primary
structure of all thought & language, which as consciousness will itself
undergo a series of transformations. These transformations occur in four
"worlds," before & after creation. Beginning in *atsilut* (the world of
emanation) as all possible combinations & permutations of the Hebrew
alphabet, it undergoes an increasing literalization & evolution into the
"torah" (written & oral "law"), which has formed the basis of the "normative" religion. The mapping of this primary structure (see below), its
visualization & recovery, was a major move in the poetics of Jewish
mysticism.

Solomon ben Ḥayim Eliashu (Hebrew, 1841–1924), after Israel Sarug

THE PRIMORDIAL TORAH AS THE CLOAK OF GOD

> *. . . Who cover yourself with light as with a garment*
> *Who stretch out the heavens like a curtain*

(Psalm 104.2.)

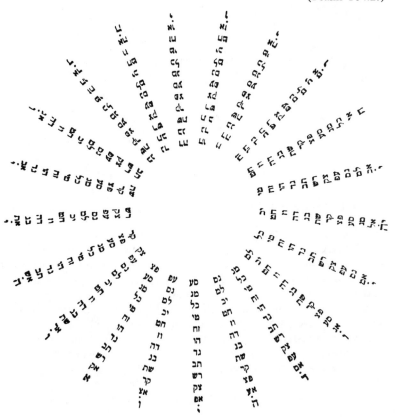

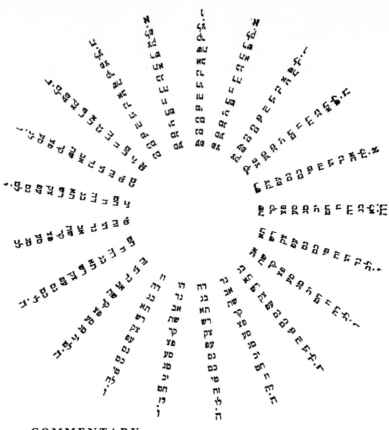

COMMENTARY

(1) "According to [Israel Sarug, a major interpreter of the kabbala of Isaac Luria], the *zimzum* was preceded by processes of an even more inward nature within *Ein-Sof* itself. In the beginning *Ein-Sof* took pleasure in its own autarkic self-sufficiency, and this 'pleasure' produced a kind of 'shaking' (*ni'anu'a*) which was the movement of *Ein-Sof* within itself. Next, this movement 'from itself to itself' aroused the root of *Din* [judgment], which was still indistinguishably combined with *Rahamim* [mercy]. As a result of this 'shaking,' 'primordial points' were 'engraved' in the power of *Din,* thus becoming the first forms to leave their markings in the essence of *Ein-Sof.* . . . As the light of *Ein-Sof* outside this 'engraving' acted upon the points within it, the latter were activated from their potential state and the primordial Torah, the ideal world

woven in the substance of *Ein-Sof* itself, came into being. This Torah, the linguistic movement of *Ein-Sof* within itself, is called a *malbush* ('garment'), though in fact it is inseparable from the divine substance and is woven within it 'like the grasshopper whose clothing is part of itself.' . . . Its length was made up of the alphabets of the *Sefer Yeẓirah* ['book of formation,' see below] and had 231 'gates' (i.e., possible combinations of the 22 letters of the Hebrew alphabet in the progression [ab, ac, ad,] etc.) which form this archistructure of divine thought. Its breadth was composed of an elaboration of the Tetragrammaton [Y-H-V-H] according to the numerical value of the four possible spellings of the fully written names of its letters, viz., the 'name' 45 (יוד, הא, ואו, הא), the 'name' 52 (יוד, הה, וו, הה), the 'name' 72 (יוד, הי, ויו, הי), and the 'name' 63 (יוד, הי, ואו, הי), which were the 'threads' and the 'weave' that were originally situated in the hem of the garment. . . . The size of this garment was twice the area necessary for the creation of all the worlds. After it had been woven, it was folded in two: half of it ascended and its letters stood behind the letters of the other half. The 'names' 45 and 52 were arranged behind the 'names' 72 and 63, and consequently the last *yod* (י) of the 'name' 63 was left without a partner in the folded garment. This folding constituted a contraction (*ẓimẓum*) of the garment to half its area, and with the removal of half of it from its previous place, something was created in *Ein-Sof* that no longer partook of its substance. All that remained in this primordial square was the unmatched *yod*, which now assumed the dynamic task of transferring the light of *Ein-Sof,* which spread in circles, to the area produced by the act of *ẓimẓum.*" (Gershom Scholem, *Kabbalah,* pages 132–33.)

The first portion of the visualized emanation, above, shows the "names" 72 & 63 in the outermost ring, while the second portion shows the "names" 45 & 52 with the blank space of the "missing *yod.*" (For more on *tsimtsum, Ein-Sof,* etc., see above, pages 4 & 12.)

(2)   The visualization, above, is a later version by Solomon Eliashov & an example of a traditional "concrete poetry" as revelation of the presumed inner dynamics of linguistic process: the interplay of sign & meaning. Scholem further points out the closeness of all this "to the ideas that later developed in modern idealist philosophies, such as those of Schelling & Whitehead"; the reader may also note the resemblance to the binomial structuralism of, e.g., Lévi-Strauss.

(3)   It is the "primordial torah" which rests behind its own gates, "guarded" against those who make the "descent into the *merkaba.*" So there is also an image of the "doorkeepers," & a mystery of same.

the 7th palace
standing at the gate
    & angry
                 war like
       strong
   harsh
               fearful
       furious
the height of mountains
brightness of the peaks
with bows strung stood before them
sharpened swords in hands
the play of lightnings out of eye balls
balls of fire from their nostrils
torches coals from mouths
wore helmets crowns
& iron coats
            spears
      javelins
width of their arms
these keepers of the gates
o these with horses
    they would ride now stand
    side of the stables troughs of fire
    coals of juniper
    they eat o fire of the mangers
    drops like 40 bushels in one mouthful
    horses mouths each mouth
    3 stables of Caesarea
    each stable was the width of

Caesar's Gate
& rivers also fire ran beside
the stables horses drank from
like fullness of the water works
in Kidron
cistern that contains
the rain that ever fell
down all Jerusalem

J.R.

INTERLUDE

Franz Kafka (German, 1883–1924)
BEFORE THE LAW

Before the Law stands a doorkeeper. To this doorkeeper there
comes a man from the country and prays for admittance to the
Law. But the doorkeeper says that he cannot grant admittance at
the moment. The man thinks it over and then asks if he will be allowed in later. "It is possible," says the doorkeeper, "but not at the
moment." Since the gate stánds open, as usual, and the doorkeeper
steps to one side, the man stoops to peer through the gateway into
the interior. Observing that, the doorkeeper laughs and says: "If
you are so drawn to it, just try to go in despite my veto. But take
note: I am powerful. And I am only the least of the doorkeepers.
From hall to hall there is one doorkeeper after another, each more
powerful than the last. The third doorkeeper is already so terrible
that even I cannot bear to look at him." These are difficulties the
man from the country has not expected; the Law, he thinks, should
surely be accessible at all times and to everyone, but as he now takes
a closer look at the doorkeeper in his fur coat, with his big sharp

nose and long, thin, black Tartar beard, he decides that it is better to wait until he gets permission to enter. The doorkeeper gives him a stool and lets him sit down at one side of the door. There he sits for days and years. He makes many attempts to be admitted, and wearies the doorkeeper by his importunity. The doorkeeper frequently has little interviews with him, asking him questions about his home and many other things, but the questions are put indifferently, as great lords put them, and always finish with the statement that he cannot be let in yet. The man, who has furnished himself with many things for his journey, sacrifices all he has, however valuable, to bribe the doorkeeper. The doorkeeper accepts everything, but always with the remark: "I am only taking it to keep you from thinking you have omitted anything." During these many years the man fixes his attention almost continuously on the doorkeeper. He forgets the other doorkeepers, and this first one seems to him the sole obstacle preventing access to the Law. He curses his bad luck, in his early years boldly and loudly, later, as he grows old, he only grumbles to himself. He becomes childish, and since in his years-long contemplation of the doorkeeper, he has come to know even the fleas in his fur collar, he begs the fleas as well to help him and to change the doorkeeper's mind. At length his eyesight begins to fail, and he does not know whether the world is really darker or whether his eyes are only deceiving him. Yet in his darkness he is now aware of a radiance that streams inextinguishably from the gateway of the Law. Now he has not very long to live. Before he dies, all his experiences in these long years gather themselves in his head to one point, a question he has not yet asked the doorkeeper. He waves him nearer, since he can no longer raise his stiffening body. The doorkeeper has to bend low towards him, for the difference in height between them has altered much to the man's disadvantage. "What do you want to know now?" asks the doorkeeper; "you are insatiable." "Everyone strives to reach the Law," says the man, "so how does it happen that for all these many years no one but myself has ever begged for admittance?" The doorkeeper recognizes that the man has reached his end, and to let his failing senses catch the words, roars in his ear: "No one else could ever be admitted here, since this gate was made only for you. I am now going to shut it."

WILLA & EDWIN MUIR

COMMENTARY

(1) "It was believed by the later Kabbalists that the Torah contained 600,000 different meanings & aspects, one for each of the 600,000 primordial souls present [at Sinai &] in every generation of Israel. To each of these souls one letter of the Torah is assigned as their own property. This letter is the individual's root & determines the way in which the Torah will be revealed to him. Its meaning is reserved specifically for him & no one else." (Charles Poncé, *Kabbalah,* page 29.)

(2)   from "the notebooks"   10/75   for Kafka   dying in the cold   I said   come in come in   we could have been together   he the poet was a friend the one who gave us that image of Amerika   but writing out of Prague   the law of worlds   no the made law of the world we know descends on him   splinters the skull   poor brains & lungs spill out   as we are only meat upon the earth   but lovers   sometimes   voices   rise in us we didn't know   o Kafka   take me one step further in the book   who wrote his father   taunted with visions of what crazy torah   as a child   when they would open up the ark   *reminds me of the shooting galleries   where a cupboard door would open in the same way   any time you got a bullseye   only with the difference   something interesting would come out there   but here   the same old dolls   & headless* called it torah also   in the darkness   stood before the law   we whispered visions   of faces   messengers   who came for him   the silent *sons of god*   (j.r.)

(3) "They were given the choice of becoming kings or the kings' messengers. As is the way with children, they all wanted to be messengers. That is why there are only messengers, racing through the world and, since there are no kings, calling out to each other the messages that now have become meaningless. They would gladly put an end to their miserable life, but they do not dare to do so because of their oath of loyalty." (Franz Kafka, *Reflections on Sin, Suffering, Hope & the True Way.*)

   Thus: "angel" (Greek *angelos*) = messenger; Hebrew *malakh* = messenger, angel; *bene elohim* = angels, sons of god, gods.

From THE BOOK OF ENOCH   "Visions of the Sons of God"

& my spirit hidden
then I climbed into the sky
I saw the holy sons of god

who stepped on flames of fire
whose clothes were white
whose faces shone like snow

I saw 2 streams of fire
light bright as hyacinth
I fell before the lord of winds

& angel Michael seized my right hand
lifted led me up to all the secrets
showed me the secrets of the right hand

& the secrets of the farthest sky
& rooms with stars & shining bodies
go out from there before the holy faces

& brought me to the sky of skies
I saw a structure made of crystals
& between those crystals living tongues of fire

& saw a yoke around that house of fire
on its sides four streams of living fire
yoked around that house

& fire angels
    & wheel angels
        & enfolded angels
& none of them would sleep
but guard the Throne of Glory

& angels I had lost the count of
thousands of thousands & 10,000 times 10,000
would surround that house

& Michael & Rafael & Gabriel & Fanuel
angels of power from above the skies
would enter & would leave that house

& now they came out from that house
Michael & Gabriel Rafael & Fanuel
& many angels I had lost the count of

& the Head of Days
whose head was white & pure as wool
& clothes were indescribable

& fell down on my face
my body was relaxed now
& my spirit was transfigured

J.R.

COMMENTARY

"From every utterance that goes forth from the mouth of the Holy
One Be Blest an angel is created, as they say: *By the word of Yahveh
were the heavens made, & all the host of them by the breath of Yahveh's
mouth.*" (Talmud: *Ḥagiga* 14a.)

Tristan Tzara (French, 1896–1963)
ANGEL

color recomposes
the liquid hanged men
worms of light in the vapor
where the clarinets grow
the bell glides under the boat
below the town flame bandages
squeeze squeeze tightly
the feldspar gleams in the speed
on holiday
mechanic of necrologies
staging of the menageries
then throws at her husband's head

meeeeeteeeeoooorooooloooo-
giies
the sun glides tangent of the atmosphere
skating dimensions

flows between the spaces
rainbow swing
where our durations are visible
woman pregnant with satellites
burning green ball
caress the centrifugal wound
bellies' acids and plant
angel mechanic
windmill
negro head
and of friendships
a bowl of vitriol
let's go to the other
meteorologies

glide aureola

PIERRE JORIS

COMMENTARY

(1) And Rilke: "Every single angel is terrible. . . ." Or again: "This 'angel' . . . has nothing to do with the Angel of the Christian heaven (rather with the angelic figures of Islam) . . . in whom the transformation of the visible into the invisible we are performing already appears complete . . . therefore 'terrible' to us, because we, its lovers and trans-

formers, still depend on the visible." Thus: "The world, regarded no longer from the human point of view, but as it is within the angel, is perhaps my real task, one, at any rate, in which all my previous attempts would converge." (1925, 1915.)

(2) "Said Rabbi Simeon: Alas for the blindness of the sons of men, all unaware as they are how full the earth is of strange & invisible beings & hidden dangers, which could they but see, they would marvel how they themselves can exist on the earth." (*Zohar* I.55a.)

Moses of Burgos (Hebrew, 1230/1235–c. 1300)
From THE BOOK OF THE LEFT PILLAR

> . . . & he set up the pillars in the porch of the temple   he
> set up the right pillar & named it Jachin & set up the left
> pillar & named it Boaz . . .

(I Kings 7.21.)

as the idea arose in the mind of God & in his pure thought to create a holy & a pure reality, the foundation & the pillar of perfection, to let all good things pour forth from his majesty . . . so the idea arose in his divine & pure will to create real beings according to an order & arrangement too diverse, too darkly wonderful, too distant & too strange for its logical comprehension by any of the masters of rational knowledge & of exegesis : but there is a reliable tradition, a kabbala passed on to all the masters of the hidden wisdom, that reality as a whole could not exist except through real beings, beings that do good & that do evil, that bring things into being & sustain them, that terminate & that obliterate, that give rewards & punishments : & THE ELOHIM HAS DONE THIS SO THAT MEN SHOULD FEAR BEFORE HIM (Ecclesiastes 3.14) as Solomon has said THE ONE AS WELL AS THE OTHER ELOHIM HAS MADE (Ecclesiastes 7.14) : & our wise ones, may their memory be a blessing, said: HE CREATED THE RIGHTEOUS, HE CREATED THE WICKED, HE CREATED PARADISE, HE CREATED HELL, TO SHOW THAT HE CREATED ALL THINGS & THEIR OPPOSITIONS (Talmud: Ḥagiga 15a) : & the Prophet said I FORM THE LIGHT & CREATE DARKNESS, I MAKE PEACE & CREATE EVIL, I YAHVEH DO ALL THESE THINGS (Isaiah 45.7) : & listen : from the meaning of these verses we can understand & we can know that He, the Holy One Be Blest, made all things & also made their contraries, & perfectly he did his perfect work perfecting his perfection for the good ones, those whose hearts are straight : & he created evil : a new reality of being appointed to bring suffering & punishments on rebels & on sinners & on all who walk the dark & gloomy road : the unpaved way

J.R./H.L.

COMMENTARY

(1)   "Without Contraries is no progression. Attraction and Repulsion, Reason and Energy, Love and Hate, are necessary to Human existence.
   "From these contraries spring what the religious call Good & Evil. Good is the passive that obeys Reason. Evil is the active springing from Energy.
   "Good is Heaven. Evil is Hell."
   (Thus Wm. Blake, "The Marriage of Heaven & Hell," circa 1790.)

(2)   With Moses of Burgos, etc., we are straining the limits of the "normative," non-dualistic religion. But the move occurs again & again, even erupts (with Jewish gnostics & inspired heretics, say) into the idea of a true counter-force: the "powers" of the world we know as the essential contraries of *Ein-Sof,* etc.: i.e., like the Nobadaddy & "rational" world-maker of Blake's visions, the source of repressive law, false Torah. And it is that split in turn that lays the groundwork for a virtual "poetics of liberation."

While such a formulation tends as here to remain a moral metaphor, it can be read more interestingly as a dialectic & "metapoetics" (G. Quasha): a complex imagery of worlds & counter-worlds. Thus the world of the "right side" is matched point for point by a world of the "other side" (the so-called *sitra aḥra*) or left side, left hand, or left pillar —spinning like anti-matter in the opposite direction. Moses of Burgos even supplies names for the counter-*sefirot* (see above), although the designations seem more spooky than substantive, viz.:

THE 10 SEFIROT OF THE LEFT ACCORDING TO MOSES OF BURGOS

(1)
T'omi'el   or Twin El   maybe : twin of Keter
or
Tumi'el : Complete El

(2)
'Ugi'el : Encircled El
or
Go'iy'el : the Bleating El

(3)
Sitri'el : the Secret El
or
Harasi'el : Destroyed El

(4)
Ga'ashkala : Shaking to the End

(5)
Geyvlahav : Backfire

(6)
Tagiriron : the Challenge

(7)
'Arav Tsarak : maybe Spurned the Sweets   (wrote Rambam)   as "God's Sweetness"

(8)
Sama'el : Defiant Rebel
Sama'el : Gives Death[1]

(9)
Gamali'el : Weaning Camel
Naḥashi'el : Snake El : camel with its legs cut off

(10)
Lilith : the Night Wailer : match her up with Malkhut as a female presence : the Shekinah of the Left

[1] By "notarikon" (see below, page 431).

INTERLUDE

David Meltzer (b. 1937)
From HERO/LIL   "The Third Shell"

And behold, that hard shell (i.e. embodiment of evil), Lilith, is always present in the bedlinen of man and wife when they copulate, in order to take hold of the sparks of the drops of semen which are lost—because it is impossible to perform the marital act without such a loss of sparks—and she creates out of them demons, spirits and Lilin. . . . But there is an incantation for this, to chase Lilith away from the bed and to bring forth pure souls . . . in that moment, when a man copulates with his wife, let him direct his heart to the holiness of his Master, and say:

> *"In the name of God.*
> *O you who are wrapped in velvet*
> *You have appeared.*

Release, release!
Neither come nor go!
The seed is not yours,
Nor in your inheritance.
Go back, go back!
The sea rages,
Its waves call you.
I hold on to the Holy One,
Wrap myself into the King's holiness."

From: *Emek Ha-Melekh*
(*Sha'ar Tikkune Ha-teshuvah*)

(1)

L	Y	L	Y	T
30	10	30	10	400

*

30 10 30 10 400 = 480 = 12

*

The book within the book.
All year long. Night & day.

(2)

The embrace.
Locked in love.
Man inside woman,
Woman inside man.
Yod in Hay,
Hay in Yod.
The halves made whole.

(3)

Lilith: process.
One end of the imagination to the other.
Start & stop in her core.
Fill her bowl with light.
She is song.

Song goes thru
Seed in her womb.
Her womb is Aleph.
First woman. Before Eve.
Last woman.
Matronita, Shekinah.
Brides of God.
Within me.
The process.

(4)

Into the Hay of her, the Hay within the Hay within the Hay of her, as thru door after door of her. All combinations of her interchange. Face into face. Sex into sex. All sparks & specks sing a multitude of possibility. Into the Hay of her, the Hay within the Hay within the Hay of her.

Her grace made more so by completion.

Upper & lower cherubic spheres extend & pipeline light thru all our veins. Birth the triumph, creation the song of it.

Flesh vanity. A shell our eyes touch & appraise. Skin deep.

Before & after each pass, praise her invisible tongue.

(5)

"To banish his loneliness, Lilith was first given to Adam as wife. Like him she had been created from the dust of the ground. But she remained with Adam only a short time, because she insisted upon enjoying full equality with her husband. She derived her right from their identical origin."

From: *Midrash Bereshit Rabbah.*

(6)

Words thrown back.
Stars, suns, moons.
We fear her more than He.
His thunder speech
Can not hide the need for union.
We father daughters to reach her.
Words thrown back.
Man stands at root end

Pointing to her door.
Words thrown back.
Stones against her window.
Jewels thrown at her feet.
Stars, suns, moon.
Letters snow upon her gold crown as she walks by.

(7)

At night I touch her mouth with language. Afterwards. I move against her. She spends all day dressing for night, preparing her face. I am a farmer. She asks me to light her pipe. We are married by flashlight. She stands in a circle of racoons. I drive a machine of letters. We are behind the wheel. The radio's on. She caresses my shoulder blades. A field of corn turns into mercury sheets her body swims under. Law is reversed at night, black is white & white black. She wants words only after sunrise. I touch her mouth with language. Afterwards. I move against her.

(8)

"You have made a mistake."
"Try the other door. It's really locked."
"You only think it's God."
"Your name has been reversed."
"No tricks."
"Don't ever get used to being cheated."
"It still hasn't been said. Give her another kiss."
"No book should be longer."

(9)

"Her radiance, however, is so great that the angels must cover their faces with their wings so as not to see her. The ministering angels are removed from the Shekinah by myriads of parasangs, and the body of Shekinah herself measures millions of miles."

From: *Midrash Ha-Gadol Shemini.*

(10)

Ah you old whore
step halfway out the blue door
with Woolworth mirror bangles

& burlesque spangles
& wink at any guy
passing by
minding his own
business.

We all know Lilith
as she moves

COMMENTARY

(1)   from "the notebooks"   10/75   a letter to Meltzer for his 3rd visit
to Milwaukee

. . . .

how you first came
will come the day after these words
are written
typing your poem of *Hero/Lil*
reading it again
I wonder
what this *zeitgeist* is
drives us to still believe in "chance"
that brings you when my thoughts are bound
with yours
your name has called you
—that would have been the magic once—
you David singer thru your father's side
but thru the mother's too
wonders of the old books we both read
those martyrs to the images
mad Jews whose words
splintered the ONE into diversity who
robbed of freedom
dreamt it back to life
high spirits   friends
as you saw Lilith

equal woman
power in the earth
o good & evil still
persisting
a poetry of changes
as the Zohar tells us
THERE IS SAMAEL
& THERE IS SAMAEL
& THEY ARE NOT THE SAME   (j.r.)

(2) THE HERETIC (from the Babylonian Talmud). Aḥer mutilated the
shoots. The Writings say of him: SUFFER NOT THY MOUTH TO
BRING THY FLESH INTO GUILT. —And what's that all about?— He
saw that permission was given Metatron to sit down while writing the
merits of Israel. So he said: There's a tradition up in heaven that there
should be no sitting & no emulation & no back & no weariness. Maybe—
God forbid!—there are two divinities! And right after that they took
Metatron out & they punished him: they whipped him sixty times with
fire & they told him: How come you didn't rise up when you saw him?
Then they also gave him permission to strike out Aḥer's merits. The
voice's daughter—the *bat kol*—rose up, saying: RETURN, BACKSLID-
ING CHILDREN—all except Aḥer. Right after that he said: As long as
this here boy has lost the world beyond, I better get some pleasure out of
this one. So Aḥer got off on bad ways. He went & found a whore &
propositioned her. She said: Aren't you Elisha ben Abuya? But when he
tore a radish out of its bed on a Saturday & gave it to her, then she
said: This must be some other Aḥer. After his break, he questioned his
old pupil, Rabbi Me'ir. He asked him: What's the meaning of the verse:
GOD HAS MADE THE ONE AS WELL AS THE OTHER? He an-
swered: It means that for everything God created he also created a
counterpart. He created mountains, so he created hills: he created seas,
so he created rivers. Then Aḥer said to him: Rabbi Akiba, your master,
didn't explain it like that but like this: He created the righteous, he created the wicked, he created Paradise, he created Hell. . . . When Aḥer
died they said: LET HIM NOT BE JUDGED & LET HIM NOT ENTER
THE WORLD TO COME. Let him not be judged because he engaged in
the study of Torah, but let him not enter the world to come because he
sinned. Rabbi Me'ir said: It would be better for him to be judged so he
could enter the world to come. When I die I'll make smoke rise from his
grave. When Rabbi Me'ir died smoke rose from Aḥer's grave. Rabbi
Yoḥanan said: What a mighty deed to burn his master! There was just

one like that among us, & we couldn't save him. If I were to take him by the hand, who would snatch him from me! And he said: When I die I'll extinguish the smoke from his grave. When Rabbi Yoḥanan died the smoke stopped from Aḥer's grave. The public mourner began his oration for him, saying: EVEN THE JANITOR OF HELL COULD NOT WITHSTAND THEE, MASTER. (Talmud: *Ḥagiga* 15a, 15b.)

For more on Aḥer (Elisha ben Abuya), etc., see page 269, below.

✿

The Sethians, per Hippolytos (Greek, c. 3rd century A.D.)
THE 3 OF BEGINNING: LIGHT, DARK, SPIRIT

---

        spirit where light and dark void each other
clear and unconfounded
                no wind blowing gentle breeze
     ointment or perfume
             it steals into things
                better than words

       light above dark below spirit between

               light the sunray on dark beneath
        in molten fire everywhere incenses
              the subtleties of spirit
      to lead powers of both alive
into dark whose fearful water drinks light
              in spirit essence
     thinks and thinks over

                              if light leaves
she knows herself isolate invisible shrouded asleep heartless inert
                    willing her to assemble within
                                        glints and chromes of light
                                                to the spirits lifting
                    (image:
                              the eye's vitreous dark
                    spirits light
                                        down its black hole)

                    patrolling for light
                         dark desires outward splendor to see
                                   and bind his emissaries
                                             freckling night sea

        light and spirit
                    empower themselves to stand
                              towards each other
                                        embracing
                              plunging into dark
                                        the strong down water

                                                              C.D.

COMMENTARY

(1)   Among early "gnostic" groups such as the Sethians—often described
as largely Jewish sects—a second energy, emerged as "evil," "darkness,"
that seems in retrospect like the natural expression of an "imperfect" &
"destructive" universe. Where an actual dualism was asserted, the straight
response—as in the story of Aḥer (Rabbi Elisha ben Abuya, above)—
was to isolate the "heretics," ultimately to drive them from the community. But the gnostic tension, which unquestionably goes back to pagan
Jewish sources, etc., remains a strong element in the mystical writings:
as a kind of "torsion," or twist in direction, that continued to shape the
imagery & bring the mind to an evolving series of mythic revelations.
All of that as perhaps a basic poetic process, in which the recognition of
contraries conditions & is conditioned by a pressure toward their reconciliation.

(2)

> "when you make the two one
> "& make the inside like the outside
> "& the outside like the inside
> "& the upper side like the under side
> "& make the man & woman be a single one
> "so the man is not the man & the woman not the woman
> "when you make eyes in place of an eye
> "& a hand in place of a hand
> "& a foot in place of a foot
> "an image in place of an image
> "then you will go into the kingdom

(Thus Jesus in the Gospel of Thomas, a document apparently used by the Naasenes, a Christian gnostic group said to have been predominantly Jewish. And here too, for all the expected dualism, we get the counter-image of a unity to be restored.)

CODA

Solomon ibn Gabirol (Hebrew, c. 1020–c. 1057)
From THE CROWN OF KINGDOM (I–IX)

> May man profit by my prayer
> may he learn the right and straight through it
> I have told the wonders of living El in it
> in brief   not at full length
> I set it above all my other praises
> I call it the Crown of Kingdom

I.

How wondrous your doings my soul knows well
Greatness is yours Adonai   and might and beauty
                                        infinity and splendor
Rule is yours Adonai   and overall and richness and honor
The created things are yours   witness above and below
for as they disappear you wear on
Might is yours
our very thought wears out getting at its secret
You are so stronger than we
The mystery of might is yours   the hidden and the hide

Yours is the name hidden from sages
            the power which carries the world over nothing
            the ability to bring the hidden to light
Yours is the mercy
which rules your creatures
            and the good   hidden for those who fear you
Secrets are yours
which thought and reason cannot hold
and life which is unending
      the throne rising over all over
      the pleasance hidden in the height of mystery
Reality is yours
in its lit shade being is

we have said it: "We will live in His shade."

You have drawn a border between two worlds and both are yours:
one for doing and the other for reward
The reward of you you have kept for the righteous
                                        kept hidden
for you saw its good and stored it up

II.

You are one   the beginning of all count
            the base of every structure
You are one   the sage of heart gape at your oneness
                        and its secret   for they cannot know it

You are one   your unity cannot be diminished or added to
                        it cannot want or gain
You are one   not as counted and dealt are one
                        for extent and change cannot reach you
                        nor description nor reference
You are one   My logic tires setting a limit for you and a law
               so I must guard my way from my own tongue's error
You are one   higher and over low and fallen
               no one   alone   to fall

III.

You are real   but earhear and eyesight cannot reach you
               how and why and where have nothing to do with you
You are real   but to yourself
               and noone takes part
You are real   before all time you were
               and dwelt without place
You are real   your secret hidden and who çan catch it?
               Deep   deep   who can find it?

IV.

You live   not from fixed time
           not from known date
You live   soulless   spiritless
           you are soul's soul
You live   not as man lives   in vain
           his end moth and worm
You live   Who comes towards your secret finds eternal delight
                        lives forever   if he eat of it

V.

You are huge   in the face of your hugeness everything of size
                        shrinks
You are huge   greater than any thought   higher than the Chariot
                        itself
You are huge   greater than large   higher than praise

VI.

You are might   of all your creatures and makings
                 there is none can do as you or as your might
You are might   changeless   only   total might is
                 yours alone
You are might   from your height you can forgive from your wrath
                                    endure sin in your anger
You are might   the mercy you show your creatures   all
                 this is the eternal might

VII.

You are highest light
eyes of clear soul see you   clouds of sin hide you from sineyes
You are hidden light
in this world   open in the visioned world
                    "mount of Adonai   it will be seen"
You are eternal light
eye of mind longs   and is startled at you
                             seeing only the edges   never all

VIII.

You are he   Elohei Elohim   Adonei Adonim   ruling high and low
You are Eloha   all creatures your witness
                 all creation made to serve you   honoring this name
You are Eloha   all the made things are your servants and serve you
                 no glory lost where others worship without you
                 the desire of all is to reach you
                 though they are like the blind who seek the highway
                 and stray from the way
                             This one drowns in ruin pit
                             this falls in holes
                     yet all think they have struck their wish
                     yet reach waste
    Your servants are openeyed   walking the right way
                             never turning off   right or left
                             till they come to the palace yard

You are Eloha   keeping made things by your Godness
                feasting creatures on your Oneness
You are Eloha   no different in your Oneness and your Godness
                        or your Firstness or your Being
It is all one secret
                and even if all the names are changed
it all comes back to one place

IX.

You are wise   wisdom is the source of life and flows from you
               all men are too stupid to know your wisdom
You are wise   the first of every first
               wisdom grew up with you
You are wise   not learn from without you
               not have it from some other
You are wise   shone fixed will from your wisdom
                        a worker and an artist   pulling something
                                                from nothing
                        as the light is drawn out from the eye
                        drawn from lightsource   without a tool
                        working without any tool
                        split and chop
                        cleanse and true
                        call to nothing and split it
                            to being and fix it
                            to timeworld and divide it
                        measure skies by hand
                        a hand joining tents of orbit
                        joining the films of creature
                        with rings of might
                        power beaming on to the edge of creation
                                        the lowest
                                        the farthest away
                                        the curtain's hem

                                                H.L.

THE END OF "A BOOK OF POWERS"

A Book of Worlds

(beginning)   these are the generations of the skies & earth   when they were created   the day when Yahveh Elohim made earth & skies.   (Genesis 2.4.)

(Greek, 4th–6th century A.D.)

From THE HIDDEN SACRED BOOK OF MOSES
CALLED "EIGHTH" OR "HOLY"

. . . .

the 7 Laughs of GOD
Hha   Hha   Hha   Hha   Hha   Hha   Hha

each laugh he gave
engendered the 7
god   god   god   god   god   god   god

the Fore-Appearers
who clasp everything one

C.D.

COMMENTARY

(1)   Beside the "work of the chariot," a second process ("work") appears called *ma'ase bereshit*, "the work of creation." This is not fixed either, not locked in its ur-text, but plays off against it, unwinding as a continuity, a variety of forms & transformations that the written word disguises but cannot expunge. The text is (so-called) Jewish heterodox: retains the image of the "gods" (here seven that his laugh creates) & strains the limits we would later see as Jewish. Creation comes through breath, through laughter here, to form a sound, a name, that turns up elsewhere as the name ההא (hey hey alef): which laughter the Greek-Jewish poet (like the poet of the Hindu Upanishads) acknowledged as itself creation.

And this, in turn, would tie up with the laughing/crying gods of Canaan, & an exuberance ("lightheadedness" the Talmud's word for it: joy bright with sexuality) never absent from the Temple celebration of the seasons as the re-enactment of Yahveh's own "creation . . . conceived as a kind of cosmic rutting season, when the rain came down, mated with the earth, and fructified it." (Thus: Patai, *Man & Temple,* page 69.)

(2)   Again, the image is one of transformation, viewed as play: a god of changes still related to the "trickster" of the shaman-poets, as the final self-transformer: hidden in "torah" as elsewhere in that "tao" (or "way") inscribed on the pillars of the Chinese synagogue in K'ai-fêng:

> The ever-living Lord, Who produces life without ceasing
> *Shêng shêng pu yi, ch'ang-shêng Chu*
> The creating Heaven, Whose transmutations never end
> *Hua hua wu ch'iung, tsao-hua T'ien*

making by translation a Hebrew-Chinese torah/tao of metamorphosis, a mind whose emptiness casts up a world of forms where nothing else existed.

Edmond Jabès (French, b. 1912)

From ELYA   "The Disappearance"

*

The day's freedom consists in the light's secret climb back to the beginnings of the shores deserted by men.

The heart beats in the emptiness of the astonished body. Its form will come from the *other*.

Thus the world will form the world in freeing it.

Thus God, within Himself, will come to terms with the Face.

The sage dipped his reed pen into the inkwell, pulled it out, and held it for a few moments, as if in doubt, above the page where he had not noted anything yet that day. Then, to his pupil's surprise, he drew a small circle in a corner of the blotter he always kept within reach.

"This circle," he said, "which the blotter has made into a point invaded by night, is God."

"Why did you want the circle to turn into a black point? And why should this stain among so many others on your blotter be God?" the disciple asked.

"Your question is that of the Lord," replied the sage.

"If my question is that of the Lord," said the disciple, "I know now that God has created me in His image."

*

At this time before time, when life was only a bare death with weak lungs, one insignificant point in space contained, like a bubble, all the wanderings of the worlds.

When it burst it freed the universe, but gave form to exile.

God had disappeared, existing only in Creation.

Being the Principle of Unity—a circle tightening in infallible memory of the circle—He was going to become the dazzling center of clear absence.

Never again will we escape exile.

The book is among its true stages.

ROSMARIE WALDROP

Joseph Gikatilla (Hebrew, 1248–c. 1325)

THE WITHDRAWAL, THE EXILE

(the semicircular line of print reads): a dot the nations of the world surround the circle are outside & Israel's the middle of the dot.

(1)   The image of *tsimtsum* (see above, page 12) is the world defined by God's withdrawal. Pinpoint at center of the circle. Empty space. With creation, emergence, it enters history, exists now in the consciousness that grows around it. The world we know begins: a world of growth, division into shapes & species: builds toward the myth of exile: Jewish, gnostic. But the point is there for each of us, renewed at each conception, flashes up, ovum ignited, swelling, screaming our entry into light. This is birth: creation felt by the created. Surrounded, absent in ourselves, each one the dot, the focal point, the center. Each one of us is now called Israel, now fills the place of exile with our absent god.

(2)   In Gikatilla's visualization the third line toward the center is the single word (נקודה) NKVDH = point or dot, while the top line is the god-name (אהוי) AHVY, spelled out as Alef-Hey-Vav-Yod.

Simeon bar Yoḥai (2nd century A.D.)
per Moses de Leon (Aramaic, c. 1240–1305)

THE *YOD* OF CREATION

---

an egg of truth
drops from the bird who lives
in fire
bursts out on 4 sides
2 emerge from it
1 is depressed
1 overflows into a sea

J.R.

COMMENTARY

(1) The *yod* (ʾ), small letter, is itself a point, an opening through which creation, as another letter (number) in the shape of *yod*, can enter. (For one version of the myth of same, see pages 50–51, above; compare as well the orphic egg-of-origin, etc.)

(2) from "the notebooks"   10/75   two points mark that name   yod yod of childhood   I remember from the prayerbooks   the Yod Hey Vav Hey gone   no sound no sound but this   in the reduction   & no YaHVeH   but one of these perhaps the shadow of the other   white on white   or black on black   were like the mystic paintings of our time the pointings   maybe male & female   when the absent yod   yod's shadow   's pierced by yod   all movement   growth   begins   there is no mystery in where the light converges   or the mind   that lonely thing   emerging   in a ring of pain   (j.r.)

Cid Corman (b. 1924)

From LIVINGDYING

On the blank
paper a
speck, in it

almost, it
seems, but to
my eyes—not

always re-
liable—
it moves at

an immense
distance at
great speed and

yet has not
moved at all—
for the white

space clings to
it as to
a meaning

COMMENTARY

(1)   "That which exists through itself is what is called the Meaning."
(Charles Olson quoting Master Lu Tzu in the 9th-century Chinese *Secret
of the Golden Flower*. And he adds in the margin of his copy: "I am /
that I am / The Great One is that which exists through itself; nothing
is above it because it is contained in the Light of Heaven.")

(2)   "There is no space free of the Divine Presence, not even a thorn-
bush." (Rabbi Joshua ben Karḥa, *Exodus Raba* II.9.)

A PROLOGUE TO "THE TORAH OF THE VOID"

On a day shortly before his death, the Rav asked his grandson:
"Do you see anything?"
The boy looked at him in astonishment. Then the Rav said: "As
yet I see only the divine nothing which gives life to the world."

Nachman of Bratzlav (Hebrew, 1772–1810)
From THE TORAH OF THE VOID

God,
for Mercy's sake,
created the world
to reveal Mercy.
If there were no world
on whom would Mercy take pity?

So—to show His Mercy
He created the worlds
from *Aziluth*'s peak
to this Earth's center.

But as He wished to create
there was not a *where?*
All was Infinitely He,
Be He Blessed!

The light He condensed
sideways
thus was *space* made
an empty void.

In *space* days and measures
came into being.
So the world was created.

This void was needed
for the world's sake,
so that it may be
put into place.

Don't strain to understand
this void!
It is a mystery—not to be realized
until the future
is the *now*.

*

Once there was *light,*
much and powerful,
holy *light,*
and it was in vessels
—too much *light,*
too much power—
and the *vessels* burst!

When the *vessels* burst
the fragments
of Holiness
took form
becoming the *outered* sciences.

So,
even of Holiness
there is offal:
Just as there is sweat
and hair and excrement,
so Holiness too
has its offal.

Holy Wisdom too has offal.
Outered wisdom
is the offal of the holy.
And when this offal is used
to twist the world,
you have sorcery.

Once, also, *source-ery*
was rooted
in a high wisdom.

He who can
should strive to avoid
the trap
of the *outered* sciences.
But whoever falls
into the trap
is not lost forever.

Seeking God
one can find Him there,
in the shards of Holiness
which give life to the sciences—
even in the very symbols
in which the sciences
express themselves.
For as long as there
is reason and rhyme—
and words—
there is Holiness
in the form of sparks.
As long as there is life
in the word, God is there.

*

And the void?

It is nothing but
the *no-thing* which takes up
no *space* at all.
All it does is separate
between the Divine which *fills*
and the Divine which *surrounds*
the world.

Without the void
all would have been One.
But then
there would not have been
any creature—any world.
So the void is a kind of

Divine Wisdom of not being
so there can be division
between one kind of being
and another.

This wisdom of not being,
the wisdom of the void—
cannot be realized!
It is not a *something*
but it makes all *somethings* possible.
Each something is infused with
God
and surrounded by God:
There is in between
a void that is not.

*

All creation comes from
the WORD:
"By the word of God
Heaven was made,
and by the breath of His mouth
all their hosts."
In words inhere wisdom
and sense.

All speech is bordered
by the five limits
of the mouth.
All creation is a limiting
in three dimensions
and in time
and in substance:
"In wisdom hast Thou
made them all."

The void has no limits,
no echo.
Burning questions
are not answered there.

Martyrs who want to know *Why?*
are told "Silence."
Thus is the decree of the *Thought!*
Such *thought* is not given
to words.

*

How is the void made?
By strife!
One *zaddik* says this
and the other that,
and *between*
there is strained a void.

*

A *zaddik* sings.
If he is a "Moses"
he can raise souls
lost in the void.

Each science
has its own song:
Each science
issues from a melody.
Even the void's Unwisdom
has a melody of its own.

"What was wrong with the heretic?"
"When he rose,
Greek song books fell from him.
All day he hummed
the Greek's song."

The song and the heresy—
each depends on the other—
the wisdom and its tune,
the science and its scale.

For heresies fall
in bookloads
from one who sings the tune
of heresy.

*

And through the *zaddik*'s *niggun,*
when in him tonguetied Moses
sings,
all lost souls
rise from the abyss,
find their way from the void.
All tunes are reabsorbed in
the song of silence,
all heresy integrated and dissolved,
Tune and word
in the THOUGHT SONG.

*

"Moses came to Pharaoh"
—the void—
"and said
Tomorrow—
see—
I bring the *arbeh,*
the swarms
of locusts
into your midst."
For *tomorrow*
is the time
of the reward receiving.

What is the reward all about?
To perceive great perception
to have cosmic insight,
today unattainable.

And then we will know
how the void
was like the locust,
its cloak and being one,
all veils and garments
but He
outer, inner He
word and wordless He
end and endless He
Tune and singer He
Most high and abyss He
void He, fullness He
I-He
You He
He
He!

        —Amen!

ZALMAN SCHACHTER

COMMENTARY

(1) The fullness of "God" described as *ayin,* "nothing"—*for* ayin *combines a thing & its opposite* (thus Abraham Kalisker, circa 1800). This is a further meditation on the image of the "point": the empty (or full) center of the circle: a condensed mass of light or energy about to burst. Yet the idea of the empty center is, however glossed over, a reminder that in a world of contingencies, there are no answers, only questions. Thus Gertrude Stein on her deathbed: "What is the answer?" (Silence.) "Well then, what is the question?"

(2) THE BREAKING OF THE VESSELS. In the vacuum left by God's withdrawal (*tsimtsum*), lines of light pour in, irradiate, collide. Crystal vessels form, which can't contain the light but burst, leaving dark shards behind. The shards (*klipot*) are the basis of all matter & represent the forces of the "other side" (the *sitra aḥra*): the uncleansed "doors of perception" of the familiar world (Wm. Blake). Within them are "sparks"

or "seeds" of light, & the intention of the process that follows is the freeing of that light.

The basic formulation—but more complex & image-filled than that given here—is Isaac Luria's. Like gnosticism—to which it is related—it traces the condition of a broken (i.e., imperfect) universe away from man & back to "source" as "god" or "nothing." The "breaking of the vessels" is also called "the death of the kings."

Joseph Gikatilla (Hebrew, 1248–c. 1325)
NOTHING

I.

COMMENTARY

(1) In Hebrew: AYIN (אין) / Aniy (אני), an anagram in which the pronoun *aniy* (I) is a name of God, as *ayin* (nothing) is his attribute in *tsimtsum.* On the use of pronouns (I, He, Thou) as names of God, the reader may want to check the *Zohar;* e.g.: "It is written, 'I, the Lord, am the first and with the last: I am He' (Isaiah 41.4). Everything is He: He is the name concealed on all sides." (130a.) Or again: *"And Thou shalt rule over him:* the word 'thou' contains a mystical allusion to the Almighty, who is also called THOU." (I.37a.)

(2) "Men have addressed their eternal *Thou* with many names. In singing of Him who was thus named they always had the *Thou* in mind: the first myths were hymns of praise. Then the names took refuge in the language of *It;* men were more and more strongly moved to think of

and to address their eternal *Thou* as an *It*. But all God's names are hallowed, for in them He is not merely spoken about, but also spoken to.

". . . He who speaks the word God and really has *Thou* in mind (whatever the illusion by which he is held), addresses the true *Thou* of his life, which cannot be limited by another *Thou,* and to which he stands in a relation that gathers up and includes all others.

"But when he, too, who abhors the name, and believes himself to be godless, gives his whole being to addressing the *Thou* of his life, as a *Thou* that cannot be limited by another, he addresses God." (Martin Buber, *I and Thou*.)

Shên Ch'üan, of Hua-t'ing (Chinese, late 17th century)
From THE VERTICAL INSCRIPTIONS

Before the Great Void, we burn the fragrant incense,
   entirely forgetting its name or form

Tracing back to the Western world,
   we resist our evil desires,
       and solely attend to purity and truth.

W. C. WHITE

COMMENTARY

"Concerning the origin of the religion of Israel (*Yi-tz'u-lo-yeh*), it has come from a distant past.

"It began with Adam (*A-tan*), who was a descendant of P'an-ku in the nineteenth generation, and it was continued, at first by Noah (*Nü-wo*), and then by Abraham (*A-wu-lo-han*).

"Abram (*Lo-han*) comprehended the purpose of the union of Heaven and man, as well as the principles (*yüan*) of moral cultivation and of human destiny. He knew also that the Way (*Tao*) of Heaven 'has neither sound nor smell' [Confucian Ode, *235:7; Doctrine of the Mean, 33:6*], and is very mysterious and profound, and that from it creatures are endowed with movement and with life, and are transformed and nourished [*Doctrine of the Mean, 22*] in orderly manner. That is why he modeled no images, nor did he allow himself to be deluded by ghosts and spirits. He made the honoring of Heaven as the only principle, leading men to 'develop completely their minds' [*Mencius, bk. vii: I, chap. 1:1*] and to conform to Heaven, so that they could follow their minds and see the Way (*Tao*)." (From the Stone Inscription at the K'ai-fêng synagogue, dated 1663 & composed by Liu Ch'ang, "specially promoted to the dignity of Kuang Lu Ta Fu, Second Classical Tutor of the Emperor, First Tutor of the Crown Prince, formerly President of the Board of Punishments, and now President on leave of the Board of Public Works.")

Franz Kafka (German, 1883–1924)
FRAGMENT

"Never will you draw the water out of the depths of this well."
"What water? What well?"
"Who is it asking?"
Silence.
"What silence?"

ERNST KAISER & EITHNE WILKINS

(Hebrew, 3rd–6th centuries A.D.)
From THE BOOK OF FORMATION   "Numbers"

With 32 wondrous ways of wisdom
       YAH
       YHVH TSEVA'OT   (O HOSTS)
       ELOHEI YISRAEL   (GOD OF ISRAEL)
       ELOHIM ḤAYIM   (LIVING GOD)

```
EL  SHADAI            (OMNIPOTENT  GOD)
RAM  VE-NISA          (RAISED  HIGH)
SHOKHEN  AD           (ETERNAL  DWELLER)
```

His Name high and holy

                                    carved, covenanted,

drilled, and created his world,

through three Sefarim:

```
            Sefer      (book) = writing
            Sfor       (counting) = number
            Sippur     (telling) = speech
```

Ten Sefirot (numbers) made of Nothingness
Twenty-two foundation Letters

Ten Sefirot as the number of the ten fingers
5 paralleling 5
                    the Covenant set in the middle
the way the tongue makes the word   the Naked Word

Ten Sefirot of Nothingness   Ten and not Nine   Ten and not Eleven
        Understand this wisely   Search it out intelligently

        Measure with them   Search out from them

        Know and consider   then Be Silent:

        Set the Word at its Origin & return the Maker to His Place

For He is the Maker   creating alone   He has no peer
and Their number is Ten   and They have no end

Ten Sefirot made of Nothing
                        Brake your heart from thinking too
                            quickly
                        Brake your mouth from speaking

                        If your heart races ahead
                        return
                        for it is said

"the creatures ran and returned"

The Covenant was made for this

Ten Sefirot made of Nothing

Their end is lodged in Their beginning
Their beginning in Their end
a flame and a coal

Know
then consider then Be silent:

that the Lord is unique
the Maker is one
He has no peer.

What number comes before One?

Ten Sefirot made of Nothing

Their number is Ten and They have no
end

The range of beginning
The range of end

The range of good
the range of evil

The range of height
the range of depth

The range of east
the range of west

The range of north
the range of south

Only Lord
God Faithful King
Patent of all
from the Residence of His Holiness to Eternity

Ten Sefirot made of Nothing

Their appearance is the look of
lightning

Their disappearance: They have no end

His Word is in them as they come and
  go
At his command They race like the
  whirlwind
and bow before His throne

Ten Sefirot made of Nothing
Twenty-two Foundation Letters
Three Mothers
Seven Doubles
Twelve Simples

The Spiritwind in each of them

Ten Sefirot made of Nothing
                    The first: The Spiritwind of Living
                        God
            His throne set from the beginning
            Blessed the Name of Eternal Life   forever continually
            Voice   and Spiritwind   and Speech

            The Speech   the Holy Spiritwind
            Origin without beginning
            End beyond ending

Ten Sefirot made of Nothing
                    The first: The Spiritwind of Living
                        God

                    The second: Wind from the Spiritwind

                    The third: Water from the Wind

                    The fourth: Fire from the Water
                        and height and depth
                        and East and West
                        and North and South

The second: Wind from the Spiritwind
                    He carved and lawed by them:
            the four winds of the skies

          East and West
          North and South

          The Spiritwind in each of them

The third: Water from Wind
                    He carved and lawed by them:
          Tohu and Bohu
          Mud and Clay
          He made them a garden
          Set them a wall
          Roofed them with plaster
          Poured snow upon them   and it became dust
          as it is said:
          "He said to the snow 'Be earth' "

          Tohu a green line which surrounds the world
          Bohu stones leveled and sunk in the Deep
          water comes out from between them

The fourth: Fire from Water
                    He carved and lawed by it:
          Glory Throne
          Serafim
          Ofanim
          Creatures of Holy   they are the
          Serving Angels

          From the three of them He founded His place
          as it is said: "He makes His angels spiritwinds
                    His servants a flaming fire"

The fifth: Sealed the height
                    He chose three of the Simple letters
                    fixed them by His Great Name YHV
                    sealed by them the six directions:

          He turned Up   Sealed it by HYV

The sixth: Sealed the under
                    He turned Below   Sealed it by YVH

The seventh: Sealed east

| | Turned before | Sealed it by VYH |

The eighth: Sealed west

| | Turned behind | Sealed it by VHY |

The ninth: Sealed south

| | Turned right | Sealed it by YHV |

The tenth: Sealed north

| | Turned left | Sealed it by HVY |

These are the ten Sefirot made of Nothing:

> The first: The Spiritwind of Living God
>
> The second: Wind from the Spiritwind
>
> The third: Water from the Wind
>
> The fourth: Fire from the Water
>
> > and height
> > and depth
> > and East
> > and West
> > and North
> > and South

H.L.

COMMENTARY

(1) The *sefirot* (emanations) appear here in their earliest form, as numbers, quantities emerging from the void. This antedates the *sefirot* as descriptive qualities, etc. (see above, page 11) by many centuries. Thus the *Sefer Yetsira,* or *Book of Formation/Creation,* emphasizes number (*sfor*) as ground of the creative process, a kind of Jewish pythagoreanism that will not disappear but will later, in the mystical physics of the *Zohar,* be equated with light as energy, the universal constant of a possibly related physics in our own time. The book proceeds without explanations, goes from the primal numbers mentioned in the opening section printed

here to the 22 letters (numbers) of the Hebrew alphabet as constituents of the known world, & maintains sufficient condensation & tension to generate a whole literature derived from its images. But number & sound may also be read as the basis of any actual poetics. (For which, see below, page 423.)

(2)   There is the possibility that the *Sefer Yetsira* served on its "practical" side & through the equation of *sefirot* with the elements, etc., as a manual for the construction of new forms & structures in the world of matter. So, the first known account of a "golem" (see below, pages 318, 462) refers to a *"Sefer Yetsira"* ("book of creation") as source:

> For Rava created a man & sent him to Rabbi Zera. The rabbi spoke to him & he did not answer. Then he said: You must have been made by the companions; return to your dust. . . . Also Rav Hanina & Rav Oshaya busied themselves on the eve of every Sabbath with the *Book of Creation*—or in another reading: with the instructions concerning creation. They made a calf one-third the natural size and ate it. (Talmud: *Sanhedrin* 65b.)

(3)   The *Sefer Yetsira* is attributed to the Patriarch Abraham. Its power as a pre-scientific tract on "golem making" reaches nearly to present times—a reminder of the turns taken by the "work of creation" in the service of an aggressive technology. In the legend the golem, created with the word [GOD IS] *EMET* (truth) written on his forehead, takes a knife & scratches out the initial *E* (alef), so that the word now reads: [GOD IS] *MET* (dead). Says the golem maker—the prophet Jeremiah in one version: "Truly, one should study these things only in order to know the power & omnipotence of the Creator of this world, but not in order really to practice them."

Albert Einstein (1879–1955)

E

---

mc^2

from "the notebooks"   11/75   (a dream)   the Alphabet came
to me in a dream   he said   I am Alphabet   take your light from
me   & I thought   you are numbers first before you are sound
you are the fingers' progression & you end in the fist   a solid mass
against the world   but the alphabet was dark like my hand writing
these words   he rose not as light at first though issuing from light
but fear a double headed body with the pen a blacker line at center
   A began it but in Hebrew not a vowel   a choked sound it was
the throat the larynx stopped the midrash said contained all sound

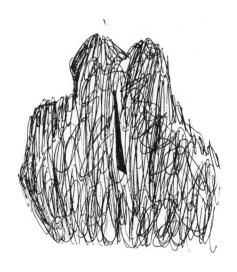

sound of alphabet initial to all speech   as one or zero   called it
WORK OF CREATION in my dream   a creature more than solid more
than space or mass or distance   & he said   all numbers & all
sounds converge here   but I knew it   I said that I would count my
way into the vision   grooved thus with numbers & with sound   the
distances to every side of us   as in a poem   (j.r.)

Nelly Sachs (German, 1891–1970)
From GLOWING ENIGMAS

These millennia
blown by the breath
always in orbit around an angry noun
out of the sun's beehive
stinging seconds
warlike aggressors
secret torturers

Never a breathing space as in Ur
when a people of children tugged at the white ribbons
to play sleep-ball with the moon—

In the street with wind's haste
the woman runs
to fetch medicine for the sick child

Vowels and consonants
cry out in every language:
H e l p !

MICHAEL HAMBURGER

David Slabotsky (b. 1943)

THE MIND OF GENESIS

Rabbi Mikhal used to say: "For the study of Torah, one must have
the Mind of Genesis, otherwise one becomes lost in the doctrine."
Illustrating the Mind of Genesis, Rabbi Mikhal related the following
tale:

"Rabbi Yehuda lived in the ghetto of Zlochtov where he studied
Talmudic law at the hand of Rabbi Lev. A dedicated man, Rabbi
Yehuda would stay in his room for days on end with a single phrase
which Rabbi Lev had assigned to him. Yet it was clear to Rabbi
Yehuda, in spite of his devotion, that his soul would ultimately
perish in the elegant disputes of Talmudic law, for while his fellow
disciples grew strong in their faith, scholarship merely succeeded in
leading him farther and farther away from the source of the Torah,
and rather than bringing a deepening joy to his daily life it was turning him into a bitter sage and souring his faith.

"Rather than come to grief through the wisdom of others, Rabbi
Yehuda devised the following plan: Since the Torah was equally holy
in all Its parts, every word and every letter possessed the gateway
into eternal life and profound understanding. Choosing a single
letter, he could reach in its union with the Sacred Name to the Sacred
Name itself. Not knowing which of the letters to choose, he settled
upon the aleph, the first in the alphabet.

"Rabbi Yehuda drew the aleph on his wall with a piece of chalk
and sat before it with great devotion, representing as it did the entire
Torah. He no longer visited Rabbi Lev and was never seen in the
study hall or synagogue of Zlochtov. The aleph had become his only
resource, his only form of worship. The aleph sustained him even on
the Sabbath and the Day of Atonement.

"Time passed and Rabbi Yehuda discovered that he was no longer
able to distinguish between the aleph and the wall on which it had

been drawn, and rather than discontinue meditation he simply included the wall along with the aleph in his mental devotions.

"Time passed and Rabbi Yehuda discovered that he was no longer able to distinguish the wall on which the aleph had been drawn from the adjoining walls of his room, and rather than discontinue meditation he simply included those walls along with the first and the aleph in his mental devotions.

"Time passed and Rabbi Yehuda was forced to include the entire ghetto of Zlochtov along with Rabbi Lev and the disciples, all of Galicia, Poland and Russia, Europe, America and the orient. In fact he carried in his mind at one time the entire creation including the planets and the kingdom of heaven.

"Time passed and the universe proceeded without interruption from its source through the mind of Rabbi Yehuda, who, sustained by the Sacred Name, no longer sought out the doctrines or laws of his faith."

Concerning this tale a student asked Rabbi Mikhal: "Regardless of his perfection can one be called a rabbi and not participate in the doctrine or law?" Rabbi Mikhal replied: "What participation could you expect from such a man? His mind is the Mind of Genesis. The sun may rise and set, the days are days and the nights are nights, but still in Rabbi Yehuda's mind the Lord has not as yet divided between them."

Harvey Shapiro (b. 1924)
TIME

1. Souls from the world
   Of formlessness
   Are up before me,
   Moving through the house,
   Waiting for me
   To make the attempt
   (As I do each morning)
   Which they enjoy and nullify.

2. What are you looking for?
   Anything
   To bind the soul
   To its roots.

3. In the Book of the Revolution of Souls
   Which we are now writing
   Willing or not.

   Tell me, declare the phantom
   Of your heart. The gods
   Are all equal.

   Every night climbing
   Out of that nothingness
   Into that nothingness.

In the beginning God created the heavens and the earth.

(Samaritan Hebrew)

THE TEN WORDS OF CREATION

In the beginning God created. And said
God, Let there be light. And God said,
Let there be a firmament. And God said, Let be collected
the waters. And God said, Bring forth grass
the earth. And God said, Let there be

lights. And God said, Let swarm
the water. And God said, Bring forth
the earth. And God said, Let us make
man. And God said, Behold I have given you.
And God saw all that
he had made, and behold it was very good. And he said, I
am the God of thy father, the God of Abraham
and the God of Isaac and the God of Jacob.
YHVH, YHVH, a God merciful and gracious, the Existent, YHVH.

JAMES A. MONTGOMERY

VARIATIONS ON GENESIS

(1) IN THE BEGINNING GOD CREATED THE HEAVEN
AND THE EARTH: you shouldn't read BERESHIT as *in the beginning* but BERA SHIT, *He created six*. If the Writing says BERA
SHIT, that means he created six letters; and through them were the
heavens and the earth formed, as it is said: FOR THROUGH YH
YHVH He formed the worlds. YH are two letters, YHVH are four,
thus there are six. So you must understand that it is through six letters that God created the heavens and the earth. If you say, is it
only the heavens and the earth that were created through these six
letters, through the writing THROUGH YH YHVH HE FORMED
THE WORLDS, understand as well that two worlds were created
by these six letters: the world here and now, and the world that will
be. (From *The Baraita of the Work of Creation*.)

(2) BY MEANS OF A BEGINNING IT CREATED GOD   was
zohar once again   because it sowed a seed would show its beauty
like the silkworm self-enclosed in palace   made it for use & beauty
   the Mysterious Unknown by means of this "beginning" made this
palace   called it Elohim   (this god)   "by means of a beginning it
created Elohim"   (*Zohar:* Genesis 15a.)

(3)   At the first of the gods' making skies and earth, the earth was
a mixedup-darkness on top of deepness: so wind-of-the-gods swept
down on the waters.

The gods said LIGHT so there was light, and the gods liked the
light so they made it different from the darkness:

> they called the light Day
> called the darkness Night:
>
> so that was Evening
> and that was Morning
> the first Day.

(Genesis 1.1–5.)

COMMENTARY

The "work of creation" appears here as continuous, a process uninterrupted by its codification in a literal text. Two points should be made:
that the work of mything (& not simply as a fiction—"lie"—in Plato's
sense) remains active to the present, & that the literal text itself, the act
in this instance of biblical "genesis," is made to open again & again by
re-reading, re-sounding, re-exegesis, in which the transmitted account is
taken as an occasion for new departures, the mind & voice in constant
motion. And this is the case exactly where we would have most expected
stasis, frozen thought; or, as the *Zohar* tells it in the voice of Simeon
bar Yoḥai: "The stories of the Torah are simply her outer garments, &
woe to the man who looks on those garments as the Torah itself, for
such a man will have no portion in the world to come. For David said:
'Open my eyes that I may behold wondrous things out of Thy law'
[Psalm 119.18], i.e. the things beneath the garment."

So also in the work of heretics & poets. A book of questions, changes.

(Hebrew, c. 8th century A.D.)

From THE PIRKE DE RABBI ELIEZER

. . . .

(1)

THE ORIGIN OF SKY

was from the light of his own robe
he took & stretched it
like a robe the skies
were rolling out from
he figured that should do it
in Shadai's words   "shall do"
—became his name then—
then firmed it up (they say)
"thy covering of thyself
"with light
"is like a robe
"the way thou stretchest the sky out
" 's like a curtain

(2)

THE ORIGIN OF EARTH

took snow or ice
—'twas underneath his throne—
& dropped it on
the waters
then they became congealed
earth's crust was formed from it
(they say)
"he tells the snow
"be earth

J.R.

Allen Ginsberg (b. 1926)

THE END

I am I, old Father Fisheye that begat the ocean, the worm at my
    own ear, the serpent turning around a tree,
I sit in the mind of the oak and hide in the rose, I know if any
    wake up, none but my death,
come to me bodies, come to me prophecies, come all foreboding,
    come spirits and visions,
I receive all, I'll die of cancer, I enter the coffin forever, I
    close my eye, I disappear,
I fall on myself in winter snow, I roll in a great wheel through
    rain, I watch fuckers in convulsion,
car screech, furies groaning their basso music, memory fading in
    the brain, men imitating dogs,
I delight in a woman's belly, youth stretching his breasts and
    thighs to sex, the cock sprung inward
gassing its seed on the lips of Yin, the beasts dance in Siam,
    they sing opera in Moscow,
my boys yearn at dusk on stoops, I enter New York, I play my jazz
    on a Chicago Harpsichord,
Love that bore me I bear back to my Origin with no loss, I float
    over the vomiter
thrilled with my deathlessness, thrilled with this endlessness I
    dice and bury,
come Poet shut up eat my word, and taste my mouth in your ear.

Rochelle Owens (b. 1936)

From THE JOE 82 CREATION POEMS

to learn everything
the V   of the sun   springing
& did it die afterwards?   the Lord God made the heav'n
& the earth
what matters
if a kid does not seethe in its mother's milk!
& the glass   is the dream   interlocking with
the fire   from   the sand   it owes
its genus/
O wild-man ate up
a fig   from   an egyptian
dancing girl's
hand/   Sweet one!   he called out.

this stage   is explanation   proving
the unequal steps   taken   by our big-footed
elders.
O I am the Grand Explorer!

& then he took a big pot & laid it down
on the ground & let the blood from
the rhinoceros
plop swiftly &
surely & let it gush &
flow as niftily as
the water from
His side!

whosoever believeth in me On my Name
is as the wind blowing thru the grass.
        & so jumping between leaves
          & roses & cat
turd/   he pondered on the land of His
captivity/

         & stuck his hand twixt his
green thighs & Lo!
—the thighs were quite dry!

               up sprang the herbs
& up the green corn (O like His thighs!) &
up the seeds & the humans &
      St. Victor & the false
      Jewish one &
       the Correct
       one & all
        that
         squirm
on the ground.   O Lord, salvage mine iniquities!
O Lord, if it please thee!

A PROLOGUE TO THE ELEMENTS OF CREATION

Said Rabbi Simeon: Mark this well! Fire, air, earth and water are
the sources and roots of all things above and below, and all things
above, below, are grounded in them. And in each of the four winds
these elements are found—fire in the North, air in the East, water
in the South, earth in the West; and the four elements are united
with the four winds—and all are one. Fire, water, air and earth:
gold, silver, copper and iron: north, south, east and west—altogether
these make twelve; yet they are all one. (*Zohar:* Exodus 23b.)

Yannai (Hebrew, c. 6th century A.D.)

FIRE-POEM: "& THEN AN ANGEL OF THE LORD
APPEARED TO HIM IN A TONGUE OF FIRE"

Fire eating
Fire carbonized in snow & smoke
Fire its look is like the face of
  mirrors
Fire flaring roaring

Fire flying in a storm wind
Fire every day renewal
Fire higher than its branches
Fire . . . .
Fire the iron bars of . . . .
Fire fevers in Sheol under
Fire black as raven

Fire burning dry & wet things
Fire of a crouching lion
Fire with assurance that it won't
  go out
Fire burns around turns back on
  self
Fire kindled without branches
Fire other fires don't swell out
Fire's sparks like lightning
Fire . . . .
Fire . . . .
Fire . . . .
Fire heaps of color like the rain-
  bow

*

. . . & changes image crowds on image
on the Burning Bush in flames
Sinai with torches
overhead were kindling sparks
below it licking light rays
inside it the domain of seraphim
who aren't burnt thereby
& from the sweat they sweat
a fire river conduit of light
whose sinews are nodules   snow
the fire doesn't boil off snow

is itself not doused by snow
for fire's maker snow's creator
ordered peace between the fire & snow
o judgment by fire o judgment by snow

J.R./H.L.

COMMENTARY

"It is a well-known fact that the Master of the Book Yetsira described
the right-hand side, Our Lady of Mercy & Compassion, as water, since
everything needs water; & as the Master of the Book Yetsira described
the right-hand side as water, so he described the left-hand side as fire."
(Moses of Burgos, *Sefer Amud ha-Smoli,* or the Book of the Left Pillar.)

Eleazar ha-Kallir (Hebrew, 7th century A.D.)

WATER-POEM: A PRAYER & INVOCATION TO THE PRINCE OF RAIN

Af-Bri
     sign
          name of
               rain's angel
clouding
       vaporing
            emptying
                raining

sprouts
       of water
           crown
              this valley
won't stop
       compact
           goes on
              unyielding
shielding them
        faithful
            beggars for
               rain

& you my hero forever Yahveh my god you wake the dead many
times you save us

be watchful
       send down
           rain from
              rain rivers
melt
   the face of
        earth
          with clear opals
water
    your power
        your mark
           written down
like drops
     reviving
        those who blow
            breath
you restore
     who invoke
        powers of
           rain

. . . .

(invocation thru the fathers priests & tribes)

: our Elohim & Elohim of our fathers

remember the father
                    you drew behind you
                                    like water

you blessed like a tree
                    planted by streams
                                    of water

you shielded
            saved him from fire
                            & water

you would guard
                when he seeded beside
                                every water

because of him don't stop your water

remember words of his birth
                        let him drink
                                the small water

you told his father to kill him
                        his blood spilt
                                    like water

as he was ready to spill
                his heart
                        like water

to dig & to find
            wells
                of water

because of him pour down your water

remember
        who carried his stick across
                            Jordan's water

one-hearted
            rolled stones from the mouth of the well
                                        of water

when he wrestled the prince

114   THE WAYS

                              mixed from fire
                                        & water
till you promised
                    you would stay with him
                                        in fire & in water

because of him don't stop your water

remember the one they drew out
                              from a reed boat
                                        in the water
they commanded
                    & didn't he water his flock
                                        with water
the people you chose
                    when they thirsted
                                        for water
he beat on the rock
                    it opened & gave out
                                        water

because of him pour down your water

remember the temple priest
                              who bathed 5 times
                                        in water
who walked
          who washed his hands in holiness
                                        of water
reading
      sprinkling purifying
                              water
kept distant
          from a people violent
                                        as water

because of him don't stop your water

remember the 12 tribes
                    you made to cross
                                        the water
for whom you sweetened

               bitterness
                     of water
whose generations
             spilt their blood for you
                     like water
o turn our minds
             encircled by
                that water

because of them pour down your water

for you are Yahveh are our elohim you make the wind blow & the
rain fall down

                                            J.R./H.L.

COMMENTARY

"Water is the original glyph of the universe, and what occurs in the
hoary bosom of the sea will divulge far more to man than the knowledge
of the ground and its vegetation." (Edward Dahlberg, *Reasons of the
Heart*, 1965.)

(Hebrew, after 3rd century A.D.)

From THE HEBREW BOOK OF ENOCH
[*Sefer ha-Hekhalot*]

Air-Poem: These Are the Many Winds That Blow Under the Cherubs' Wings

(1)
The Brooding Wind

the wind of god
brooding
on the waters' face

(2)
The Strong Wind

yahveh made the sea go back
strong wind blowing
all that night

(3)
The East Wind

east wind brought
the locusts

(4)
The Wind of Quails

wind came out
from yahveh
brought the quails

(5)
The Wind of Jealousy

the wind of jealousy
upon him

(6)
The Wind of Earthquake

& after that
a wind of earthquake
yahveh not inside

(7)
The Evil Wind

the evil wind
has left him

(8)
The Wind of Rain

of north wind
bringing rain

(9)
The Wind of Lightnings

he makes lightnings
for the rain
brings wind out of his storerooms

(10)
The Wind That Breaks the Rocks

yahveh walks by
a strong wind splits
the mountains
breaks rocks to dust

(11)
The Wind That Assuaged the Sea

god made a wind
pass over
earth
assuage the waters

(12)
The Wind of Anger

from wilderness
a wind came
struck the corners of the house
it fell

(13)
The Storm Wind

storm wind
that completes his word

J.R.

COMMENTARY

(1) "God produces Air from the Spirit"—literally WIND—"& turns it into twenty-two sounds, the letters of the alphabet: three of them are mothers, seven of them are double letters, & twelve of them are simple. But even above these does the Spirit stand in worth." (Charles Poncé, *Kabbalah:* paraphrase from the *Sefer Yetsira,* for which, see pages 92–98, above.)

(2)   Adds the text of *Sefer ha-Hekhalot,* after naming the winds around the Throne (above): "And Satan is standing among these winds, for 'storm wind' is nothing else but 'Satan,' & all these winds do not blow but under the wings of the Cherubim, as it is written: 'And he rode on a cherub & he flew   oh yes he did   he flew that quickly   —on wings of wind' (Psalm 18.11.)."

Armand Schwerner (b. 1927)

From THE DOMESDAY DICTIONARY   "Earth"

Earth, Pherecides teaches, is the primal element.

Of the four essential qualities—Heat, Cold, Moisture, and Dryness—Earth incorporates Cold and Dryness, and corresponds to the Humour Melancholy, which results from a disproportion among the four Humours, including in addition, Phlegm, Blood and Choler. Melanelius, out of Galen, Rufus, and Aetius, describes it to be a *bad and peevish disease, which makes men degenerate into beasts.*

Earth is the heaviest element. Like Water, it tends to go down. That explains its position in the center of the universe, toward which everything falls. Fire, Air, Water and Earth are arranged in giant concentric layers. Using the egg as metaphor, Fire is the shell, Air the white, Water the yellow, and Earth a little fatty drop in the middle of the yolk. At the point of greatest pressure lies the Abyss where Hell sits.

In a good man the elements are well mixed; Christopher Goodman has written:

> Though the present condition of man be earthly, made of the earth, feeds on the earth, and is dissolved to the earth, and therefore the soul doth less discover herself by her proper actions than doth the material body; yet it is not unknown to philosophy that there is an ecstasy of the soul . . .

Earth is ornamented with stones, mountains, beasts and plants.

The diamond is a great stone, though no bigger than a filbert. It comes from India. The Greeks called it "the untamable force." The diamond when it is near iron counteracts the activity of the magnetic stone; it also discloses the presence of smallpox. Dioscorides teaches that the diamond is the stone of love and reconciliation. A woman who wears the diamond finds favor with her husband. If the diamond is placed under the head of a sleeping woman, it tests her faithfulness: faithful, the woman turns toward her husband; otherwise she rolls to the other side. When the diamond is carried on the left side, it protects against phantoms, bad dreams and the devils who sleep with women in the guise of men.

The magnetic stone, an iron-colored stone, is found in the region in India where the troglodytes live. The magnetic stone attracts iron and glass. In Ethiopia there is a kind of magnetic stone which from one side attracts iron, and from the other repels it. There are mountains of magnetic stone that attract ships. The magnetic stone cures sickness in the spleen, and dropsy.

Certain parts of Earth are hollowed into caverns where the imprisoned winds occasionally rage. This, Aristotle teaches, is the cause of earthquakes. Where the east wind dominates is a region abundant in flowers and fruits. The west wind is cold and humid, less favorable. The north wind is cold and dry; that is why men of the North are tall and good-looking. The south winds make men timorous.

As for mountains, some say that at the beginning Earth was smooth and lacked them. Herbs from the mountains are better for animals than herbs of the valleys; fruits are less plentiful there than in other places, but excellent. Aristotle teaches that it rains very little on very tall mountains, because the vapors turn into rain before reaching the peaks.

It is good to remember the beasts, how they are. Certain animals were given to man for food—the deer and the sheep, for instance. Others were put on Earth to help him, like the horse and the camel; others yet, to amuse him, such as monkeys and dogs. Some animals remind him of his fragility: the flea does. And others allow him to remember the power of God: such are the bear, the snakes, and the lion.

COMMENTARY

from "the notebooks"   11/75   for Schwerner   as introduction to a series of poems about the world earth foremost in our thoughts   the way the words come: "down to earth"   as if to signal passage   that we leave that world where mind breathes purely   & come down to find

again materials   a space that comes up solid to my hand   o matter
matter   consciousness is also touch   creation is creation of this place
    image of what we are   life felt most sharply where the dead wait
where our fathers do not sleep   do not not-sleep   earth that the book
has led us down to   will show the way home at last   a world of obstacles   —"that crush me" Kafka wrote—   in beautiful pursuit   procession into sun moon stars   the tree outside the house becomes the road
to heaven   shamans climb it with our children   fathers did too   whose
beards entangled in its branches   animals & people in a world we knew
    soon to be wrested from us by invasion   of some darker mind   be-
yond that time   knowledge by which we named our animals   or named
ourselves   for animals   a language shared   pleasures   fulfillments
in a world of nouns   (j.r.)

Carol Bergé (b. 1934)

DOUBLE MEMORY

---

in the caves, inland, we transfix
on the blind lizards: newt-like,
encapsulated, delicate as infants,
their gills reminders of origins,
their sight of the sea. darkness
does not surprise them, they move,
have grown fine feathery antennae,
the exquisite spines show white
through cold, glasslike flesh: we,
gifted, swim in with our ghosts.

David Rosenberg (b. 1943)
PSALM 19

The heavens declare the glory of God; and the firmament sheweth his handywork

The universe unfolds
the vision within:
creation

stars and galaxies
the words and lines
inspired with a hand

day comes to us
with color and shape
and night listens

and what is heard
breaks thru deep silence
of infinite space

the rays come to us
like words
come to everyone

human on earth
we are the subjects
of light

a community
as it hears
the right words

creating time
the space of the sky
the face of the nearest star

that beats like a heart
in the tent where it sleeps
near the earth every night

then rises above the horizon
growing in our awareness
of the embrace

of inspiration
we feel as we turn
toward the warmth

starting at the edge of the sky
to come over us
like a secret love we wait for

love we can't hide
our deepest self-image
from

nobody holds back that fire
or closes the door
of time

words My Lord writes shine
opening me
to witness myself

conscious and unconscious
complex mind
warmed in an inner lightness

that moves me
to the simple beat
of time

testimony
of one author
speaking thru history's pages

commanding my attention
bathed in light
around me

clean perfect notes
hearts play
make us conscious

we become the audience
amazed we can feel
justice come over us

our minds become real
unfold
the universe within

silence becomes real
we hear
clear words

become the phrasing of senses
lines of thought
stanzas of feeling

more lovely than gold
all the gold in the world
melting to nothing in light

sweet flowing honey
the right words
in my mouth

warming your subject
as he listens
breaking thru his reflection

his image in the mirror
. what mind can understand the failure
waiting in itself

silent self-image
created in the dark alone
to hold

power over others!
but justice comes over us
like a feeling for words that are right

absolutely
a mirror is pushed away
like a necessary door

we're free to look at everything
every shape and color
light as words

opening the mind
from nightmares of social failure
desperate routines

we're inspired above
the surface parade
of men dressed up in power

we see the clear possibility
of life growing
to witness itself

let these words
of my mouth
be sound

the creations
of my heart
be light

so I can see myself
free of desperate symbols
mind-woven coverings

speechless fears
images hidden within
we are the subjects of light

opening to join you
vision itself
my constant creator.

(Hebrew, 4th/5th centuries A.D.)

From THE BOOK OF MYSTERIES   "Rites for the Sun"

FOURTH HEAVEN heaven of the angels of the sun lies stretched
out in a storm wind stands on fire pillars wearing crowns of flame is
filled with storage chambers of the powers treasuries of dew &
angels in the corners lightly gallop gallop & in it there are seven
rivers fire water & beside them angels standing on both sides
are numberless

from this side fire angels burning flames & on the other water angels
frozen into hail they do not put each other out do not ignite each
other but these dip in the fire rivers those dip in the water rivers
calling making songs & praises to the one who lives forever made
them to express his strength

& this heaven houses the sun's canopy is full of light & fires come together fire angels ringed with power who surround him drive him through the day & water angels bodies like the sea their voice is like the voice of water fierce with beauty drive him through the night

. . . .

if you long to see the sun by day easy in his chariot & rising watch & guard yourself & purify yourself for 7 days avoid all victuals & all drink & everything unclean

& on the 7th day stand before him in the hour that he rises make a smoke before him an incense of spices 3 shekels in weight & call on the names of angels 7 times who drive him through the day & if these don't answer 7 times go back & call them backwards 7 times & say

I CALL ON YOU ANGELS WHO DRIVE THE SUN YOUR ENERGY YOUR POWERS DRIVING THE SKY ROAD THAT ILLUMINATES THE WORLD BY HIM WHOSE VOICE SHAKES THE EARTH WHO SHIFTS MOUNTAINS IN HIS ANGER HAS STRENGTH TO CALM THE SEA HIS GLANCE WOBBLES THE PILLARS OF THE WORLD WHO CARRIES UNIVERSES ON HIS ARM INVISIBLE TO EYE OF ANY LIVING THING WHO SITS UPON THE THRONE OF GREATNESS OF THE KINGDOM OF THE KABOD OF HIS HOLY HOLY ROAMING OF THE WHOLE WORLD BY HIS NAME O GREAT O TERRIBLE O BRAVE O HUGE O FIERCE O POWERFUL O HOLY O STRONG O WONDERFUL O HIDDEN O RAISED UP O LUMINOUS I CALL YOU BACK & CALL ON YOU TO DO MY WILL MY LONGING AT THIS TIME & SEASON TO REMOVE THE CENTER OF THE SUN ITS CORE THAT I MAY SEE HIM FACE TO FACE THE WAY HE IS BENEATH HIS CANOPY & LET ME NOT CATCH FIRE FROM YOUR FIRE BUT GIVE HIM LEAVE TO DO MY WILL

& when you finish calling you will see the sun under the canopy will ask if life or death will follow or if good or evil when you seek to send the sun back then remember your first oath & say

I CALL ON YOU RETURN THE SUN'S CORE TO ITS PLACE
THE WAY IT WAS & MAY THE SUN GO ON ITS WAY

. . . .

if you long to see the sun at night & going on a northern path purify
yourself 3 weeks of 7 days avoid all victuals & all drink & everything unclean stand at the night watch the third hour & wrapped in
white cloth speak the sun's name & the names of angels 21 times
those who drive him through the night & say

I CALL ON YOU ANGELS FLYING IN THE AIR ALONG THE
FIRMAMENT BY HIM WHO SEES UNSEEN HIMSELF THE
KING REVEALING EVERYTHING UNSEEN WHO SEES ALL
HIDDEN THINGS THE CHIEF WHO KNOWS THE SECRETS
OF THE DARKNESSES WHO TURNS DEEP DARKNESS INTO
MORNING MAKES NIGHT AS LIGHT AS DAY ALL HIDDEN
THINGS MADE KNOWN BEFORE HIM LIKE THE SUN &
NOTHING IS TOO WONDERFUL FOR HIM & BY HIS NAME
THE HOLY KING WHO GLIDES ON WINGS OF WIND &
BY THE LETTERS OF HIS SECRET NAME REVEALED TO
ADAM IN THE GARDEN RULES CONSTELLATIONS &
THE SUN & MOON BOW DOWN LIKE SERVANTS TO THEIR
MASTER BY THE NAME OF HIM THE GOD OF WONDERS
NOW I CALL ON YOU TO MAKE KNOWN THIS GREATER
MIRACLE & LET ME SEE THE SUN IN POWER IN THE
COMPLEX WORKINGS OF HIS WHEELS NO PORTION OF
THESE UNSEEN THINGS TOO WONDROUS FOR MY EYES
A WHOLE DAY LET ME SEE IT ASK HIM WHAT I LONG
FOR LET HIM SPEAK WITH ME THE WAY A MAN SPEAKS
WITH HIS FRIEND TO TELL ME SECRETS OF THE DEPTHS
MAKE KNOWN THE HIDDEN THINGS TO ME BUT NOTH-
ING BAD TO HAPPEN NOTHING BAD

& as you finish speaking you will hear a voice the thunder from the
north & something will appear like lightning worlds will shine before
you you will see it & bow down & falling earthwards on your face
will pray this prayer

(a Greek hymn for Helios the sun god)

I ADORE YOU HELIOS
     CLIMBING THE EAST
GOOD SAILOR
KEEPING THE FAITH
HIGH DRIVER
LONG AGES YOU PRIMED YOUR GREAT GLOBE
O HOLY ASSEMBLER
YOU GOVERN THE MESSENGERS
LORD
SHINING DRIVER
KING WHO SETS OUT THE STARS

& I PLONY BEN PLONY HURL MY PLEAS AT YOU MAY
YOU BE SEEN BY ME REVEALED TO ME UNFRIGHTENED
NOTHING EVER BE CONCEALED FROM ME BUT EVERY-
THING I ASK YOU SPEAK

then stand on your feet you will see him up north moving east & turning your hands back behind you & bending your head will ask him
everything then raise your eyes up to the sky & say

URPALI'EL I CALL ON YOU BY HIM WHO MADE YOU
FOR HIS GLORY & HIS MAJESTY MADE YOU TO LIGHT
HIS WORLD TO RULE HIS WORLD THAT YOU NOT DAM-
AGE ME NOT FRIGHTEN ME THAT I NOT BE AFRAID OR
TREMBLE & YOU TURN BACK ALONG YOUR ROAD IN
PEACE REVOLVING THAT YOU NOT BE KEPT FROM MO-
TION NOW & FOR ALL TIME AMEN SELAH

J.R./H.L.

COMMENTARY

(1)   The worship of the sun—& other powers of earth & sky—persists in spite of efforts to desacralize the image in favor of the one god. The Hebrew word for sun is *shemesh,* sun-god of the Babylonians, whose cult Ezekiel spies out in the Temple, still vivid as a memory of same in later ritual; thus, after Patai, *Man & Temple* (page 30): "at the Eastern Gate / they looked back / said / 'our fathers stood here / backs turned to the temple / faces east / & bowed before the Sun.'" But the text adds later: "As for us, our eyes are turned to the Lord."

   Yet the issue, in popular, magical & meditative Judaism, is (like much other nature-related mythopoeia) far less resolved than that. The Greek prayer to Helios, above, is transcribed in Hebrew letters & is part of a widespread Jewish & Hellenistic convergence. Of a roughly contemporary manifestation, E. R. Goodenough writes: "We have all along known that the Essenes addressed prayers to the sun." And in the fragment from the Dead Sea scrolls that follows, two other astrological beings appear among the constellations—to remind us of the abundance of such in the ongoing Jewish *poesis*.

(2)   "Therefore take heed to yourselves—lest you lift up your eyes to heaven, & when you see the sun, & the moon, & the stars, & all the forces of the sky, you should be pressed to worship them, & serve them, which the Lord your God divided among all nations under the whole heaven." (Deuteronomy 4.15, .19.)

(Hebrew, c. 1st century A.D.)

THE CODE OF DAY & NIGHT

A Fragment

---

(1)

* * . . .
h . . .
. . . .
& a man who would become . . . .
broad & rounded . . .
mixed & not the flesh of . . .

(2)

. . . . unclean
. . . . hard stone
. . . . a man of . . .
. . . . . clean
& thighs are long & thin & toes
are thin & long was from the second vault
spends 6 parts in the house of light 3 in the pit
of darkness is his time of birth the festival
of taurus will grow poor his beast is taurus

(3)

wa * h . . . .
& the head . . . .
of terror . . . wingy teeth & fingers of
his hands are thick thighs thick & hairy
toes are thick & short spends 8 parts in the house
of darkness 1 part in the house of light a man . . .

J.R.

COMMENTARY

Here the original message was written down in code: "a cipher [that used] the comparatively simple expedient of reversing the order of the letters of the words & employing a combination of alphabets." (J. M. Allegro, "An Astrological Cryptic Document from Qumran.") The resort to cryptography was symptomatic: a move from an open relationship with sky & stars to a hidden one, in which the old images had become not only awesome but demonic: the natural world a presence man must defeat & master, or with which he must traffic outside the law, in secret. Writes Robert Kelly of "that wisdom outlawed & made criminal by the city of Rome," etc., a condition of separation suffered by the Jews as well: "The traditional sciences became 'occult' when the city took on its modern sense. . . . Just as the sky over a modern city is occulted by smoke & industrial throwaway, its proper atmosphere, so that antique science based on the inspection of the sky becomes mythologized, & hence a fossilized, hence a despised, science, rather than an open possibility. . . . There are no ready pragmatic ways of inferring the Pleiades. They go unseen, their dance ignored. And we are cut off."

This is the condition of the lost garden, as also of the city deprived of its cosmic model, etc., still to be sighted in the coded poem; for which, in the variety of their Jewish manifestations, see page 431, below.

Richard Grossinger (b. 1944)
From TALISMANS: STAR MAGIC

The stars are a veil, an arras that hangs down over another universe; it appears to be a curtain woven with flowers, a tapestry of horsemen and castle; it appears to be a gown, a robe sewn with the zodiac, but as we approach it, it is too hot to touch; it dissolves into planets and suns; we thought we were within an arm's length of touching it, but now it lies beyond us a billion, and a billion more, light years away. We take a step back, and the curtain hangs loosely, hiding an adjacent room. We are born and find the stars at hopeless distances, but behind them is another universe, closer to the earth, one that we can hold in our hands as a deck of cards, and deal, one after another, without changing our place, star by star coming up into the masked sky. Lift the veil, and beneath it is a woman's face, a fire burning, a bright yellow field of grain; a king sits on his throne motionless for twenty-five thousand years; this is a star; this is one portion of the mapped sky. Lift the angel on the Star Card and the five senses are lifted too, plucked like buds from their earthly counterparts; it is a single picture, but the cards drawn from it are unlimited. The tarot clings like flesh to the throbbing underbelly, the exposed sheath of nerves; rip up the card and the blood flows from the wound; a spring dance of odd colors forms, a mushroom grows. The card lies over an always-burning fire, and the veil is not made of red pomegranates but electrons, and we cannot touch them and cannot eat them. The card lies between neuron and image, between astrum and star. Lift the card without touching it; look thru the image into another image; the woman becomes a naked dancer, a winged sorceress; the woman opens the door of a constellation and lets you into a room. You climb the staircase to an attic, and out beyond it lies a field, a sky above the sky. The lines along which the universe opens are infinite.

Moses de Leon (Aramaic, c. 1240–1305)

From **THE ZOHAR**   "Moon"

Then Rabbi Simeon said:

The secret of Solomon's wisdom was in the name of the moon when blessed from every side.

In his days the moon was magnified & reached her fullness.

A thousand mountains rose before her, & she blew them away with a puff.

A thousand mighty rivers flowed before her, & she swallowed them at a draught.

Her nails reached out in a thousand & seventy directions, & her hands in twenty-four thousand, so that nothing could escape her.

Thousands of bucklers clung to her hair.

From between her legs a youth emerged who stretched from one end of the world to the other with sixty clubs of fire.

And his name was Enoch son of Jered.

Under him are stationed many Living Creatures, & the moon's hair's fastened under them & called "the scepter's knobs."

Her hands & feet take hold of it, she's like a lion clinging to his prey.

Her nails are those who call to mind the sins of men inscribing them with rigor & exactness.

The parings of her nails are those who do not cleave to the King's Body & suck from the side of uncleanness when the moon begins to wane.

So Solomon, after he had inherited the moon in its fullness also desired to inherit it in its defective state, to gain the knowledge of the spirits & the demons, inheriting the moon on every side.

Clarisse Nicoidski (Ladino, 20th century)
THREE POEMS

To Federico García Lorca

(1)

    A horse broke into a gallop
under
the snow it found the bodies of young men

& your mouth
which spoke for them
              of a lost mother
                a house
                a love
a ravaged truth

the horse took it all the way to the moon
the dead applauded

but the moon hid herself
the horse sunk to the bottom of
the sea

(2)

I met you on the road of words
   you gave me your water to drink
   so hot it made me thirsty
   you gave me your bread to eat
   so dry it made me hungry
   you gave me your roads
   & out of them came a forgotten woman who called
      your land her own

—did she look like me?
—And I never knew.

(3)

Down came the stars when
the blood gushing from your mouth wrote words in the sand

we read them

some of them lit their lights
glowing gleaming
who knows when they'll burst into flame

KEVIN POWER

David Antin (b. 1932)

From THE BLACK PLAGUE

. . . .

the constellation————————————————

the location—

        between the Scorpion and Hercules in the
           southeastern quarter of the summer sky
        draw a line / from Ras Algethi in Hercules
           to Antares in the Scorpion
        it will pass through a topaz star of the 2nd
           magnitude this is Alterf / or the Owl's Eye

the mythology—

        "our mind is related to the most knowable
           things in Nature as an Owl's Eye to the
           Sun"

A BOOK OF WORLDS   137

the Owl is represented with outspread wings breaking its fall as it dives upon its companion constellation of the Rat / which is depicted as already struggling in its Claws // perhaps due to their sombre coloration / their silent ghostlike flight / their hootings and screechings / and their large glaring eyes / they have always been regarded as creatures of ill omen / holding a position among birds precisely equivalent to that of lemurs among mammals // they subsist entirely upon living prey //

the Rat is a trapezoidally shaped constellation / the only conspicuous object in which is the pale emerald star Meyid / marking the rodent's snout // this star α-Ratti is alternatively known as Shahadet / the Witness / whereas the entire constellation has also been known as the Slave or the Victim / while the constellation of the Owl has also come down to us as the Torturer or the Executioner //

for the naked eye————————————————

in the year 453 A.D. a Nova of reddish hue rivalling Mars in brilliance appeared below the Claws in the Rat's back and vanished in three weeks time // this area is now occupied by a faint reddish cluster known as The Burst //

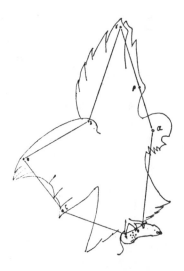

sweep the field south of Algienah in the northern wing / to
find the Dark Nebula / a jet-black cloud of cosmic matter /
whose sharp-cut silhouette has the form of a knout //

the sole object of interest in the constellation of the Rat is
α-Ratti / known to the Arabs as The Witness // El Fergani
was much struck by the curious cold green color of this star /
which is approaching the earth at an incredible speed //

the most remarkable feature of this part of the sky is Alterf
// the Owl's Eye is a yellow supergiant that has proved to be
an extremely irregular Long Period Variable // its fluctuations
in luminosity from 2nd to 3rd magnitude over a period of
several centuries are due to occultation of the brighter star
by a smaller dark companion with which it orbits about a
common center // the occultations have in the past been
associated with various terrestrial phenomena

> ". . . black bands cross the golden star
> Rat's feet traverse the land
> black spots beneath the arm
> on the face of the Sun
> holding the sea in its Claws
> the planets in their course
> the Sun dives on the sparrow
> in the Owl's yellow Eye"

COMMENTARY

(1) "the terrible thing Gedaliah said would be if all our ideas of reality
were based on the evidence of 200 years of experimentation and measurement and the constitution of the universe was changing all this
time." (D. Antin, from "autobiography 2.")

(2) He mounted a tower in the Street of the Jews & examined the comet
at close range, then he announced: "Its tail points toward Vienna!"

Samuel ha-Nagid (Hebrew, 993–1056)
POEM WITH SKY & EARTH

I look up at the starry sky
and down at the creatured earth
with heartfelt understanding of how
well and wisely made they are.
The heavens seem an enormous tent
hung by loops and hooks,
moon and stars a shepherdess
guiding her flock to pasture;
then a lonely moon glides
through the clouds like a ship;
or the clouds move like a girl
watering her garden and trees;
and the dew settles as from a woman
who shakes her wet hair over the ground.
Like the animals people seek their rest
in mansions or in stables;
they flee the *timor mortis*
like doves the diving falcon.
At last it all seems like a great dish
that's been smashed into a thousand pieces.

GEORGE ECONOMOU

Paul Celan (German, 1920–70)

AND WITH THE BOOK FROM TARUSSA

All poets are Jews.
——MARINA TSVETAYEVA

Of the
constellation of Canis, of the
bright-star within and the dwarf-
light that also weaves
on roads mirrored earthwards,

of
pilgrim-staffs, there too, of the south, alien
and nightfiber-near
like unsepulchered words,
roaming
in the orbit of attained
goals and stelae and cradles.

Of things
sooth-said and fore-told and spoken over to you,
of things
talked upwards,
on the alert, akin to one
of one's own heart-stones that one spewed out
together with their in-
destructible clockwork, out
into unland and untime. Of such
ticking and ticking amid
the gravel-cubes with

(going back on a hyena spoor
traceable upwards)
the ancestral
line of Those-
of-the-Name-and-Its-
Round-Abyss.

Of
a tree, of one.
Yes, of it too. And of the woods around it. Of the woods
Untrodden, of the
thought they grew from, as sound
and half-sound and changed sound and terminal sound, Scythian
rhymes
in the meter
of the temple of the driven,
with
breathed steppe-
grass written into the heart
of the hour-caesura—into the realm,
the widest of
realms, into
the great internal rhyme
beyond
the zone of mute nations, into yourself
language-scale, word-scale, home-
scale of exile.

Of this tree, these woods.

Of the bridge's
broadstone, from which
he bounced across into
life, full-fledged
by wounds—of the
Pont Mirabeau.
Where the Oka doesn't flow. Et quels
amours! (Cyrillic, friends, I rode
this too across the Seine,
rode it across the Rhine.)

Of a letter, of it.
Of the one-letter, East-letter. Of the hard and
tiny word-heap, of the
unarmed eye that it
transmits to
the three
belt-stars of Orion—Jacob's
staff, you,
once again you come walking!—
on the
celestial chart that opened for it.

Of the table where this happened.

Of a word, from the heap
on which it, the table
became a galley-seat, from the Oka River
and its waters.

Of the passing word that
a galley-slave gnash-echos, into the late-summer reeds
of his keen-
eared thole-pin:

Colchis.

JOACHIM NEUGROSCHEL

COMMENTARY

from "the notebooks"   12/75   a letter to Paul Celan : of how your
poems arise in me   alive   my eye fixed on your line   "light was • salvation" I remember   (in the simpler version)   Paris   nineteen sixty
seven   in cold light of our meeting shivered to dumbness   you said
"jew"   & I said "jew"   though neither spoke the jew words   jew
tongue   that both of us had known   neither the mother language
loshen   the vestiges of holy speech   but you said "pain" under your
eyebrows   I said "image"   we said "sound"   & turned around to silence

lost   between two languages   sat & drank wine's words   like blood
we didn't drink toward vision   still could not speak without a scream
    a guttural   the tree out of the shadow of the white cafe was not "the
tree"   roots of our speech above us   in the sun   beneath the sewers
language of the moles   "who dig & dig   do not grow wise   who make
no song   no language"   into the water silence of your death   the pink
pale sky of Paris in the afternoon   that held no constellations   & no
life   no knowledge of the sun as candelabrum   as a tree   menorah
"light knotted into air   with table set   chairs empty   in sabbath splendor"   the old man stood beside in figure of a woman   would raise his
arms to reach it   the axis of the world   bring the air down solidly &
speak   no sound   the way you forced my meaning to your poem   now
gone   words of which still press against my tongue   "drunk   blest
gebentsht"   (j.r.)

MENORAH

---

1   she lights the lights

2   the bridegroom moves to her

3   the tree of life
     is upside down

4   the sun

5   illumination of the bride

6   whose light is sarah

7   lighting fires
     making love

COMMENTARY

(1) The tree of life, which represents the mystery of consciousness & link, or ladder, between earth & sky, appears here as the menorah or great seven-branched candelabrum of the Jewish temple. Thus the earthly tree is also sky tree, whose seven lamps were long ago read as the seven planets: "the eyes of Yahveh looking on the earth," the book says (Zechariah 4.10). Yet the latent imagery is also strongly sexual, for the tree's sap, which fed the lamps of the menorah, is elsewhere seen as semen, blood, or milk, the true *elixir vitae*. And this is acknowledged in the accompanying rituals, from the strenuous, near acrobatic movements of the temple priests who climbed ladders to fill & light the bowls with wicks made from the High Priest's underwear, to the domestic candle-lighting of each sabbath, which Safed kabbalists & others celebrated as a marriage between God & his bride: "an almost complete identification of the *Shekhinah,* not only with the Queen of the Sabbath, but also with every Jewish housewife who celebrates the Sabbath" (G. Scholem.) *She who lights the lights.*

(2) "& yahveh spoke to moses told him you will make a candlestick of pure gold beaten work its shaft its branches its knobs its flowers all one piece six branches coming from its sides by three and three three bowls like almond blossoms in one branch a knob & flower in the other branch three bowls like almond blossoms & a knob & flower —for the six branches coming from its sides— & in the candlestick four bowls like almond blossoms each with knobs & flowers & a knob under two branches all one piece & a knob under two branches all one piece & a knob under two branches all one piece —for the six branches coming from its sides— their knobs & branches all one piece a single beaten work of pure gold you will make the lamps for it be seven they will light the lamps for it will let the lamp light shine around it & the tongs for it will be pure gold the snuff dishes will be pure gold a talent of pure gold will do to make it that & all its vessels see that you make it in this mode this is being shown you on the mountain" (Exodus 25.31–.40.)

Simon Magus (Samaritan/Greek, c. 20/30 A.D.)

From THE GREAT SENTENCE "Fire/Tree"

(1)

Torah

> *the Lord thy God is a consuming fire*
> *burning fire*
> *Body thy leich devouring fire:*

principle
LAW
begins all
fire : Power   that takes no limit   that makes the
Book of the Showings Forth of God   using
He Voice
She Name
Second   Syzygy

fire : rooted in Mind of A-bounding Strength
raging sealed concealed
in the house the root of all holds

this house : this man   born the root   giving this house
in him   lives   A-bounding Strength
Who grows these roots
Whom Universe Order provides

His Strength   and   Strength of that fire

(2)

fire   treasure of all that is   giving it its
treasure   upthere   upthere   heaven's light

great   tree   visited on Nebuchadnezzar in sleep

> *I saw a tree in the midst of the earth,*
> > *the height thereof was great.*
>
> *The tree grew, and was strong,*
> > > *the height thereof reached heaven,*
> > > > *sight thereof the end of all the earth.*
>
> *Its leaves were fair,*
> > > *fruit thereof much,*
>
> *in it meat for all:*
> > > *beasts of the field shadows under it,*
> > > *fowls of the heaven homes in*
> > > *the boughs thereof,*
>
> *all flesh was fed of it:*

fire   tree of life the universe fleshes
        trunk branch leaf bark   the
skin   seen heard touched tasted smelt   brought to
fire   set to burning by flames's A-bounding Strength
        that *devours* all   consumes all
fire   laid inside the tree
        tamed   dying   bound to end
fire   fruit this tree bears
        image coating body
        there in the granary   not to be burnt
        fruit from the barn   feeds all flesh   the
        chaff eaten by
fire   fruit of the tree
        child kindled in the trunk
fire   living

C.D.

COMMENTARY

The tree of life, which here—in vision of the Samaritan messiah & "first gnostic," Simon Magus—contains the child of light & heat (= messiah = the anointed one with oil of olives), is imaged elsewhere in the Garden mysteries, the burning bush as seen by Moses, the menorah of the Jewish temple, the cross that passes into Christian cult, the sefirotic "tree" of the kabbala. In *poesis,* which is itself the *ma'ase bereshit* ("work of creation" as renewed beginning), the tree is consciousness, the brain & spinal tree inside us, at whose base the serpent (= yoga "kundalini") waits. Writes Gaston Bachelard: "The imagination is a tree. It has the integrative virtues of a tree. It is root and boughs. It lives between earth and sky. It lives in the earth and in the wind. The imagined tree imperceptibly becomes the cosmological tree, the tree which epitomizes a universe, which makes a universe." This is the tree of the first garden: two trees united (in another telling) that the fall of man, our entry into (or away from) consciousness divides, creates a schism between mind & knowledge, as burden of the severed intellect, beginnings of abstraction. In Nebuchadnezzar's dream (Daniel 4.10–.12), which Simon Magus quotes, the vision, now unchanneled, turns to madness, & the king is overwhelmed by living forms:

> the dream fulfilled on him
>   drove him away from men
> now ate the grass like oxen
> body wet with sky dew
> hair had grown to eagles' feathers
> nails like claws of birds

Yvan Goll (German, 1891–1950)
THE INNER TREES

The drunken trees
The trees of my life drunk with death and hot
Are leaping up out of my head
Full of fruit, using roots
Hands and suns
Nimble and thoughtful animals

Saturn's light is burning
In the eye of the golden frog
All the time the comets
Blossom in the pastures

ROBERT BLY

Larry Eigner (b. 1927)

A POEM & A COMMENTARY ON CREATION,
DESTRUCTION, PRESERVATION, ETC.

The closed system
  Of earth
    Of the Ark

          Love
Mercy

    shut him up carefully
in it   like involved self the
  wandering spot with
    the man   family   beasts

          the needs   after predictions of
                     your own acts

           rise up   go forth

      on the water beyond

        the walls that

          can be made

       creation

        and the floods

the more there is the more

begins

a kind of chain

firecrackers or

burning woods

having defined a thing

and called it Evil

in all proportion

the outsized man

. . . .

I first saw a chumesh Oct 1970 at a Bar
   M. where the kid's sedrah was where Noah boards the Ark—
     Pentateuch and Haftorahs (Soncino), annotated by J D
      Hertz; from notes I learned Elohim orders Noah to get in
      the ship and YHVH shuts him up carefully ("very mighty,"
      capable) and lovingly inside. ("being", concern) purpose,
      I guess   involvement
         goal—priority—setting, judgement, feedback, grk justice
         due proportion and balance
  "The Ancient Rabbis," says Hertz, had it Elohim and YHVH are
inseparable ("Shema . . . echod . . ." ?). And it figures, purpose
and involvement, a lot of one without any or enough (there's the
rub) of the other is fanaticism, hang-up, or else getting flooded
(unless, everything being serious and a game in inverse proportion,
you can afford more or less to be indecisive and tentative, can afford "negative capability" amid one kind of abundance or another—
only thing for me here, by the way, virtually no decisions have the
old folks ever allowed me, which by now seems a good thing, so far,

day-to-day living my only forte). Anyway, purpose and involvement always, may be pretty much like creation/destruction/preservation (together with the Whole of Existence the Trimurti), beginning/ ending/continuing. There's morning baths in the Ganges and other rivers and tubs, "Day By Day Make It New" . . .

A PROLOGUE TO THE WORKS OF ADAM

this is the book of the Works of Adam   on the day that Elohim created Adam   he made him to resemble Elohim   he made them male & female   blessed them   named them Adam   on the day of their creation

(Hebrew, c. 3rd–4th century A.D.)

From THE FATHERS ACCORDING TO
RABBI NATHAN

& the Holy One Be Blest
his great name blest forever world & time
whose wisdom & whose understanding built the world
made skies & earth
beings up high & down below
& made in man all things made in his world
made forests in the world & forests in man (man's hair)
made evil beasts in the world & evil beasts in man (man's lice)
made channels in the world & channels in man (man's ears)
made a wind in the world & a wind in man (man's breath)
a sun in the world & a sun in man (man's forehead)
stagnant waters in the world & stagnant waters in man (man's
    rheum)
salt water in the world & salt water in man (man's tears)
streams in the world & streams in man (man's piss)
walls in the world & walls in man (man's lips)
doors in the world & doors in man (man's tongue)
sweet waters in the world & sweet waters in man (man's spit)
stars in the world & stars in man (man's cheeks)
towers in the world & towers in man (man's neck)
masts in the world & masts in man (man's arms)
pegs in the world & pegs in man (man's fingers)
kings in the world & a king in man (man's heart)
clusters in the world & clusters in man (man's breasts)
counselors in the world & counselors in man (man's reins)
millstones in the world & millstones in man (man's stomach)
mashing mills in the world & mashing mills in man (man's spleen)

pits in the world & a pit in man (man's navel)
flowing waters in the world & flowing waters in man (man's blood)
trees in the world & trees in man (man's bones)
hills in the world & hills in man (man's ass)
pestle & mortar in the world & pestle & mortar in man (man's joints)
horses in the world & horses in man (man's legs)
angel of death in the world & angel of death in man (man's heels)
mountains / valleys in the world & man (erect / reclining)
: thus to know that when the Holy One Be Blest
made all things in the world
he made all things in man

COMMENTARY

(1)   The account proceeds by riddling, following the typical view of man as miniature world, *imago mundi,* etc. In later kabbalistic *poesis,* the whole man came to be equated with "tree," both "man" & "tree" serving as visualizations of the ten stages (*sefirot*) of God's descent to consciousness. The two appear interchangeably as that which first emerges in the play of lights within *tehiru,* the space voided by the "limitless," *Ein-Sof,* at the start of creation. (See above, page 12.) This "primordial man" (Hebrew: *adam kadmon*) was the archetype for mankind made in God's likeness: himself, by a final anthropomorphism, a god "both male & female." The exile of man from the "garden" thus had its model, probably its inception, in the lost lights shining from the eyes of Adam Kadmon, which burst the vessels designed to hold them & became trapped in matter—an anthropomorphic retelling of the "breaking of the vessels / death of the kings," for which, in an alternative form, see above, page 88. And this was then replayed in the separation of male from female in the birth of Eve, the separation of the trees of life & knowledge, of man/woman from the garden, of the Shekinah (as "female principle") from God, etc. The result was "exile" (*galut*), which later came to define not only the Jewish experience as such, but a universal condition: human, existential, ultimately gnostic. At the boundaries of *galut,* the tree of life becomes the tree of death, & man (as tree, etc.) the bearer of death consciousness. The Shekinah changes from loving mother & bride, & assumes a terrifying aspect as the occulted moon goddess: she who "tastes the other, bitter side, whose face is dark." In this world of ambivalences & metapoetic transformations—of that dual-

ism which normative Judaism thought of as the ground of all "heresy"—
the snake at the bottom of the tree/spine is both devil & messiah. (See
below.)

(2) "When the Holy One Be Blest created man, he created him as an
androgyne." [*Midrash Genesis Raba.*]　　(3) "Rabbi Oshaya said in the
name of Rav: The first man, his body came from Babylon, his head from
the land of Israel, & his limbs from the other countries." [Talmud:
Sanhedrin 38a–b.]　　(4) "In man I see the moon, the plants, blackness,
metal, the star, the fish. Let the cosmic elements slide symetrically. De-
form, boil." [Tristan Tzara, "note sur l'art nègre."]　　(5) "And Adam
climbed the bank of the Wellspring and his glory burst forth over the
worlds. Then he arose and sat by a well of vain imaginings and said 'I
am a king without a peer! I am Lord of the whole world!' " [Mandean
gnostic text, in E. S. Drower, *The Secret Adam.*]　　(6) "God created
man and men created God. So it is in the world, that men create gods
and they worship their creations. It would be fitting for the gods to worship men according to the truth." [From the gnostic Gospel of Philip,
84–85.]

Justin the Gnostic (Greek, c. 1st century A.D.)
From THE BOOK *BARUCH*　　　　　　　"The Garden"

Yahweh Good Pap Priapos Straight Cock Herding Lady's Thing
　　　　who sees what will be before it is

　　Elohim the FatherorMother
　　　　　　who can't see this
　　　　　　　　but invisibly
　　　　is allowed to father himself everywhere

　　Eden Israel SnakeWoman

                    who knows as little as FatherorMother
                              but can she feel!
                                thinking twice
                                  two body
                          cunt up woman
                          cunt down snake

they are the roots the fountains
                    without &
                    thanks to whom nothing everything the way it is
                        and continually being made up and taken away

FatherorMother looked at Eden half woman Israel the rest snake
                    "got to have her"
          "Elohim
                I want you too
                              just as much
                                        more maybe"

     bed

     love

     fuck

     children
                    the 12 father's angels

                      Michael Amen
                          (*these things says the Amen,*
                            the faithful and true witness
                          the beginning of the creation of God)
                              Baruch Gabriel Esaddaios . . .

                    the 12 mother's angels

                    Babel Achamoth Naas Baal Belias Satan Sael
                    Adonaios Leviathon Pharaoh Carcomenos Lathen

the father's are Elohim's   the mother's Eden Israel's

all of them in the Paradise
                              the Lord God planted
                              east of Eden
            turned toward her face
                    so she could see it
                            and see her angel children

  the trees of the garden these angels
                                    to say one word for another
                                              the trees are angels

            tree of life : Baruch
            tree of knowledge of good and bad : Serpent Naas

Paradise is made of the married joy of Elohim and Eden
where their angels enroot earth's loveliest plots

now earth is Eden Israel but not the snake torso
                      from cunt above groin in wife body
                      gentle mild to gaze at
                      she made man out of her dirt meat

out of snake springs below cunt she took wild beasts animal creation

men and women chain in flesh the love of FatherorMother and Earth

            "take my windair" she says to Adam
              "my fire" he says   to him

            "I give her airwind
                my picture cuts her size" :
                                    Eden to Eve

      "give her my fire" said Elohim

Adam   signed sealed delivered the covenant still endures
       and Eve:
                   "we are one   soul and spirit
                        and between you"

       "multiply and divide
                       make up by fucking
                               the numbers of the dead
                   until they even out the living"

                                                              C.D.

COMMENTARY

(1)   Here the roots & the performers are still "Jewish," but the mytho-
poetics of the piece runs toward combinations that are quickly beyond
the boundaries of Jewish orthodoxy. A new departure even for "gnosticism," etc., the hidden, inaccessible god (*Ein-Sof*) or "good" is later
revealed as Priapos, the ithyphallic god of Greece. The rulers of the gar-
den-paradise are the male Elohim & female Eden-Israel (as old earth-
goddess, snake-woman, cp. Aztec Coatlicue, etc.), who fuck & bring to
birth twelve angel-trees apiece: the trees of Elohim led by the angel
Baruch (= tree of life), those of Eden-Israel (the "left" or "evil" side) by
Naas = serpent (Hebrew: *naḥash*). In the later separation of Elohim &
Eden—male & female—the terror of the world we know is set in motion.

(2)   "The Garden, says Simon Magus, must be the womb, and scripture
will teach us that this is true when it says, *I am he that moulded thee in
thy mother's womb* (Isaiah 44.2). The Garden must be the womb, and
Eden the placenta, and *the river which comes out of Eden to water the
Garden* (Genesis 2.10) the navel. . . . This is the Law which Moses laid
down, and each of the books is written about this same law, as their titles
make clear. . . . The title of the second book is Exodus, for the child
that is born must pass through the Red Sea and come into the desert—
and the Red Sea, they say, is blood and tastes of bitter water. . . . But
when changed by Moses, that is by the Word, that bitter substance be-

comes sweet. And that this is the case, one may hear from all men generally when they repeat the poet's words: *It was black at the root, but its flower was like milk; and the gods call it moly; and it is difficult to dig for mortal men; but the gods can do all things* (Homer, *Odyssey* X 304–6)." (Simon Magus, *The Megale Apophasis,* as paraphrased in Hippolytos, *Refutation of All Heresies.*)

Asa Benveniste (b. 1925)
GREEN

---

what the serpent said within the garden
I have already outwritten you all
boasting of his lightning satan'az
his mouth in contact with dust
as he moved over the ground
crooked in form who spoke
first after God followed by the woman
and last of all the man
                          which is what
nahhash intended
                   I have already
written all the words in my own dirt
avoiding the grace of smooth surfaces
though he believed himself a beauty
under tappuah
                the maker
the language
             leveller
who took spheres from his mouth

unto theirs
             so poetical
in seduction click clack
the animals too at that expulsion
finding their first fears

finding their own dreams

Per Hippolytos (Greek, 3rd century A.D.)
From THE NAASENE COSMOLOGY   "The Serpent"

. . . .

Naas the Serpent Whom We Wear

     you can   make   7   from the brain

            valuted room

                wings   on either side
            wind blows on

    through blood pipes

                to Pine Nut

          down   Spine Sperm

      tailing in cock cunt

   where brain kern sleeps in secret blood

this is in small Serpent Naas   who made us

        brain the dragon head

                    six other coiling lines from there
                              bind the corpse
spine   containing the well-head   the stinging tail
                              the seventh

. . . .

    "If you knew what to ask
              he would give you living bubbling water"

into this water every breath enters choosing itself forming shape
                        peculiarity   desires   each nature
                              more than iron   the magnet
                        or gold the sea falcon's backbone
                                    and chaff   amber

through Naas the blind man will see Paradise Park

                              planted with every tree

                              and fruit of the Tree

            water sighing through the trees and fruits
        will see from one and the same water

                              olive tree drink
                                    and draw oil
                              vine curve down
                                    and find wine
                              so on and so forth forever

    The Perfect Man is unknown in this world
                    betrayed by the ignorant
                    who are as a drop in a cask
                        small dust in the balance pan

Pass through the third gate
            receive the proof of things unseen
                    that who you are is all you are not

                                            C.D.

COMMENTARY

(1)   This "Naasene cosmology" & that from Justin's Baruch (above, page 155) give contrastive views of the serpent as destroyer/preserver: a clash of symbols among two gnostic groups close to their probable origins in Jewish heterodoxy. The Naasenes get their name from the Hebrew word for "snake" transformed to Greek *naas,* & the event in the garden is the bringing of knowledge (gnosis) in a positive sense; thus the related Ophites: "We venerate the Serpent . . . cause of Gnosis for mankind." Suppressed in Judaism—as by other prevailing orthodoxies—the idea never wholly disappears.

(2)   "Know & believe that the Serpent, at the beginning of creation, was indispensable to the order of the world. . . . It is he who moves the spheres & turns them from East to the West & from the North to the South. Without him there would have been neither seed nor germination, nor will to produce any created thing." (Joseph Gikatilla, *Mystery of the Serpent,* c. 1300.)

Nathan of Gaza (Hebrew, c. 1643–80)
SERPENT

Messiah.

(by *gematria*)

T. Carmi (Hebrew, b. 1925)

From ANATOMY OF A WAR

Serpent, serpent,
go tell the Supreme Serpent
we're all choking underneath our old skins.

Serpent, serpent,
go tell the Supreme Serpent
our baby eyes are hardening in our foreheads

our old hands are like rusty pliers,
our old mouths are like shoes in the desert,
our old tongues are like deformed keys,
the old venom seethes in our lungs.

Serpent, serpent,
go tell the Supreme Serpent
to give us back the seasons of the year,
summer and spring, winter and fall

and the moon at night.

MARCIA FALK

Harris Lenowitz (b. 1945)

THE WIND   TWO TREES   MEN AND WOMEN

Shabbes Bereshis: for Tamar

Ruah elohim *wind of
god*   nefesh
haya *living breath
living creature* ne-
shama *the wind soft-
blowing huffed into
the Adam*   Yahweh *the
puffer comes to
visit the Adam   a
friendly call* le-ruah
ha-yom *at the breezy
part of the day just
towards evening* ruah
elohim   nefesh   ne-
shama   Yahweh   le-
ruah ha-yom *a warm
breath   bound on hare
hare's breath in wind
   the wind carries
spoor*
Va-yikra yahweh elo-
him el ha-adam *Yah-
weh of the gods calls
the Adam   to serve*

The woman sees that the tree provides
good food, is easy on the eyes and charms
toward wisdom, takes of its fruit and eats,
also giving some to her man with her
and he eats   The eyes of both of them
open and they know they are naked (eyrumim)
They sew fig-leaf into belts for themselves
They hear the voice of Yahweh going about
in the garden at the breezy time of the day
(le-ruah ha-yom) and the Adam and his woman
hide from the face of Yahweh of the gods
among the trees of the garden   Yahweh of
the gods calls to the Adam "Where are you?"
And he answers, "I heard your voice in the
garden, was afraid because I was naked
(eyrom) and hid" So He said, "Who told you
you were naked? Have you eaten from the
I-commanded-you-not-to-eat-from-it tree?"
The Adam said, "The woman you presented
to be with me   she presented me from the
tree and I ate"

*Yahweh knows where the Adam is   to service   passing for fate   to
memory* zikharon *of ruin-will-be*   zakhar *is* zikharon *man is memory
Now   naked* eyrom   *the Adam sees his prick*   zakhar   *and the
woman's hole* (isha *woman   one breath longer than   man* ish) (*her man*
ishah)   *they are naked   now know they are naked   their knowledge*

is arum *subtile   they are* eyrum *naked Yahweh pants after them*
pants after him   the Adam   the knows remembering zakhar   arom
eyrum   va-yipah be-apav nishmat hayim   va-yehi ha-adam le-nefesh
haya   *when Yahweh of the gods huffed breath to life* zakhar u-nekeva
prickandhole he made them   but before naase adam be-tsalmeynu
ki-dmuteynu . . . va-yivra   elohim et ha-adam be-tsalmo   be-tselem
elohim bara   oto *in his image he made him/it   The god is woman/man*
    the Adam was   lonely   couldn't find a completion   a perfection
    an incompletion   sleight of hand   makes two halves more than
one whole   forget   go to deepsleep va-yapeyl Yahweh elohim tardema
al ha-adam *forget   Creation   imperfect   by design! Correct*
it   the very try is evil   is good   From basar ehad *one flesh*
two flesh two bone   the Adam CHOOSES ve-davak be-ishto *to stick by*
his own bone   gives up

But recalls   in the breezy evening   to Thou   a fix   plan
    says ha-isha asher natata imadi hi natna li min ha-eyts
va-okheyl *she gave me it   the one you gave   to be with me*
Rabbit flashing teeth   no alibi   no excuses   no forgiveness
challenge   We are man   we remember   we are one for all your
test   It will do me in But I remember why   You failed   feared
tricked   And Yahweh of the gods cannot still the voice or the wind
fears his image   the power of himself   knowing himself   like
the man knows the woman   remembering other battles   other gods:
va-y omer Yahweh elohim   heyn ha-adam haya ke-ahad mi-menu la-daat
tov va-ra   ve-ata pen yishlah yado ve-lakah gam me-eyts ha-hayim
ve-akhal va-hay le-olam   va-yeshalheyhu Yahweh elohim mi-gran eyden
Keep him   now he knows   from being one of us   living forever

The Evil sits still with the Good   Yahweh elohim is one   Even with
the help of man   granting logos   shekhina   can never be two trying
to be one   The man and the woman have their halfdom knitting to-
gether   melting   making the old One   bringing more to make Onetry
knowing   remembering   when making   game of harehound

COMMENTARY

from "the notebooks"   12/75   for Harris Lenowitz & as a first prologue
to the Book of Job

o has the work of creation ended?
ended & plunged us into terror
eye of your god still lurking there
like snake in its hole
mad snake
when will you strike again & be beautiful
& shining like the rainbow

sign of god & peace   you who were meant to be man's lover   (the old
texts say)   *our houses full of cherished snakes   high beings   angels
with cocks & eyes*   o the dream of the voluptuary is still   still true   the
snake still splendid in   world of his emanations   your mysteries no less
than ours   you prince of coils   of circles   urge to make life that drives
you snake as well   o impulse to create   to be prolific   & the good
(they said) rests on this evil too   what's at the center then?   the face of
the devourer   blood-smeared face stares back at us across our terror
   auschwitz   hiroshima   & we ask   who are the panthers in the temple?   what is the pain Job feels   & why?   the answer   SILENCE
until the mute man cries   in self-denial   makes his god speak through
madness   as the wind of Yahveh

yammered
called to Job
o has the work of creation ended?
in clash of contraries
it starts again
the words of Yahveh raised against us
*for you have not spoken of me
the thing that is true
as my servant Job hath*
in which the work resumes

(j.r.)

Louis Zukofsky (b. 1904)

THE IYYOB TRANSLATION FROM "A-15"

An
  hinny
by
  stallion
out of
  she-ass

He neigh ha lie low h'who y'he gall mood
So roar cruel hire
Lo to achieve an eye leer rot off
Mass th'lo low o loam echo
How deal me many coeval yammer
Naked on face of white rock—sea.
Then I said: Liveforever my nest
Is arable hymn
Shore she root to water
Dew anew to branch.

Wind: Yahweh at Iyyob
Mien His roar 'Why yammer
Measly make short hates oh
By milling bleat doubt?
Eye sore gnaw key heaver haul its core
Weigh as I lug where hide any?
If you—had you towed beside the roots?
How goad Him—you'd do it by now—

My sum My made day a key to daw?
O Me not there allheal—a cave.

All mouth deny hot bough?
O me you're raw—Heaven pinned Dawn stars
Brine I heard choir and weigh by care—
Why your ear would call by now Elohim:
Where was soak—bid lot tie in hum—
How would you have known to hum
How would you all oats rose snow lay
Assay how'd a rock light rollick ore
Had the rush in you curb, ah bay,
But the shophar yammer *heigh horse'*

Wind: Yahweh at Iyyob 'Why yammer,'
Wind: Iyyob at Yahweh 'Why yammer
How cold the mouth achieved echo.'
Wind: Yahweh at Iyyob 'Why yammer
Ha neigh now behēmoth and share I see see your make
Giddy pair—stones—whose rages go
Weigh raw all gay where how spill lay who'
Wind: Iyyob
'Rain without sun hated? *hurt no one*
In two we shadow, how hide any.'

(Hebrew, c. 7th century B.C.)
From THE BOOK OF JOB   "Whirlwind"

. . . for ye have not spoken of me the thing
that is right, as my servant Job hath

Then God answered Job out of the whirlwind:

Do you dare to deny my judgment?
   Am I wrong because you are right?
Is your arm like the arm of God?
   Can your voice bellow like mine?
Dress yourself now like an emperor.
   Climb up on a throne.
Unleash your savage justice.
   Humiliate the rich and mighty.
Make the proud man grovel.
   Pluck the wicked from their perch.
Push them into mass graves.
   Throw them down to Hell.
Then I will admit
   that your own strength can save you.

Look: the Beast beside you:
   he eats grass like a bull.
Look: the power in his thighs,
   the pulsing sinews of his belly.
His penis stiffens like a pine;
   his testicles bulge with vigor.
His ribs are bars of bronze;
   his bones—iron beams.

He is first of the works of God,
   who created him as a plaything.
He lies under the lotus,
   hidden by reeds and shadows.
Though the river rages, he is not alarmed;
   he is calm though the torrent beats against his mouth.
Who then will take him by the eyes
   or pierce his nose with a peg?

Will you catch the Serpent with a fishhook
   or tie his tongue with a string?
Will you pass a rope through his nose
   or crack his jaw with a pin?
Will he plead with you for mercy
   and timidly beg your pardon?
Will he come to terms of surrender
   and promise to be your slave?
Will you play with him like a sparrow
   and put him on a leash for your girls?
Will merchants bid for his carcass
   and parcel him out to shops?
Will you riddle his skin with spears
   and split his head with harpoons?
Go ahead: attack him;
   you will not do it twice.

Look: hope is a lie;
   you would faint at the very sight of him.
Who would dare to arouse him?
   Who would stand in his way?
Who under all the heavens
   could fight against him and live?
Who could pierce his armor
   or break through his coat of mail?
Who could open the gates of his mouth?
   His arched teeth are terrible.
Flames rush from his mouth;
   smoke pours from his nostrils.
Power beats in his neck,

    and terror leaps before him.
Iron to him is like straw,
    bronze like rotten wood.
Swords and arrows tickle him;
    slingstones hit him and crumble.
Clubs are like splinters to him;
    he laughs at the quivering spear.
His belly is spiked, jaggèd;
    he drags the swamp like a rake.
He makes the ocean boil;
    he spits up the sea like a geyser.
No one on earth is his equal—
    a creature without fear.
He looks down on the highest.
    He is king over all the proud beasts.

STEPHEN MITCHELL

THE END OF "A BOOK OF WORLDS"

ב

THE VISIONS

Nothing, only an image, nothing else, utter oblivion.
Slanting through the words come vestiges of light.

—FRANZ KAFKA

If you are "my witnesses," I am the Lord
& if you are not my witnesses
I am not, as it were, the Lord

—SIMEON BAR YOḤAI

A Book of Beards

Gertrude Stein (1874–1946)
From PATRIARCHAL POETRY

Their origin and their history patriarchal poetry their origin and their history patriarchal poetry their origin and their history.

Patriarchal Poetry.

Their origin and their history.

Patriarchal Poetry their origin and their history their history patriarchal poetry their origin patriarchal poetry their history their origin patriarchal poetry their history patriarchal poetry their origin patriarchal poetry their history their origin.

That is one case.

Able sweet and in a seat.

Patriarchal poetry their origin their history their origin. Patriarchal poetry their history their origin.

And Adam was living for a hundred years and thirty years.
Then he was begetting someone in-his-image in-his-likeness.
He called him Seth.
The days of Adam after Seth's begetting were eight hundred years.
Begetting sons and daughters.
All the days of Adam's living were nine hundred years and thirty
    years.
Then Adam died.

And Seth was living for a hundred years and five years.
Then he was begetting Enos.
after Enos's begetting Seth was living for eight hundred years and
    seven years.
Begetting sons and daughters.
All the days of Seth were nine hundred years and twelve years.
Then Seth died.

And Enos was living for ninety years then Enos was begetting
    Cainan.
After Cainan's begetting Enos was living for eight hundred years
    and fifteen years.
Begetting sons and daughters.
All the days of Enos were nine hundred years and five years.
Then Enos died.

And Cainan was living for seventy years then Cainan was begetting
    Mahalalel.
After Mahalalel's begetting Cainan was living for eight hundred
    years and forty years.

Begetting sons and daughters.
All the days of Cainan were nine hundred years and ten years.
Then Cainan died.

And Mahalalel was living sixty years and five years.
Then he was begetting Jared.
After Jared's begetting Mahalalel was living for eight hundred years and thirty years.
Begetting sons and daughters.
All the days of Mahalalel were eight hundred years and ninety-five years.
Then Mahalalel died.

And Jared was living for a hundred years and sixty-two years.
Then he was begetting Enoch.
After Enoch's begetting Jared was living for eight hundred years.
Begetting sons and daughters.
All the days of Jared were nine hundred years and sixty-two years.
Then Jared died.

And Enoch was living sixty-five years.
Then he was begetting Methusaleh.
Enoch was one who walked with God
three hundred years past his begetting of Methusaleh.
Begetting sons and daughters.
All the days of Enoch were three hundred years and sixty-five years.
He was one who walked with God.
Then he was not.
For God had taken him.

And Methusaleh was living for a hundred years and eighty-seven years.
Then he was begetting Lamech.
After Lamech's begetting Methusaleh was living for seven hundred years and eighty-two years.
Begetting sons and daughters.
All the days of Methusaleh were nine hundred years and sixty-nine years.
Then Methusaleh died.

And Lamech was living for a hundred years and eighty-two years.
Then he was begetting a son.
He called him Noah
saying: this one will be a comfort to us in our work
the labor of our hands upon this soil
the Elohim had cursed.
After Noah's begetting Lamech was living five hundred years and
ninety-five years.
Begetting sons and daughters.
All the days of Lamech were seven hundred years and seventy-seven
years.
Then Lamech died.

And Noah was five hundred years old.
Noah was begetting Shem and Ham and Japheth.

J.R.

COMMENTARY

(1)   "And why was the world created with a single man then? To teach
that if any man has caused a single soul to perish, it is as though he had
caused a whole world to perish. And if any man has saved a single soul,
it is as though he had saved alive a whole world." (*Mishna: Sanhedrin*
4.5.)

(2)   "If what is supposed to have been destroyed in Paradise was destructible, then it was not decisive; but if it was indestructible, then we
are living in a false belief." (F. Kafka.)

Rossana Ombres (Italian, b. 1931)

THE SONG OF LILITH

(that has no ending)

Eve suffered still from a repulsive
fetal stench: for she came
from a swamp's seething womb.
The palms of her hands were pink with blood
that still rushed, childlike and unruly,
outside its ducts:
on her udders
the nipples were phalanges of adult ring fingers
with a hornlike plug
meant to fall off with the first milk.
Eve had the look of an herbivorous animal,
a suspicious and stolidly furry beast
—rabbit or hare—
her wonderless mouth was agape
and the tip of her tongue (Eve didn't yet speak)
hung out like a worm from a rotting cherry.

Adam hung around
with the constructive curiosity of a mole
covered with the sad color of a tawny dog:
after copulating
with a bat-bellied griffin
and giving vent to his remaining spasms
in the abandoned nest of a hermit-crab,
he had to try now—he was under strict
orders—to use his sex
with the new creature. But Eve

had smooth skin
without the sheep's fleece, all golden nests,
without the marine gleam of shells
without the ibis' anfractuous frenzy
and then
it was exasperating her not uttering a sound
not even a wave's faint roar
from Eden's farthest beach.

How beautiful it was when he, Adam, seduced
spotted panthers, and in the giant
thistle forest, played with sheep
—their expression was so patient and beatific—
or when he caught
wind-drunk gazelles
and carried them deep inside a large
storm-cooled anemone!

But now a dark Angel
with shiny locust-wings
(Mzpopiasaiel was his name, he said,
the righteously choleric one)
had given him Eve
decreeing—what voice of wood-crackling-in-the-fire
had that cup of holy wrath!—
decreeing her to be
not his food but love companion.

But he, Adam, wasted time counting
the tiny collars of a tedious creeper
biting into peaches and boning
red mullets fished with acanthus leaves
spitting out, with the widest possible arc,
clingstone and cherry pits
pissing on sluggish lettuce leaves:
hoping
(and time for him till now
had been only a wait for orders)
that from the beheaded cloud, to the right of the apple tree,

there should come to him
flying—like other times—a new signal.

When he saw Lilith, the sweetest demon,
shining with female form
hooded by a labile ring of alchemic stars
advancing in bright fierceness
preceded by an incredible animal
—certainly a residue of other
more meticulous creations—
sporting a single high horn
on its celestial forehead . . .

But the new eve of sodomy is looking for
other demons in her likeness: no
feigned clawing attacks, no
festive howlings:
the mythical new eve
beautiful in the acrobatic cadence of her walk
unknown to Eden's other animals,
hurls stones, hooded by alchemic
stars, beautiful, hurls stones.

Man's daughter she is not, nor Angel's bride:
beyond paradise's prolific marshes
waiting to be milked
the unicorn
carries her, Lilith, who already knows
the mysterious form of the mandrake root
and the golem that grows in the kernel! She knows
that jasper placed in henbane
causes a mortal sleep, drier and stranger
than the one fastening on Orpheus' back,
that in the starred moray's vulva
there is a mermaid's embryo
in the tiger lily the latex
that will beget Amazons, and one hundred
female deities are waiting in the steeped firtree
in the shape of gold ducklings

another hundred female deities
will be nursed by unicorns and their blood
will be white to contagion, prescient to fire.

How many lexicons
Lilith already knows!
She speaks seventy tongues
awakening in their dens and subduing
dead alphabets of creations at once perfected and consumed!
She has no dealings with snakes,
merchants of shabby knavery, and from condescending
magmatic chasms
she learned mystic delights.

The day will come when she, Lilith . . .

EDGAR PAUK

COMMENTARY

(1) "No she-demon has ever achieved as fantastic a career as Lilith who started out from the lowliest of origins, was a failure as Adam's intended wife, became the paramour of lascivious spirits, rose to be the bride of Samael the demon king, ruled as the Queen of Zemargad and Sheba, and finally ended up as the consort of God himself." (Raphael Patai, *The Hebrew Goddess,* page 207.)

(2) from "the notebooks" 12/75 a discourse on Lilith who she is her force her power that they would call "demonic" she the woman fought to be above the man at least be equal in that game her sex a thwarted thing female presence seated in proud exile dispossessed would cry for vengeance in death of little children seduction of those men away from home estranged from Eve the wife our Lady of the Contract Lilith breaks loose on the other side —o moon nightwailer— rages in the laundry roaming through your house at dawn (a poltergeist) she hurls dishes from cupboard sits among them scraping at your sores sometimes a comfort otherwise a joke an old obsession like that furry animal who pisses in your soup free spirit (j.r.)

(Aramaic, 50 B.C.–50 A.D.)

From THE GENESIS APOCRYPHON   "The Mystery"

] . . . . . . and with the planting
   ] . . Moreover, the mystery of evil which
   ] . . . and the mystery which

JOSEPH A. FITZMYER

COMMENTARY

(1)   "And it came to pass, when men began to multiply on the face of the earth, & daughters were born to them, that the sons of God saw the daughters of men that they were fair: & they took them wives of all which they chose." (Genesis 6.1–.2.)

(2)   "And all the others together with them took wives unto themselves, & each chose for himself a wife, & they began to enter them & to defile themselves with them, & they taught them charms & enchantments, & the cuttings of roots, & made them acquainted with plants. And they became pregnant, & they bore great giants, whose height was three thousand ells: who consumed all the acquisitions of men. And when men could no longer sustain them, the giants turned against them & devoured mankind. And they began to sin against birds & beasts & reptiles & fish, & to devour one another's flesh, & drink the blood. Then the earth laid accusation against the lawless ones." (The Book of Enoch, 7.1–.6.)

I saw a dream o a dream o I will show my dream to you my son
    & Enoch lifts his voice
                he speaks to his son Methusaleh
my voice to you
        he says
now hear me this dream-vision of your father's
   how in bed (your mother Edna not yet with me)
      I saw a bull (look look) come from the earth a white bull
        then a heifer & two more bulls with her one black one red
the black bull gores the red one
  chases the red bull across the world
     I do not see him now
but see the black bull growing
  the heifer with him many oxen looking like
     his children
         followers
that cow has gone to hunt the red one
  doesn't find him
     weeps
      & weeps in hunting
(as I looked)
  then the first bull comes & quiets her
    she doesn't cry
but bears another white bull
  later many bulls
       & black cows
in my sleep
  that white bull grew became a large one
    who fathered many white bulls like him

& the white bulls fathered white bulls
    more like him
        like one & then another
                                many
*

my eyes saw sleeping from the sky above a star
    falls from the sky
        becomes one eating pasturing among the oxen
black oxen swelling changing stalls
    & pastures
        lived among each other
saw & looked up to the sky saw many stars
    come down from heaven
        threw themselves around the first star
            who were cattle too & pastured
(looking seeing)
    saw their cocks swell down like horses
        mount the oxen's cows
            who swelled gave birth to elephants
                & others
                    camels   asses
whom the oxen feared
    fearful they began to bite
        their teeth tore devoured
            goring with their horns
& swallowed down the oxen
    children of the earth were trembling
        shook before them
                        fled

                                                    J.R.

COMMENTARY

(1) "Dream-vision," says the text, then follows with an allegory of those events set out in the preceding commentary (see above). And in back of it there is the sense of some previous disaster ("ecological crisis," we might now say) that would lead to plant & animal domestication as the first great human steps toward fixing up the world. It is, from the present vantage, a lot less comfortable, this propaganda for the new agriculture as the solution to a presumed population explosion among hunters, gatherers, nomads, etc., which had led already to species extinction & depletion—a solution that would set up cycles of relief & expansion toward the global crises now upon us. So, the first paradox of the "holy book" itself comes with God's opening thrusts to man & woman: BREED A LOT & FILL THE EARTH / & TAKE IT OVER // RULE: / THE FISH OF THE SEA / THE FLIER OF THE SKIES / ALL LIFE THAT CRAWLS UPON THE EARTH (Genesis 1.28): an incitement to the very condition that brings the flood & the new beginning with Noah, himself the father of agriculture, etc., & with his sons who found the later city-states & kingdoms. The incoherence of the *logos* is a circumstance that leads to the greatest questioning of the mind behind the act (see the present anthology, *passim*) or, failing that, the fiercest injunctions to keep silent.

(2) " 'The sons of God saw the daughters of Adam.' Thus it is said in the Book of Joshua: 'Two men, spying secretly, saying.' And who are the daughters of Adam? It is written [I Kings 3.16]: 'Then came two women, prostitutes, to the king.' Of them it is written: 'They saw that the Wisdom of God was in Solomon.' Then they came, but not before; the majesty of his royal estate caused them to cry out for mercy. These two had been embracing one another in the world above, but they descended to the world below & inherited dust. They lost the good portion that had been theirs. The sons of God had been crowned with compassion, but instead they came to be crowned with a battered cluster of grapes." (From *Zohar: The Book of Concealment,* tr. Roy A. Rosenberg.)

(Aramaic, 50 B.C.–50 A.D.)

From THE GENESIS APOCRYPHON   "After the Flood"

Column X

. . . the ark settled (upon) one of the mountains of Ararat . . .
. . . I atoned for all the land . . .
. . . I burned incense on the altar . . .

Column XI

. . . you must eat no blood . . .

Column XII

[and became the father of] Arpachshad two years after the flood,
    . . . all the sons of Shem
. . . Put and Canaan . . . . . .
I and all my sons began to cultivate the earth and I planted a
    vineyard . . . on Mount Lubar and in the fourth year it pro-
    duced wine for me . . .
And I began to drink it on the first day of the fifth year . . .
I invited my sons and the sons of my sons and the wives of all of
    us and their daughters and we gathered together and went . . .
. . . to the Lord of the heavens, to the Most High God, to the
    Great Holy One, who rescued us from destruction . . .

JOSEPH A. FITZMYER

Louis Zukofsky (b. 1904)

From BOTTOM: ON SHAKESPEARE

---

* * *

'Hath not a Jew eyes?'

M.V.,I,iii, 72;III,ii,61

After the flood were born to Noah's sons—Shem, Ham and Japheth —their sons who mixed eyes sometimes, sometimes heads. Of the whole earth they were still seen some time having one language in one plain. Then differentiated speech scattered them, spelled out upon the earth's face about its channels, the Great Sea, the Red, the Salt, Chinnereth.

Son of Japheth, Javan (Ionians).

Pythagoras, in whom green pulse of pod and flame seeded nine spheres of number and tone, saw thru the hindsight of five Changes of himself his incarnation before Troy and heard his latest voice, that of Zaratas the Chaldean. Xenophanes was simpler. He talked with the Medes among whom he wandered, the strays, had the rainbowed earth—for his feet. Clean cup and table, sang the season—winter. *A good glance—Stop beating that dog, he's a friend, I knew as I heard his voice:* the words as reproachful as the herdsman of Tekoa's, *sold the poor for a pair of shoes.* Less Javan, and alive two centuries earlier, he might be Amos foreseeing *days the mountains shall drop sweet wine, and all the hills shall melt.*

Whether or not Ocellus Lucanus learned from Pythagoras, when Ocellus is read beside Shakespeare the eyes exist thru two millennia, suffer none of the changes of the mind's eye, and persist in the changes called *Los Cantares,* 90 and so on, into America 1956:

hardly forgotten Ocellus—little *oculus,* the Latin diminutive used to praise excellence.

'Whole earth . . . of one speech' fed Kung's eyes anew. The same continent turned Prince Siddhartha's downward to worlds of lotus blossoms—a way from headiness, yet twisting to it as with Pythagoras (whom Ovid in the recaptured Changes of love praised curiously for the intellect into which he turned the gods his mortal eyes did not see). The Asians Kung and Buddha flourished about the time 50,000 exiled Jews came back with Zerrubbabel to live for the second Temple at Jerusalem under Cyrus. (536 B.C.)

'Beréshīt bara Elohīm ēt hāshāmayim v'ēt hāāretz.'

Genesis,I,i

The word *ēt,* untranslatable, but always used in Hebrew with the definite grammatical object that follows it, has it may be said ineffable presence for strange tongues. Its grammatical thought shadows the grammar of a voice that effects in previous time to have muffled a *seen* object, so making how many millennia to *ēt? Aleh hādvārim (Deut.,I,1)—These are the words.* In Hebrew the word for *word* is also the word for *thing.* The roots and stems of grammar are foresights and hindsights so entangled that traditions and chronologies mean little if not an acceptance, a love of certain, living beings for words as seen things. *Being and Non-being before the Void* —Rig Veda X (ca. 1000–800 B.C.) is the same vision and entanglement—more distilled or 'philosophical'—of the Asian mainland that sent its later European avatar to the Ionian Sea and Syracuse.

From THE BOOK OF FORMATION   "The Father"

When Abraham our Father came into this life
> He looked
> He saw
> He explored
> He articulated
> He placed
> He engraved
> He combined
> He structured & he elevated with his hands
& the Lord of All appeared to him in vision &
> He set him in His Bosom &
> He kissed him on his head &
He called him "Abraham my Love" &
He cut a covenant with him & with his seed forever &
He cut a covenant with him between the ten fingers of his
> hands which is the covenant of tongue &
He cut a covenant with him between the ten toes of his feet
> which is the covenant of circumcision &
He tied the twenty-two letters of the Torah in his tongue &
He revealed to him His secret:
> He drew them through Water
> He burned them in Fire
> He shook them through Air
> He kindled them in the Seven
> He led them through the twelve constellations

J.R.

from "the notebooks" 1/76 first of those crazy Jews o cockeyed pappa
with Yahveh's kiss hot still on your throat you ramble through
camps of *goyim* in shadow of a small hut hung with herbs fresh licorice
betwixt your lips & scorn their idols dolls you squawk *o Din o*
Judgment on my killers they Nimrod's folk who threatened me at child-
birth 'twas from these I hid out in my momma's throat sucked milk from
the angel's little finger now they do call me Abba Abie Baby I swing
mine axe my heart is wed to procreation plentiful as sand 's my seed
rammed up the holes of countless generations will form a people like
yourself a world of wanderers in movement through worlds themselves
in movement & the others ask who is this crazy Jew learns all these
secrets magic words by conversation tongue into God's mouth betrayed once by his father (salty idol fucker) holds a knife still to his own
son's throat in fire of whose eyes an altar blossoms becomes the happy
garden he can plant in peace (j.r.)

(Aramaic, 50 B.C.–50 A.D.)

From THE GENESIS APOCRYPHON "Of Sarah"

---

how splendid & how beautiful the form of her face
& how fine the hair of her head
how clear are her eyes & how pleasant is her nose
& the full radiance of her face
how lovely are her breasts & all the whiteness of her skin
her arms: how beautiful
her hands: how perfect
& how welcome the appearance of her hands
how soft are her palms
    how long & narrow all the fingers of her hands

her legs: how beautiful
how rounded are her thighs
no virgins & no brides beneath their canopies more beautiful than
    she
her beauty far beyond all women
beauty high above them all
& wisdom in her too
all that she holds is lovely

COMMENTARY

"When Sarah gave birth to Isaac in her old age, the nations of the earth said, *He is really the son of her maidservant, & she makes believe that she is suckling him.* In instant reply to them Abraham said to Sarah: *This is no time for modesty. For the hallowing of the Name arise & show your breasts.* Sarah arose & showed her breasts, & her two nipples were pouring out milk like two jets of water, as is written, *And she said: Who would have said unto Abraham that Sarah would give children suck?* (Genesis 21.7) . . . At sight of Sarah's milk the nations of the earth brought their children to her to give them suck. . . . And how is the expression *give children suck* to be interpreted? That these children of the nations of the earth became children of Israel. . . . Accordingly, all Gentiles throughout the world who accept conversion & all Gentiles throughout the world who fear God spring from the children who drank of the milk of Sarah." (From *Pesikta Rabati* 43.4.)

Thus, as "bride" & "mother-of-the-nations," Sarah continues the tradition-of-the-goddess common to the surrounding mythologies. While some such tradition is often explained by assuming a "matriarchy" prior to the rule of the male "elders" (= Hebrew "beards"), the reader should consider the advantage to the ancient patriarchies in the deification of the female principle as mother, bride, etc.—at least that the relation between mythic & actual rule may be trickier than the simpler telling would allow.

After these events it was
God tested Avraham
and said to him
Avraham
He said
Here I am
He said
Now take your son
your only-one
whom you love
Yitzhak,
and go-you-forth to the land of Moriyya,
and offer him up there for an offering-up
upon one of the mountains
of which I will tell you
Avraham arose early in the morning
he saddled his ass
he took his two boys with him and Yitzhak his son
he split wood for the offering-up
and arose and went to the place of which God had told him

On the third day Avraham lifted up his eyes
and saw the place from afar
Avraham spoke to his boys
You remain here with the ass
I and the boy will go yonder
we will prostrate ourselves and then return to you
Avraham took the (pieces of) wood for the offering-up
he laid them upon Yitzhak his son
in his hand he took the fire and the knife

Thus the two of them went together

Yitzhak said to Avraham his father
He said
Father
He said
Here I am my son
He said
Now here are the fire and the wood
but where is the lamb for the offering-up
Avraham said
God will see-for-himself to the lamb for the offering-up my son
Thus the two of them went together

They came to the place of which God had told him
There Avraham built the altar
and arranged the wood
and bound Yitzhak his son
and laid him on the altar atop the wood
Avraham stretched out his hand,
he took the knife to butcher his son
But HIS messenger called to him from heaven
and said
Avraham Avraham
He said
Here I am
He said
Do not stretch out your hand against the boy,
do not do anything to him
For now I know
that you stand in awe of God
you have not withheld from me your son   your only-one
Avraham lifted up his eyes and saw
Here   a ram caught behind in the thicket by its horns
Avraham went
he took the ram
and offered it up for an offering-up instead of his son
Avraham called the name of that place
HE sees

EVERETT FOX

COMMENTARY

"In the community of Worms, some eight hundred souls were killed in the course of two days at the end of the month Iyyar 1096. Among these were some who 'offered up sacrifices of righteousness, who with whole heart took their sons and slew them for the Unification of His Glorious and Awesome Name. . . . Now there was a unique person there whose name was Rabbi Meshullam bar Isaac, and in a loud voice he called out to all those standing by and to his lifelong companion, Mistress Zipporah: 'All you great and small, hearken unto me. Here is my son whom God gave me and to whom my wife Zipporah gave birth *in her old age: Isaac* is this child's name: and now *I shall offer him up as Father Abraham offered up his son Isaac.*' Whereupon Zipporah besought him: 'O my lord, my lord, *do not* yet *lay thy hand upon the lad* whom I raised and brought up after having given birth to him *in my old age*. Slay me first so that I shall not have to behold the death of the child.' But he replied, saying: 'Not even for a moment shall I delay, for He who gave him to us will take him away to his own portion and lay him to rest in Father Abraham's bosom.' *And he bound his son Isaac, and picked up the knife to slay his son,* and recited the blessing appropriate for slaughter. And the lad replied, 'Amen.' And the father slew the lad. Then he took his shrieking wife and *both of them together* left the room; and the vagabonds murdered them. Over such as these, wilt Thou hold Thy peace, O Lord?" (Shalom Spiegel, *The Last Trial:* from a medieval chronicle, *Ma'ase ha-Gezerot ha-Yeshanot,* circa 1100.)

Howard Schwartz (b. 1945)

THE SACRIFICE

It is said that as he grew older Isaac put the journey to Mount Moriah out of his mind. Even to Rebecca, his wife, he would not speak of what had happened. So circumspect did he become that by the time of his marriage at the age of forty no one could remember the last time he had been heard to speak on the subject. So it seems likely that during the period in which his wife was expecting a child the old memory came to his mind even less often, for Rebecca had grown ripe with her waiting, which was already much longer than the old wives had estimated.

On one such night, while he and Rebecca were sleeping side by side, Isaac dreamed for the first time of the sacrifice that had taken place almost thirty years before. But this dream was even more real than the actual incident, for then his confusion had saved him from his fear, and now all the terror he had not noticed was with him as a faceless man chained him to a great rock and held a knife against his neck. He felt the blade poised to press down when the sun emerging from behind a cloud blinded them both, and at the same time they heard the frantic honking of a goose whose grey and white feathers had become entangled in the thorns of a nearby bush. It was then that the fierce and silent man, whom Isaac now saw was his father, put down the blade and pulled the bird free from the thorns and berries, and as he brought it back Isaac saw how it struggled in his hands. Then, when the goose was pressed firmly to the rock, Isaac watched as his father pulled back the white throat and drew the blade. He saw especially how white was the neck and how cleanly the blade cut through. At last Abraham put down the blade and unbound his son and they embraced. It was then that Isaac opened his eyes, felt the arms of his wife as she tried to wake him, and heard her whispering that the child was about to be born.

When Isaac understood he sat up in bed and hurried from the room to wake the midwife who had been living with them for almost three weeks. Two hours later Rebecca gave birth first to one son and then to another, the first who was hairy, his skin red, the second who came forth with his hand on his brother's heel. Isaac found himself fascinated as he watched the midwife wash the infants in warm water. The first son, whom they came to call Esau, was born with an umbilical cord that was dark purple, the color of blood. But his second son, whose name became Jacob, had a cord that was soft and white as pure wax. It was this perfectly woven rope that Isaac found most intriguing, for reasons that he could not comprehend. And he sensed a strange terror as he unsheathed a knife and drew the blade to sever this last link between what was and what will be. For it was then the dream of that night came back to him, and he saw in the same instant how the hands of his father had held down the goose, and how the sharp blade had cut across its neck, soft and white, like the severed cord he held in his own hands.

(Hebrew, Bible, c. 10th century B.C.)

From THE BOOK OF GENESIS   "Jacob & the Angel"

> *Look! the Angel that made a man of Jacob*
> *made Israël in His embrace*
>
> *was the Law,   was Syntax.*
>
> (Robert Duncan.)

On that night he arose
he took his two wives and his two maids and his eleven children
and crossed the Yabbok crossing,
he took them and sent them across the river and sent across

that which was his
Yaakov remained behind alone
Now a man wrestled with him until the break of dawn
When he saw that he could not prevail against him
he touched the socket of his hip
and the socket of Yaakov's hip was dislocated as he wrestled
   with him
Then he said
Let me go
for the dawn is breaking
But he said
I will not let you go
unless you bless me
He said to him
What is your name
And he said
Yaakov
Now he said:
Not Yaakov/Heel-Sneak shall your name be said henceforth
but rather Yisrael/Fighter of God
for you fought with Godhood and with mankind
and prevailed
Yaakov asked
he said
O tell me your name
But he said
Why do you ask about my name
And he blessed him there
Yaakov called the name of the place Peniel/God's-Face
for
I have seen God
face to face
and my life is saved

EVERETT FOX

COMMENTARY

(1) Jacob as trickster goes through the change of name to Israel, here translated "fights-with-God" but elsewhere "man-who-sees-God." The "elders" move between worlds, as recognizable, limited beings but also as men approaching "god." The line between sight & vision vanishes: the man who fights the angel-god becomes the angel Israel himself. Thus, in the later "Prayer of Joseph," Jacob says:

I Jacob who am speaking to you am also Israel: an angel of God & a ruling spirit. Abraham & Isaac were created before any work. But I Jacob, whom men call Jacob but whose name is Israel, am he who God called Israel & meant a man who sees God: the firstborn of every living thing that God gives life.

And again, to the "angel" with whom he wrestles:

Are you not Uriel, the eighth after me & I Israel, the archangel of the power of the Lord and the chief captain among the sons of God? Am I not Israel, the first minister before the face of God?

Similarly Isaac, in Philo's Hellenistic approach to Judaism as mystery religion (thus: E. R. Goodenough, *By Light, Light*), becomes the son-of-god born-of-a-virgin, Logos, married to Sophia, model (like the others) for self-transformation. But said transformation as *poesis* is only meaningful where the human is maintained as point-of-origin—i.e., where there exists a truly double vision—or like Duncan (in the context of the epigraph here appended by the present editor) in "wrestling with form to liberate form." Within the larger Jewish enterprise, the work is either transferred to Israel as "chosen" people (that in itself a paradox), or it remains a construct of the imagination, the work of poet heretics & mystics.

(2) *"And God went up from Jacob in the place where he spoke with him.* Rabbi Simeon said, From here we learn that Jacob formed the Holy Chariot, together with the other patriarchs, further that Jacob constitutes the supernal Holy Chariot that will restore the full light of the moon & that he forms a chariot by himself." (*Zohar*, I.173b.) Or earlier, Simeon ben Lakish (3rd century A.D.): "The patriarchs *are* the Merkaba."

For more on the *merkaba* (chariot or throne of God), see above, page 20.

(Hebrew, 2nd century B.C.)

From THE TESTAMENTS OF THE 12 PATRIARCHS

"Joseph & the Bull"

> *& Joseph dreamed & told it to his brothers (said) see I*
> *have dreamed a dream: & see the sun & moon & the 11*
> *stars bow down to me: & told it to his father & his*
> *brothers: & his father turned on him & said: what is this*
> *dream you dreamed? shall I & shall your mother & your*
> *brothers come to you & bow down to the earth?* (Gen-
> esis 37.9–.10.)

words of our father Jacob (said)
    my sons   run everywhere
    grab what your hands can hold
    thrust in my sight
we thought   said
    what can we make our own?
    we only see
          the sun
              the moon
                  the stars
he said
    whatever your hands can hold
Levi first grabbed a stick
he raised it up
jumped on the sun
& rode it
which Judah saw
he saw him
raised a stick himself

then rode the moon
the nine tribes followed each one
rode his star his planet
in the sky
        left only Joseph
on the earth
our father Jacob said
    my son why did you not do
    what your brothers did
he thought   said
    I am a man
            born to a woman not
                    sky's child
    my end will be
            returning standing
                    back on earth
& speaking   looked   he saw
a great bull near him
wings were like a stork's
his horns the reem's horns
Jacob said
    you mount him Joseph son
    you ride upon his back
which Joseph did
he mounted on the bull
when Jacob left him
Joseph then rode four hours gloried
in the bull   the bull
flew up with him his hand
reached for a stick
started to strike his brothers

                                            J.R.

COMMENTARY

(1) from "the notebooks" 1/76 whose true denial wins us hero
child of the earth the stars elsewhere are distances inside our heads
we travel in astral corridors "my place is with her" Joseph says
born from her hole his words accept our death played out where we
find ourselves then rides the bull like Mithra military god the Romans
swooned on nobly the eyes of Jew & Gentile seek the sky "immortal"
    kept from the true denial Gilgamesh offends the goddess finds his re-
ward in death o do they know they hug the earth still easy riders
    Baal & Yahveh in image of her children tribes of earth *night of the*
earth & fish like Olson's Merry there in Dogtown I drove past with
Kahn outlaw & free among the redmen & Israel you gonif of the
purple sage may you be earthbound too my people know no gods
but earth & what the mind throws back in dreams her mound *her*
part that takes him in *vast earth* Jerusalem of many hills (j.r.)

(2) As elsewhere the "sons of Israel" are both individuals & tribes. The
dream of Joseph takes us backward to a world of gods & titans: the
elders towering in childhood visions. Within his dream-time world, the
man as hero moves among the stars, plays out a ritual in which the possible is real, the wish fulfilled. The brothers are the founders, sons-of-
origin, & one of them (the chief) recalls still how the human line goes
back to earth. And hidden in that line the secret of the totem shows the
tribes related to the other children of the earth. These are the animal-
powers, summoned elsewhere in the praises of the fathers, as when
Jacob names his sons in blessing them (Genesis 49, J Document); thus

1

JUDAH

a lion's whelp

you fatten on
your prey

crouch like a
waiting lion

child of the lioness

who will stir him up?

2
ISSACHAR

a rawboned ass
between the sheepfolds
crouching

saw how good
it was to
rest there

pleasant country

bent his shoulder
to the wheel

willing serf

3
DAN

a roadside serpent
horned snake in
your path
      strikes at
the horse's heel
rider goes tumbling
backward

4
NAPHTALI

a hind set
free

father of lovely
fawns

5
JOSEPH

wild colt by
a spring &
on the hillside
the wild asses

hostile bowmen
　　　shot at him

　　　their bows unsupple
　　　bow-arms quaver

In the dance of the fathers, then, the bearded ones appear as children,
playing games of metamorphosis & marveling at themselves.

George Oppen (b. 1908)
EXODUS

Miracle of the children　　the brilliant
Children　　the word
Liquid as woodlands　　Children?

When she was a child I read Exodus
To my daughter　　'The children of Israel . . .'

Pillar of fire
Pillar of cloud

We stared at the end
Into each other's eyes　　Where
She said hushed

Were the adults　　We dreamed to each other
Miracle of the children
The brilliant children　　Miracle

Of their brilliance　　Miracle
of

A PROLOGUE TO THE WORKS OF MOSES

. . . .

Moses said: "I am only flesh & blood & cannot look upon the angels." But Metatron changed Moses' tongue into a tongue of fire, & his eyes he made like the wheels of the heavenly chariot, & his power like that of the angels, & his tongue like a flame, & brought him up to heaven. 15,000 angels were on the right hand & 15,000 on the left, Metatron & Moses in the middle.

(Samaritan Arabic, c. 16th century)

From MOLAD MOSHEH   "The Birth of Moses"

Mount Sinai said:
You will receive while upon me the Book of Truth and there will be
   revealed to you
secret things, and visions will be disclosed to you. The good news
   regarding you will be spread about
in all the countries. The lights will be increased manifold, for
   you
will step upon me in the curtain of fire. This is the honor, glory
and respect all of which will appear for you in public, by the decree of the One God,
the Victorious. For this reason I offer you, O chosen one,
continual salutations: peace both night and day, as many as there
   are birds that light
and fly.

. . . .

Then Night and Day began to glorify him
with the tongue of circumstance in public. They said, Today
is the greatest festival: today our joy is without sorrow.
Our light has lighted up, appeared and shone forth at the coming to
existence
of the Master of the human race, the Master of all male and female
beings, we were
waiting for this great day from the time of the beginning of creation.
We offer you the finest greetings: peace, O prophet who is one who
talks with God.

. . . .

Then the Sun came forth and in its praises said,
Peace to you, O prophet, famous for brilliance
and light until the end of time, for your light will never be extinguished.
All lights obtain light from your light. All the lights
at times are put out and at times are lighted up, your light will
never be extinguished.
So to you from me be peace forever.

. . . .

And when the Sun had finished its words and what it had recited in
the finest poetry
the Moon stepped forth and said, Give ear to me, O you greater than
me for I will have one night of
fullness every month, then I begin to dim, decline and disappear
but this new born babe will have perfection, beauty
throughout the passing of the centuries and ages, and through all
the passages of time.
How can he not be perfect, free from imperfection,
since he is the moon of day and night, the light of all the stars
along their courses
and all the lights like these spread in the highest places.
This Master's light will never dim in earth

and sky. For this I chant your salutations: peace forever
and forever. O you perfect Moon, you beacon in the darkness,
O you intercessor with your Lord upon the Day of Resurrection,
O you exalted in your dignity, O you most high
in rank: our trust is on you, trust of Him of Mercy,
you O Moses you the son of Amram.

SELIG J. MILLER/J.R.

COMMENTARY

(1) "What does this mean: 'The Lord of hosts, he is the King of
glory'? —It means that he apportions some of his glory to those who
fear him according to his glory. —How so?— He is called 'God,' and he
called Moses 'god,' as it is said, 'See, I have made you a god to Pharaoh.'
[Exodus 7.1] . . . And the Holy One Be Blest said to Moses, 'I have
made you a king,' as Scripture says, 'He became king in Yeshurun'
[Deuteronomy 33.5]. Just as they blow trumpets before the King when
he goes forth, so in your case, when you go forth they will sound
trumpets: 'Make for yourself two trumpets of silver.' " (*Midrash Tan-
huma* IV, 51f.)

(2) "What then? Didn't Moses enjoy an even greater partnership with
the Father and Maker of the universe, being deemed worthy of the same
title? For he was named god and king of the whole nation. And he was
said to have entered into the darkness where God was, that is, into the
formless and invisible and incorporeal archetypal essence of existing
things, perceiving things invisible to human nature." (Philo Judaeus, *Life
of Moses*, i.155–58.)

(3) "The Patriarchs, and especially Moses, are [according to Philo] the
great revelation of the higher Way. . . . Each reveals a different aspect
of the struggle to rise, or of mystic achievement. But each Patriarch is
really one who has achieved the end of the Mystery. . . . The Mystery of
Moses abandoned the material world and led the worshipper above all
material association; he died to the flesh, and in becoming reclothed in
a spiritual body moved progressively upward through the *kosmos noetos*,
the Powers, and at last ideally to God himself, being at each stage identi-

fied with the spiritual existence at that stage. . . . Moses, who put off his physical nature, went into the darkness naked, and so had communion in a constant way with the Monad, as a result of which he became the true initiate, hierophant of the rites, and teacher of divine things." (E. R. Goodenough, *By Light, Light*, pages 96, 238, describing Philo's view of Judaism as a mystery religion, centered in "initiation.")

For an example of a Hellenistic Jewish mystery play, circa 2nd century B.C., see below, page 493.

Eleazar ben Judah of Worms (Hebrew, c. 1176–1238)
THE IMAGE OF SPEECH AT SINAI

---

the Creator lowered fire on the mountain   great glorious magnificent   they say   *Mount Sinai was completely smoke for YaHVeH dropped on it in fire*   surrounded it with cloud & mist & darkness
    a black cloud   they say   *made darkness his hiding place*   the voice mixed with fire & the voice came out in fire   image of the voice seen in a cloud   a word emerging chiseled in its bounds a letter wavered in the air   the people saw the speech the image of the letters   then they knew that he was carving light from darkness
because the fire blazed   it flamed like light that breaks out of the surrounding dark   they say   *YaHVeH speaking to you from middle of the fire*   thus   as if a man was speaking to you on a cold day letters coming from his mouth & cutting up the air to leave their image   when he spoke at Sinai *you could hear his voice then in middle of the fire*   thus   an inner fire that burned beside his speech
    the flowering of your word illumines wrapped in darkness   so they could not see the voice   the speech would enter   in the hearer's heart   & then he thought he heard the voice speak mouth to mouth   thus:

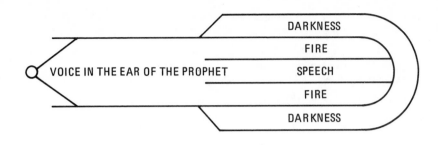

DARKNESS
FIRE
VOICE IN THE EAR OF THE PROPHET   SPEECH
FIRE
DARKNESS

J.R./H.L.

COMMENTARY

"Now Moses would stand and the word would come into his ear as through some sort of pipe, so that none other of the Children of Israel could hear it. When Moses' face flushed, however, they knew that the word had come to him." (*Pesikta Rabati,* 5.11.)

(Hebrew, Bible, c. 12th century B.C.)

From THE BOOK OF EXODUS   "Song of the Sea"

---

now Moses & now Israel's children sing this song
to Yahevh   saying
I would sing this song to YAHVEH
                        glorious in glory
            horse & rider hurled into the sea
my strength my song are YAHVEH
victory is YAHVEH
            THIS ONE is my god

                    I give my field to
                  is my father's gods
                    I raise him up
         YAHVEH is a man of war
         YAHVEH's name is YAHVEH
              pharaoh's chariots
                                 his army
                    hurled into the sea
           his master drivers
                       sinking in the reed sea
                                       red sea
    's deeps have covered them
    they drop into its shadows like a stone
              your right hand
                         YAHVEH
                    beautiful with power
              your right hand
                         YAHVEH
                    shatters your enemies
    & by your endlessness of glories
    those who stand against you
                    you put down
    your anger issues
                    you eat them up
                         like straw
    & by the winds your nostrils blow
    the waters gathered
              stood
                    became a flowing hill
    depths clotting in the heart of sea
    the enemy had said
              I will pursue them
                    I will catch them
                         I will divide the spoils
         my life will be fulfilled in them
              my sword be bare
                    my hand be their inheritor
    you blew them with your wind
              the sea has covered them

                    they sink like lead in mighty waters
who is like you
                    YAHVEH
          among the gods
who is like you
                    strong   withdrawn
                              feared in our praises
                                   doing wonders
you bent down your right hand
               earth ate them up
     became our lead in kindness
                    took this people to you
     you our guide in power
                         to your holy field
the people heard
                    would tremble
     writhing of the people of Philistia
     the chiefs of Edom shaken up
     the gods of Moab chattering
     men of Canaan melted
fear & terror on their heads
the power of your arm has made them
               still as any stone
     until your people has passed over
                    YAHVEH
     when this people has passed over
                         whom you bought
               you bring
          you plant them
     on the mountain
               your inheritance
     a place set up
          for you to sit in
     a place you worked
       a holy place of ADONAI our masters
               your hands set up
                    o YAHVEH
YAHVEH will be king
o world o time

(coda)

& Miriam the seer Aaron's sister
took drum in hand
the other women moved behind her
beating drums & dancing
Miriam responded
"sing to YAHVEH
                    "glorious in glory
          "horse & rider hurled into the sea
"my strength my song are YAHVEH

J.R./H.L.

COMMENTARY

(1) "In that night when Israel crossed the Red Sea / the angels desired to sing a song before God / but the Holy One forbade it & said to them / My legions are in distress & you would sing a song in my presence?" (*Deuteronomy Raba* 2.14.)

(2) "Moreover he saw a skull floating on the face of the water, he said to it: For drowning others you were drowned, & in the end those who drowned you will be drowned." (From Talmud: *Pirke Avot,* "the sayings of the fathers.")

(Hebrew, c. 8th–10th century A.D.)
A DIALOGUE. THE DEATH OF MOSES. COME-DOWN.

: in my mother's womb
you saw me perfect
chose me to be your voice
why should I die?

: so no one says
the man of God went up
to God
he has become like God

INTERLUDE

(Hebrew, Bible, c. 11th century B.C.)
From THE BOOK OF PSALMS   "12 for Yahveh"

1
at Yahveh's rising
his enemies
        scatter
   enemies run from his sight
like smoke

like the passage of smoke
like wax that melts
        in his fire

2
from Yahveh
an oracle
      (thunder)
   brings joy to
  the armies
(o stars!)

3
THE STARS

the kings & their armies
bow down
      bow down
the meadows share in
division of spoils

4
THE SUN-DISK

a dove's wings
silver plated

feathers
yellow gold

5
MOUNT ZALMON   /   THE DARK ONE

when Shadai loomed
over the kings
snow fell on Mount Zalmon

6

o mountain of the gods
                    o Bashan
                                o mountain
o mountain with the peaks
                    o Bashan
                                o mountain
o shake with envy
                o mountain with your peaks
at the mountain he chose
                    o home of god Yahveh

7
THE BATTLE

Yahveh kicked in the heads of
            his enemies
        split open skulls
as Yahveh roared down in anger

8
washed your feet in their blood
        the tongues of
                your dogs lapped
enemies' blood

9
see
        the processions of Yahveh
my sweet lord's processions
                my king
marches down from his stronghold

10
singers come first
then drummers

surround
        the young girls
    beating drums

11
    he turned back
the beast in reed thickets
            herd of wild bulls
    with their calves
trampled my people
            were hungry for
    silver
(war hungry)
            stampeded all in their path

12
they bring blue cloth
        out of Egypt
even Cush heaps its produce on
                        Yahveh
all kings
    bring you gifts

                                        J.R./H.L.

(Hebrew, Bible, c. 10th century B.C.)

From THE FIRST BOOK OF SAMUEL

"After the Shamans"

now Samuel was dead   all of Israel did the rites for him   & buried him in Ramah   his own city   & Saul had put away the ones that spoke with ghosts   the shamans   he sent them from the country

& the Philistines all came together   camped in Shunem   Saul & Israel together in Gilboa

& when Saul saw the army   of the Philistines   he was afraid   his heart was trembling

when he called to Yahveh   Yahveh would not answer   not by dreams   & not by oracles   & not by seers

then Saul told his servants   *find me a woman who can speak with ghosts   that I can go to   make her sound her shaman bag   can speak through her*   his servants said   *well yes   there is a woman mistress of the shaman bag   at Endor*

& Saul disguised himself   he changed his clothes   he went   & two men went with him   at night   they came to where she was   Saul said to her   *show me divinings   sound your bag   raise up for me the one I name*

the woman said to him   *well yes   you know what Saul has done   you know he banished those who speak with ghosts   the shamans   yes*   she said   *why must you lay a trap for me   cause me to die*

Saul swore to her by Yahveh   *as sure as Yahveh lives   no one will punish you for this thing* then the woman said *who should I bring you* & he said *bring up Samuel*

& when the woman saw Samuel she cried   her voice was loud   she spoke to Saul   she said   WHY HAVE YOU TRICKED ME   YOU ARE SAUL

he said to her   the king *don't be afraid what did you see*   the woman told him *I saw gods ascending from the earth   saw elohim*

he said to her *what form is he*   she said *an old man comes up covered with a mantle*

& Saul perceived that it was Samuel   Saul stooped   his face was to the ground   he bowed himself

J.R.

COMMENTARY

(1)   "Beforetime in Israel, when a man went to inquire of God, thus he spake, Come, & let us go to the seer: for he that is now called a Prophet was beforetime called a Seer." (I Samuel 9.9.)

(2)   "Then the Lord put forth his hand & touched my mouth. And the Lord said unto me, Behold, I have put my words in thy mouth." (Jeremiah 1.9.)

(3)   "Thou shalt not suffer a shaman to live." (Exodus 22.18.)

David Meltzer (b. 1937)
From TOHU   "Shaman"

Shaman denies fat pleasure.
Holes-up in a cave to fast.
Ghost animals come at night &
sing ghost animal songs about
Animal Heaven where earth is meat
on a fiery bone devoured
hour after hour in the barking Void.
He deciphers light songs sung by
the farthest star, the nearest spark.
Reads a quick light flash
passing over loon's eyes.
Shaman de-codes all glyphs & gyres
& translates rainbow tract
dazzling in dragonfly's spread wingspan.
Shaman bent over each vowel like a watchmaker.
Flame-crazed by code, see him crawl
over hallucinating boulders & bake in the sun.
See shaman go for words where no words are.

O let earth & all earth's critters know
I was here & I am hers too
Make use of me, sweet Mystery
Make use of me from toe to lotus!

          Days later
see Shaman in no-self daze
stumble into town
xylophone-ribbed, tobacco-leaf brown.

People make room for Shaman,
watch all his moves with inner cameras,
confused how his bloody fingers move out
to touch invisible shapes.
Shaman knows beyond knowing
Shaman knows man beyond man
& when Shaman is ecstatic & righteous
Shaman sings a song that is the song of earth.
There is no better one.

and the wood of an outside room, and they are utterly consumed with fire in the sitting. II Sam. 23

And David, the son of Jesse, was wise, and a light   Apocryphon: David's Compositions
like the light of the sun, and literate,
and discerning and perfect in all his ways before God and men. And the LORD gave
him a discerning and enlightened spirit. And he wrote
3,600 psalms; and songs to sing before the altar over the whole-burnt
perpetual offering every day, for all the days of the year, 364;
and for the offering of the Sabbaths, 52 songs; and for the offering of the New
Moons and for all the Solemn Assemblies and for the Day of Atonement, 30 songs.
And all the songs that he spoke were 446, and songs
for making music over the stricken, 4. And the total was 4,050
All these he composed through prophecy which was given him from before the Most High.   Ps. 140

To the choirmaster. A Psalm of David. Deliver me, O LORD,
from evil men; preserve me from violent men, who plan evil things in their heart,
and stir up wars continually. They make their tongue sharp as a serpent's, and under their lips is
the poison of *a spider.*

Guard me, O LORD, from the hands of the wicked; [preserve me] from [violent] men . . .

COMMENTARY

(1) "While still in his mother's womb, David recited a poem . . . he contemplated the day of death & recited a poem." (Talmud: *Berakhot* 10a.)

(2) "[In] the central painting of the Dura-Europos Synagogue [circa 250 A.D.] . . . a large tree or vine is represented. . . Halfway up the vine or tree sits Orpheus with his lyre, playing to the animals. That this figure was called by the name Orpheus in the synagogue is as unlikely as

that its pagan name was kept in Christian catacombs. The figure was Christianized by being called Christ. It would certainly have been toler-ated in the Jewish synagogue only if it bore a Jewish name, and several scholars have suggested that that name could have been David." (E. R. Goodenough, *Jewish Symbols in the Greco-Roman Period,* volume 2, page 170.)

(Coptic, before 6th century A.D.)

THE DAVITHEA INCANTATION

ISEOSIS   KAI   AISEOS   AURIOUKKEKMAROUK

do it   Uriel
do it   Michael

I call you down to me this day
holy Father
having in you
angel's lilting voice
archangel's singing
heaven's children's enraptured eyes
turned towards you
Hymn of the Father

down to me
Davithea you
lying there on the bed of the tree of life
right hand ringing the golden bell
left plucking the harp of breath
calling all angels
"salute the Father of us all"

down to me right now
Davithea Eleleth

naming the seven holy
the FirstAngels
Michael Gabriel Suriel Raphael Asuel Saraphuel Abael
standing by the Father's right arm
ready to do his every desire
who hear all my mouth pours forth
my hand beckons turns winks
they comply

come down upon this cup in front of me
fill it full of grace
of sacred breath
make it grow within me
a sacred plant inside my heart
for I am (*your name here—out loud*)

if the seven do not hear
do not obey the signals of my hand
I will turn my face East
hold back the sun in the East
moon in the West
struggle against the creatures of heaven
saying to heaven
"turn copper : shed no dew on Earth"
saying to Earth
"turn iron : give no fruit"
until the Father hurls his lance of light
Father sitting on his throne
sends me his dean
great and strong his strength
who is Davithea
who comes to me in this holy place
where I am who am (*your name again—out loud*)

Davithea
shall give me voice
that does not hiss snap break
voice ascending there on high
lends me tongue to sing with every instrument
gently breathes

voice that makes music ring
its sweetness to the people around me

seven
make my face lovely worthy
the love of all who see me
make me as the voice of harper David
when played inside his Father's tent

let them not look
upon my face and run away
but leave their work return
come back to look me
in the face

A I O!   A I O!
I name you here to me
by the seven vowels
carved on the Father's chest :   A A Z
                                    E Z
                                  E E Z
                                    I Z
                                    O Z
                                    U Z
                                  O O Z
A I O!   A I O!
that you hear the tidings of my mouth
this hour while it is still within the hour
before another takes its place

shine on me in vision
that does not sink me in fear
thank the strength of the Father

Yak   Meyak   Semyak
you three deans strong in your strength
lying there on the bed of the tree of life
put sweetness in my throat's grooves
I, Severus, Anna's son

yes yes   quick quick   now now now

THE IMAGE

THE   DAUEITHEA   RACHOCHI   ADONIEL

(*in regular letters:*)

thapsiorie . . . . thapsiopse   /
thapsiorirar : thapsior : psior //
iriaathenneos tache tache adu——
                    (quick quick now——)

(*under the picture:*)

you draw the phylactery in honey, pure, without
water, without fire, on an alabaster tablet.
rinse in white wine.
21 white grapes.
male mastic gum.
Cancarippos, called Claw.
a large white cloth.

Offer:

male frankincense.
male mastic gum
sowbread primroses.
full.

C.D.

COMMENTARY

(1)   "Davithea or David, at one point called Davithea Eleleth. This per-
sonage, with his lyre and golden bell, plays and sings in 'the tent of the
Father,' as David did in the tent of Saul. He is the leader of the heavenly chorus who gathers all the angels to hail the Father. . . . Here it
must be pointed out that in the charm the function of David is ideally
to turn the magician into a *mousikos anēr,* a man who, like Socrates and
many Greek mystics after him, hoped for immortality through learning
to 'make music' in harmony with the celestial music. David also sends
his grace and spirit, or the grace and spirit of the Father, into a cup
which gives divine life to those who drink. That is, David is the heavenly
Savior, whether in terms of the musical voice 'without harshness' which
he gives, of the Tree of Life whose power he grants, or of the cup which
is the vehicle of that tree. . . . David for the rabbis was also a prophet,
and they said that the Psalms consist of compositions made in ecstasy as

the Holy Spirit came upon him." (E. R. Goodenough, *Jewish Symbols in the Greco-Roman Period,* volume 2, pages 168, 170; volume 9, page 94.)

The Davithea charms come from Hellenistic magical papyrî. For more on the Tree of Life, etc., see page 147, above.

(2) "It is, as we have learned, that God has another David who is in command of many celestial hosts and legions: and when God desires to be gracious to the world He looks upon this David with a smiling countenance, and he in turn sheds light and grace upon the world through his beauty, his head being a skull of gold broidered with seven ornaments of gold." (*Zohar* 3.84a.) Adds Gershom Scholem, in the *Encyclopedia Judaica:* this other David is the Shekinah.

(3) "The Throne immediately underneath the God of Israel is in the form of Jacob, and the Throne below in that of David." (*Zohar* 2.242a.)

INTERLUDE

Nelly Sachs (German, 1891–1970)
"IF THE PROPHETS BROKE IN"

If the prophets broke in
through the doors of night,
the zodiac of demon gods
wound like a ghastly wreath of flowers
round the head—
rocking the secrets of the falling and rising
skies on their shoulders—

for those who long since fled in terror—

If the prophets broke in
through the doors of night,
the course of the stars scored in their palms
glowing golden—

for those long sunk in sleep—

If the prophets broke in
through the doors of night
tearing wounds with their words
into fields of habit,
a distant crop hauled home
for the laborer

who no longer waits at evening—

If the prophets broke in
through the doors of night
and sought an ear like a homeland—

Ear of mankind
overgrown with nettles,
would you hear?
If the voice of the prophets
blew
on flutes made of murdered children's bones
and exhaled airs burnt with
martyrs' cries—
if they build a bridge of old men's dying
groans—

Ear of mankind
occupied with small sounds,
would you hear?

If the prophets
rushed in with the storm-pinions of eternity
if they broke open your acoustic duct with the words:

Which of you wants to make war against a mystery
who wants to invent the star-death?

If the prophets stood up
in the night of mankind
like lovers who seek the heart of the beloved,
night of mankind
would you have a heart to offer?

RUTH & MATTHEW MEAD

Amos the Prophet (Hebrew, Bible, 8th century B.C)
A VISION IN THE VOICE OF YAHVEH

> *The Lord God has spoken;*
> *Who can but prophesy?*
> Amos 3.8

this is what Yahveh Adonai
showed me:
a basket of summer fruit

asked me: Amos what is this?
I said: a summer basket
he said: a summary for Israel
my people
never will I let it pass

but they will squawk their palace songs
that day
I say it Yahveh Adonai
there will be bodies everywhere
& silence

listen: you who suck
life from the poor man
drive him from his work

you say: when will the new moon pass
so we can sell grain?
when will the sabbath end
so we can show our wheat?
you weight their baskets light
weigh your coins heavy
you cheaters with lying scales

you buy the poor for money
paupers for a pair of shoes
sell chaff for grain

God swears it by the pride of Jacob:
will I always be
forgetting?

will the earth shake some day—
all alive on her lament?
she'll rise up like a river
wholly
flooding drowning
like the Nile

that day the word of Yahveh Adonai
says:
I will make the sun turn back
at noon
earth will grow dark in daylight

will turn your feasts to mourning
songs to howls
wrap everybody's laps in sackcloth
everybody's head be shaved
be bald
will make it like grieving
for an only child

a bitter day to end it
days are coming
—says the word of Yahveh Adonai—
a famine in the land
will be no hungering for bread or water
but for Yahveh's words

J.R./H.L.

COMMENTARY

(1)   Arising at a time of invasions & internal conflicts, the work of the prophets marked a shift in *poesis* toward new extremes: the delineation of moral pain, in which the poet (prophet) stands as alienated conscience, accuser of his race. However the words might seem in later, written form, as speech they struck against the going, still repressive institutions of the state. The discourse that resulted, a late & particular development of the prophetic frenzy, was devastating: a discovery of "history as nightmare" (Heschel) & of a "moral madness" in the face of human cruelty, which cast the prophet in the role of rebel but also led, one fears, to the creation of a new, cruel monster in turn—as in the Yahvists' push to eradicate their own predecesors & contemporaries among the shamans & the prophets of Baal, etc. What is evident too is a gradual movement from vision to voice, from "seers" to "hearers" & "speakers"; thus, as Blake wrote of Isaiah & Ezekiel: "The voice of Honest Indignation is the voice of God." The breakthrough is like a controlled paranoia in which "even a minor injustice assumes cosmic proportions." Writes an editor of the *Encyclopedia Judaica*: "The parallel to 'prophet' is 'madman' (*meshugga*)," a resemblance mentioned in the Bible & not unheard of in the poetics of our own time, etc.

(2)   "Who could bear living in a state of disgust day & night? The conscience builds its confines, is subject to fatigue, longs for comfort, lulling, soothing. Yet those who are hurt, and He Who inhabits eternity, neither slumber nor sleep. . . . The prophet is human, yet he employs notes one octave too high for our ears. He experiences moments that defy our understanding. He is neither 'a singing saint' nor a 'moralizing poet,' but an assaulter of the mind." (Abraham J. Heschel, *The Prophets,* pages 9–10.)

Says prophet Jeremiah: "There is something in my heart like a burning fire / Shut up in my bones / & I am weary with holding it in / & I cannot" (20.9). And Menahem Mendel of Kotsk, a Hasidic master of the 19th century: "When a man has a reason to scream, & cannot though he wants to—he has achieved the greatest scream."

(Aramaic, Bible, c. 170 B.C.)

From THE BOOK OF DANIEL   "Night Dreams"

---

in the year One   the years of Belshazar the king of Babylon   Daniel dreamed a vision   visions in his head   asleep   then drew the dream with words   he said

how Daniel spoke & said   I had a dream   among my visions   night dreams   here it is   the 4 winds of the skies are boring thru the Great Sea

4 living creatures leave the sea   each one is different from the other

first up is like a lion   but eagle-winged   I kept on watching him
   until they stripped his wings   & pulled up from the earth   on 2 feet like a man   they stood him up & put a man's heart in him

& here another one   a second creature   looking like a bear   they
raised up on one side   3 ribs were in his mouth between his teeth
   they say to him   get up   eat flesh excessively

afterwards   I had a vision   here it is   another   like a shiny cat
this creature had 4 wings   like birds wings   & 4 heads   was given
power

afterwards   I had a vision   visions of the night   a fourth   a creature much more powerful   that causes trembling   teeth of iron
very large   with which it eats & crushes   stomps on the remainder
with its feet   & different from the creatures from before   it has
10 horns

had a perception of those horns   & look   another smaller horn
   comes up among them   & 3 horns   3 of the horns before   are
pulled up by the roots before it   & look   a man's eyes on this horn
   a mouth that says great things

I had a vision
            before the thrones dropped down to earth
                        ANCIENT OF DAYS was seated
                              dressed like pale snow
& head hair like white fleece
            his throne was flames of fire
                        wheels of fire burning
                              fire rivers flowing
going out from where he sat
            a thousand thousand serving him
                        ten thousand times ten thousand waiting
                        judgments set
                              books opened

had a vision   then   a voice came from the words   the great ones
   that the horn spoke   had a vision   lasted till the killing of the
creature   the concretions of his body broken   given to be burnt in
fire

& power taken from the other creatures   but they gave them length
of life   up to a time   a season

I had a vision   visions in the night
            upon the clouds the sky
                        is someone looking like a man
                                    o manchild
comes up to
            ANCIENT OF DAYS
                        they bring him near
                                    they give him powers preciousness
                                                a kingdom
peoples nations tongues
        to worship
                        power power for a world's length
                                    never ending
                                                kingdom which will never
                                                            be destroyed

I   Daniel   felt my wind was hurt in me   inside its sheath   the visions in my head now turbid   turbid

J.R./H.L.

COMMENTARY

(1)   *Poesis* as dream-work persists even "after the shamans" (see above,
page 217). The position of the prophets is here ambiguous: poets, in
Blake's recognition, they are in conflict with the still existing guilds of
seers & the poets/prophets of the old gods, as in Elijah's battle with
Baal's prophets (see below). The idea established & perpetuated through
the written word is that of the monolithic state, the monolithic god
whose word is gathered, frozen, into a single "sacred" book. The vision
itself, as in the Book of Daniel, moves toward allegory "in the service of
the state." Thus, in the explanations that follow these visions (Daniel
7.16–.28), the beasts are the "four kingdoms" (dominating nations), &
the dream, while still the literary frame, has more & more the sound of
fiction, even poetry-as-propaganda. Says Ezekiel, whose great vision (see
above, page 16) is at the heart of Jewish mysticism: "Ah Lord God,
they are saying of me: Is he not a maker of allegories?" (Ezekiel 20.49.)
    It is the present editor's sense that the Jewish past (like the human past
in general) consists of all of these conflicted forms; & the reader at his
present remove may choose to find *poesis* ("language as the act of the

instant and [not] language as the act of thought about the instant"—
C. Olson) wherever it rings most true. He may later see how the written
word itself becomes a tool against its own literalness.

(2) from "the notebooks" 2/76 the power of a dream we read
through Daniel once again asleep awake the dream has come into
the world around us *make an object of a dream*—Breton surrealist master taught—*then call the dream a poem* the boundaries to be an-
nihilated : this that binds me to the dream work to the prophets
shamans in service of the state no unity but conflict at the poem's
heart the masters of *my* revolution sit in Paris 1920 with eyes of other
prophets they plot their future deaths new murders the monocle of
Tzara in the snow (he thinks) what turn is taken now? o poets
whose vision realized is vision spurned (j.r.)

(Hebrew, from 5th century A.D.)

A DREAM SERVICE

. . . .

o master of the world I am yours & my dreams are yours I dreamt
a dream & don't know what it is but would want o Adonai o my El
o El of the ancestors all dreams to work for my good for the good
of this people (o Israel) dreams of myself or dreams about
others or dreams others dream about me if the dream is good let
it work like dreams of Joseph the Saint but if it needs healing then
heal it o healer who healed King Hezekiah healed Prophetess
Miriam's leprosy Naaman's leprosy sweeten these dreams like the
waters of Marah by Moses Jericho's springs by Elisha for you
who turned Balaam's curses to blessings will turn my dreams to joy
  for myself for Israel guard me be good to me want me
amen

J.R./H.L.

(Hebrew, Bible, c. 9th century B.C.)

ELIJAH & THE PRIESTS OF BAAL   "in a time of famine"

vayehi
many days
the words of YaHVeH to Elijah
in the 3rd year (saying)
GO
let Ahab see you
I will truly bring down rain upon
Earth's face

· · · · · · · · ·

vayehi
the moment Ahab saw Elijah
Ahab said
are YOU the troublemaker
here in Israel

he said
I made no trouble here
in Israel
it's YOU your kinsmen
YOU left the rule of YaHVeH
YOU pursued the Baals

now send now gather all of Israel
at the mountain called GOD'S VINEYARD
450 of Baal's prophets
400 of Ashera's
those who eat with Jezebel

· · · · · · · · ·

vayehi
Elijah told the people
I remain
I stand as YaHVeH's prophet
I alone
Baal's prophets are 450 men

(he said) that they will give us
two young bulls
that they can choose the one bull for themselves
& cut it slice it in pieces put it on the branches
BUT SET NO FIRE TO IT
& I will do one bull will put it on the branches but SET NO FIRE
    TO IT

& you will call in the name of your elohim
& I will call in the name of YaHVeH
& the elohim that answers with fire is THE ELOHIM

(then everyone answered & said
that it was good)

& Elijah to Baal's prophets
CHOOSE ONE BULL & GO FIRST FOR YOU ARE MANY
& shout in the name of your elohim
BUT SET NO FIRE TO IT

& they did they took the bull he gave them they did it up they
    shouted in Baal's name
from morning until noon they shouted saying
ANSWER US O BAAL
(no voice no answerer they leaped over the slaughter-place he
    made for them)

vayehi
at noon Elijah minced beside them
(said)
SHOUT LOUDER LOUDER maybe your elohim is speaking maybe
    traveling 's on a journey maybe sleeping MAYBE WAKE HIM UP

& they shouted LOUDER LOUDER
they slashed themselves the way they do it with swords & spears
letting the blood flow over them

vayehi
when noon was passing
they still prophesied
until the offering of the seed
but got no voice
no answer
no one listening

then Elijah spoke to all the people
COME AROUND ME
all the people came around him
(he was healing YaHVeH's broken altar)

took 12 stones
(the number of the tribes
of Jacob's sons
YaHVeH's words had come to
told him
ISRAEL WILL BE YOUR NAME)

Elijah built an altar
out of stones
in YaHVeH's name & dug
a trench (2 troughs of seed
in width) around it

he spread out the branches
cut the bull in pieces
put it on the branches (saying)
FILL UP 4 JUGS WITH WATER
POUR WATER ON THE FIRE OFFERING
& ON THE BRANCHES

he said it twice
they twice
then thrice
they said it thrice

(water was then
around the altar
also he filled the trench
with water)

vayehi
the time of *minḥa*
of the offering of the seed
Elijah PROPHET came up close
& said

YAH ELOHIM
(of Abraham Isaac Israel)
today
let them find out that you
are ELOHIM are GOD in Israel
& I your slave
whose words
only were YOUR words

YaHVeH answer
answer me
this people then will know
YOU YAHVEH ARE THE ELOHIM
YOU WHO HAVE TURNED THEM UPSIDE DOWN

& Fire-of-YaHVeH fell
it fell devoured
the burnt offering
the branches
the stones & dust
licked up the water in the trench

the people saw it
fell down on their faces
saying
YAHVEH IS THE EL
YAHVEH IS THE ELOHIM

Elijah said to them
NOW GRAB HOLD OF BAAL'S PROPHETS
(let none of them escape)
& they grabbed hold of them
Elijah brought them down to Kishon Brook
& slaughtered them

he said to Ahab
GET UP & EAT & DRINK
THERE IS A SOUND OF HEAVY RAIN
(so Ahab went to eat & drink)

Elijah climbed up to the top of Carmel
crouched down on the earth
he put his face between his knees
& told his boy   GO UP NOW
look out towards the sea

(went up & looked
he said) not even a small trace
he told him
do it 7 times

vayehi
the 7th time
he said
a little cloud there
like a man's hand
on the sea

he said
move on now say to Ahab

HITCH IT UP
COME DOWN
THE RAIN WON'T STOP YOU

vayehi
the sky had darkened up
with clouds & wind

vayehi
a big rain
Ahab riding in the rain
towards Jezreel
the place they call
"god's seeding"

J.R./H.L.

COMMENTARY

(1) "& the Children of Israel did what was wrong in Yahveh's eyes
   they served the Baals the Ashtoreths the gods of Syria the gods of
Sidon the gods of Moab the gods of Ammon's sons the gods of the
Philistines they turned from Yahveh they abandon Yahveh" (Judges
10.6.)

(2) Thus: the struggle between Yahveh & the (so-called) "strange
gods" runs from here throughout the Bible. But the question persists, if
the intrusions are merely foreign (Baal's prophets, above, are more than
likely Jews) or are variants in fact of the Hebrew-Jewish vision in conflict with each other. Writes Raphael Patai: "Let us here stress the fact
that in addition to 'official' Judaism—that crystallization of the religion
which represented the consensus of most of the religious leaders of a
certain time and place—Judaism has always comprised heterodox variants as well. . . . There can be no doubt that down to the very end of
the Hebrew monarchy the worship of old Canaanite gods was an in-

tegral part of the religion of the Hebrews. . . . The reason is not far to seek. The image of Yahweh, in the eyes of the common people, did not differ greatly from that of Baal or other Canaanite male gods. Often it would have been difficult to determine whether a certain cult was legitimately Yahwistic, heretically Yahwistic, or unequivocally pagan. The worship of Yahweh thus easily merged into, complemented or supplanted that of the Canaanite male gods." (*The Hebrew Goddess,* pages 20, 25.)

Even more so, the persistence of the goddesses: Ashera, Anat, Ashtoreth, as bride of God (*El*) & Queen of Heaven.

(3) For more on Jewish rain-making—another survival of shamanic traditions, etc.—see above, page 112, below, page 470.

(Ugaritic, c. 1400 B.C.)

From A POEM ABOUT ASHERA:
HOW SHE GOES TO BULL GOD EL
TO SEEK A HOUSE FOR BAAL HER SON

So Ashera sets out
toward El

at the Flowing of the Two Rivers,
near the Fountain of the Two Deeps.

She arrives at the Field of El.

She walks onto the platform
of the KING
the FATHER OF YEARS.
She bends, then
falls.
She bows.

She pays homage to him.

As soon as El
discovers her,
his narrowed lips part,
and he laughs.

He puts his feet up
on a footstool.

He twiddles his thumbs.

He raises his voice
and calls,

"What has Lady Ashera of the Sea
come for?
What has the Queen of the Gods
come for?

You must be hungry?
You're surely thirsty?
Have something to eat
or drink.
There is food on the tables,
drink in the goblets,
wine in a golden cup,
trees' blood,
if the affection of KING EL
stirs you,
if the BULL's love
moves you."

Lady Ashera of the Sea says,

"EL
your word is wise,
eternal with wisdom:
happiness and your word are one.
Our King is
Almighty Baal,

our Judge,
and there is none over him.
So by our cry
fill his jug,
fill his cup
as we cry to you.

He calls loudly
to BULL EL
his father,
EL his KING

                     who made him.

He calls to Ashera
and her sons,
to the goddess
and her mass of offspring,

'Look, there is
no house for Baal
as the Gods have,
and no court
as Ashera's sons have.

EL's home is a shelter
for his son:
the home of Lady Ashera of the Sea
is a home

                     for the untouched brides:
                     Pidraya's home,
                     the daughter of Light,
                     Talaya's home,
                     the daughter of Rain,
                     the home of Artsaya
                     daughter of Y'bdr.' "

                     And EL of the GENTLE
                     HEART says,

"Am I to be an agent of Ashera,
to carry hods?

If Ashera will be a slave
making bricks
a house will be built
for Baal
as the other Gods have,
with a courtyard
fit for a son of Ashera."

And Lady Ashera of the Sea
says,

"Lord of the Gods in wisdom,
the grey of your beard has surely taught you something."

H.L.

COMMENTARY

"The Goddess Asherah was worshipped in Israel from the days of the first settlement in Canaan, the Hebrews having taken over the cult of the great mother goddess from the Canaanites. . . . It appears that of the 370 years during which the Solomonic Temple stood in Jerusalem, for no less than 236 years . . . the statue of Asherah was present in the Temple and her worship was a part of the legitimate religion approved and led by the king, the court and the priesthood, and opposed only by a few prophetic voices crying out against it at relatively long intervals. . . . One cannot belittle the emotional gratification with which she must have rewarded her servants who saw in her the loving, motherly consort of Yahweh-Baal, and for whom she was the great mother-goddess, giver of fertility, that greatest of all blessings." (Raphael Patai, *The Hebrew Goddess,* pages 42, 50, 52.)

For more on the goddess, in her role as Queen of Heaven, see above, page 36. The most likely identification there is Anat, lady of battles.

Raquel Jodorowsky (Spanish [Chilean], contemporary)
IN THE MOUNTAIN OF THE SONG THAT SHOWS

In the Mountain of the Song that Shows
My City
there is an old woman under the sea
whose power can protect the world
instructing animals
in active mythical scenes
whose power can guard men
with her termite skins reflecting
the show of life
In her journeys of the eye
She goes inside the ocean
in search of information
her ferocious appearances
intending to lead the salmon
to her place of origin,
and the hungry hunters
in the vast deserts
ask for the answer
of the time of Beauty.
In the Mountain of this necessary Song
the Wife of Turquoise
sets her faces in the house of the sun
distinguishing warriors
who offer their sufferings to the earth
and she follows it all day long around the sky
as far as the birth of the poles.
It is thus that she grasps this eagle of fire
and arrives here.
But men, grain of giants,

dispensers of all the bad that is written
with separated heads
used in dances with ceremonial drugs,
have determined that the Lady does not exist
since no stranger could see her.
. . . O Invisible, Beloved Benefactor,
acting between liquid and solid,
do not return to any of them
whose heart of lies injures your waters
and whenever there is danger·
change your name entirely.
Though you possess no formal authority
all who remain listen as you speak.
Lady Messenger do not rest
dispense your perfume among us
give the children a part of your mystery
Then bruskly take away your hands
from the knees of God
Far off we are already weeping
when your song ends.

DAN GERBER

o Ephraim you have played the harlot—
Israel is defiled

(Hosea 5.3.)

(Hebrew, medieval)

From THE ALPHABET OF BEN SIRA   "The Birth"

As it is written HE DOETH GREAT THINGS PAST FINDING
OUT, YEA, MARVELOUS THINGS WITHOUT NUMBER.
(Job 9.10.)
   Now see how great are the deeds of the Holy One Be Blest for
if it says HE DOETH GREAT THINGS PAST FINDING OUT
why should it say MARVELOUS THINGS WITHOUT NUMBER &
if it says MARVELOUS THINGS WITHOUT NUMBER why
should it say HE DOETH GREAT THINGS PAST FINDING
OUT? What does it mean? And so our wise men may their memory
be blest explained: HE DOETH GREAT THINGS PAST FIND-
ING OUT why this pertains to all the works of creation & MAR-
VELOUS THINGS WITHOUT NUMBER why this pertains to
those three born without their mothers lying with a man. And those
three were Ben Sira & Rav Papa & Rabbi Zira: all of them total
saints & all great wise men.
   And this is what they say about them. First about Rav Papa &
Rabbi Zira: that in all their lives they never carried on an idle
conversation: that they never slept in the study house no not even
for a cat nap: that no man ever got down to the study house before
them nor ever found them sitting quietly but rather sitting studying:

that no day passed but that they made it holy & never did they gossip about friends & never did they profit by a friend's misfortune never did friends curse them on their death beds & never did they look upon a crucifix & never took a bribe: for they were like a sturdy mast fulfilling what was written LEADING THOSE WHO LOVE ME & FILLING UP THEIR TREASURES. (Proverbs 8.21.) And how did it happen that their mothers should have given birth without a husband? Here they say: one time they went down to the bath house & a seed of Israel went up into their holes & they were pregnant & they gave birth but the children never knew who was their father.

But Ben Sira did know who his father was & how his mother gave birth without a man to do the man's thing. This is what they say about her: she was the daughter of the prophet Jeremiah & once when Jeremiah went to the bath house he spied some rough trade from the tribe of Ephraim all of whom were beating out their own seed making waste of it but the whole tribe of Ephraim in that generation was full of such as these as written: HE HAS DONE THE EVIL THING IN GOD'S EYE. And when Jeremiah saw them he began to call them down & they immediately moved in on him they said: WHY SHOULD YOU CALL US DOWN LIKE THAT? LONG LIVE THE WAY OF BEERSHEBA. And they said: WE WON'T LET YOU GO FROM HERE UNTIL YOU DO IT JUST LIKE US. He said: JUST LET ME BE I SWEAR TO YOU I'LL KEEP IT SECRET. But they said back to him: DIDN'T ZEDEKIAH SEE NEBUCHADNEZZAR EAT A LIVING RABBIT & DIDN'T HE SWEAR TO HIM BY GOD'S DECREE HE'D KEEP IT SECRET & DIDN'T HE THEN GO & BREAK HIS OATH? AND YOU WOULD TOO. BUT NOW IF YOU JUST DO LIKE US WE'LL LET YOU GO BUT IF YOU DON'T WE'LL SODOMIZE YOU LIKE OUR FATHERS DID IT IN THEIR WEIRD RELIGIONS & IF THEY DID THAT MUCH IN THEIR WEIRD RELIGIONS WE'LL DO IT EVEN MORE ON YOU. He was so frightened then so fearful that he did it right off just as they had said but then as soon as he had gotten out of there he cursed his day the way it's written CURSED BE THE DAY WHEN I WAS BORN (Jeremiah 20.12) & went off & fasted 248 fasts one for each part of a man's body. But a drop of this very saint remained until the daughter of this very saint went to the bath house & it got into her hole & after seven months she bore a son equipped with teeth & talking. Once she gave birth she felt ashamed: people she felt would think that she had come to it by whoring. But then the child opened his mouth he said to his mother: WHY DO YOU FEEL ASHAMED FOR PEOPLE? Then he told her: I AM SIRA'S SON. She said to him: WHO IS THIS SIRA? He told her: JEREMIAH. And she asked: WHY CALL HIM SIRA? He said: BECAUSE HE IS A SIRE ABOVE ALL SIRES A PRINCE ABOVE ALL PRINCES: IT IS HE WILL GIVE HIS NAME TO EVERY PRINCE & KING BE-CAUSE WHEN YOU COUNT UP SIRA & JEREMIAH BY GEMATRIA THEY COME OUT EQUAL. Then she said to him: MY SON SHOULDN'T YOU HAVE BETTER SAID I AM A SON OF JEREMIAH? He said to her: I WOULD HAVE SAID IT BUT THE THOUGHT WAS TOO REPUGNANT SAYING THAT JEREMIAH COVERED HIS OWN DAUGHTER. She said to him: MY SON ISN'T THERE A PROVERB THAT WHAT HAS BEEN IS WHAT WILL BE? (Ecclesiastes 1.9.) YET WHO EVER SAW A DAUGHTER PREGNANT FROM HER FATHER? He said to her: O MOTHER NOTHING IS NEW UNDER THE SUN: AS LOT WAS EVERY INCH A SAINT SO WAS MY FATHER & AS WHAT WAS DONE TO LOT WAS DONE BY FORCE SO WAS IT TO MY FATHER. She said to him: YOU FRIGHTEN ME. HOW DO YOU KNOW THESE THINGS? He said to her: DO NOT BE FRIGHTENED BY ME BECAUSE NOTHING IS NEW UNDER THE SUN. LOOK AT MY FATHER JEREMIAH THIS IS WHAT HE DID TOO WHEN HIS OWN MOTHER BENT TO HEAR HIM YES HE OPENED UP HIS MOUTH HE CALLED HIS FATHER FROM THE BELLY OF HIS MOTHER & SAID I won't come out until they tell me what my name is. THEN HIS FATHER OPENED HIS MOUTH HE SAID: Get out your name is Abraham. HE SAID: That's not my name. HE SAID TO HIM: Your name is Isaac Jacob IN THAT ORDER NAMING ALL THE TRIBES & ALL THE FIGURES OF THAT GENERATION BUT HE SAID That's not my name. UNTIL ELIJAH MAY HIS MEMORY BE BLEST PASSED BY HE SAID: Your name will be called Jeremiah which is Yirmiyahu which is God Will Lift for in your days the Holy One Be Blest will raise an enemy & he will lift his hand against Jerusalem. HE SAID TO HIM: That really is my name & you because you said my name my name will be like yours Elijah which is Eliyahu I will take the Yahu from it for my name of Yirmiyahu which is Jeremiah. AND JUST AS HE CAME OUT SPEAKING I CAME OUT SPEAKING JUST AS HE CAME OUT PROPHESYING FROM THE BELLY OF HIS MOTHER AS THE SAYING GOES: Before I made you in the belly I did know you (Jeremiah 1.5) SO I CAME OUT PROPHESYING. AS HE CAME OUT FROM THE BELLY OF HIS MOTHER WITH A NAME SO I CAME OUT FROM THE BELLY OF MY MOTHER WITH MY NAME. AS HE MADE A BOOK AROUND THE "ALFA-BETA" SO I WILL MAKE A BOOK AROUND THE "ALFA-BETA." SO DON'T BE FRIGHTENED BY MY WORDS. She said to him: MY SON DON'T BRAG THE EVIL EYE MAY OVERPOWER YOU. He said to her: THE EVIL EYE WOULD HAVE NO CAUSE TO OVERPOWER ME SO NOW DON'T GO ON SPEAKING ABOUT ME BECAUSE I'M ONLY DOING WHAT MY FATHER DID. THERE IS A SAYING ABOUT ME THAT AS A SHEEP FOLLOWS A SHEEP A SON'S DEEDS FOLLOW ON HIS FATHER'S. (Talmud: *Ketubot*.) She said to him: MY SON WHY WOULD YOU STOP MY SPEAKING? He said to her: BECAUSE YOU KNOW THAT I'M HUNGRY BUT HAVEN'T GIVEN ME TO EAT. She said: HERE ARE MY BREASTS FOR YOU FOR EATING & FOR DRINKING. He said: NO NO I DO NOT CRAVE YOUR BREASTS GO IN- STEAD & SIFT FLOUR FIND A CHICKEN KNEAD FRESH BREAD GET MEAT & OIL & OLD WINE & COME EAT WITH ME. She said to him: HOW CAN I BUY THESE THINGS? He said to her: MAKE CLOTHES & SELL THEM SO THE VERSE WILL BE FULFILLED THROUGH YOU: a sheet she made & sold (Proverbs 31.24) & IF YOU NOURISH ME FOR A YEAR THE OTHER VERSES WILL BE FULFILLED THROUGH YOU: many a valiant daughter but you above them all. (Proverbs 31.29.)

So she began to make clothes & sell them & she brought him bread & meat oil & old wine & she nourished him a year.

J.R./H.L.

COMMENTARY

(1)   from "the notebooks"   2/76   here at the center of the world—he writes—the gathering grows most intense   if only the imagination holds it   sodomites walk past with Jeremiah   perfumed men & prostitutes they show their sex freely   the wind rises over Jerusalem moves between the women's legs & lifts their odors to the altar   seeds & blood engulf the priest   so beautiful   so like a boy bride   in whose smoke serpents reappear   the cherubim great creatures of the mind are twined in love   they will not leave you   lurk in jewish holes & *tantra* the message blown from east to west   in the prophet's words the secrets of their nature again alive   as Yahveh cried out for his lost brides   —o the god that knows all knows this too—   *these women gone two sisters daughters of one mother whores that I knew in Egypt they would let men squeeze their tits would suck on their virgin tits o tender tender as their names were* : vision of Ezekiel   in the temple built by Solomon lover king whom the priest's beauty now recalls   a trace of semen in the *mikvah* this power that can lift us to the god   (j.r.)

(2)   "The world like Great Sodom lies under Love
        and knows not the hand of the Lord that moves"

—Robert Duncan

Meshullam the Great ben Kalonymos (Hebrew, 10th century)
A POEM FOR THE HIGH PRIEST, SUNG THERE-
AFTER ON THE DAY OF THE *KIPPURIM,*
AS HE WAS CELEBRATED ALSO
IN *THE WISDOM OF BEN SIRA*

like a tent
     stretched tight
               around the ones who live
                         above
was the appearance of the priest

like lightning
        breaking from
               the brightness of
                    his beasts
was the appearance of the priest

like knots
     the knotting at
              the four
                 extremities
was the appearance of the priest

like the rainbow's
            image
          in middle of
                 the cloud
was the appearance of the priest

like the splendor
        which
          he wrapped
             o Rock

                                    around his fashionings
was the appearance of the priest

like a rose
          set in
             the middle of
                         the garden
                                    of sweet love
was the appearance of the priest

like a headband
                set upon
                      the forehead
                               of a king
was the appearance of the priest

like the love
           that settled on
                         the bridegroom's
                                        face
was the appearance of the priest

like the clear light
                  set within
                           his turban's
                                  light
was the appearance of the priest

like the man who sits
                 in secret
                        to entreat
                                 a king
was the appearance of the priest

like the star
           called brightness
                         at the limits of
                                    the east
was the appearance of the priest

                                        J.R.

COMMENTARY

(1) "There is a teaching in the name of Rabbi Yose, saying: When the priest spreads forth his hands it is forbidden to look at them, for the reason that the Shekinah is hovering over his hands. . . . At that moment there is a whisper followed by silence throughout the universe. So when a king is about to join his queen, all his attendants are agog and a whisper runs through them: Behold, the King is about to meet his Matrona." (*Zohar* 3.147a, 146a.)

(2) "We are told that a priest not beloved by the people ought not to take part in blessing the people. On one occasion, when a priest went up and spread forth his hands, before he completed the blessing he turned into a heap of bones. This happened to him because there was no love between him and the people." (*Zohar* 3.147b.)

Yehuda Amichai (Hebrew, b. 1924)

From TRAVELS OF A LATTER-DAY BENJAMIN OF TUDELA

. . . .

On Fridays they sewed my handkerchief
to the corner of my pocket, to prevent me carrying it
on the Sabbath and sinning. On festivals priests blessed me
from the white caves of their shawls, with cramped
epileptic fingers. I looked at them
and God didn't thunder. Since then his thunder
has retreated and become a great silence.
I looked at them and my eyes were not blinded.
Since then my eyes have opened wider and wider
from year to year, beyond sleep,
to the rim of pain, beyond eyelids, beyond clouds, beyond years.

Death is not sleep but open eyes, the whole body
gaping with eyes, pressed in the narrow space of the world.

. . . .

Not one finger of God but ten
choke me. "I won't let you let me leave you." That too
is a meaning of death.
You forget the way you were.
Don't blame the Chief Butler who forgot
the dream of Joseph! Hands still sticky with candle wax
forget Channukah. My face's wrinkled masks
have forgotten Purim. The body mortifying itself
on Yom Kippur forgot the High Priest (as beautiful
as you, this night), forgot the song of praise:
the appearance of the High Priest is like the sun,
like an onyx, a topaz. The appearance. Also your body
is Urim and Thumim. The nipples, the eyes,
the nostrils, dimple, navel, mouth, your mouth—
all these blaze for me like the Priest's breastplate,
all these spoke to me and prophesied what I should do.
I run away. Before your body
prophesies the future, I run away.

RUTH NEVO

Jerome Rothenberg (b. 1931)

THE CHILDREN OF THE FLOWERS OF THE PRIEST-HOOD: 4 Poems with Commentary for the Temple

to Paul Blackburn (*1926–1971*)

THE POEMS

1

tall golden candelabra
each had 4 bowls
filled with oil
4 ladders placed against
4 branches
children of the flowers of the priesthood
would climb up
        with pitchers
for the outer lamps
wicks made of worn-out
drawers & sashes
of the priests
for inner wicks they used
the high priest's
drawers
& women sifted wheat by this
illumination

2

joy of the Levites
seated on the 15 steps
with drums harps cymbals lyres trumpets
they sang above the crowd
the 15 songs of climbing
at cockcrow blew
2 trumpets

3

SONG OF THE COCKCROW

teki'ah
teru'ah
teki'ah

4

at the Eastern Gate
they looked back
said
"our fathers stood here
"backs turned to the temple
"faces east
"& bowed before the Sun

THE COMMENTARY

1

that I would write a poem called
Children of the Flowers of the Priesthood
made out of memory
of some incredible racial unconscious
how can I rip it from my chest?

I ask you
now that we're both certain
memory
begins there
like a flower blossoming
from esophagus
words seeking air
as flowers in
Aztec codex
my good friend the poet died from
when his esophagus closed up
& left him without his verbs & nouns
dear Paul
my loyalty is with you
Children of the Flowers of the Priesthood
maybe
even now the roots
stir in our thoughts
together
where there is neither Greek or Jew

2

exiled in Salamanca
& driven mad by
Image of the Temple

Salamanca, N.Y.
19.xii.73

COMMENTARY

(1)   Descriptions, after Patai's *Man & Temple,* of the ceremony called
"joy of the house of water-drawing," as performed by young & old
priests in the Jerusalem temple. Outbursts of sexuality &/or *kalut rosh*
("lightheadedness" so-called) marked the occasions, including ecstatic
dances in which the "pious men," rabbis & others, "whose great hour

this was, began to dance with burning torches in their hands. It is told of the venerable Rabban Shimeon ben Gamliel himself, that he used to dance with eight golden burning torches; he threw them high up into the air and again caught them alternately, and so great was his skill that no torch ever touched another nor did any torch ever fall to earth. Nay, even more than that, Rabban Shimeon ben Gamliel could perform, alone of all men, the following form of prostration: he threw himself forward upon his face, supported himself for a moment with his two thumbs stuck to the floor, kissed the floor and immediately jumped back to standing position. Other sages performed similar feats and entertained the audience with enigmatic sayings." (Patai, *Man & Temple*, pages 28–29.)

Dances of this kind, associated with mystic rites from David's time on, break out again in events like Jesus' "round dance" (below), the processionals of Safed, & the ecstatic dances of the Hasidic rebbes (below, page 334). For other rain-feasts & fertility ceremonials, see above, pages 112 & 236; below, pages 470–71 & 537.

(2) "Leopards break into the temple and drink to the dregs what is in the sacrificial pitchers. This is repeated over and over again. Finally it can be calculated in advance, and it becomes a part of the ceremony." (Franz Kafka.)

(Syriac, c. 3rd century A.D.)

From THE ACTS OF SAINT JOHN

"The Round Dance of Jesus"

"A praise poem
"we sing now
"will go to meet what is to come
& had us form a circle
we stood in with folded hands

himself was in the middle
(said)   You answer
Amen
then started singing
praises   saying
"Praises   Father
circling & we answered him
Amen   (said)
Praises   Word   (said)
Praises   Grace
Amen   (said)
Praises   Spirit   (said)
Praises   Holy Holy   (said)
O thee transfiguration   (said)
Amen   (said)
Thank you   Sunshine   Light
no darkness   (said)
"I will inform you now
"the reason for this thanks
(then said)
I save
& will be saved
Amen
I free
& will be freed
Amen
I hurt
& will be hurt
Amen
Am born
& will give birth
Amen
I feed
& will be food
Amen
I hear
& will be heard
Amen
I will be known

all knowing mind
Amen
I will be washed
& I will wash
Amen
all Grace Sweet Mind the Dance is round
I blow the pipe for
all are in the Round Dance
I will pipe
all dance along
Amen
I will moan low
all beat your breasts
Amen
the One & Only Eight
plays up for us
Amen
Old Number Twelve
stomps up above
Amen
the Universe controls
the dancer
Amen
whoever isn't dancing
's in the dark
Amen
I will go
& I will stay
Amen
I will dress thee
& I will dress
Amen
I will be Oned
& I will One
Amen
I have no house
& I have houses
Amen

I have no place
& I have places
Amen
I have no temple
& I have temples
Amen
I am a lamp to thee
who see me
Amen
I am a mirror to thee
who view me
Amen
I am a door to thee
who come thru me
Amen
I am a way to thee
wayfarer
Amen   (said)
"Follow
"my Round Dance
"& see yourself in me
"the Speaker
"& seeing what I speak
"keep silent on
"my mysteries
"or dancing think of what
"I do
"make yours the suffering of a man
"that I will suffer
"yet powerless to understand your suffering
"without a word
"the Father sent language thru me
"the sufferer you saw
"& saw me suffering
"you grew restless
"shaken
"you were moved toward wisdom
"lean on me

"I am a pillow
"who am I?
"you only will know me
"when I'm gone—
"but am not he for whom
"I am now taken—
"will know it when you reach it
"& knowing suffering will know
"how not to suffer
"I am your god
"not the betrayer's
"will harmonize the Sweet Soul with my own
"the Word of Wisdom speaks in me
"says
"Praises   Father
& we answered him
Amen   (said)
Praises   Word   (said)
Praises   Grace
Amen   (said)
Praises   Spirit   (said)
Praises   Holy Holy   (said)
"& if thou wouldst understand that which is me
"know this   all that I have said I have uttered
"playfully   & I was by no means ashamed of it
"I danced
"& when you dance in understanding
"understand & say
"Amen

J.R.

COMMENTARY

The figure of Jesus emerges, dark & shining in the pattern of other Jewish messiahs from then to present, & enters history. With him he carries the older metaphors of transformation: *I will make you a god to Pharaoh . . . the Patriarchs are the Merkaba . . . Israel the first born, logos . . . son of God*—working the change not only on himself but on his fellow Jews as well. For it is from this point on that *we* are drawn into the paranoia of the *other:* are transformed ("betrayers," "murderers") & locked into a system of thought, of action & response, which dominates & robs us of control over our lives.

The Jews, by Jesus' time, had aready moved into the world outside Judaea. With the wars of that first century the land itself was taken from them—irrevocably in the Christian triumph that would follow. The visible Jewish response was further to literalize the Torah, to bring all into the domain of the written: to replace the broken temple with the studyhouse, the rites of sacrifice with those of prayers & exegesis. But beneath that surface other forces stirred: a secret transmission or kabbala that kept alive a poetics of liberation & an anger that produced further messiahs, further failed revolutionaries & mystics, fantasies of escape from exile, & a continuing dream of freedom in a world in which "a fence was built around the Law."

For the later messiahs Jesus remained a covert model. Multiphasic from the start, he appeared in a variety of forms to the early Jewish Christians, including the dancer-of-the-mysteries & playful trickster in the gnostic Acts of Saint John. Thus he was himself a creature of the *nous poetikos* (creative mind) that would proliferate his image through the world. But the source of that image was still Jewish: prophetic & visionary & sharing that other side of the Jewish psyche that Gershom Scholem describes for Sabbatai Zevi, messiah of a later age: "[a movement] with its doctrine so profoundly shocking to the Jewish conception of things that the violation of the Torah could become its true fulfillment . . . [yet] a dialectical outgrowth of the belief in [his] Messiahship. . . . Not only . . . a single continuous development which retained its identity in the eyes of its adherents regardless of whether they themselves remained Jews or not, but also, paradoxical though it may seem, a specifically *Jewish* phenomenon. . . ." (From *The Messianic Idea in Judaism*, page 84.)

For more on the "heretical" messiahs, see below, pages 311–16, 321–28, & commentaries in "Sources, &c." But the conflict & dance were felt among the early rabbis as well—as in the following.

Armand Schwerner (b. 1927)
From PROLOGUE IN SIX PARTS

II

a kind of outside

There were four who entered Paradise: Ben Azzai, Ben Zoma, Elisha ben Abuyah and Akiba. Ben Azzai saw more than one is permitted to see, and paid for it with his life. Ben Zoma lost his mind. Elisha ben Abuyah became an apostate and sought to destroy the divine plants . . . only Akiba remained safe and sound.

In recognition of the danger and the destructive effects of this sort of speculation, the saying was coined:

If one directs his mind to the following four things, it were better for him if he had never been born: what is above, what is below, what was before creation, and what will take place at the end of the world.

(*Hag.* 2:1, *Hag.* 11a)

III

the dance

not unlikely that his body
should shake like this,
                              accustomed,
in old goings-away from itself
for other lakes,
                   to agues and worse.
The whole man is a holier

man, he knew,
                    from the keen violence within,
                                        filling him
with disquieting pleasure, pleasure of an old sort
wandering among foreign
lakes, likely
images,
          Indians of a sort,
                              o you sad Rabbis
tracking away like geese, if you only knew it,
after a goose. No jumping theodicists could have missed
any more
of what you'd left gratefully behind
in the crowded clanks of brutal towns.
                                   Relieved, so
relieved, you stand up straight,
                         o heroes,
missing it all, under the pushed
grassland, the droughtless pastureland,
greening . . .
and all around the African grass,
                                   insect passes
play tiny rounds, violent with a lovely
violence, striplings
vocal and clear to the bending
Akiba, opening to smallest music.
Inept Ben Azzai, blunt angel of the chase,
                                        father
of a more foolish violence, and foolish
fond old man
what could you have seen,
all furtive and booted, that laid you so low
failing of expectation?
O I see you three hold hands in the warm savanna
as on the roof of the world
terrified beasts lunge, watching for corners,
not at home, not
treading easy,
              my heart, bold Ben Azzai,

right in your keeping. You leave me
for nothingness. Down you go, or up, changed
for good from what you were in your exploring
premises.
                    It was a promise fulfilled
                                        unexpectedly,
loss of all names alike to common air, you, you, you've been
nowhere. If you had only . . .
                            Forever, my waking dream, no end
to this and my parcel of self,
Good Akiba, stands dreaming on the plain with you,
no martyr marvel, finding merely what you'd brought,
                                                bent
a little from the burden of not having pined
for the last horizon
white weather in the final mind.
                        And you,
Abuyah, in your quashing hobnails
angry at the grass, poor Rabbi,
                        what
did it ever do to you, as to the white hands
of Ben Zoma, mind gone, all color and laughter gone.
Akiba, angel of the will, teach me
how to listen, the stance a little down, the proper
movement toward the bare ground, a return
alive, the keepings of a name
by the satisfactions of regular breathing
not utterly drowned in common air.

COMMENTARY

For Abuya's apostasy ("mutilating the shoots"), see above, page 67. Two further stories thereon:

1

It is reported that once while studying the law in the valley of Genusan, he saw a man climbing a tree. The man found a bird's nest in the tree, & taking the mother with the young ones he still departed in peace. He saw another man who finding a bird's nest followed the Bible's command to take the young only, allowing the mother to fly away. And yet a serpent stung him as he descended, & he died. "Now," he thought, "where is the Bible's truth & promises? Is it not written, 'And the young thou mayest take to thyself, but the mother thou shalt surely let go, that it may be well with thee & that thou mayest live many days.' Now, where is the long life to this man who followed the precept, while the one who transgressed it is unhurt?"

2

During the fearful period of religious persecution, the learned Rabbi Juda, whose life had been passed in the study of the law & the practice of God's precepts, was delivered into the power of the cruel torturer. His tongue was placed in a dog's mouth & the dog bit it off. So Ben Abuya said, "If a tongue which uttered only truth can be so used, and a learned, wise man be so treated, of what use is it to avoid having a lying tongue & being ignorant? If these things are allowed, there is surely no reward for the righteous & no resurrection of the dead."

(Jerusalem Talmud)

Akiba, who maintained his "sanity" in Paradise, reasoned in the first instance, above, that the man's days would be long in the future world "where all is happiness."

On that day Rabbi Eliezer brought all the proofs in the world, and
the masters would not accept them.

He said to them: If the law is according to me, let this locust tree
prove it.

The locust tree moved a hundred cubits. (And some say: four hundred cubits.)

They said to him: The locust tree cannot prove anything.

Then he said to them: If the law is according to me, let this stream
of water prove it.

The stream of water turned and flowed backward.

They said to him: The stream cannot prove anything.

Then he said to them: If the law is according to me, let the walls
of the House of Study prove it.

The walls of the House of Study began to topple.

Rabbi Joshua reprimanded them:

If scholars are disputing with one another about the law, what business is it of yours?

They did not fall down out of respect for Rabbi Joshua, and did not
straighten up out of respect for Rabbi Eliezer, and they are
still inclined.

Then he said to them: If the law is according to me, let the heaven
prove it.

A voice came forth from heaven and said:

Why do you dispute with Rabbi Eliezer?

The law is according to him in every case.

Rabbi Joshua rose to his feet and said:

"It is not in heaven" (Deuteronomy 30.12)

What is the meaning of: "It is not in heaven"?

Rabbi Jeremiah said:

The Torah has already been given once and for all from Mount
   Sinai,
we do not listen to voices from heaven.
For You have already written in the Torah on Mount Sinai:
"After the majority must one incline." (Exodus 23.2)

Rabbi Nathan came upon Elijah.
He said to him: What was the Holy One, blessed be he, doing at
   that moment?
Elijah said to him:
He was smiling and saying: My children have defeated me, my chil-
   dren have defeated me!

NAHUM GLATZER

COMMENTARY

From Edmond Jabès, *The Book of Questions:*

He answers every question with another question. (Reb Léma)

*My name is a question. It is also my freedom within my tendency to
question.* (Reb Eglal)

. . .

*The time of the earth is that of a question we have tried in vain to an-
swer.* (Reb Diab)

"God is a questioning of God." (Reb Arwas)

(Hebrew, traditional)

A POEM FOR BAR YOḤAI

o you Bar Yoḥai
                        you in oil
            be happy
oil joy from
                        your friends
o you Bar Yoḥai
            holy
                        oiling you with oil
you oiled
            & measured holy
                        you hold up
a leaf from Holy Crown
            held on your head
                        your beauty
o you Bar Yoḥai
            your good home
                        you homed in
the day you ran
            you roamed
                        Hole of the Rocks
you hid in
            gave you glory
                        halos for your head
o you Bar Yoḥai
            circle of whose trees surround
                        lore of Adonai
study
            wondrous light
                        o hearthlight

glows for you
       your teachers
             teach you
o you Bar Yoḥai
       o you flew
             you in the applefield
you drew flowers
       odors
             o secrets of
the Torah
       buds & branches
             you for whom we speak
o you Bar Yoḥai
       wore your power
             in faith's war
fire
       at its gates
             pulled sword
from sheath
       you drew against
             your enemies
o you Bar Yoḥai
       where the stones were
             marble
you were there
       before the lion
             you who saw the bear's
crown jewel
       (saw
             but who saw you?)
o you Bar Yoḥai
       in holiest of
             holies
green line
       months made months
             the seven sabbaths
secrets of the fifty
       linked the links of *shin*

                    your links
o you Bar Yoḥai
          wisdom's ancient *yod*
                    you saw
into his glory
          32-fold path
                    o onset of high offerings
a cherub enters
          oiled & shining in
                    your light
o you Bar Yoḥai
          wondrous light
                    o high above you
frightened
          past all sight
                    & hidden
call it nothing
          call it sleep
                    eyes cannot see

                                        J.R./H.L.

COMMENTARY

(1)   A pupil of Akiba's (mid-2nd century A.D.), Simeon bar Yoḥai came
to be identified with the ecstatic side of *poesis,* itself not separated from
the developing Jewish otherness, resistance. Sentenced to death for talk
against the Roman state during Bar Kokhba's war (see below, pages 299,
603–4), he hid with his son Eleazar in a cave for twelve years; was
credited much later as "author" of the *Zohar.* The anniversary of his
death has been celebrated since at least the 16th century as a festival
(*hilula*) in the village of Meron in Israel; marked by a night-long series
of potlatch-like fire events (in which money, costly garments, the first-cut
locks of three-year-old boys, etc., are thrown into a great fire), accompanied by singing & ecstatic dances, healing rites & fire-handling. Bar
Yoḥai's hymn (the *ashrekha*) is sung as a series of ten strophes corresponding to the ten *sefirot,* & new songs in Hebrew & Arabic are still
composed for the event.

(2)   from "the notebooks"   5/76   what do you mean to me Bar
Yoḥai   old man in cave you fled to   hating "even the best of gentiles"

there returned to the primeval world   lost poems rose before you
    words in your exile hurt because you made them   not fit not be
what the others heard   (they said) the Jew is stubborn in his hole
drove you to see your Jew's face other's face of exile at world's center
    you would say (o universal Jew fierce rabbi brother) we are all one
man the cry of vision covers our last escape   from otherness   from
birth   cry when we first saw light   (j.r.)

(Hebrew/Aramaic, written c. 499 A.D.)

From THE BABYLONIAN TALMUD   "Beauty That
                                                                        Withers"

Rabbi Eliezer was sick. Rabbi Yohanan came to visit him.
He saw Rabbi Eliezer lying in a dark house.
Rabbi Yohanan bared his arm, and the room lit up.
He saw that Rabbi Eliezer was crying. He said to him: Why are
    you crying?
Is it for the Torah in which you have not learned enough?
We have learned: Do more, do less, it matters not,
so long as one's heart is turned to heaven.
If because of the provisions you lack—
not every man merits two tables.
If because of the sons you have not—
see, this is the bone of my tenth son.
Rabbi Eliezer said to him:
I am crying over this beauty of yours, which is to wither in the
    dust.
He said to him:
You are right to cry over that.
And they wept together.

NAHUM GLATZER

(Hebrew/Aramaic, written c. 499 A.D.)

THE GREAT LAMENT

for the Rabbis

The columns of Caesarea ran with tears, roof gutters ran with
blood, stars were visible in the daytime
All cedars were uprooted
All trees were uprooted
Fiery stones fell from heaven
All images were effaced and were used as stone pillars
All statues of humans were torn out of position
Seventy houses were broken into by thieves at Tiberias
Hail stones fell from heaven
The rocks of the Euphrates kissed each other
The rocks of the Tigris kissed each other
The palms were laden with thorns

THE END OF "A BOOK OF BEARDS"

A Book of the Wars of Yahveh

Rochelle Owens (b. 1936)
From I AM THE BABE OF JOSEPH STALIN'S
DAUGHTER

DIN

who am i floating
above cows
YAHOEL AM I
whiter than   white
animal skins   unblemished
lambs.   my blood
so red & light salty
Isaac Resnikoff
the pious scribe
studies my .word.

"A Book of the Wars of Yahveh" is also the "Book of the Exile": an assemblage of voices in anger & pain, rebellion & madness, hatred of other & of self.
Here "history" is truly "nightmare" (see page 231, above), & the face God
shows is that of *DIN* or JUDGMENT. The book sketches a record of *poesis*
(vision, voice) as the struggle for human survival in a world of mind-forged
manacles & racial bondage. It moves from the political & religious upheavals
under the Romans (Jesus & other "messiahs," destruction of Temple & city,

                    it is as if sacred white scrolls
          encase my holy legs   Rising I Rise

                    over this peculiar

                              continent
                                        I float
                    above cities   singing glory glory
    I am living prayer &

                              THEY give me their
              .love.

                              I Am That I Am
                    DIVINE STERNNESS
                         *

                         J U D G M E N T
                    DIN

Shekinah's withdrawal from same into years of sterility) to new rebellions,
enforced diaspora, medieval visions of heaven & hell, dreams of new zions,
messiahs & mystics who work within a web of cruelty & persecution, bending
the Law to their visions or striking against it toward a growing concern with
liberation: mystical, secular, radical, zionist, subterranean, criminal, etc. The
terror, if not the triumph, is both Jewish & human: the disasters of a civilization that moves along the road to Auschwitz, Hiroshima. The editor has
chosen not to supplement these texts with commentary: the basic statements on
poesis & myth have occurred elsewhere, & whatever other information is
needed will be found in the notes. The events, as in "A Book of Beards," are
roughly chronological—the writings about those events from various times &
places. The participants throughout are Jews, not saints.

Charles Reznikoff (1894–1976)

PALESTINE UNDER THE ROMANS

Israel is like a bird
that a creeping weasel has wounded in the head
or a man knocked against a wall—
the cattle have trampled it but still it flutters.
If there is bone enough to make the tooth of a key,
and ink enough to write two letters of the alphabet—
the house is sold and the door but not the key;
the ship is sold, the mast, the sail, the anchor, and all the means
    for steering,
but not the packing-bags or lading.

Go with a staff and a bag and a scroll of the law,
and fear not the rush of tramping shoes at the sound of the
    shouting!
In the evening, until midnight, until dawn,
as soon as we can tell between blue and green,
between blue and white,
when we lie down and when we stand up,
each in his own way
(though we stop to return a greeting or greet a man out of respect,
    out of fear),
bringing grapes in baskets to the winepress or figs in baskets to
    the drying-place,
trampling the grain and binding it into sheaves,
or the women spinning their yarn by moonlight,
a workingman on the top of a tree or a course of stones,
or a bridegroom on the first night,
or he whose dead lies unburied before him,
and they that bear the bier and they that relieve them—
if our faces cannot, our hearts
turn towards Jerusalem
and you, the God of our fathers,
of Abraham, Isaac, and Jacob.

Abba Yose ben Ḥanin (Hebrew, 1st century A.D.)

A POEM FOR THE MASTERS

Oy from the Boethusians!
Oy from their bludgeons!
Oy from the Kantherites!
Oy from their libels!
Oy from the Amanites!
Oy from their snake hisses!
Oy from the house of Ishmael ben Phiabi!
Oy oy from their fists in our faces!
They themselves are high priests
& their sons are treasurers
& their sons-in-law are captains of the Temple
& their servants beat the people with sticks!

J.R./H.L.

School of John the Baptist (Greek, c. 60/70 A.D.)

From APOCALYPSE   "The Woman"

I saw a sign in Heaven:
a woman clad in Sun, Moon beneath her feet,
twelve stars her crown, child in her belly,
crying her pangs, aching to bear.

I saw: a great dragon, color of flame, seven heads, ten horns,
seven diadems, tail dragging a third of the stars,
hurling them against Earth.

Began birth: snake faced her to eat her son
who is to shepherd every tribe,
crook hard as iron from the stars,

whom they carried quickly to God: to His great Seat.
She ran to the desert where He had made her a home,
where she will be cared for 260 days.

I saw war in Heaven: Michael and his angels
against snake and his: who fought, who lost,
whose place up above, find it no more: angels thrown down,
old snake named Accuser, Satan who miscarries all the world.

I heard a shout in Heaven: "now salvation, strength—
our God's reign, kingdom of Messiah His Anointed, comes to birth.
Who accused our brother, accused him day and night
to our God's Face, thank the Lamb's blood,
Word of those who witness, loving life no more than death, he
's been beaten, the serpent thrown off:

A BOOK OF THE WARS OF YAHVEH   281

Heavens, rejoice! And smile, all camped there:
but Earth, Sea, woe, woe:
down towards you in anger the accuser comes,
knowing he has but little time."

Cast away on Earth snake came for the woman
who, given great eagle's wings, soared into the wastes
where she is sheltered a season, seasons, half a season
far from serpent's mouth:
he spat water, a river to drown her.
Earth her rescue: opened wide, drank down
the torrent he belched. Woman-maddened snake
left to fight her seed's remnants
because they keep God's Law, making
Jesus' witness theirs.

Snake came to the beach and stopped.

C.D.

Jesus ben Hananiah (Hebrew/Aramaic, 1st century A.D.)
THE PROPHECY OF JESUS BEN HANANIAH

---

a voice from the sunrise
a voice from the sunset
a voice from the 4 winds:

cry for Jerusalem & the temple
cry for the bridegroom & the bride
cry for all of their people

1

back then • the government of Israel was in a woman's hand a woman's hands whose name was Helen • in the temple stood the stone called Stone-That-Yah-Set-Up that had the letters of the Holy Name cut in • *who learns these letters can do anything* the wise ones thought • they were afraid the young ones if they learned them would destroy the world • the wise ones were afraid they bound two dogs of brass to the two iron pillars at the Gate of the Burnt Offerings (said) *whoever comes in here & learns the letters let the dogs howl at him then let the letters leave his mind* • well in comes Jesus • then he learned the letters wrote them on a parchment slit his thigh & laid the parchment in • he felt no pain • no pain the flesh closed up around it • going out the dogs bound to the pillars howled the letters left his mind • he went back to his house & with a knife he cut his flesh & lifted out the writing • how he learned the Name

2

rebellion growing • great division throughout Israel • then Jesus leaves for Upper Galilee • the wise ones come before the Queen they say *Our Lady this one is a sorcerer he leads the world to ruin* • well she sends her horsemen after him they find him stirring up the men of Galilee he says *I am the son of God* he says *it says so in your Torah* • well the horsemen try to take him but the men of Galilee resist • a war starts • Jesus tells them *you don't have to fight just trust the power of My Father In Heaven* • well the Galileans had been making birds from clay then Jesus spoke the letters of the Name & just like that they flapped their wings • right then the men

fell down before him • then he tells them *bring a millstone* • so they
roll it to the seashore where he speaks the letters sets it on the sea &
just like sitting in a boat he's floating on the water • horsemen
dazzled • Jesus says to them *you tell your lady tell her what you
saw here* • then he makes the spirit lift him from the water & put him
on dry land • when they go back to the Queen & tell her then she is
amazed & trembling • she really is amazed

3

*then the Elders of Israel took a certain man whose name was Judas
Iscariot & brought him into the house of the holy of holies* • & he
learned the letters of the Ineffable Name which were engraved on
the foundation stone : & he wrote them on a small parchment slit
his thigh & laid the parchment in • he felt no pain just as Jesus had
felt no pain before him • then when Jesus & his men came in before
the Queen & the wise ones she had told to be there Jesus spoke up
first he said *Of me the prophecy was made : dogs encompassed me
about I did not fear them* • then the wise ones came in with Judas
they began accusing him & he accusing them & saying to the Queen
of me King David said : I will ascend to heaven • & he wrote :
he shall receive me (selah) • well he raises up his hands like eagles'
wings & takes off • everyone's amazed they say *how can he fly there
between the sky & earth* • the elders say to Judas *sound the letters
& fly after him* • then Judas does it just like that he flies into the
sky & everyone's amazed *how both of them can fly like eagles* •
until Iscariot grabs hold of him & flies up higher soars can't force
him down to earth • neither one can beat the other with the Name
the Name shared equally between them • but when Judas saw that
this was so he played it dirty yes he pissed on Jesus even buggered
him until he got unclean & down he fell to earth & Judas with him •
well they weep about this on their night they cry for what he did to
him • & right away they seized him & they said to Helen : *Let him
be destroyed* they said : *Or let him say who beat him* • & they put
a coat over his head & banged on him with pomegranate branches •
well he didn't know a word to use against them • how they knew the
power of the Name had left him

J.R./H.L.

Lenny Bruce (1927–66)
CORPUS CHRISTI PLAY

I wanted to do a film showing—because I'm sure that day in the cell, it's just like in the tank, like four, five, six people in the cell there, and there was Cestus, Distus, and this guy who was probably crapped out in the corner:

GUARD: O.K.—you two.

GOOD THIEF: What?

GUARD: You get crucified today.

GOOD THIEF: Get my file down here. That's bullshit.

GUARD: O.K. Get ready all you guys. You're all getting crucified in this cell.

GOOD THIEF: I'm the good thief. Whaddayou bullshittin me for? I'm in here for checks!

GUARD: Come on, you. Get ready. You're gettin crucified.

GOOD THIEF: Heh heh. I'm *not* getting crucified. Get my file down here. I'm the good thief. I'm here for petty theft. Understand? *Checks.* How can I get crucified now? I dunno what the hell that guy's doing, but . . .

O.K. Now he sees they're getting him all ready and they're moving him:

GOOD THIEF: *Hey!* What the hell, are you kidding with this shit? I'm not getting cruc—hey mister! Do me a favor? There's a mistake here. They think that I'm with you, for some reason here.

And Christ says

CHRIST: Don't worry—you'll be with me.

GOOD THIEF: Come *on* with that! I'm *not* with you. Tell them. Come on, it's no joke now. We're going up the hill.

But he's praying, everybody's pushing.

GOOD THIEF: Well come on! Hey! Get the public defender. Come on, this is bullshit now, ahh . . .

O.K. Now. Up on the cross.

GOOD THIEF: Hey mistuh! Please, before it's too late. Do me a favuh, O.K.? Tell them?

CHRIST: Don't worry, you're with me . . .

GOOD THIEF: STOP SAYIN THAT! Will ya? I'M *not with you,* O.K.? I mean, I'm with you, I like you, but stop telling these assholes I'm *with* you. They think "I'm with you" means that I'm *with* you, I conspired with you, I dunno . . . Look Don't be pushy. I like you, O.K.? I dunno what you're talking about, I woke up, all I know I'm getting crucified—I'm here for checks, I *can't* get crucified. I'm being denied due process, I'm entitled to do my time for checks first. And I don't wanna get crucified. I *can't* go now. O.K.? I'll meet you later. . . . Come on. Don't be pushy now, O.K.?

O.K. *Mop.* They all went. And then when the guy came back,

"Hey . . . you were *right* . . . I knew you weren't bullshitting, but, uh, heh, heh, I had alotta faith in you, but you get to meet alotta weird people in the joint, you know? . . . You relax; I'll talk to the press. That's all."

Remember this: I'm dying for your sins. For your sins and your kids' sins. I'm dying, so—well, just *shape up!* That's all. I'm dying so that, in the future, things will be right, so you just realize what the values are. Good things—remember the good: remember that being born is an original sin. And once we scrub that dirt off you with lye, a few of you will stray and do it again. Try to fight it. Try to fight it, and remember that the physical is not the most desirable. The spiritual—that's the thing to look for, since spiritual trim—I'm getting off here now, cause I see that dying for you does no good. You don't appreciate I'm dying for you. That's what I've done, I've suffered my whole life for you, and whaddaya do, ya run away with some cheap *shicksa*. Go be nice to people! Go get crucified! Look at my hands: I'm Helena Rubenstein. That's who she really is—*corpus christi*.

Simon Magus, per Irenaeus (Latin, 1st/2nd century A.D.)
THE STORY OF SIMON & HELEN

Simon Magus, the famous witch
given a god's glory
taught "I am the one
showed myself to the Jews
as Son, as Father
touched earth in Samaria
to all others
the Holy Spirit

Strength beyond strength
Father standing above all
call me any Name you like"

had with him her
named Helen bought
redeemed from an easy house in Tyre
said "Helen names

First Thought my mind had
Universe Mother   in the beginning
through her I thought
I made angels, archangels:
I am her Father
she is my Daughter
my will desired:
she journeyed down
creating those Strengths and Angels
who made make up this shameless world

they hated her
captive under their eye
complained 'we have no mother
Simon—who's he?'
so my Thought chained
these Powers who streamed from her
shaming her every way they could
kept her from coming back to me

finally humbled to woman
locked in female
they poured her soul like water
from one body jug to the next

My Thought was in Helen of Troy
for whom the heroes fought
who blinded Stesichorus
for mocking her in his poems
until in his Palinode he took it back
'yes, you did not go to Troy'
so she gave him back his eyes

My Helen now one woman now another
always shamed always humble
at last took flesh in a brothel
she is the Lamb who went astray
why I'm here:

to lift her up strike off her chains
saves you seeing who
she is"

the Angels and the Powers
so misruled because
each wanted to be god one and only
Simon came to refresh this world
borrowing shape like the Strengths', Energies', Angels'
himself in disguise
one man among men yet no man
suffered in Judea
yet did not suffer

the Angels of the world
dictated to the prophets
so if you look for hope
from Simon and his Helen
forget the Angels and the writings
they inspired:
you are free
do what you like
his grace buys freedom
not what you do in nature
there is nothing
good you can do all's
pure luck

the Powers who made this place
delivered commandments
that teach you to be
law-abiding slaves
Simon sez
"follow me
I will smash the world
untangle you from the scripts
of its false begetters"

the wise men, priests of his mysteries
live through their senses
working magic, casting out devils, weaving spells
brewing elixirs of love, seductive glamors
raising familiars
bringing on spirits of enchanted dreams
they have a statue of Simon as Zeus
another of Helen as Athena, goddess of wisdom
the Simonians started *gnosis*
they say so themselves

C.D.

(Greek, 1st century B.C.–3rd century A.D.)

A SPELL FOR A BLASPHEMING WOMAN

take a lamp not painted red with seven wicks & make a wick from
rope out of a shipwrecked boat & on the first wick write with myrrh
ink IAO on the second ADONAI on the third SABAOTH on the
fourth PAGOURĒ LADY CRAB on the fifth MARMOROUTH on
the sixth IAEO on the seventh MICHAEL putting olive oil into the
lamp & set it on the window sill that faces south a coil of wormwood
on the lamp along the edge & say

great powers   gods
giving your lives this moment
yes this day I call on you
I aim words at this godless woman
says Iao has no ribs
Adonai is knocked out by his own raging
Sabaoth has squawked 3 times
says Crab Lady is hermaphroditic

Marmorouth's balls are clipped
Iaeo wasn't buried in sarcophagus
says Michael's a hermaphrodite
not I not I who say this
Lord but she unholy woman lead her
to me   burning   passionate
subdued & helpless
until she gets to me

: this seven times & if the first light sputters know the demon seized
her : if the second that she's wandering out : the third she's walking : the fourth she's coming close : the fifth she's at the door :
the sixth she springs the latch : the seventh she's inside the house :
& use it for those across the sea for this the lamp's set in a little
water in the open air papyrus floats under the lamp the spell is
said six times

J.R.

Charles Reznikoff (1894–1976)

From JERUSALEM THE GOLDEN

The moon shines in the summer night;
now I begin to understand the Hebrews
who could forget the Lord, throw kisses at the moon,
until the archers came against Israel
and bronze chariots from the north
rolled into the cities of Judah and the streets of Jerusalem.

What then must happen, you Jeremiahs,
to me who look at moon and stars and trees?

(Hebrew, c. 7th century A.D.)

A KARAITE DIRGE FOR THE FALL OF JERUSALEM

For the palace that has been forsaken
   We sit alone & weep
For the Temple that has been demolished
   We sit alone & weep
For fences that have been breached
   We sit alone & weep
For my sanctuary that has been burned
   We sit alone & weep
For the roads to the Temple that have been uprooted
   We sit alone & weep
For bolts that have been snapped
   We sit alone & weep
For the killers who have conquered
   We sit alone & weep
For the shame that has grown great
   We sit alone & weep
For stone colonnades that have been scorched
   We sit alone & weep
For friends who have been scattered
   We sit alone & weep
For priests who have stumbled
   We sit alone & weep
For sacred studies that have been forbidden
   We sit alone & weep
For kings who have been scorned by God
   We sit alone & weep
For nobles who have been humiliated
   We sit alone & weep
For the poor who have been decimated

We sit alone & weep
For the redeemed who have been kidnapped
We sit alone & weep
For the saints who have been trampled
We sit alone & weep
For the rains that have been abolished
We sit alone & weep

LEON NEMOY

Yehuda ben Idi (Hebrew, 3rd/4th century A.D.)

THE WITHDRAWAL OF THE SHEKINAH FROM HER HOME IN THE TEMPLE

---

after Yoḥanan bar Nappaḥa

from the ark cover she moved onto the Cherub
from the Cherub onto the other Cherub
from the second Cherub onto the threshold of the Temple
from the threshold into the court of the Priests
from the court onto the altar in the court
from the altar onto the roof of the Temple
from the roof onto the wall
from the wall into the city of Jerusalem
from the city onto the Mount of Olives
from the Mount of Olives into the desert

RAPHAEL PATAI

A SONG OF THE MOURNERS OF ZION

1

Rabbi Ishmael ben Elisha said: Since the day the temple was destroyed & since the day a kingdom's harsh decrees first fell upon us, there is a rule we have imposed upon ourselves: that we will not take a wife or bring forth children. So it will be that Abraham our Father's seed will perish.

Better that Israel cease: better that Israel err than do evil

2

THE SONG OF THE MOURNERS

o peasants seed no more
           no more surrender of your harvests earth
     but shut your bounty up within you
you vine why should you give more wine?
     they offer no more wine in Zion
     they bring first fruits no more
& you skies you should hold back your dew
           you should block up your rain
     your treasure
& sun you should hide your rays of light
& you moon should extinguish your great light
     why should light shine when Zion's light
           is dark?
& bridegrooms you should not go forth
you brides should not adorn yourselves for love

you women should not pray for sons
you who are mothers now should mourn
        why did you bear in pain?
   so you should bury them with groans?
& all these men here
    what do they want with sons now?
why should they speak about a man's seed
when the mother is abandoned   her sons dragged off?

J.R./H.L.

INTERLUDE

Arlene Stone (b. 1930)

From THE SHULE OF JEHOVAH

The Initiation   On his bed of lion pelts,
               unkosher
               but adorable,
               young David Joseph lies,
               dreaming of the ark,
               clitoral light.

               His rainbow robe slips open,
               the honeyed eel falls out,
               its deviated septum
               capped
               by hard-boiled egg,
               a profligate
               as salty as the seas
               of Canaan.

The guru Moses lifts his hand;
the rod of Aaron stiffens
from serpent's crook
to wand. The Red Sea dams
in menopause, but overflowing
menses boil Egyptian rivers,
and black plagues cataract
with frogs, flies, crickets,
daggered hail
until our David pants,
alone on blooded sheet—
Sweet Bull brought down
by cow murrain.

The Vigil   Deborah's apron tents the river
by David's caravan—
his camel neck
dry-docked
where waves ride out to sea
beneath the hibernating stars.

Bits of tin leap
zestful—
mosaic angels playing
hide and seek—
a fusillade of birds
flung like charred barley—
Deborah moors her son
to dock with lifelines:
garters,
hooks and eyes—

My David's roots ascend a Jacob's ladder;
his cock, that serpent lax with grapes,
sprawls below a crater.
His pupils bottle wine
in dusty cellars,
the lashes droop like spiders.

Goliath vaults the slingshot!
(A black blood pressure armband).
His sweat electrifies
a rocksalt trunk—
Barbed wire his hair,
his eyes
swastikas.
He fires his cannon snout.
Below the nuclear equator,
the Pig Jaw opens—
tongue a plane self-immolating,
radio still going
(a last asthmatic call for space)
Line up and take your places
in the oven, oven, oven
oven, oven . . .

(Hebrew, after 63 B.C.)

From THE WAR OF THE SONS OF LIGHT AGAINST THE SONS OF DARKNESS

For the man of understanding. War rule. Beginning.

"The conquest of the sons of light shall be undertaken firstly
"against the lot of the sons of darkness, against the army of Belial
"against the band of Edom & Moab & of the sons of Ammon
"& the multitude of the sons of the East & of Philistia
"& against the bands of the Kittim of Asshur & their people
"who shall come to the aid of the wicked of the Covenant
"sons of Levi & sons of Judah & sons of Benjamin
"The Deportation of the desert shall fight against them
"for war shall be declared on all their bands
"when the Deportation of the sons of light returns from the desert of the peoples
"to camp in the desert of Jerusalem

A. DUPONT-SOMMER

Simeon Bar Kokhba (Hebrew, 2nd century A.D.)

A LETTER & A DIRGE TO MARK THE ENDING OF THE SECOND ROMAN WAR

. . . till the end . . .
. . . they have no hope . . .
. . . my brothers in the south . . .
. . . of these were lost by the sword . . .
. . . these my brothers . . .

(Hebrew, traditional)

A CURSE & ANGRY POEM AGAINST THE NATIONS

this word is spoken at
the open door:
for the Prophet Eliahu

1

THE CURSE

pour out thy wrath upon the nations that do not know thee & upon
the kingdoms that call not upon thy name for they have eaten
Jacob & laid waste his dwelling: pour out thy wrath upon them : &
may the kindling of thine anger overtake them : pursue them with
anger & destroy them from under God's skies

2

not to us Adonai not to us
but to your name
be praises

for love of us
for truth's sake

why should the *goyim* say:
where is their god?

& our god in the skies

all that he wanted
done

their idols
gold & silver

workings of the hands
of man

whose mouths
are wordless

eyes are sightless

ears are deaf

nose dead to smell

hands without touch
feet without motion

can't utter sound
thru throats

like these be those
who made them

J.R.

Moses de Leon (Hebrew, c. 1240–1305)

From MIDRASH OF THE ABSENT   "Messiah"

---

the Garden has three walls all made of fire   an outer wall that holds
the righteous of the gentiles   a second wall that holds all those who
wait upon Messiah who see Messiah once a day   on Friday from
the time Israel begins its rests all the palaces inside the Garden
shake   & the inner palace is Messiah's & is called the Bird's Nest
     & Messiah come out from there & the tsadikim come out with
him   & Messiah wears clothes of vengeance for the coming victory
of Israel   & all come in with him & he comes out there with the
Fathers   then he stands there in middle of the Garden   he stands
where the pillar stands there in the middle   & he grabs the 4 rings
at the 4 corners of the Garden & lifts his voice   the dome over the
Garden vibrates & the 7 Angels called before him say   CHOSEN
ONE OF YAH BE STILL   FOR THE TIME IS HERE WHEN
THE EVIL KINGDOM WILL BE TORN OUT FROM ITS
PLACE   & they hear a voice out of the synagogues & studyhouses
a cry of power   AMEN MAY HIS GREAT NAME BE BLEST
FOREVER   then the Holy-One-Be-Blest shakes all the domes &
drops 2 tears into the Great Ocean   & the tsadikim come back &
Messiah comes back with them to the palace called the Bird's Nest

in the Garden   on the side of the East Wind   there is a palace
hidden & shut tight   & this one is called the Palace of the Glow
this one this palace built "like the pure substance of the heavens"
from the walls around it letters burst & sparkle rising & descending

flying up from one side coming to rest at the other   exchanging
places but without confusion   & no one can stand beside them for
they do not stop their motion not even for a moment   & flowers
spun from the 4 colors of the glow spark toward the palace   on the
sabbath Messiah comes there with the Fathers   & the letters quiet
down the letters speak the letters sing a joyous song   but nobody
knows what it is

& there inside that palace is an opening   & there behind the curtain there are images of those killed at Lod   & images of the 10
killed by the Kingdom   Messiah rises up & enters there & sees those
images & lifts his voice & bellows like a lion   & the whole Garden
shakes & the tsadikim shake   & the pillar in the middle of the Garden shakes up & down   & 4 Angels of the Wheel are called & catch
hold of the 4 rings & the dome is spinning & a voice sounds from
the heights   & the Holy-One-Be-Blest lets 2 tears fall directly
down   & the wheels come in to the Messiah & all the Fathers come
in through the opening in the Eastern Gate inside that palace   &
there they see the varying degrees of the tsadikim killed at Lod &
the 10 killed by the Kingdom   & all stand with Messiah   & the
wheels lift up & raise them to the King the King of Kings the Holy-
One-Be-Blest who swears that he will put on clothes of vengeance
he will execute his vengeance on the gentiles   for they say "he will
judge among the gentiles   he will fill the earth with corpses"   &
they come back to Messiah

J.R./H.L.

(Hebrew, 10th century)
PIYUT: "A GREAT MUSIC"

Ah people do do shake off dust do rise do
Go to Jerusalem see she is praised do
Ride over flagstones break through new roads do
Eat curds eat honey eat up whole rivers do
Add to your stores by their riversides do
Take do plunder the Goyim's prize do
Meet the rays from Shekinah's face do
Use up inherit Jerusalem's fields do
See sun & moon shine their lights do
Illumine with music do sing your songs do
Close with your enemies smoked out burnt off like dew

as written *you have sold yourselves cheap no money can buy all
this back* (J.R., after Isaiah 52.3.)

J.R./H.L.

Judah ha-Levi (Hebrew, c. 1075–c. 1141),
per Charles Reznikoff
From JEHUDA HALEVI'S SONGS TO ZION

My heart in the East
and I at the farthest West:
how can I taste what I eat or find it sweet
while Zion
is in the cords of Edom and I
bound by the Arab?
Beside the dust of Zion
all the good of Spain is light;
and a light thing to leave it.

And if it is now only a land of howling beasts and owls
was it not so
when given to our fathers—
all of it only a heritage of thorns and thistles?
But they walked in it—
His name in their hearts, sustenance!—
as in a park among flowers.

In the midst of the sea
when the hills of it slide and sink
and the wind
lifts the water like sheaves—
now a heap of sheaves and then a floor for the threshing—
and sail and planks shake
and the hands of the sailors are rags,
and no place for flight but the sea,
and the ship is hidden in waves
like a theft in the thief's hand,
suddenly the sea is smooth

and the stars shine on the water.

Wisdom and knowledge—except to swim—
have neither fame nor favor here;
a prisoner of hope, he gave his spirit to the winds,
and is owned by the sea;
between him and death—a board.

Zion, do you ask if the captives are at peace—
the few that are left?
I cry out like the jackals when I think of their grief;
but, dreaming of the end of their captivity,
I am like a harp for your songs.

Abraham Abulafia (Hebrew, 1240–c. 1291)

HOW HE WENT AS MESSIAH IN THE NAME OF ANGEL RAZIEL TO CONFRONT THE POPE

Naḥmanides: *And so when the eskaton arrives   the messiah will come to the Pope   by command of the Name and will say   "Send out my people that they may serve me"   and then he will have come*

(from an argument between Naḥmanides
and Paolo Christiani   Barcelona, 1264)

This *Book of Witness* is the fourth book of Raziel's explanations . . . until this year he had not composed a book which might be called "prophecy" . . . and in that good year the Name awoke him to go to great Rome   He commanded him in Barcelona   in the year "These" and five thousand [1280] . . . in going he passed

through Trani and was taken captive by goyim   because of slanders
Jews had laid against him   but a miracle was done him   YHVH
aided him   and he was delivered . . . went through Capua . . .
and in the month of Av came to Rome . . . and determined to go
before the Pope the day before Rosh Hashana   And the Pope commanded his guards   while he was in Soriano   a certain city a day's
walk from Rome   that if Raziel should come there to speak with
him in the name of all Jewery   that they should take him immediately   and that he would not see him at all   but that they should
take him out of the city and burn him by fire   and there was the
firewood behind the city's inner wall   but this thing was announced
to Raziel   He paid no attention to the words of the speakers   but
went away by himself   and saw sights   and wrote them   and
made this new book   and called it the *Book of Witness*   it being a
witness between him and the Name who delivered him from the
hands of his enemies   For on the day of his going before the Pope
two mouths spoke to him   and as he entered the outer gate of the
city a messenger came out towards him and told him the news   that
the one who sought his life had died sudden death   instant   in
that very night he was slain   and died   and he was delivered
and then caught in Rome by the Little Brothers   and stayed in
their college "Strength" days [= 28]   and went out on the first day
of Marḥeshvan   and I have written this here to say the praise of the
Holy One Blessed Is He and His miracles and wonders with Raziel
and His faithful servants

H.L.

Ḥayim Vital (Hebrew, 1542–1620)

THE MUSLIM: A DREAM

Friday   full moon in Adar   5355   a Sabbath evening   dreamt that
I was in Jerusalem. A Muslim with a brilliantly white cap came up
to me. He smiled. Salaamed. He placed a hand over my head
& said in a soft but audible voice   "Rise up   o God   & scatter all
thine enemies."   Then Rabbi Yakob Massod led me to the house of
Rabbi Ashkenazi. He rose for me   bowed down   & sat me at his
right side. He took the *Zohar* in his hand & told me   "Let us
study."   There was a passage that he couldn't understand but I explained it. It was a section of the *Zohar Shemot* that tells about a
man who danced for Rabbi Eleazar & so showed him he would enter
Paradise

*

In the dream I thought the Muslim was the prophet Elijah

J.R.

(Hebrew, medieval)

THE RAINBOW CALENDAR OF ISAAC LURIA

. . . & I have set my rainbow in the cloud
(Genesis 9.13.)

NISAN   if you see the rainbow from the east side • an eastern king grows angry with his minister • & if the west • beasts in the field to die • wool be abundant & grapes & lentils bring success :

IYAR   if from the east side • the world stays on its course three years • & if the west side • a western king to turn against his minister • & he will seize his wealth • beasts in the wilderness to die • much rainfall :

SIVAN   if from the east side • heavy sadness for the nations & much rain • & a famine in the land of Persia • & if in the west much wheat throughout the world :

TAMUZ   if from the east side • nations will be destroyed • thereafter peace & quiet in the land • & if the west side • forecast of good things for the poor & destitute :

AV   if from the east side • famine throughout the world & emptiness of pocket & war between the kings of Egypt & Media at the end they will make peace : & if the west side • famine in Media lasts three years • speakers of lies to multiply :

ELUL   if from the east side • war in Persia with the men of India & the men of India succeeding • & if the west side • successes in the villages :

TISHREI   if from the east side • great bounty in Assyria & in Rome • & death will be throughout the world • & if the west • great quarrels break out in the world • slaves to rebel against their masters :

ḤESHVAN   if from the east side • & stars are visible by day this sign shows famine there will be death three years • & if the west side • a certain king to kill another :

KISLEV   if from the east side • wheat in abundance & all sorts of seeds • & it will rain three months • & this foretells a sickness among men • & if the west • a certain king to go to war & to succeed :

TEVET   if from the east side • a king will catch hold of overcome & kill the men who caught him • & the vineyards will succeed • & if the west • fruits will succeed & in Media wars :

SHEVAT   if from the east side • great abundance comes • & a king his princes & his soldiers go to war against a western king • & if the west • fruits will succeed • & in Media many wars :

ADAR   if from the east side • much rain in the desert • & travelers will succeed • & if the west • the rain to multiply to fullness • great sorrow in the deserts

J.R./H.L.

(Yiddish, 17th century)
"1648": FOR COSSACKS

                    bitter times
the cossack Krivno
            in the town of Bar
stood with Lysenko
all those decent people
            set a cross up
            led our brothers
            doomed men   broken boned
            out of a dark pit
            a black grave
Krivno who comforts them
says
            "spoke to your old men
            "your bosses
says it   gives forth a laugh
            "now I speak final words
            "both for my men & you
            "whose wives & children
            "suffer long from
            "hunger   thirst   cold
            "ask you to bow to
            "cross   end blindnesses
            "happily live on earth
Jews answer
            "silence   evil man
            "no other words
            "better you kill us here
            "no change of minds   nay nay
            "mind's bright as sunlight

"evil man   can't work it
"mind knows no other faith
"though we be cut up   burnt
"at stake et cetera
image of terror
follows
o genocide for Holy Name
& leaves a desert
wilderness
strewn with the bones of
Jewish prey

J.R.

Nathan of Gaza (Hebrew, c. 1643–80)
From THE VISION OF RABBI ABRAHAM:
THE BIRTH & CIRCUMSTANCES
OF THE MESSIAH SABBATAI ZEVI

& I Abraham had shut myself in for 40 years had grieved over the
power of the Great Dragon lying in middle of his rivers when *the
voice of my beloved knocketh* saying look a son is born to Mordecai
Zevi in the year 5386 & they will call him Sabbatai Zevi he will con-
quer the Great Dragon take the strength out of the piercing serpent
& the crooked serpent he will be the true messiah :   while I still was
wondering at this vision look a man appeared to me he looked like
polished brass from his loins on down he had the brightness of a
fire from his loins on up was like bdellium transparent like the body
of the sky he called LOOSEN THE KNOTS OF THE DEMONIC
POWERS MAKE WAR AGAINST THEM & PREPARE A REF-

UGE THERE ARE NO PROVISIONS HERE : I fell into a deep sleep then a horror of great darkness over Egypt then a ferret & chameleon appeared & brought a great light *light that hides his power* & a man was there his size was one square cubit & his beard one cubit long his penis was a cubit & a span he held a hammer in his hand & tore up a great mountain ten by six score thousands & the man went up the mountain where a pit was that went down it to the bottom & he fell & fell inside : the man who looked like polished brass said don't you grieve over Messiah's fall for you will see the power of this man only now I couldn't hold my grief in now I fell into a heavy sleep I saw no other vision for a month

*

. . . blessed art thou o lord our god king of the universe who permittest that which is forbidden.

(s.z.)

Isaac Bashevis Singer (Yiddish, b. 1904)

From SATAN IN GORAY   "The Faithful"

. . . From that time on, Goray indulged in every kind of license, becoming more corrupt each day. Assured that every transgression was a rung in the ladder of self-purification and spiritual elevation, the people of Goray sank to the forty-nine Gates of Impurity. Only a few individuals did not join in but stood apart watching Satan dance in the streets.

And the deeds of the Faithful were truly an abomination. It was reported that the sect assembled at a secret meeting place every night; extinguishing the candles, they would lie with each other's wives. Reb Gedaliya was said to have secreted a whore sent him by the sect in Zamość somewhere in his house without the knowledge of his wife, Rechele. A copper cross hung on his breast, under the fringed vest, and an image lay in his breast pocket. At night Lilith and her attendants Namah and Machlot visited him, and they consorted together. Sabbath eve, dressing in scarlet garments and a fez, like a Muslim, he accompanied his disciples to the ruins of the old castle near Goray. There Samael presented himself to them, and they all prostrated themselves together before a clay image. Then they danced in a ring with torches in their hands. Rabbi Joseph de la Reina, the traitor, descended from Mount Seir to join them in the shape of a black dog. Afterward, as the legend went, they would enter the castle vaults and feast on flesh from the living—rending live fowl with their hands, and devouring the meat with the blood. When they had finished feasting, fathers would know their daughters, brothers their sisters, sons their mothers. Nechele, Levi's wife, strolled about unclothed, consorted with a coachman before the eyes of all the company—and of her own husband too. . . .

Goray became a den of robbers, an accursed town. The old residents were afraid to leave their homes, for children, who were also numbered among the Faithful, threw stones at the rival group. The children were particularly spiteful. They placed nails on the prayer-house seats of the old residents, causing them to tear their clothing; they cut the fringes of their prayer shawls, and molested their goats. Some boys even poured a bucket of slop down the chimney of a house and contaminated the vessels and food. The Faithful went so far as to write the government, charging their opponents with disloyalty, and they spilled oil on their goods; they even avenged themselves on small children. A woman who was returning from the bathhouse was ambushed in a back street by some hoodlums who attempted to rape her. She screamed and they ran away.

God's name was everywhere desecrated. In the villages the peasants already complained that the Jews had betrayed their faith and were behaving exactly like gypsies and outlaws. The priests were inciting the masses to a holy war. They foresaw all devout Christians gathering together, sword and spear in hand, to exterminate the Jews, man, woman, and child, so that not a trace should be left of the people of Israel (God save us!).

(Ladino, after 17th century)

4 POEMS FOR SABBATAI ZEVI [SHABTAI TSVI]
THE TRUE MESSIAH AS DRAWN FROM HYMNS
SUNG BY HIS FAITHFUL FOLLOWERS AFTER HIS
CONVERSION TO ISLAM FOR THE GREATER
GLORY OF THE GOD OF ISRAEL:

. . . I am the Lord your God Shabtai Tsvi

1

a glow of true messiah
whose faithful saw joy   light
his rising from the nether depths
spear set on rock
o he was light
was hidden   drowning in the sea
struck the crooked serpent
swallowed oil—was pure
oil of messiah—
day that they stole his clothing
from the sea of blood
then dressed up with his crown
cast lots for it
they called it "purim"
Barzilay his strong disciple crying
crying until night
who brought him clothing from his house
—for gayness to King David's son—

2

. . . .

"mitsrayim"
    the name for Egypt
called it "mitsray yam"
        the boundaries of
                the sea
    once the son of Amram
            opened
    pushed his people thru it
Shabtai the winding serpent
        the winding serpent
    gave us freedom
        the boundaries of the sea he made
                wide as the god
        the son of Amram opened
    Shabtai Messiah no one else
opened his own mouth
        a pen spoke from it
        (instant scripture)
            opened
        the Matronita's GOODNESS
            shown
    extended Torah's days
        already shrunk
once the son of Amram opened

3

was born   the child of life
lit up high mountains
days since he crushed that snake
lit up high mountains

lit up the moon by daylight
redeemer who wore his crown
lit up high mountains
darkness was here no longer
—had not come from holy places—
redeemer showed the way the torah
lit up high mountains
was born   the sun that heals
healed the Shekinah
her wisdom came on us
lit up high mountains
he MY REMEMBRANCE says   I'm faithful
to believers in Zevi Sultan
my belief in him a tree
lit up high mountains
days since he crushed that snake
lit up high mountains
lit up the moon by daylight

4

(Coda)

· · · · · · · ·

Sabbatai is myrrh root
is King David Jesse's son
the fourth leg of the chariot
went down into the sea
fought Samael
the king said   living   being

· · · · · · · ·

opened the jet for us
freed us from cruel commands
expunged all griefs
King Sabbatai Zevi

J.R./H.L.

(Yiddish, traditional)

THE SONG OF THE SEXTON

at dawn going from house to house &
knocking at the shutters chanting:

get up jews
sweet holy jews
get up bow down to god
god is in exile
shekinah is in exile
the people is in exile
get up work for god

David Meltzer (b. 1937)

From THE GOLEM WHEEL

•

E'mes: Truth
Mes: Death

•

Shem ha-me forasch to begin
& to end remove *Shem,*
the life-principle.

•

5340 (1580)

•

in answer to the Rabbi's dream question:

*At Bra Golem Devuk Hakhomer
V'tigzar Zedim Chevel Torfe Yisroel*

(Make a Golem of clay & you will destroy
the entire Jew-baiting community)

•

to the correct form
in accord with the *Zirufim*
in the *Sefer Yetsirah*

the words & numbers,
a meditation of imagination
whose best works are God

with the Rabbi who was song
went two men of fire & water
to the Moldau's banks

there from the 4th element
in the night holding candles
they intoned divine words
to bring forth life

•

Rabbi Judah Loew of Prague
        as Jacob wrestled with God
in himself & for his tribe
        made the golem
to guard Prague Jews from Christian redbeards
        sneaking thru the ghetto
spying for sacred butcher blocks where
        Christ's pure maids were
                beheaded.
        Their virgin pure blood
poured into buckets hidden in the synagogue
        basement &, at Pesach,
passed about in gold goblets,
        drunk as sacrament

        • • •

The Jew in me is the ghost of me
hiding under a stairway

or returning home to a hovel
to find table & chair
wrecked by Golem's fist

bed broken, my black rags
hanging from his teeth.

        •

Goylim, Golem,
what to do?
There is no Golem earth
nor earthly city to rest in.

In the movie
he was played by
Harry Bauer, a German,
who also played Raskolnikov

in another movie I saw when younger (O
I am always younger) in Hollywood
many years ago.

Movies rob you of your birthright,
your tribe denounces you.
Frankenstein, The Mummy
bury their faces behind your mask.

Golem, *goylim,*
what to do?
Vengeance soothes before the act
& after its fact. Then what?
What to do?
Goylim, Golem
what to do?

Golem was without friends
standing at the town gate
stiff from resurrection.

Golem was without a soul
& howled his pain
& stomped on a little boy & girl
who stood beneath him in the rain.

Jacob Frank (Hebrew/Polish, 1726–91)
From THE BOOK OF THE SAYINGS OF THE LORD

[These are some of the sayings of Yankiev Leivitch, Yakov ben
Lev, who called himself Yakov Frank and whom some called Wise
Jacob. Frank was a creature of Podolia, Turkey, Poland-in-its-dis-
integration. He traveled. His father was a traveling preacher. Frank
was a peddler too and spoke everybody's language: Balkan,
Turkish, Yiddish, Polish, Ladino, with quotations, citations, and
language play from Hebrew and Aramaic. He joined up with Sabbateans, followers of the messianic movement begun by Shabtai Zvi
and Nathan of Gaza, continued through Barukhya, and temporarily
short one messiah. With them, he turned against the Talmud, into
the Zohar, and out through the Sabbatean pore. He added some
things to the movement: a new emphasis on the Virgin, a passage
through Christianity, after the passage through Islam which Shabtai/
Nathan originated, on the way to Esau. Perhaps more sex. He
became a messiah to thousands of Jews. —H.L.]

It is in your ancient books that there is an island hidden in the
sea & that by it a very great ship waits full of weapons & on that
island live kabbalistic Jews awe-filled & devoted & every month
they take boats out to the great ship to ask & seek if the time has
come for them to go out to the four corners of the world to wage
war On that same island there is a great & very fearful mountain
that no man can ascend & on the mountain there is a golden
staff A strange man will come & strike the ship & then the hour
will have come to begin the war

I have told you things you regarded as folly & ignorance But see
it is well-known: when Italian nuts are gathered the outer shell is
green & bitter & stains the hand Then one comes to the center

I must wipe out your names Even your sons will not be called
by your names I give you new names you & your sons

There is no other people in the whole world has gone as bad as
the Jews . . . They're like snakes & vipers no love no friendship
   no peace among them only hate and strife I have brought you
out from the midst of the Jews so that you might not learn to do as
they do

My uncle Yakov told me that when I was a 2-year-old & he would
take me to his bed I would keep him up till he said "Good night"
with me to all the creatures: to big spiders & little ones to all the
snakes to the animals in the woods to the birds I said "Good
night" to all of them

When I was little I saw a children's book All the customs were
written in it & there were different pictures like pharaoh washing in children's blood & so forth We children took a knife & began
piercing & gashing not only what was bad but everything that was
good as well until we made that book a sieve

I had a little band of peasants' sons We went to the synagogue
and stole the shofar From there we went to the river & blew the
shofar like they do in the synagogue

In Sniatyn I saw that the beadle was accustomed to go from
house to house & would rap three times with the hammer in his
hand to announce penitence So I gave him a few coins & he gave
me the hammer I got up at midnight & went from house to house
   from Jews to peasants from peasants to palaces even to a well-
known nobleman & to Catholic priests & to all the inhabitants of the
city & woke them from their sleep They were alarmed & all of them
got up & called out in a loud voice "What do you want?" & I answered them "Arise for penitence!" & they ran after me & I fled &
I rapped twice on a Jewish gate & they woke up & called "Blessed is
the True Judge" & asked me "Who died?"

When I saw the sight it seemed to me I heard a voice call "Go &
lead Jacob the Wise to the Chambers & when you bring him to the
First Chamber I warn you the command is upon you to open all
the windows & doors before him" So there I was flying in the

wind & on my right & left were two virgins the like of whose beauty has never been seen   In those chambers I saw mostly women & Virgins   in a few of them there were groups of teachers & students & when I had heard just one word of their discourse I immediately understood everything they intended to say   & there were many of these Chambers & in the last I saw the First (I mean Shabtai Zvi) seated as well   like a teacher with his students   wearing the clothes of a Frank   & he turned to me & asked "Are you this Jacob the Wise? I have heard about you   that you're a hero & have soul   I too went to the place you're going   but I don't have the strength to go on   If you want to   be strong!   & the Name will help you   Many Fathers have taken this burden on & failed"

& there he showed me through the window a depth like the Black Sea covered in a fearsome dark   & to the side of the depth I saw a great mountain   reaching up into the heart of the sky   & I called out

> "Come what may!
> I'm going!
> God help me!"

Another time   I came to the synagogue in Salonika where around 1200 well-to-do Jews were gathered   & the gabbai called men up to the Torah   "Let such-&-such get up" according to the custom of the place   & I called out in a loud voice "Don't a single one of you dare come up to the Torah   or I'll kill him & lay him waste right here!"

When they heard this awful impudence all of them became disturbed & began to grumble & mutter against me

So then I grabbed the lectern in front of me & warned them again that I would murder any man who moved up to the Torah with the lectern & then I took the scroll of the Torah & sat on it . . .

& the Jews were completely terrified & fled from the synagogue

Today you make fun of me   but I tell you that the number of Jews that will follow me will be as great as the hairs on your heads

Since I could find no lodging I was forced to curl up in sewers & caves & to spend the night lying in refuse   I bore all this & suffered it on account of my love for the Name   to do His will

. . . but the sea would not take me & vomited me up on to the dry land

I will go & I will enter Poland   for the place of the Ascent is in Poland   There a building will be built   more beautiful than man has seen since the world was created

There is a certain tree whose branches are spread out behind the wall which surrounds it   & whoever looks at the wall from the outside seems to see many trees   But he who sees from behind the fence knows that there is no more than one tree there   So we must know & desire one tree & not seek many trees

When the water is turbid it is good to catch fish   & so when the world is filled with bloodshed we will be able to hunt the thing that belongs to us

A certain man had a pearl without flaw   & traveled from city to city seeking an artisan who could pierce the pearl & not ruin it promising a great wage to the one who would do it   & no artisan would take upon himself to do this craft   & this man even tried to pay the greatest of the artisans a thousand gold pieces   but he didn't want it   & so this man didn't know what to do with his pearl & went to the artisan's helper when the artisan was not at home   & not telling the whole story   took out the pearl & gave it to him & said   "Take it & put a hole in it & I'll pay you good money"   & the helper took the pearl & pierced it fearlessly   & the man paid him his wage & went his way joyful   So is my case   Many wisemen wished to pierce & were unable because they feared   But I was chosen to make the Great Repair & diminish the Shard because I am ignorant   & I will pierce & I will do what is necessary

Since the world was being newly made there has been no man could recognize the true God   His Name is not yet known   & no man has uncovered the place of His Glory   But there is much of the Godhead in this world & Its Aspects reveal Themselves in the images of creatures & They see & are not seen

. . . the Shekhina . . . the Virgin . . . most beautiful of women

You see my daughter   Know that she is a queen!   But do not
think that it is on account of her beauty we call her "queen"
   No!   She is really a queen   In reality

This world is the Gate of Shells   Every grain has a shell that en-
closes it   You see that the whole world calls out "Eternal Virgin!"
says that she is the Redeemer & Savior   She has suffered alongside
Him since the beginning & has had no place of rest   & has gone wandering with Him & has fled with Him to Egypt   She comes before
the fruit which will come into the world soon   that all the kings of
the world will bow to

when you hear that I'm in great distress & that the people walking
behind me are in trouble & being chased from place to place & are
without bread or clothes   know that it's God leading us

Eve tells me that there's a treasure in the mountain   six hundred
million pieces of gold the Catholic priests know nothing of   & I
wanted to order you to go to a certain cave near Czestochowa   &
there you'd have found six hundred tailors sewing clothes   & on
every garment gold coins would be attached so loosely that when one
wearing them passed through the streets gold coins would fall off   &
the people would come running from right & left to gather the
coins   & I would have ordered that the clothes be made ready &
the carriages before we left the prison   but we would have taken
nothing from the treasure & only would have divided it out among
the believers according to their needs   & when we left the prison
I would have been sitting with her in the carriage & no man
would've seen her but me & you   & as we passed through the streets
of Warsaw the gold would've fallen left & right   & all the people of
Warsaw would've been gathering up the gold   & you would've called
out in a mighty voice "Long live the King!"   & all the lords &
people would've called "Here is our King!"

One day he asked those who know the secrets   Issakhar & Mor-
dekhai   to explain Shabtai Zvi's death   The men said to him

> Shabtai Zvi came to taste everything in the world
> So of course
> he had to taste the bitterness of death

But he said

> The answer is good
> But if he came to taste it all
> why did he not taste the sweetness
> of rule & reign

I will teach you the manners of kingship for I want to give a crown to every one of you

In a dream in Czestochowa I saw the goddess who came to me appearing as a beautiful virgin & I brought you before Her & when you came you turned back at the door & two of you fell to the earth & when they came back again She leaned Her head away from one of them completely & from the other only partially & for this reason I have not rejected him completely Be unified from now on & heed me perhaps the salvation will come again I have brought you to the nations it's a custom of theirs to plow in order to seed & now that you've spread scandal & revealed this secret to the nations you have driven me out of the inheritance of the Name in Poland

I tell you that all the Jews are in big trouble now because they wait for the coming of the Redeemer & not the coming of the Maiden Look upon the peoples how they dwell peaceably in their possessions for they trust their Maiden who is only the reflection of the image of our Maiden

When people change their faith what's it like? Like pouring oil from cruse to cruse Thus I left the faith of Ishmael & entered the Christian faith & hid it from no man that I was previously of Ishmaelite faith The day will yet come when I return to it again & then my holy name will be revealed to all the world

When the Name comes to my aid I will buy a beautiful house & fill it with beautiful furnishings & set special rooms apart for my daughter & dress her in queenly robes & precious jewels & I will not permit any man to come near her only I myself will take pleasure in her & I'll drink & eat with her & only when gentile guests come will I invite them to eat with her too & I'll sit with her day & night & tell her what I know so she will come to understand the greatness of our faith   For until today I have not said even one thing about it to her   It's in my mind to raise her up to the status of a man / an adam so everything that's happened to me will happen to her

Every man is bound & tied to his fortune by a strand   & there's no difference between man & man except that one is bound to his fortune by a cotton thread while he whose fortune is great is bound to it by a golden thread

I wanted to take you out from under the name Israel   for this name has no good fortune   & I wanted to bind you to the thread of gold   But what can I do if you entangle yourselves in the thread of cotton?

You have not yet entered into the knowledge for the knowledge is stored away   & the meaning of the word "knowledge" is "knowing" : "Know before whom you stand!"   If you'd already come into that knowledge then no sin could have caught you nor no illness   no wound   pox or death   & a man must draw near & enter this knowledge in purity & light & cast off from himself the yoke of all the evil laws & faiths & customs   & must also stand in higher degree regarding the good qualities than other men   & I have yet to find this in you   & therefore I have brought you simply to conversion   & I have accompanied you myself

In a dream I saw the Christian lawmaker sitting   & around him Catholic priests   by a fountain of good pure water   & when I looked closely I saw that the fountain flowed out from there & came to me

The soul has a man's form & has been hidden in a secret place since the creation of the world   & there has not yet been a man with a soul in him   Even the Holy Fathers & Jacob our Father that was greater than all of them & all the great ones & holy ones had no souls   For there is in every man an inner lack   & he does not feel his lack   & on account of this we wear ourselves out trying to reach to the degree of whole man   for only the whole man will be fit for a soul to be in him   The Name   who is altogether good cannot come into this world which has an end   & on account of this we are obliged to try & turn everything into dust & ashes

I told you: be wary of the cross for the way of the cross goes here & here & divides into four ways & it's possible to make a mistake

I say to you that even if all the kings of all the nations come to me it is nothing in my eyes My sole intent & desire is that the Jews come to me The Jews are destined to come to me in multitudes No rank of the camp will be less than ten thousand
Every troop will have its own flag in its own colors the black flag & the blue will come last On the flags new things will be revealed & seen & the world is destined to come to me & say what they saw on the flags You are invited to come under my flag because we will be marching towards a known thing with this flag & therefore I have called you my brothers because you're destined to be my flag bearers & I too will carry the flag though my hands are heavy I say to you : when these Jews come you must go out to meet them humbly & meekly your heads & eyes to the ground
& then you will come to know what the Name has done in His world

H.L.

F. T. Prince (b. 1912)

From DRYPOINTS OF THE HASIDIM   "The Baal Shem"

1

To believe is above all to be in love,
And suffer as men do who are in love.

  The story has it that one day
One Friday, when the zaddik makes
  His self-examination
                        a disciple found the Besht

So emptied of himself and crushed, in darkness
And dereliction
                    the last breath
Of life had almost left him:

And was so terrified all he could say
Was
    'My master and my teacher . . .'

But those words were enough
To reach his heart and bring it back from death.

2

There you have everything
                            that name
A kind of joy surrounding it,
    The Baal Shem Tov.

The Master of the Good Name,
    A healer in the name of God

A poor man and not learned;
    But he could overcome division
Between clean and unclean
                        the holy sparks
    And evil urge within a man:

    'The process lies in giving shape
To formless forces, dragons, *kelipoth* . . .'

And he could shake the worlds in prayer,
                                that could be seen
When wheat-grains trembled, trembled in an open sack
    And water in a jug

And he could offer them the prize
    Of heart-prayer, with the sudden burst of light—
Fire light honey light—
    And silent music and invisible eyes
That shut the eyes of the mind and yet give sight.

3

With that they have new thoughts of good and evil,
   And evil as cast or withered good
                           that come
After the deep wound dealt by that deceiver
   Sabbatai Zevi
             —Who also had belonged
Like all such prophets and themselves
                     to 'the last times'
Of impiety and confusion,
   And had brought about the fall
Of many in Israel whom he told to sin
   Freely, because the last times were at hand.

                   Yet so it was
   That after he had damned himself and them,
Israel ben Eliezer the Baal Shem
   Could say
          'In evil also we find good':

'Torah the seed of justice
   Like the sun giving light
Builds upon evil,
            and the powers of evil
Are but a throne for good'

   He also said
         'The man who sins
Burns the whole Torah in the eyes of God.
   But we should say
         It is enough for me

'*If he has this or that good quality*'

4

   For if the holy sparks in things
Are separated from God, so are the Jews:

Everything is in exile,
                                  everything will return
Because everything desires to be redeemed—
    Everything in the world and worldliness—

    Not to be emptied of itself or worldliness
But to be hallowed in the *kawannoth*.

                                  And Israel

Seeming helpless in dispersal
                              soiled
    And failing of the Law and prayer
Can be that suffering consciousness,

And bid for the return of all
                              the 'turning'

    (And Bunam in that stinking room
At Danzig, where he had turned in to pray
    Went pale and shrank and turned away

But turned back, for he said
                              'The very walls

'Would arraign God, if I rejected them')

Howard Schwartz (b. 1945)
RABBI NACHMAN'S DREAM

In my dream I woke up in a forest. The forest was boundless; I wanted to return. One of you came to me and said: *This is the forest you have forgotten. It is so long, it is infinite. Nothing could be named until you found your way back to this forest.* And one of you showed me the way to a garden. The distance was endless; I wanted to turn back. And one of you took me aside and said: *Without you the letters inscribed in every scroll inside every Ark were separated from the spirit that animates them like the spirit that inhabits a body, and the words on the scroll had no more meaning to us than the languages of the builders of the Tower of Babel, after they had lost the right to comprehend the holy tongue.* And one of you brought me a torch and said: *This torch has been handed down from father to son; its light alone has saved us from total darkness; its flame has never gone out.* And I took the torch, and its flame rose up into Heaven.

Denise Levertov (b. 1924)
ILLUSTRIOUS ANCESTORS

The Rav
of Northern White Russia declined,
in his youth, to learn the
language of birds, because
the extraneous did not interest him; nevertheless
when he grew old it was found
he understood them anyway, having
listened well, and as it is said, 'prayed
                    with the bench and the floor.' He used
what was at hand—as did
Angel Jones of Mold, whose meditations
were sewn into coats and britches.
                    Well, I would like to make,
thinking some line still taut between me and them,
poems direct as what the birds said,
hard as a floor, sound as a bench,
mysterious as the silence when the tailor
would pause with his needle in the air.

(Yiddish, traditional)

FIVE FOR THE REBBE

1

The rebbe went dancing
& lost all he had
When his hasidim found it
he gave them a sign
Then he took it all back

2

The rebbe was a good old boy
when he drank a toast
all his hasidim used to fight
to catch the droppings

3

When the rebbe dances
the walls dance with him
the hasidim clap hands
They clap hands when the rebbe dances

4

The rebbe sits & sweats
& the shekinah hovers over him
Then the hasidim sing & dance & jump
They love the way the rebbe looks

5

days of messiah
king   the rebbe
eldest
wears his hair long

like a hermit
sweet bread   buns
grow on the trees
with corn cob pipes
for branches
& tobacco leaves
hasidim can light up on
not in prayer huts
made of clay brick
but built with
stews & noodle puddings
whiskey fountains
in the rebbe's kitchen
Nebukhadnezzar
come himself from Babylon
into Yerushelayim
crying to the rebbe
life   life
all that they drink is life

J.R.

*

"All rabbis look like savages," Langer said. (F. Kafka)

Isaac Babel (Russian, 1894–c. 1939)

THE CEMETERY AT KOZIN

The cemetery of a little Jewish town. Assyria and all the mysterious stagnation of the East, over those weed-grown plains of Volhynia.

Carved gray stones with inscriptions three centuries old. Crude high-reliefs hewn out in the granite. Lambs and fishes depicted above a skull, and Rabbis in fur caps—Rabbis girt round their narrow loins with leather belts. Below their eyeless faces the rippling stone line of their curly beards. To one side, beneath a lightning-shattered oak, stands the burial vault of the Rabbi Azrael, slain by the Cossacks of Bogdan Khmelnitsky. Four generations lie buried in that vault that is as lowly as a water-carrier's dwelling; and the memorial stone, all overgrown with green, sings of them with the eloquence of a Bedouin's prayer.

"Azrael son of Ananias, Jehova's mouthpiece.

"Elijah son of Azrael, brain that struggled single-handed with oblivion.

"Wolff son of Elijah, prince robbed from the Torah in his nineteenth spring.

"Judah son of Wolff, Rabbi of Cracow and Prague.

"O death, O covetous one, O greedy thief, why couldst thou not have spared us, just for once?"

Rajzel Zychlinska (Yiddish, b. 1910)
POOR PEOPLE

Being poor has one color
Everywhere.
Poor people walk over the earth silently
Speaking to the worms.
From beneath all the rocks
Death looks at them
And calls.

LUCY S. DAWIDOWICZ & FLORENCE VICTOR

Peretz Markish (Yiddish, 1895–1952)
TWO POEMS

1

I don't know whether I'm at home
or homeless.
            I'm running, my shirt
unbuttons, no bounds, nobody
holds me, no beginning,
no end

my body is foam
smelling of wind

Now

is my name. I spread my arms, my hands
pierce the extremes
of what is. I'm letting my eyes roam around
and do their drinking from the foundations
of the world

eyes wild, shirt ballooning,
my hands separated by the world, I don't know
if I have a home
or have a homelessness,
or am a beginning or an end

2

I won't put on a light all night
the wall disappears in tears and quiet
from the blue dovecot of my prayed-out face

ripped out of my eyes, the dove,
by itself, and gone.
                    A rope
circles my head. My head is the shame
under a rope. And my hands, my cheated hands . . .

loneliness, I'll make up a bed for us
on the threshold. Would you
caress me? if you would caress me, caress
me

will the dove come back in the morning?
she will. I'll kiss you, world, your fingers,
and close my eyes
and splash out
your blue secret.
                    Thank you, God.

the wild dove ripped itself
from my eyes. It flew. Somewhere my walls

walked quietly off.
and where did you hide your hands?

I won't put on a light all night
in the blue dovecot of my mourned-out face.

ARMAND SCHWERNER

(Anonymous, Yiddish)

ZARITSKY'S CHILDREN, & OTHER POEMS
FOR THE RICH

1

Zaritsky with 10 children
10 children
the rest of us who sweat
to feed them
woe o woe o wind
sweet children
locked in factories
o worse off than his dog

2

derision of the working class
the poor
what was a working girl to them
o money   money's
wisdom in this world
past all reproach

3

o mother o mother
cat's licking the butter
hen's laying eggs
bride's got a veil
groom wears a prayer-shawl
poor man stays poor
children suck fingers
women die starving

4

bosses with hearts of stone
lived in distrust of
workers   a poor working man
would drink a little whiskey
called him a drunkard
to his face
            cheap whiskey was
their wine   a golden goblet
is no cup
a working man's no master
in his house
o fatherer of worlds
where does it end?

5

A POEM FOR MILLIONAIRES

viz Rothschild   face of gold
conspicuous consumer
died like any beggar
once went to his vault
for money   speculation
trapped inside
all doors were closing on him
seven days of hunger   sucked

blood from his own fingers
Rothschild   Rothschild
strutted before kings
he said he couldn't die
of hunger
ended like the rest
he lies there
broken into pieces
bag of bones

J.R.

*

Samuel said, & some say, Rav Joseph: Poverty is becoming to Jews, like a red halter on a white horse.

Rochelle Owens (b. 1936)

THE VOLUMINOUS AGONY OF KARL MARX

Izzy sells out the workers party!
I'm the prophet! The dreamer!
The mystic! The plumber! The plumber
of fat sweet sweet revolution!
I love my family! I want them to laugh!
I have all the perception & intelligence
to write the book on economics!
I will sit—I will sit on my boils
in the British Museum & write on economics!
I am the coming judgment! Economics!
My veins are religious with economics!

Who is Karl Marx! I am Karl Marx!
I hate the passage of time without revolution!
I want to cheat the day & the night!
Yahweh! Yahweh! I am a fish sticking out
of the hand of God! I would like a new
gold watch for Christmas! Yahweh! Yahweh!
I have pain! I have pain! I am abused by
historical forces! Revolution which is past
& revolution which is to come! Yahweh!
Let me play Karl Marx! Let me play a workman!
I have got big calluses! Boils! Calluses! Boils!
Calluses! Yahweh! I do a jig for thee!
I have a big izzy in my pants—let me hang
it out for thee! Give me back my foreskin,
Yahweh! I have heard of the Socialist Party!
I've never heard of the Socialist Party!
Look in my eyes! Do you see politics in my eyes!
Or economics! Rage! Rage & pain! Yahweh! Yahweh!
You gave me boils! A family to support.
Six mouths to fill up with groats & milk!
Hate is stuffed into me with my Jewish mother's
milk! I want to write the philosophy that will
burn down all other philosophies! I want to
kill all those who see ideas! Not economy!
Yahweh! Yahweh! Am I right! Yahweh! Yahweh!
Give me the weapon! Give me the weapon that
will kill! Give me the force! Give me the force!
Give me the force to set my teeth on edge &
eat fire! Please! Please let me be able
to sit down like a man should—without pain!
Please let me be able to write the book! Please
take away the filthy boils! Yahweh! Yahweh!
You piss-stink filthy Babylonesch bastard
are you powerless to heal!

Sholem Aleichem (Yiddish, 1859–1916)

A LULLABY FOR TSARS

*Scene : Petersburg. Tsar Nicholas rocking the infant
prince to sleep*

sleep sleep o beautiful child
o Tsar's heir
will grow up to have a sack of money
cities   villages   be wiser
than your father   me   o king of kings
me with a kingdom called Siberia
will have inns & prisons
endless churches   gendarmes   cossacks   guards outside your door
can whip & beat a man's flesh without tiring
o thou sweet Tsar's heir have no terrors
of Japan he thinks that I'm a fool but Russia
lives still still a Tsar is needed
o mad socialists who think they can abuse us
no no we'll shoot them torture them
pretend to constitutions yes we'll throw a bone
a fig (a finger) let the tears
& blood flow o thou my Tsar's heir only
knowing that you're well
spite of the howlers
journalists & poets singing songs
of what?
even the bombs exploding there
are old   no news
is good news in the end
we'll catch them beat them may even string them up
by ones o Tsar's heir
clubs & knouts & police & spies
are everywhere
fill up my kingdom

J.R.

Harry Lieberman & Roger Welch

From GINIVISHOV, POLAND—1885: MEMORY MAP

[The following are excerpts from an interview with Harry Lieberman, age 96, made on September 29, 1973, at the John Gibson Gallery in New York. The artist asked him to describe his childhood home (which was Ginivishov, Poland) as he remembered it from 1885. A map was then created from his memory. This work was one of four Welch created for his exhibition at the Gibson Gallery in September–October 1973.]

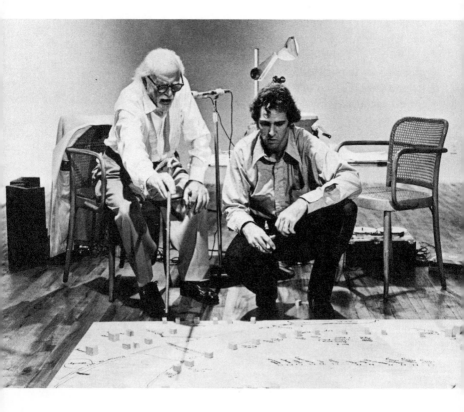

HARRY LIEBERMAN: "I want to call your attention. My ears are 96 years old. You're used to talking very low, but to me, you have to talk very loud."

ROGER WELCH: "O.K. . . . This is the top of the hill?"

H.L.: "Yes, this is the top of the hill. The fact is, the whole town is built on the top of the hill . . . the whole town."

R.W.: "But then the synagogue is at the bottom?"

H.L.: "The synagogue is in the bottom. And the reason is, let me explain it to you. The reason that the synagogue is in the bottom is —King David has got it in his book, 'In the depth of the space, I am praying.' That's the reason most of the Jews in the old country made the synagogues in the bottom."

R.W.: "Yes."

H.L.: "Understand? And in America, it's different. In America everything is on the *top!*"

*

H.L.: "Now let me say it in plain words. Mostly 99% is Jewish people in the whole village all around. See? When it's coming to the bottom, it is mostly the Gentile people and the poor people who have no business. They're living in the bottom around here."

R.W.: "Yes, so let's see, I would like to make another sketch."

H.L.: "What would this be?"

R.W.: "Here would be the village and the market."

H.L.: "And this will be the bottom?"

R.W.: "Yes."

H.L.: "Well, in the bottom . . . in here . . . you will make the

GINIVISHOV, POLAND — 1885

JEWISH HOUSES

GOATS SHEEP CHICKENS COWS GOATS CHICKENS SHEEP COWS GOATS CHICKENS SHEEP SHEEP COWS CHICKENS

DIRT ROAD

GENTILE HOUSE

WAGONS

CHICKENS GEESE

SALOON LEATHER GOODS METAL IRON GOODS

WAGONS

GENTILE HOMES

JEWISH HOMES

DIRT ROAD

STANDS

MEN'S CLOTHING WOMEN'S CLOTHING SHEEPSKIN CLOTHING PEASANT HATS HATS SHOES CANDY LACE

STANDS

NEEDLE CUTTING BUTTONS SCARFS SMALL REMNANTS BUTTONS LACE CANDY

GENTILE HOMES

JEWISH HOMES

PINCUS-JACOB WHEAT MERCHANT TERNE HOME PIECE GOODS STORE MERCHAL VADES DAIRY STORE STAND FOR SELLING CAPS AARON PINCUS-JACOB GENERAL MERCHANDISE STORE PIECE GOODS STORE MOYSHE KAKES PIECE GOODS STORE SHYRAN KOSZAK PIECE GOODS STORE

TOP OF HILL

DIRT ROAD

STARCH TANKS BARN

PATH

BOTTOM OF HILL

RABBI'S HOME

CURING TANKS TANNERY

GENTILE HOMES

LAKE

Ginivishov, Poland – 1885
Drawn from Harry Lieberman's
description – Sept. 29, 1973

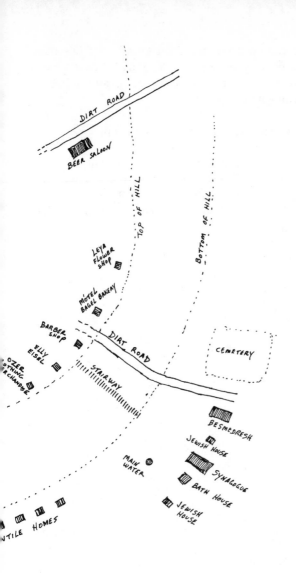

DIRT ROAD

BEER SALOON

TOP OF HILL

BOTTOM OF HILL

LEYA
FLOWER
SHOP

MOTEL
BAGEL BAKERY

BARBER
SHOP

DIRT ROAD

CEMETERY

OZER
CLOTHING
MERCHANDSE

ELLY
EISEL

STAIRWAY

BESMEDRESH

JEWISH HOUSE

MAIN
WATER

SYNAGOGUE

BATH HOUSE

JEWISH
HOUSE

NTILE HOMES

Roger Welch
September, 1973

place where they are getting the water. You know what this place usually is in the old country? A square. You understand what I mean? This is a square with a rope hanging down and a bucket, and the people are coming here to get the water."

R.W.: "That was right down here at the bottom of the hill?"

H.L.: "Yes, everything is down at the bottom of the hill. Now remember, I'm talking about a Jewish town. They got a synagogue, they got a Besmedresh, you know what I mean? Then they got a burying place where they bury people. All the Jewish people had one and the Gentile people had one."

R.W.: "Yes."

H.L.: "This is what consisted of the town."

Richard Kostelanetz (b. 1940)

From THE EAST VILLAGE 1970–1971

SECOND AVENUE

An Outhouse shoeshine stand

306 East Village Astrology Service

Below-street Hammockmaster

Much audible music, especially into the night.

Much mess on the streets, because no group feels obliged to clean, despite attempts to organize block unity.

Several investments lost trying to establish small business on this busy corner.

"Progress" → from hip to Ukrainian

The stylish wooden facade of the Cauldron, the tastiest and most congenial of the neighborhood's macrobiotics.

Henry H. Perlmutter
310
Repair Service

"It's better, and safer than before"

6th St. Block Association

Shah Bagh Indian Restaurant

Makitten Trucking 322 East Sixth St

Houses approximately similar in height, width and in their street-level facade, through two remodeled brown-stones, one a German Lutheran Church.

House, spread at night, occasionally sponsoring street sales.

Plants visible in windows.

Yossing

Yossing Bells

Community Synagogue Center

"Holy Mother o' God! Will yiz!"
"Wot?"
"There's a guy laying there! Burrhnin!"
"Naw! Where!"
"Gawd damn the winder!"
"It's on Tent Street! Look!"
"Oy! Oy Vai! Oy Vai! Oy Vai!"
"Git a Cop!"
"An embillance - go cull-oy!"
"Don't touch 'im!"
"Bambino! Madre Mia!"
"Mary. It's jus' a kid!"
"Helftz! Helftz! Helftz!
    Yeedin! Rotivit!"
— Henry Roth, Call It Sleep (1935)

SIXTH STREET

Bricklayers Tenderers 318

Local No.104 Marijka's Beauty Salon 320 E. 6th St.

Tambro Club (elderly gamblers)

Ukrainian grocer, whose living quarters are visible, through his store's back door.

Arunachala Ashrama Bhagavam Sri Ramana Maharshi Center, Inc.

Childcare under Cars parked

Cats

Barricaded liquor store 331

Wipe-Repairs

American Bar + Grill N. Shupak 334 Billiard Tables
"No Public Telephone"

Rahssed Jeweler

One psychedelic house-facade

A heavily bar.

SIXTH STREET

FIRST AVENUE

Louis Zukofsky (b. 1904)

From "A-12"

There is too much air in the air.
Too many stars too high.
A spring mattress pronouncedly spring
This is a "fall to" table, it leans
From New England, not Manhattan.
When I sit down to eat, my father drowses.
This is a "fall to" bench-trestle
It leans to the table.
My guest Henry (masculine)
What a face has the great American novelist
It says: Fie! Nancy, fiance.
I have just met him on Rutgers Street, New York
Henry James, Jr.,
Opposite what stood out in my youth
As a frightening
Copy of a Norman church in red brick
Half a square block, if I recall,
Faced with a prospect of fire escapes—
Practically where I was born.
Breathing quite affectively in the mind
Ready to chance the sea of conversation

And unshamefacedly—it has been like a warm day—
The look of a shaven Chassid,
Were it possible to either him or Chassid,
Takes an impressed step forward
Pleased, not ominous in behalf of the blind or the publicist—
Said the Chassid:
If you do not, Lord, yet wish to redeem
Israel, at least redeem the Gentiles.

I cannot be too grateful for what you did for Rutgers Street
(Or for Baltimore, "That cheerful little city of the dead")
You went down-town once
At that no beard shaking the head

    —Let me go, the dawn is on us
    —No, not until you bless me first
    —Your name?
And the sun rose (chaos to come)
And he halted.
And once before, toward Haran
Lighted upon a certain place
And stayed there, the sun had set.
Stones for pillows.
He dreamed
There were angels going up and down a ladder.
Standing over him a Voice:
—I will give you the land where you sleep on stone,
Seed the dust of the earth.
Blest. And in you everybody—
        west, east, north, south.
And awoke afraid
—How dreadful is this place
None other but His—the gate to Him.
Said: Keep me in the way I go
With bread,
A coat to put on—
To come back to my father—

In peace
200-year spruce at least
For a fiddle for Paul:
Save
The heart of the wood so to speak
And who belongs to it.
Paul to Paul,
Recall surely,
Carved, not the chips of the process,
Whence are the stems?
He sang sometimes, my son,

When we let him talk,
A chance lilt,
After prayers—
A shred, a repeated word, his whole world—
As, like Bottom,
You might blunder on *tumblesalt*
For *somersault,* Paul.
"They sang this way in deep Russia"
He'd say and carry the notes
Recalling the years
Fly. Where stemmed
The Jew among strangers?
As the hummingbird
Can fly backwards
Also forwards—
How else could it keep going?
Speech moved to sing
To echo the stranger
A tear in an eye
The quick hand wiped off—
Casually:
"I loved to hear them."

As I love:
My poetics.
"Little fish," he grieved
For his wife.
He prayed to the full moon
Over the prow
Alone on that trip
Not seasick.
He returned
For a last look
At Most
After the fire.
His boy wept
And would not let him go.
But he kissed and kissed him and crossed

The Atlantic again alone
This time to
Bring the family over.
What did he not do?
He had kept dogs
Before he rolled logs
On the Niemen.
He swam
Dogpaddle
(Dexter, Paracelsus!)
What a blessing:
He saw Rabbi
Yizchok Elchonon
Walking
On the wharf
In Kovno.
The miracle of his first job
On the lower East Side:
Six years night watchman
In a men's shop
Where by day he pressed pants
Every crease a blade
The irons weighed
At least twenty pounds
But moved both of them
Six days a week
From six in the morning
To nine, sometimes eleven at night,
Or midnight;
Except Fridays
When he left, enough time before sunset
Margolis begrudged.
His own business
My father told Margolis
Is to keep Sabbath.

"Sleep," he prayed
For his dead.
Sabbath.

Moses released the horse
For one day from his harness
So that a man might keep pace.

A shop bench his bed,
He rose rested at four.
Half the free night
Befriended the mice:
Singing Psalms
As they listened.
A day's meal
A slice of bread
And an apple,
The evenings
What matter?
His boots shone.
Gone and out of fashion
His beard you stroked, Paul,
With the Sabbath Prince Albert.
I never saw more beautiful fingers
Used to lift bootstraps.
A beard that won over
A jeering Italian
Who wanted to pluck it—
With the love
His dark brown eyes
Always found in others.
Everybody loves Reb Pinchos
Because he loves everybody,
How many strangers—
He knew so many—
Said that to me
Every Sabbath
He took me—
I was a small boy—
To the birdstore-window to see
The blue-and-yellow Polly
The cardinal, the
Orchard oriole.

Everybody loved Reb Pinchos
Because he loved everybody.
Simple.
You must, myself,
As father of Nicomachus
Say very little
Except: such were his actions.

Aleph Katz (Yiddish, 1898–1969)
BOWERY MOTIFS

1

Dust and dirt,
Bread begged for,
A dead life.

A cursed blessing,
Broken world,
Stink of money.

Man a mistake,
A ghost of lice,
Fear of mice.

An outraged city
Deafens a secret,
And laughs at God.

The mountain is high,
And the avid merchant stingy:
The market is full of buyers,
And the diver brings back few pearls.

The shadow strangles,
The glance gulps down
and dies.
The way is forbidden,
Blocked.

Wishes are trampled;
The heart, a dead body.
Alone, one surrenders and waits, trembling,
For a miracle.

JAMES WRIGHT

Arthur "Dutch Schultz" Flegenheimer (d. 1935)

From THE LAST WORDS OF DUTCH SCHULTZ

Oh, stop it! Stop it! . . . Oh, Oh, Oh, Sure, sure, Mamma, etc.

1

Please, you know me. Oh, Louie, didn't I give you my door bell? Everything you got, the whole bill. And did you come for your rest in the doctor's office, sir? Yes, I can see that. Your son-in-law, and he isn't liked, is he? Harry, does he behave? No; don't you scare me; my friends think I do a better job. Oh, police are looking for you all over; please be instrumental in letting us know. That wouldn't be here; they are Englishmen and they are a type I don't know who is best, they or us. Oh, sir, and get the doll a roofing. Please. You can play jacks, and girls do that with a soft ball and do tricks with it. Please; I may take all events into consideration; no, no. And it is no; it is confused and it says no; a boy has never wept . . . nor dashed a thousand kim. . . .

2

Two thousand; come on, get some money in that treasury; we need it; come on, please get it; I can't tell you to. You are telling the truth, aren't you, Mr. Harris. That is not what you have in the book. Oh, yes I have. Oh, please, warden. Please. What am I going to do for money. How is that; how do you like that? Please put me up on my feet, at once. Thank you, Sam, you are a boiled man; I do it because you ask me to. Did you hear me? I would hear it, the Circuit Court would hear it, and the Supreme Court might hear it. Come on, pull me up sir. All right. Cam Davis. Oh, please reply. N.R.A. If that ain't the payoff. Please crack down on the Chinaman's friends and Hitler's commander. All right, I am sore and I am going up and I am going to give you honey if I can. Look out. We broke that up. Mother is the best bet and don't let Satan draw you too fast.

3

I know what I am doing here with my collection of papers, for crying out loud. It isn't worth a nickel to two guys like you or me, but to a collector it is worth a fortune; it is priceless. I am going to turn it over to. . . . Turn your back to me, please, Henry. I am so sick now. The police are getting many complaints. Look out. Hey, Jack; hello Jack. Jack, mamma. I want that G-note. Look out, for Jimmie Valentine, for he is an old pal of mine. Come on, Jim, come on Jimmie; oh, thanks. O.K. O.K. I am all through; I can't do another thing. Hymie, won't you do what I ask you this once? Look out! Mamma, mamma! Look out for her. You can't beat him. Police, mamma! Helen, Mother, please take me out. Come on, Rosie. O.K. Hymes would do it; not him. I will settle . . . . . the indictment. Come on,

Max, open the soap duckets. Frankie, please come here. Open that
door, Dumpey's door. It is so much, Abe, that . . . with the brewery.
Come on. Hey, Jimmie! The Chimney Sweeps. Talk to the Sword.
Shut up, you got a big mouth! Please help me, Henry. Max come
over here . . . . French Canadian bean soup . . . I want to pay, let
them leave me alone. . . .

October 24, 1935

Jerome Rothenberg (b. 1931)
THE MURDER INC. SUTRA

for Robert Kelly

Pincus Tavern
which Kelly passed
as schoolboy   den
of murderers or den of Jews
as murderers
no Benya Kriks he says
but bad guys simply
rotten
in the way America
disposes   though I pretend
other Pincus Taverns meetingplaces of one-eyed
hand in caftan hardcocked
Jewish bandits
beautiful men of noses enlarged with purple veins
of still-curled earlocks from childhood
who dared to cross the border in three coats
watchbands laid out from wrist to shoulders
but beardless could whistle

lost messages in secret Jewish code
meaning
"the Tsar's asshole smells of vinegar" etcetera
& were obliged to wield knives   not only
to cut a notch off a salami
but slit a windpipe
spreading his blood across
the merchant's vest or seeing
pictures in it
of rabbis with hardons unheard of
in the secular world
real to their perceptions who were
brothel Jews & inn-
keepers
expert in management of taverns
where most would let the Polacks
drink but took a piece
themselves if pressed to it
even would suck each other off
in Polish prisons
from there to Brooklyn emanations
made the journey   sought
Golden Kingdoms
at the corner of Stone & Sutter
(Kelly thought) some lounged
in doorways   improbable murderous Litvaks
with names like Lepke   Gurrah   "Dutch Schultz"   Rothstein
   Lansky   Siegel
would drive wing'd cadillacs
with wraparound chrome exteriors of nineteen-thirty-one
to banquets on high holidays
eating turkey   chicken   goose with mushrooms
"a fish soup on which floated lakes of lemon juice"
drank velvety madeira   booze from Canada   cigars of J. P. Morgan
   sniffed cocaine   sucked oranges
or dropped peels into their vodka
would wear a deluxe striped suit made of english navy
but with a head for business
Jews moved past el trains blasting tommy guns

other Jews made movies
ran after black girls   did a buck & wing
for Roman gangsters
toasted their mothers with hunky wines
that smelled of sun & bedbugs
of which the father of the dead man wrote in journal
"my child brings solace to a heavy heart
"his intense physicality
"not Jewish truly but tendering a dream of
"strength   resilience   broken promises
"a horsecock strapped between his legs
"in tribute   & my secret joy too
"seeing his dead frame surrounded
"by a thousand blossoms roses of old Poland
"a choir like the Warsaw Synagogue
"led by Sirota   bursts into songs of angels
"flashbulbs from fifty cameras pop
"blinding the humble button operators workers
"in black jackets & silk lapels some
"with yellow shoes   milk-stained wives   outclassed
"outdistanced by that stud in coffin
"whose hair pasted back still smells of
"whorehouse evenings along Atlantic Avenue
"not Moldavanka mad Odessa nights
"remembered the enforcers lift his coffin
"sweat stains the armpits of orange-colored suits
"strawberry vests   blue leather shoes
"& under the shirtcuff of the murdered son
"a diamond-studded bracelet"   thus
Babel or an uncle
might have written though the flesh
retreats from these as other
killers Jews who frightened the round-cheeked schoolboy
with gangster visions   of concrete
bodies into Catskill lakes
their fathers stood above & threw
lint from old pockets into
praying for joy   deliverance
from America the beautiful

oppressor riding in white convertible
up streets of Brownsville
the eagle of the golden States hooked on his arm
& hungry   diving
on faces that he hates
of Jew & Gentile
first searches their hearts for "freedom"
& the happy buck

Osip Mandelstam (Russian, 1891–c. 1938)
POEM

Nothing can be done for this night
but it's still day where you are.
A black sun rises
at Jerusalem's gates.

A yellow sun is worse, worse—
oh hushaby, hushaby—
Jews were burying my mother
in a bright temple.

Jews without grace,
Jews without priests,
saying their service over her ashes
in a bright temple.

And Jewish voices
rang across her body.
I woke in my cradle,
lit by the glow of a black sun.

BURTON RAFFEL & ALLA BURAGO

INTERLUDE

For Belial jibed at vision; but at night when he craftily
crept into the dark corners of himself, he took up
the sacred books, the ultimate books of the last
indignation, and read the prophecies that were heard
by the river Chebar, and he wept.
(*E. Dahlberg*)

Edward Dahlberg (1900–77)
From THE FLEA OF SODOM

Walking in the evening air I mused, "All is basely mingled, the people, the goods and the genders, for the tender vine of remembrance is broken. Where is the street for the baker and the shops of spices? Who weighs the egg and the sweet cakes, and what idol stands guard over the flesh on the table?" And I said, "O defiled flock, take a harp, and chant to the ancient relics, lest understanding perish." Then I labored for the miracle of seeing and knowing, and thought I heard murmuring Euphrates, and perceived the first-born leaves of Eden whose savor of apple, elm and hazel-nut garnished the lips of Jehovah. But it was nothing, and my spirit was a mute tomb. Inside the 6th Avenue cafeteria were Andromache, Thais, Golem, Bedlam, Proletcult sitting at a table with the tittering art-hags of Tartarus and Pilate Agenda. Going away, I turned back, hungering as Lot's wife did for the lascivious hearths of Sodom. Would I take Cain's guilt, Ham's shame and Rahab's vileness to warm myself in the sheepfold of adhesive mediocrity? Perhaps I would go to Los Angeles, which is the orchard of Gomorrah, and not the fig of Israel. I knew I had slain my blood, for Abel was crying out of my veins. What should I do? "Sit," whispered my heart, entreating, "Will ye go away?" to which my soul and flesh replied, "Lord, to whom shall we go?"

Jacob Glatstein (Yiddish, 1896–1971)
GOOD NIGHT, WORLD

Good night, wide world,
big stinking world.
Not you but I slam shut the gate.
With a long gaberdine,
with a fiery yellow patch,
with a proud stride,
because I want to,
I'm going back to the ghetto.
Wipe away, stamp out every vestige of conversion.
I roll around in your garbage—
praise, praise, praise—
hunchbacked Jewish life.
Damn your dirty culture, world.
I wallow in your dust
even though it's forsaken,
sad Jewish life.

German pig, cutthroat Pole,
Rumania, thief, land of drunkards and gluttons.
Weak-kneed democracy, with your cold
sympathy-compresses.
Good night, electrified arrogant world.
Back to my kerosene, candle shadows,
eternal October, tiny stars,
to my crooked streets, humped lanterns,
my sacred pages, my Bible,
my Gemorra, to my backbreaking
studies, to the bright Yiddish prayerbook,
to law, profundity, duty, justice—
world, I walk gladly towards quiet ghetto light.

Good night. I'll make you, world, a gift of
all my liberators.
Take back your Jesus-Marxes, choke on their courage.
Croak over a drop of our Christianized blood.
For I have hope, even if He is delaying,
day by day my expectation rises.
Green leaves will yet rustle
on our sapless tree.
I don't need any consolation.
I'm going back to my very beginnings,
from Wagner's pagan music to melody, to humming.
I kiss you, dishevelled Jewish life,
I cry with the joy of coming back.

August 1938

RUTH WHITMAN

*when night fell the stars glittered   the pile of corpses lay in the
field   & snow came down out of the night with soft cruel
abundance • such was God's will • the presence of a god was
felt but it belonged to the goyim • there is a god in the world
but there is no god of Israel*   (Uri Zvi Greenberg)

Paul Celan (German, 1920–70)

A DEATH FUGUE

Black milk of morning we drink you at dusktime
we drink you at noontime & dawntime we drink you at night
we drink & drink
we scoop out a grave in the sky where it's roomy to lie
There's a man in this house who cultivates snakes & who writes
who writes when it's nightfall *nach Deutschland* your golden hair
    Margareta
he writes it & walks from the house & the stars all start flashing
    he whistles his dogs to draw near
whistles his Jews to appear starts us scooping a grave out of sand
he commands us play up for the dance

Black milk of morning we drink you at night
we drink you at dawntime & noontime we drink you at dusktime
we drink & drink
There's a man in this house who cultivates snakes & who writes
who writes when it's nightfall *nach Deutschland* your golden hair
    Margareta
your ashen hair Shulamite we scoop out a grave in the sky where
    it's roomy to lie

He calls jab it deep in the soil you men you other men sing & play
he tugs at the sword in his belt & swings it his eyes are blue
jab your spades deeper you men you other men play up again for
    the dance

Black milk of morning we drink you at night
we drink you at noontime & dawntime we drink you at dusktime
we drink & drink
there's a man in this house your golden hair Margareta
your ashen hair Shulamite he cultivates snakes

He calls play that death thing more sweetly Death is a gang-boss
   aus Deutschland
he calls scrape that fiddle more darkly then hover like smoke in the
   air
then scoop out a grave in the clouds where it's roomy to lie

Black milk of morning we drink you at night
we drink you at noontime Death is a gang-boss *aus Deutschland*
we drink you at dusktime & dawntime we drink & drink
Death is a gang-boss *aus Deutschland* his eye is blue
he hits you with leaden bullets his aim is true
there's a man in this house your golden hair Margareta
he sets his dogs on our trail he gives us a grave in the sky
he cultivates snakes & he dreams Death is a gang-boss *aus Deutschland*

your golden hair Margareta
your ashen hair Shulamite

J.R.

Uri Zvi Greenberg (Hebrew, b. 1894)
From GOD IN EUROPE

We were not like dogs among the Gentiles . . . they pity a dog,
They pet him, even kiss him with the Gentile mouth.
Like a fat baby, one of their very own,
They pamper him, always laughing and playing;
And when the dog dies, how bitterly the Gentiles mourn him!

We were not brought in boxcars like lambs to the slaughter,
Rather, like leprous sheep,
Through all the beautiful landscapes of Europe,
They shipped us to Death.
They did not handle their sheep as they handled our bodies;
They did not yank out their teeth before they killed them;
Nor strip the wool from their bodies as they stripped our skin;
Nor shovel them into the fire to make ashes of their life,
And scatter the ashes over streams and sewers.

Where are there other analogies to this,
This monstrous thing we suffered at their hands?
There *are* none—no other analogies! (All words are shadows of
    shadows)—
That is the horror: no other analogies!
No matter how brutal the torture a man may endure in a Christian
    country,
He who comes to compare will compare it thus:
He was tortured like a Jew.
Every fear, every anguish, every loneliness, every agony,
Every scream, every weeping in this world,
He who compares things will say:
This is the Jewish kind.

There is no retribution for what they did to us—
Its circumference is the world:
The culture of Christian kingdoms to its peak
Is covered with our blood,
And all their conscience, with our tears.

ROBERT MEZEY

David Ignatow (b. 1914)

THE STRANGER

That face grown hair, flat-lipped,
ears like pointed spears, tufts shoot from them—
this face human by virtue of our fright.   '
What stirs in us? This flat mouth talks:
Have mercy, I am of the species . . .
We shoot him on sight, he dies for us,
lies prone in our brain a terror; not human,
no, never, we with tactile skin. Kill, for God's sake.
Do not listen to the monster that will persuade us
in our accents. Fire into its throat, its magic,
its evil, its death of the human. Who was the woman
bore it? Think it woman and die shuddering,
but kill! And he conquers, rises from the dead
around him, freed by their deaths; and mourns,
bewailing his fate to be alone, to eat and sleep alone,
to adventure alone: cry of the human;
he mourns his dead and his fate, beating his chest.
And they rise, now that they are done for,
now that there is nothing to lose they take him
to their breasts; they accept, weeping.

Alexandro Jodorowsky (Spanish [Chilean], contemporary)

From EL TOPO [THE MOLE]   "The Death of the
                                          Fourth Master"

. . .

A tall pole in the desert is all the Fourth Master has for a house.[1]
El Topo boldly approaches the Fourth Master and challenges him.
The Fourth Master is an almost skeletal old man. He has long white
hair and wears only a loincloth. El Topo waits for the Fourth Master
to attack him.

FOURTH MASTER: *You want to fight me? How do you plan to do it?*
I don't have a revolver.

He digs in the sand and pulls out an old rusty revolver that no
longer works.

FOURTH MASTER: *I traded my revolver for a butterfly net. You'll*
have to fight me with your fists.

The Master assumes the comic posture of an oldtime boxer. He
challenges El Topo.

FOURTH MASTER: *Hit me. Hit me.*

[1] The possessions of the Masters have been diminishing. The First Master
lived in a tall tower, the Second Master in a wagon, the Third Master in a
lean-to. The Fourth Master has only a pole in the desert and a sheet covering
his body. The First Master had two revolvers, the Second Master one revolver
that fired several shots, the Third Master one revolver that fired a single shot.
The Fourth Master has no revolver, only a butterfly net. The First Master
had a large oasis, the Second Master a small stream, the Third Master an oval
pool. The Fourth Master has only the sand in the desert.

He pushes El Topo. El Topo is disconcerted. He decides to strike the old man. But he cannot land his punches. The Master dodges them with magical speed. El Topo becomes impatient. He tries some karate blows. All of them miss the Master. Desperate, El Topo draws his gun, as the Master picks up his butterfly net, and fires. The Master catches the bullet with his net and sends it whizzing back to El Topo. The bullet explodes near El Topo's black boots. The Fourth Master laughs.

FOURTH MASTER: *You see? My net is mightier than your bullets.* The Master stops laughing. *If you fire again, I'll return your own bullet into your heart.*

El Topo doesn't know whether or not to believe him. He starts toward him. He tries to fire, but can't. He knows he's been defeated. He lets his revolver fall to the ground. The Fourth Master falls to his knees with El Topo.

FOURTH MASTER (gently): *How could you possibly have won? I don't fight. I have nothing. Even if you'd tricked me, you couldn't have taken anything from me.*

EL TOPO: *Yes! I could have taken your life.*

FOURTH MASTER: *My life? It means nothing to me. I'll show you.*

He grabs El Topo's revolver and shoots himself in the liver. El Topo frantically takes him in his arms.

FOURTH MASTER (in great pain): *You lost.*

He dies.

El Topo cries out in pain to the Heavens. He tears at his clothes and tugs at his beard. He bolts like a madman.[2] He runs through the desert toward the places where he left the bodies of the other Mas-

[2] Think of *The Song of Roland* or the madness of Don Quixote.

ters. He comes to the tomb of the Third Master where he had left him covered with rabbits. He tries to approach the grave, but it bursts into flames. He can't bear the heat and runs off.[3]

Completely crazed, El Topo comes to the place of the Second Master. He looks for the body. On the very spot where the Master died, he sees a huge structure made of toothpicks. An irregular, deformed pyramid built by lunatics. El Topo tears down the toothpick walls with the butt of his revolver. Inside he finds the bodies of the Second Master and his Mother, her arm around her son.[4] El Topo continues running through the desert until he comes to where the First Master died. He sees the skeletons of the Master's two helpers. Green plants have sprung from their bones.[5] The trap into which the First Master fell is filled with bright yellow honey. The First Master's body floats in the honey like a foetus. El Topo falls to his knees, picks up a piece of honeycomb and squashes the cells against his face, filling his mouth with honey and screaming desperately.[6]

El Topo appears inside the octagonal tower of the First Master. He beats against the walls, trying to knock them down. He feels trapped within the bones of his skull and is beating against his head from within to open it into eight parts. The lamb from the roof of the tower is seen crucified to one of the exterior walls. El Topo manages to break open the immense tower. The walls fall outwardly like eight stone petals. Standing in the center of the fallen tower, El Topo, liberated, releases two doves, which disappear in the sky.[7]

. . .

EL TOPO'S VOICE [later, walking on a long bridge that stretches a mile across a mile-deep precipice]: *I've been spilled like water and*

[3] Parallel between the flaming grave of rabbits and Moses' burning bush.
[4] The Mother probably built the pyramid and remained trapped inside until she starved to death.
[5] Life springs from putrifaction: inspired by alchemist drawings.
[6] The wax filled with honey should also resemble a piece of flesh full of pus.
[7] Parallel between the two doves that ascend in the air and the alchemical process of evaporation.

my bones have been disjointed. My heart has melted like wax over the entrails of my body. And my tongue has stuck to my palate. And You have placed me in the shadow of death. My God, my God, why hast thou forsaken me? Why are you so distant from my salvation and the words of my plea? My God, I cry out by day and You don't answer. And by night and there is no relief.

JOANNE POTTLITZER

Bob Dylan (b. 1941)

From LINER NOTES TO *HIGHWAY 61 REVISITED*

On the slow train time does not interfere & at the Arabian crossing waits White Heap, the man from the newspaper & behind him the hundred Inevitables made of solid rock & stone—the Cream Judge & the Clown—the doll house where Savage Rose & Fixable live simply in their wild animal luxury. . . . Autumn, with two zeros above her nose arguing over the sun being dark or Bach is as famous as its commotion & that she herself—not Orpheus—is the logical poet "I am the logical poet!" she screams "Spring? Spring is only the beginning!" she attempts to make Cream Judge jealous by telling him of down-to-earth people & while the universe is erupting, she points to the slow train & prays for rain and for time to interfere— she is not extremely fat but rather progressively unhappy. . . . the hundred Inevitables hide their predictions & go to bars & drink & get drunk in their very special conscious way & when tom dooley, the kind of person you think you've seen before, comes strolling in with White Heap, the hundred Inevitables all say "who's the man who looks so white?" & the bartender, a good boy & one who keeps a buffalo in his mind, says "I don't know, but I'm sure I've seen the other fellow someplace" & when Paul Sargent, a plainclothes man from 4th street, comes in at three in the morning & busts everybody for being incredible, nobody really gets angry—just a little illiterate most people get & Rome, one of the hundred Inevitables whispers "I told you so" to Madame John. . . .

Yehuda Amichai (Hebrew, b. 1924)
NATIONAL THOUGHTS

You: trapped in the homeland of the Chosen People.
On your head a cossack's fur hat,
Child of their pogroms.
"After these words." Always.
Or, for instance, your face: slanting eyes,
Pogrom-Year eyes. Your cheekbones, high,
Hetman's cheekbones, Hetman the rabble-king.
Hassid dancing, dutiful, you, naked on a rock in the early evening
    by the canopies of water at Ein Geddi
With eyes closed and your body open like hair.
After these words, "Always."
Every day I know the miracle of
Jesus walking upon the waters,
I walk through my life without drowning.

To speak, now, in this tired language
Torn from its sleep in the Bible—
Blinded, it lurches from mouth to mouth—
The language which described God and the Miracles,
Says:
Motor car, bomb, God.

The squared letters wanted to stay closed,
Every letter a locked house,
To stay and to sleep in it forever.

ASSIA   GUTMANN

Allen Ginsberg (b. 1926)
JAWEH AND ALLAH BATTLE

Jaweh with Atom bomb
   Allah cuts throat of Infidels
Jaweh's armies beat down neighboring tribes
Will Red Sea waters close & drown th'armies of Allah?

Israel's tribes worshipping the Golden Calf
   Moses broke the Tablets of Law.

Zalmon Schacter Lubovitcher Rebbe what you say
   Stone Commandments broken on the ground
  Sufi Sam whaddya say
   Shall Prophet's companions dance circled
    round Synagogue while Jews doven bearded
       electric?
Both Gods Terrible! Awful Jaweh Allah!
   Both hook-nosed gods, circumsized.
Jaweh Allah which unreal?
     Which stronger Illusion?
      Which stronger Army?
   Which gives most frightening command?
What God maintain egohood in Eden? Which be Nameless?

Which enter Abyss of Light?
Worlds of Gods, jealous Warriors, Humans, Animals & Flowers,
Hell Beings, even Hungry Ghosts all die,
Snake cock and pig eat eachother's tails & perish
All Jews all Moslems'll die all Israelis all Arabs
Cairo's angry millions Jerusalem's multitudes
suffer Death's dream Armies in battle!
Yea let Tribes wander to tin camps at cold Europe's walls?
Yea let the Million sit in desert shantytowns with tin cups?
I'm a Jew cries Allah! Empty Budha circumsized!
Snake sneaking apple to Eden—
Alien, Wanderer, Caller of the Great Call!
What Prophet born on this ground
bound me Eternal to Palestine
circled by Armies tanks, droning bomber motors,
radar electric computers?
What Mind directed Stern Gang Irgun Al Fatah Black September?
Meyer Lansky? Nixon Shah? Gangster? Premier? King?
one-eyed General Dayan?
Golda Meir & Kissinger bound me with Arms?
HITLER AND STALIN SENT ME HERE!
WEITZMANN & BEN-GURION SENT ME HERE!
NASSER AND SADAT SENT ME HERE!
ARAFAT SENT ME HERE! MESSIAH SENT ME HERE!
GOD SENT ME HERE!
Buchenwald sent me here! Vietnam sent me here!
My-Lai sent me here!
Lidice sent me here!
My mother sent me here!
I WAS BORN HERE IN ISRAEL, Arab
circumsized, my father had a coffee shop in Jerusalem
One day the Soldiers came & told me to walk down road
my hands up
walk away leave my house business forever!
The Israelis sent me here!
Solomon's Temple the Pyramids & Sphinx sent me here!
JAWEH AND ALLAH SENT ME HERE!
Abraham will take me to his bosom!
Mohammed will guide me to Paradise!

Christ sent me here to be crucified!
Buddha will wipe us out and destroy the world.
The New York Times and Cairo Editorialist Heykal sent me here!
Commentary and *Palestine Review* sent me here!
The International Zionist Conspiracy sent me here!
Syrian Politicians sent me here! Heroic Pan-Arab
Nationalists sent me here!
They're sending Armies to my side—
The Americans & Russians are sending bombing planes tanks
Chinese Egyptians Syrians help me battle for my righteous
house my Soul's dirt Spirit's Nation body's
boundaries & Self's territory my
Zionist homeland my Palestine inheritance
The Capitalist Communist & Third World Peoples
Republics Dictatorships Police States Socialisms
& Democracies
are all sending Deadly Weapons to our aid!
We shall triumph over the Enemy!
Maintain our Separate Identity! Proud
History evermore!
Defend our own bodies here this Holy Land! This hill
Golgotha never forget, never relinquish
inhabit thru Eternity
under Allah Christ Yaweh forever one God
Shema Yisroel Adonoi Eluhenu Adonoi Echad!
La Illaha Illa 'llah Hu!
OY! AH! HU!   OY! AH! HU!
SHALOM!   SHANTIH!   SALAAM!

January 13, 1974

Edouard Roditi (b. 1910)

From THE CONSPIRACY

[1]

One day I woke up to the fact that I'm not alone to be alone. I began to recognize the symptoms of my own loneliness or lunacy in the faces and the behavior of others too. I even discovered that we, the lonely ones, constitute a secret élite in our otherwise democratically equalitarian city. We have our passwords, our almost inconspicuous signs and ways of greeting each other. We hold meetings now to which only the initiates are admitted. Should it ever become known abroad that we belong to this secret sect, we know that we have every reason to fear the worst. But what can the worst be? Have we not already experienced, in this monstrously ordered world, the very depths of degradation? We invented our own hell when we voted the reforms on which we hoped to found our own heaven.

[2]

We celebrate our unholy sabbaths in an artificial cave that manages to suggest to its inmates that they are well concealed from the unwelcome curious in the bowels of the earth or in submarine depths of the ocean. Nobody knows why we need the illusion of such womblike secrecy, nor would I be able to describe at all credibly the liturgy of our preposterous Masses. Anything I might say or write about them would immediately suggest that we must be insane to insist on such absurd precautions in concealing from the public eye such ludicrous ceremonies that anyone of sound mind would dismiss as commonplace or harmlessly infantile. Still, we have good reasons to distrust the suspicious authorities that rule us and, at the same time, we delight in our own secrecy and in our sense of doing something forbidden or subversive when we recite our pretentiously cryptic doxology in all seriousness, as if its meaningless obscurities were imbued with a magic too destructively powerful to lend itself to more public utterance.

Once a disloyal member of our fraternity was rash enough to divulge a part of our doxology to the uninitiate, who began to taunt us in public with our own secret phrases. Overnight, we were forced to change our whole ritual, after which some of our hymns, repeated to us by others in another context, soon failed to sound at all familiar in our ears. Instead of feeling that our old ritual was being profaned, we then began to dismiss it all as merely malevolent nonsense. Only in our own cave can our words sound at all meaningful. Only there can our otherwise commonplace ritual still purify us of our imaginary individual sins through participation in a greater collective sin that is sinful only because it is so secret.

*

Semite: to find a way for myself.
(G. Oppen)

George Oppen (b. 1908)
SEMITE

what art and anti-art to lead us by the sharpness

of its definitions connected
to all other things this is the bond

sung to all distances

my distances neither Roman

nor barbarian the sky the low sky

of poems precise
as the low sky

that women have sung from the windows
of cities sun's light

on the sills a poetry

of the narrow
end of the funnel proximity's salt gales in the narrow

end of the funnel the proofs

are the images the images
overwhelming earth

rises up

in its light nostalgia
of the mud guilts

of the foxhole what is a word a name at the
    limits

of devotion
to life the terrible knowledge

of deception

a lie told my loves tragically
pitifully had deceived

themselves had been betrayed

demeaned thrown away shamed
degraded

stripped naked Think

think also of the children
the guards laughing

the one pride the pride
of the warrior laughing so the hangman
comes to all dinners Aim

we tell each other the children cannot be
    alone whereupon murder

comes to our dinners poem born

of a planet the size

of a table top
garden   forest   an awning

fluttering four-lane

highway the instant

in the open the moving
edge and one
is I

THE END OF "A BOOK OF THE WARS OF YAHVEH"

ג

THE WRITINGS

Tradition, according to its mystical sense, is Oral Torah, precisely because every stabilization in the text would hinder and destroy the infinitely moving, the constantly progressing and unfolding element within it, which would otherwise become petrified. The writing down and codification of the Oral Torah, undertaken in order to save it from being forgotten, was therefore not only a protective as (in the deeper sense) a pernicious act.

—GERSHOM SCHOLEM

The book is as old as water and fire.

—EDMOND JABÈS

A Book of Extensions

Abraham Abulafia (Hebrew, 1240–c. 1291)
From THE BOOK OF THE LETTER

. . . .

      And Adonai said to
    Zechariahu the Messenger,
      Raise your voice
        with the tongue
            of your pen,
        write
the word of God, this book with
your three
fingers; and God was
with him as guide, and he wrote
all that was commanded
and he came reciting the words
of God to the Jews circumcised
in the flesh as well as the
dullheaded and poor, but
they paid no heed to the form
of his coming, spoke of him
and his god in unimaginable
terms

JACK HIRSCHMAN

(Greek, 4th–6th century A.D.)

From THE HIDDEN SACRED BOOK OF MOSES CALLED "EIGHTH" OR "HOLY"   "Vowel Poem"

```
aeêiouô
 eêiouô
  êiouô
  iouô
   ouô
    uô
    ô
    ôuoiêea
    uoiêea
    oiêea
     iêea
     êea
     ea
     a
```

COMMENTARY

(1)   From Greek magical papyrus—attributed to Jewish sources—in which vowel configurations name & summon planetary angels: as part of the fusions current in the Hellenistic world. The magic here is carried by the voiced breath: a combination & recombination of vowels, also used in naming. The Roman letters (original: Greek) permit the writing down or stabilization of the vowels, which would be part of the *oral* tradition in Hebrew, where only consonants are written down. Thus, until the masoretic vocalizations (circa 6th–7th centuries A.D.) there was no fixed Hebrew text that could be read without the oral transmission of soundings.

Compare Malinowski on Trobriand Island "garden magic": "The magic is in the breath, & the breath is the magic."

(2)   "God said to Moses, 'I will make you write most of my Torah but not all' . . . because the oral transmission is the mystery of God, & God hands over his mysteries only to the righteous." (From *Midrash Tanḥuma* 6.)

A PERFORMANCE FROM "THE SECRET BOOK OF MOSES ON THE GREAT NAME"

do it right : use
this universe map:

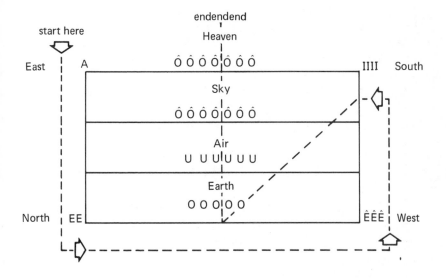

speaking

East			hands	left		go	: *A!*
North		right	fist	up			: *E!E!*
West			hands	out			: *Ê!Ê!Ê!*
South			hands	over	mouth		: *I!I!I!I!*
Earth			hands	on	toes		: *O!O!O!O!O!*
Air	eyes	front	hand	to	heart		: *U!U!U!U!U!U!*
Sky	face	back	hands	under	head		: *Ô!Ô!Ô!Ô!Ô!Ô!Ô!Ô!*
Heaven						again	: *Ô!Ô!Ô!Ô!Ô!Ô!Ô!Ô!*

. . . .

I Name You   pull You here : *yuhweuhwo ohwahwehweyh*
   YaHWoH
ahwehweyh ahwih ehweyh ahweyh yoowoh euhweyh YeHWooH
   ahweyhwoh
ohwih ohweyhwih yahweyh yohwoohweyh auhweyh uhweyhwah yoh
   yohwah-
hwih yohwahwih ohweyh ehweh ooh yoh YaHWoH goodbig Name
   now not
later : take new birth body You Lynx You Eagle You Snake You
Phoenix You Life You Strength You ForceFate You Idols the gods'
person *ahwihwoh yoh wuh YaHWoH eyhyoh ahwah oohwih*
   ahahahah eh:yuh
yoh ohweyh YaHWoH ahwih: ahwohweyh oohwehwoh ahyehweyh
   yoohweh uh-
wehyah ehyoh eyhyih uhuh eheh eyheyh ohwahwohweyh //
   khekhampshim'm
khangalash a e i o u yeyhwehwah / ohwo-eyhwo-weh z euonymous
   good
omen nomen zohyoh-yeir ohmuhruh-romromos

w i d e n   d o u b l e   YaHWoH   n a m e   follow me:
eY   YY   uHuH   eHeH   WeyHWeyH   oWaHWoWeyH

Sun inters 14th day now do this rite on gold clean licked special
plate:

                    YaHWaH   *yuh:oweyh*
   yeuhwowoh
eyhwohwih ehwo:eyh ohwuh ehweyh:uhwohweyh ohwohwoh:
   ohwohwih ohwa-
hwoh ehwoh ohweyh uhwoh now more complete: *ahwoh-euhweyh*
   owahwih yo
eyhwuhweh-ohwah oohwoh ohwo eih ooh ehwoh oiwuhwuh
   ohwuhwuh a :
                    eat these Names :

                                                      C.D.

The "naming" of God as central activity of the Jewish mystic poets (see above, page 7). But the written names were at first a notation for their sounding; later, a numinous value in themselves. In the magical papyrus, above, the directions for transformation of text to sound are evident— along with the attendant movements. Viewed in this light they offer the remains of what Dada poets & others in our century re-invented as the "sound-poem": patterns of "abstract" sound intended to be read aloud. Wrote Hugo Ball of his own first soundings (1915): "I now noticed that my voice, which seemed to have no other choice, had assumed the age-old cadence of the sacerdotal lamentation."

Isidore Isou (French, b. 1925)

THE YOUNG GIRL'S TEARS: A CLOSED POEM

M dngoun, m diahl ⊕[1]hna îou
hsn îoun înhlianhl M[2]pna iou
vgaîn set i ouf! saî iaf
fîn plt i clouf! mglaî vaf
Λ[3]o là îhî cnn vîi
snoubidi î pnn mîi
A[4]gohà îhîhî gnn gî
klnbidi Δ[5]blîglîhlî
H[6]mami chou a sprl
scami Bgou cla ctrl
guel el înhî nî K[7]grîn
Khlogbidi E[8]vî bîncî crîn

cncn ff vsch gln *ié*
gué rgn ss ouch clen *dé*
chaîg gna pca hi
Θ[9]snca grd kr di

[1] Θ = sigh
[2] M = moan
[3] Λ = gargle
[4] A = inhale
[5] Δ = rattle
[6] H = groan
[7] K = snort
[8] E = grunt
[9] Θ = sigh

COMMENTARY

Like Tristan Tzara around the First World War, Isidore Isou came from Rumania to Paris 30 years later, where he founded (along with Maurice Lemaître, Gabriel Pomerand, & others) a school of poetry called "lettrism." Of this they wrote: "To keep things moving, we desire to bring about a new sensitivity, a sensitivity to sound: attentiveness to letters & to sounds, as being without logical meaning yet filled with an insolent magic." (*La Dictature lettriste,* 1946.) At the limits of the avant garde, their manifesto still recalls the old, creative functions of the "letters" (Hebrew, etc.) working somewhere between sight & sound.

(Hebrew, after 3rd century A.D.)

From THE HEBREW BOOK OF ENOCH [*Sefer ha-Hekhalot*]

Come and behold the letters by which the heaven and the earth were
    created
the letters by which the mountains and hills were created
the letters by which the seas and rivers were created
the letters by which the trees and herbs were created
the letters by which the planets and constellations were created
the letters by which the globe of moon, the globe of sun, Orion, the
    Pleiades and all the vast lights of the heavens were created
the letters by which the throne of glory and the wheels of the
    Merkaba were created
the letters by which the necessities of the worlds were created
the letters by which wisdom, understanding, knowledge, prudence,
    meekness, and righteousness were created, by which the whole
    world is sustained.

And I walked by his side and he took me by his hand and raised me
upon his wings and showed me those letters, all of them, that are
graven with a flaming pen on the throne of glory: And sparks go
forth from them and cover all the chambers of the seventh heaven.

Abraham Abulafia (Hebrew, 1240–c. 1291)

From LIFE OF THE WORLD TO COME   "The

Permutations"

YHVH	YHHV	YVHH	YVHH	HVHY	HVYH
HVHY	HVYH	HHYV	HHYV	VHYH	VHHY
VHYH	VHHY	VYHH	VYHH	HYHV	HYHV
HYHV	HYVH	HHVY	HHVY	YHVH	YHHV
YHHV	YVHH	HVHY	HVHY	HVYH	HHYV
HVYH	HHYV	VHYH	VHYH	VHHY	VYHH
VHHY	VYHH	HYHV	HYHV	HYVH	HHVY
HYVH	HHVY	YHVH	YHVH	YHHV	YVHH
HVYH	HHYV	VHYH	VHYH	VHHY	VYHH
VHHY	VYHH	HYHV	HYHV	HYVH	HHVY
HYVH	HHVY	YHVH	YHVH	YHHV	YVHH
YHHV	YVHH	HVHY	HVHY	HVYH	HHYV
HHYV	VHYH	VHHY	VHHY	VYHH	HYHV
VYHH	HYHV	HYVH	HYVH	HHVY	YHVH
HHVY	YHVH	YHHV	YHHV	YVHH	HVHY
YVHH	HVHY	HVYH	HVYH	HHYV	VHYH
VYHH	HYHV	HYVH	HYVH	HHVY	YHVH
HHVY	YHVH	YHHV	YHHV	YVHH	HVHY
YVHH	HVHY	HVYH	HVYH	HHYV	VHYH
HHYV	VHYH	VHHY	VHHY	VYHH	HYHV
HYHV	HYVH	HHVY	HHVY	YHVH	YHHV
YHVH	YHHV	YVHH	YVHH	HVHY	HVYH
HVHY	HVYH	HHYV	HHYV	VHYH	VHHY
VHYH	VHHY	VYHH	VYHH	HYHV	HYVH

J.R.

COMMENTARY

(1) The "explicit name" or *tetragrammaton* (4-letter name), long taken as YHVH, from the Hebrew letters yod-hey-vav-hey יהוה—thus English Jehovah, Hellenistic Iao (Yah-Woh), more recent YaHVeH, etc. The original absence of vowels in Hebrew notation has retained the mystery, which was only revealed (i.e., sounded) by the High Priest on the Day of Atonement. Later the written form itself was viewed as power source & commonly reduced to YY (yod-yod יי), pronounced as *adonai* (from Semitic *adon:* lord), etc.

But also see page 5, above: the name beyond the name.

(2) Tabular permutations, as above, while clearly used for *poesis* &/or meditation, fail to catch the fast motion of expressive/ecstatic methods elsewhere used by Abulafia & followers, or the varieties of names possible from combinations & recombinations of the Hebrew alphabet. Thus, writes the anonymous author of *Sha'are Tsedek,* "Gates of Justice" (1295), regarding his own experience:

". . . During the second week the power became so strong in me that I couldn't manage to write down all the combinations of letters which automatically spurted out of my pen. . . . When I came to the night in which this power was conferred on me, & Midnight had passed, I set out to take up the Great Name of God, consisting of 72 Names, permuting & combining it. But when I had done this for a little while, the letters took on the shape of great mountains, strong trembling seized me & I could summon no strength, my hair stood on end, & it was as if I were not in this world. Then something resembling speech came to my lips & forced them to move. I said: 'This is indeed the spirit of wisdom.' "

The range of approaches & names ("the whole Torah is nothing but the great name of God"—thus, J. Gikatilla) should be clear in the images that follow. From what is in effect a sacred "concrete poetry."

Moses Cordovero (Hebrew, 1522–70)

From **THE GARDEN OF POMEGRANATES**   "The Unity
of God"

י = Y (yod)
ה = H (hey)
ו = V (vav)
א = alef = one

AMULET ON THE TETRAGRAMMATON

COMMENTARY

"An amulet for pure and concentrated thought. In order to attain great understanding, the amulet says (right side) that it is necessary for a man's thoughts to be pure. The amulet states (left side and bottom) that focusing on the characters of the design and sounding the vowels written here beneath the Tetragrammaton (ḥirik /i/, shᵊwa /ə/, and kamats /a/) will lead to that goal. Notice that the divine name produced in this reading would be /YiHVaH/.

"The amulet is called 'To Cleanse the Thought' (top line) and uses the traditional opening for a *shiviti* wall amulet (Psalm 16.8), then continues (the block letters) through spellings of and reference to the various divine names." (H.L.)

(Samaritan Hebrew, traditional)
CONCRETE POEM: "YHVH GREAT GOD"

```
Y  H  V  H  G  R  E  A  T  G  O  D  Y
H  V  H  G  R  E  A  T  G  O  D  Y  H
V  H  G  R  E  A  T  G  O  D  Y  H  V
H  G  R  E  A  T  G  O  D  Y  H  V  H
G  R  E  A  T  G  O  D  Y  H  V  H  G
R  E  A  T  G  O  D  Y  H  V  H  G  R
E  A  T  G  O  D  Y  H  V  H  G  R  E
A  T  G  O  D  Y  H  V  H  G  R  E  A
T  G  O  D  Y  H  V  H  G  R  E  A  T
G  O  D  Y  H  V  H  G  R  E  A  T  G
O  D  Y  H  V  H  G  R  E  A  T  G  O
D  Y  H  V  H  G  R  E  A  T  G  O  D
```

J.R.

Tristan Tzara (French, 1896–1963)
From LE COEUR À GAZ

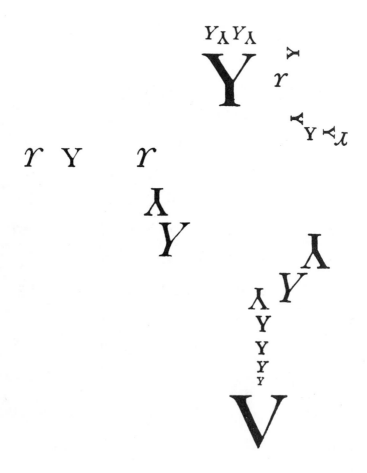

Moses Cordovero (Hebrew, 1522–70)
COMPOSITION AROUND THE INEFFABLE NAME

ויניעֵנ לזמן ומלא הארץ רעה אתה׳   אמן ואמן   כרוך ח׳ לעולם אמן ואמן

(the topmost line): ". . . He will bring us to the time when Earth is filled
with knowledge of the Name. Amen Amen. The Name be blest forever.
Amen Amen."

(the inner circle): Y-H-V-H (the tetragrammaton) in the center surrounded by its permutations in four groups of six pairs.

(outside the inner circle): [1] beginning with the larger word, הנה, &
working outwards & counterclockwise, the two circular lines concern the
transmutations of Y-H-V-H, linked (through gematria?) with the three
initial words of the Priestly Blessing, *yevarekhekha, ya'er* & *yisa* (all of
which are followed by the tetragrammaton in the blessing itself), & with
the phrases, *midat yom* (aspect of day / maleness) & *midat layla* (aspect
of night / femaleness); [2] block letters are the initial words of the Priestly
Blessing (see above) intermixed with the letters of the tetragrammaton;
beneath the first block letters are transmutations of the tetragrammaton,
& under the second block letters is the name of "72" (see below, page
405) in twelve groups of six three-letter syllables.

NAME EVENT ONE

Slice an apple in three.
Write a name on each slice & eat it.

NAME EVENT TWO

Write a name in the sand.
Have participants lick it up.

NAME EVENT THREE

1. A participant selects a piece of deerskin parchment.
2. He cuts it up to make a sleeveless garment, large enough to fall across his shoulders & his chest down to his navel & along his sides down to his loins. He also makes a hat.
3. The name of God is stitched into the garment.
4. The participant fasts for seven days, then at night he brings the garments to a lake or river, where he speaks the holy Name.
5. If he sees a green shape on the water, he begins again. If he sees a bright red shape, he walks into the water to his waist.
6. The participant puts on the name.

Abraham Abulafia (Hebrew, 1240–c. 1291)

From LIFE OF THE WORLD TO COME   "Circles"

(1)

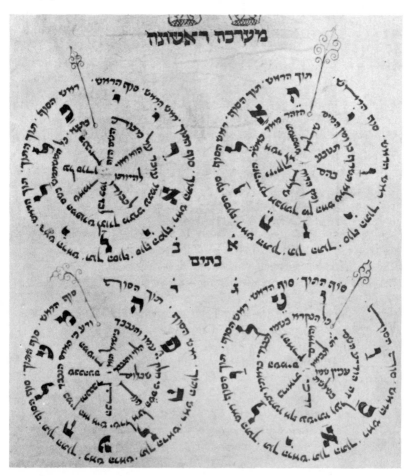

READING INSTRUCTIONS: Beginning at the marker: the outer rims read right to left; the inner rim leads to the inner spokes, & from circle into circle, right to left. The words at top = "first order."

UPPER RIGHT

outer rim: middle of the first . middle of the last . first of the last . last of the last . first of the middle . middle of the middle . last of the middle . first of the first . last of the first

middle rim (large letters): permutations of the name "72"

inner rim: **be very wary as your fathers warned you of the fire don't be burnt by it & water**

inner spokes: **not to / drown / in it / & wind / that it not / harm you / you not / use**

UPPER LEFT

outer rim: first of the last . middle of the middle . middle of the first . first of the first . middle of the last . last of the last . first of the middle . last of the middle . first of the first . last of the first

middle rim (large letters): permutations of the name "72"

inner rim: **it on condition anyone who takes the name for his own needs transgresses the command**

inner spokes: **about said name / was formed / to be / for his own glory/ only thus / the prophet / said about / its secret**

LOWER RIGHT

outer rim: last of the middle . last of the first . first of the last . middle of the last . first of the middle . middle of the first . middle of the middle . first of the first . last of the last

middle rim (large letters): permutations of the name "72"

inner rim: **whatever has my name I made it for my honor formed it worked it truly & concerning this the name informed**

inner spokes: **his prophets (be he blest) / about his name / by 3 / ways / of creation / of the skies / & earth / & man**

LOWER LEFT

outer rim: last of the first. last of the middle . last of the last . middle of the middle . first of the first . middle of the first . first of the middle . first of the last . middle of the last

middle rim (large letters): permutations of the name "72"

inner rim: **& know according to the name the one most honored is the one of Israel because the name's own portion is his people & the most honored one**

inner spokes: **of Israel is / the Levite & the most honored / of the Levites / is the / priest / & the most honored / of the priests / is the Messiah**

(2)

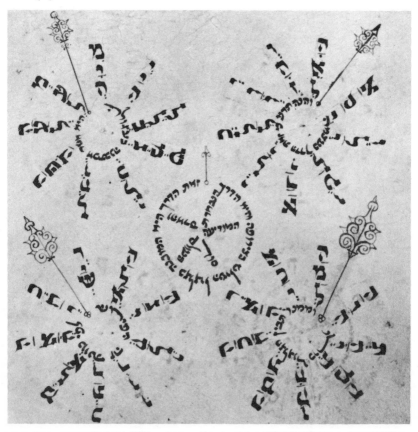

READING INSTRUCTIONS: Right to left & circle into circle toward the center. Larger letters are permutations of the name "72."

UPPER RIGHT, *the rim:* **o look here now this is the way itself**

UPPER LEFT, *the rim:* **by which you'll understand the gilgul metempsychosis complete**

LOWER RIGHT, *the rim:* **the one I now write in the circle**

LOWER LEFT, *the rim:* **the intention of the explanation**

CENTER, *the rim:* **way that may be understood as three-fold gilgul metempsychosis**

CENTER, *the spokes:* **the chosen way / disclosing / secrets / of the world / & man**

(3)

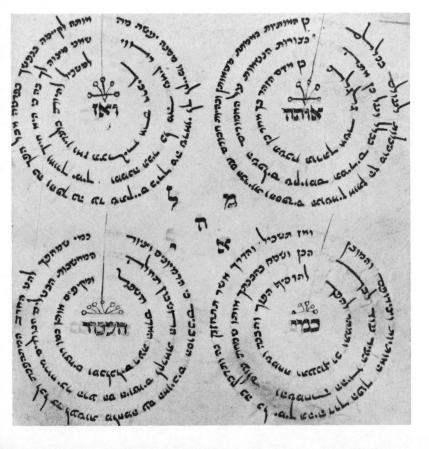

READING INSTRUCTIONS: upper rims to lower, right to left, & circle into circle.

UPPER RIGHT: so are the letters in their true essentials & when joined to people & to books that carry them are made intelligible as wholes to world & public: forms that the lowly asses carry though their existence is eternal: so then manchild you be careful that you not forget that you are working transformation of the Torah

UPPER LEFT: making it exist inside your soul in its particulars: so turn through it o turn through it & what of it is fit for your fulfillment let your hand fulfill: do what I tell you here it is your life your length of days from which you come to know what isn't fitting that a wise man be without & then your ways will be successful

LOWER RIGHT: & then you will be wise: the way that you must cleave to & be strong in all your days will be the way of turning letters & combining them: & understanding what is understood rejoicing in your understandings & eternally rejoicing this rejoicing further wakening your heart to keep on turning them & understanding: joy & pleasures as you rush to turn

LOWER LEFT: like one who turns the sword the flame that turns itself toward every side & wages war against the enemies around you: for the empty images & forms of thought born of the evil impulse are the first emerging into thought surrounding it like murderers to foul the gnosis of the lowly tortured man

(4)

·

· ·

& the secret

ITS MEASURE IS RIGHT	& LEFT
MEASURE OF ITS RIGHT	ITS LEFT
MEASURE OF ITS LEFT	ITS RIGHT
IT HAS NO IMAGE	SKIES
IMAGE OF ITS RIGHT	LEFT
IMAGE OF ITS LEFT	RIGHT
& ITS BIRTHPLACE	BEING FROM NON-BEING
FATHERING FROM NOTHING	NAMES

·

· ·

MY NAME IS OTHER THAN	
WHAT HAS NO	IMAGE
MY IMAGE IS OTHER THAN	
WHAT HAS NO	NAME
& I HAVE NO NAME	OTHER THAN IMAGE
& I HAVE NO IMAGE	OTHER THAN NAME
EN-EY-EM-EE	WRITTEN OUT FULLY
MY NAME AN IMAGINING	FOR MY TRUTH

J.R./H.L.

COMMENTARY

(1)   Abulafia's poetry of permutations (a kind of medieval "lettrism," etc.) here takes the form of nearly 200 circles, consisting of a discourse on meditation, a set of instructions for specific permutations, & the permutations of the letters themselves. In the present instance the permutations work off the so-called Name-of-72: i.e., 72 three-letter syllables "based on the three verses of Exodus 14.19–.21, each of which contains 72 letters. . . . [It] was made up by joining the first letter of verse 19, the last letter of 20, and the first of 21, to form its first triad; the second

letter of 19, the penultimate of 20, and the second of 21, to make the second triad, and so on until we have 72 three-letter terms comprising all the letters of these verses." (J. Trachtenberg, *Jewish Magic & Superstition*, page 94.) Abulafia in turn arranges the syllables in rows & columns, then sets them into circles according to instructions ("middle of the first, middle of the last," etc.), which form part of the circles as well. In this way the disciple is led into the circles, must follow their message as an act of concentration.

Abulafia himself writes of the abstracting/spiritualizing process which he then employs & by which the world is apprehended as language/ sound: "Know that the method of *tseruf* (the combination of letters) can be compared to music; for the ear hears sounds from various combinations, in accordance with the character of the melody & the instrument. Also, two different instruments can form a combination, & if the sounds combine, the listener's ear registers a pleasant sensation in acknowledging their difference. . . . The same is true of the combination of letters. It touches the first string, which is comparable to the first letters, & proceeds to the second, third, fourth, & fifth, & the various sounds combine. And the secrets, which express themselves in these combinations, delight the heart which acknowledges its God & is filled with ever fresh joy." Thus the letters—by a process called *dilug* (skipping)—become a basis for meditation "on the essence of one's thought, abstracting from it every word, be it connected with a notion or not . . . (by putting) the consonants which one is combining into swift motion." (From *Sha'are Tsedek*, for which, see G. Scholem, *Major Trends in Jewish Mysticism*, pages 154– 55.) For Abulafia & others, such processes remain essentially "oral," in the sense of open-ended: an improvisatory meditation on a fixed base (torah, names of God, etc.) whose true meanings are not "literal" but the occasion for an ongoing process of reconstruction (revelation) & sounding. In touch with Yogic currents from the East, Abulafia's intention here seems clearly mantric; but his practice of a systemic & concrete poetry also closely resembles the 20th-century lettrism of Isidore Isou, the asymmetries & nuclei of Jackson Mac Low, & the blues kabbala improvisations of Jack Hirschman, all of whom he may have influenced.

(2) "Abulafia who was never admitted into the great rabbinic canon of the Jews because in fact he was the Jews first truly modern poet / visual artist saw the abstract musical beauty of the letters of the Hebrew alphabet went for the form of the thing itself which of course was nothing but the absolute *ain* of the pinpointed pain of the elohimic struggle." (J. Hirschman.)

Jack Hirschman (b. 1933)

From ON THE HEBREW LETTERS   "Exile"

The Hebrew letters, in respect of both the so-called "chaos" and the pure abstract forms of a sensuality, are the sovereign language of poetically visual trans-literature at this time.

The letters are not merely drenched in the mysticism of poetics which signifies our time, they suggest as well the language of *the other, or Double,* in exile.

This exile has ceased to be a purely Jewish one, especially as the Israel nation seems to have been attained. It is rather the exile of modern man himself from the Eden which continues to define him, even through the interchange of east and west, the rise of interest in the sensuality of the Oriental stance and stroke, suggestive of future power struggles, future haikus of disaster, future yellow teeth.

Clear strokes, of course, are the gems of abstract beauty, and no doubt the lines of trigrams in the *I Ching* as basis for pure strokes and slashes return the *Oldest East,* the transliteration of *total modern consciousness.* The image that is most central in this is the image of Jerusalem.

Not however the image of a Jerusalem attained,

but the Jerusalem who is the emanation of Albion,

for it is Blake's glyph that sustains a power that not even Cathay can surpass.

When, that is, one comes to understand that the tomb and underworld of the human soul is not "over there" but here and present and now.

It is the image of Jerusalem, the woman, that proceeds.

Woman who announces by her very existence the realism of imaginative life as *being* itself.

The Hebrew letters thus become a realistic homage to the ancient that persists in exile. It affirms the atomic permutations of being which comprise a great chain of being new and old at once. It transcends the politics which itself contains; and with the proud 22 of its interior army, it contrives to announce that it is the middle of the east from which both east and west must draw the marcations of their future humanity.

The use of the Hebrew letters in exile tells of the immense job of sustaining the whole world from the middle pillar outward, the violence contained, the radiance emanating.

Wallace Berman (1926–76)

From IMAGE OF THE WALL

Hannah Weiner

From CLAIRVOYANT JOURNAL   "The Initiation"

THIS IS MY POEM
NO MORE 2 *JACK* HRS SLEEP.   GOOD AFTERNOON   JAPA.
If you sleep more DRINK MORE WINE YOU CAN WRITE
NOW you're writing HILARIOUS. You can GO BAREFOOT
12 times
          This is an initiation
no you saw it only 4 or 5 you *went barefoot* and TAKE OFF THE
PIN. ENJOY THE WORKING MALA BEADS.   WRITE.   CAS-
TRATION. THE INITIATION BEGINS.   You sit on the aisle 2nd
row WRITE things get a little gold CONSECRATED gold again *too
late* BIG MOMENT.   IT COULD WRITE YOU COULD BE DIS-
TINGUISHED HAPPY WRITE POEMS You dont like DOCTOR
looks or *angry* manner, concentrate on HIM hear SHE'S OK.
      DOOR
Flowers look LIKE BIRTHDAY CAKE YOU'RE OK GOD. The
altar is covered TOO MUCH fruit NOT WE DONT AGREE DO
          tootsie girl
MORE HOMEWORK THE WINDOW SILLS *oh cleaning*   NO
IMPROVEMENT YOU LOOK LIKE QUITE COMFORTABLE
          you remember this
GOD Swamiji has *altar* covered with fruits and flowers his back to
us QUITE STRONG WINDS YOU CAN CONSECRATE the green
leaves suddenly appear to have white WAIT A MINUTE flowers
USUAL hallucination YOU ARENT POOR KOL NIDRE GEMI-
NIS *very important give up* PUJA MY KINGDOM

COMMENTARY

Weiner's journals—contemporary—arise from an experience of word-visualizations reminiscent of those of the traditional poet-mystics: "I see words on my forehead, in the air, on other people, on the page. These appear in the text as CAPITALS or *underlines* (italics)." With this the reader can compare, e.g., the appearance of the Hebrew letters (above, page 391) as "great mountains," or the oral manifestation to the kabbalist Joseph Caro (1488–1575) of a *maggid* (heavenly messenger), who took the name Mishna & a persona between male & female:

> Sabbath night. . . . I had eaten & drunk very little, studied *Mishna* at the beginning of the night & then slept until dawn. When I awoke, the sun was already shining & I was grieved, saying to myself, "Why did I not rise when it was still night so that the *speech* should come to me as usual." Then I began to recite *Mishnayot* & when I had read five chapters, "the voice of my beloved knocketh" in my mouth, sounding by itself & speaking thus: "I have come to delight myself with thee & to speak in thy mouth, *not in a dream but as a man speaketh with a friend.* . . . For when thou fallest asleep amid thoughts of the *Mishna,* then my seven worlds shall keep thee; & when thou awakest after having fallen asleep amid thoughts of the *Mishna,* then it will speak in thy mouth & thy lips will vibrate."

The lack of a similar context for Weiner's experience, etc., is a condition of our time—on which no further comment.

(Hebrew, medieval)
THE MASORA CALLIGRAMS

(1) "ANIMALS & TREES"

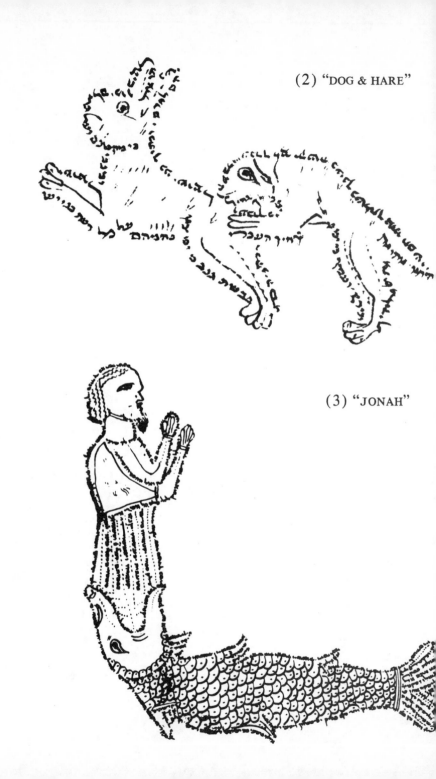

(2) "DOG & HARE"

(3) "JONAH"

(4) "FACE"

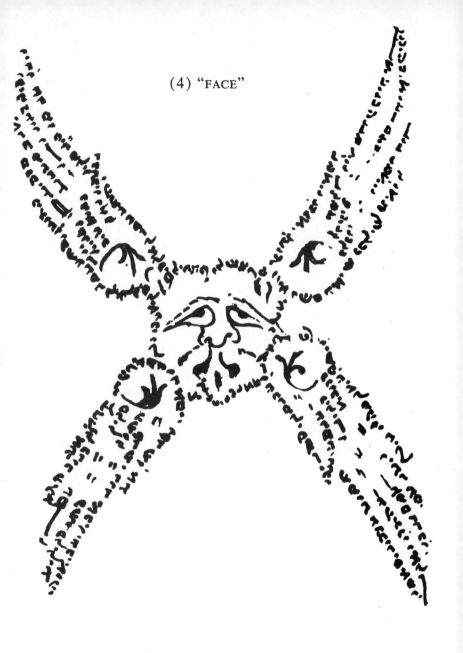

COMMENTARY

Words drawn into visual images have a near universal distribution among cultures that practice writing—more elaborate & expansive, less literal & literary than the "shaped poems" per George Herbert, etc., would lead us to believe. In Apollinaire's *Calligrammes* (circa 1914), the mode is revived—& re-shaped, smashed open—with the claim, e.g., in his "horse calligram": "You will find here a new representation of the universe. The most poetic & the most modern."

The masora "calligrams" occur here & there in traditional annotated copies of the Hebrew Bible. Writes Berjouhi Bowler (*The Word As Image,* page 128): "In some Hebrew manuscripts the massorah, which is the critical emendation found [as marginalia] on certain pages of the Bible, ceases to be the usual three lines, in minuscule letters, surrounding the biblical text. Unexpectedly . . . the massorah is shaped into patterns which generally have no particular relevance to the biblical passage or to the emendations and alternative readings [that make up their text]. The strange intrusions can appear either as a full page decoration . . . or in corners of the page. There is no apparent reason for their appearance."

Those reproduced here are in minute writing & have been greatly enlarged. Although the scribes' disregard of injunctions against iconography, etc., is obvious, the intention is otherwise unknown. Thus, Bowler again: "As the massorah proceeded, it became extremely abstruse and less understood. . . . Written by mere men to clarify the revelation of God, to safeguard the Word from the abuse of mortality and change, [the massorah] itself became the mystery. The mystery grows denser as the words themselves are swirled into these elaborate decorations. . . . As the rational content vanishes, a new communication occurs. The forms grow into these archetypal shapes and appear before us. We are invited to drop for an instant our existential alienation and join the dance." ("The Word as Ikon," *Typographica* 8, London, 1968.)

(Hebrew, medieval)

A PRAYER FOR THE KING

COMMENTARY

Reassemblage & reshaping of traditional New Year prayers, toward an address to God the King. Compare the Tzara calligram which follows —as an example of Dadaist abstraction. The prayer, above, ends with the words: "Keep us from plagues, swords, starvation, captivity, poverty, destruction, epidemics. And write down a life of goodness for the children of your faith. And all creation will thank you . . . You of good name." The relation to amulets in which prayers & psalms are shaped into menorahs, stars, etc., should be obvious.

Tristan Tzara (French 1896–1963)

CALLIGRAM

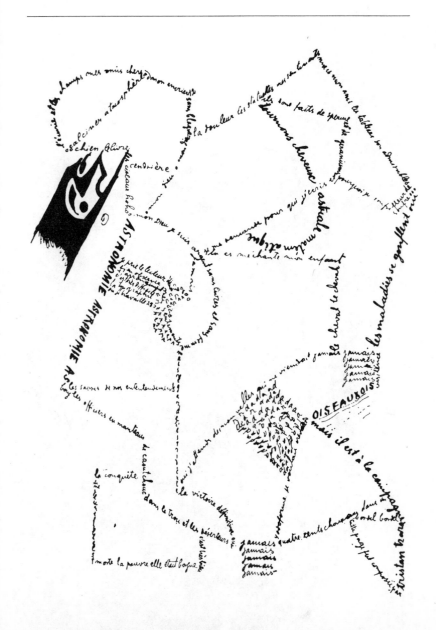

THE SCROLL OF ESTHER AS A BEAR

Jacques Gaffarel (17th century)
CELESTIAL ALPHABET EVENT

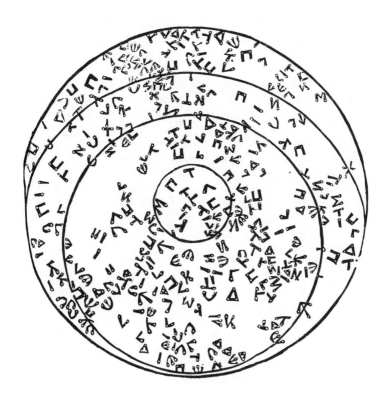

COMMENTARY

(1)   An extreme example of a language process event based on natural phenomena, this derives from Hebrew alphabetic practice projected on the night sky. The key is calligraphic: a form of the alphabet ("magic letters") going back to Hellenistic period, in which the lines of the letters culminate in rounded points (thus, א, alef, = ᙍ), permitting a later application to the night sky, where patterns of stars (points joined by "lines") can then be read as letters, groups of letters read as words, etc. In the process the sky becomes a massive concrete poem, whose words or "messages" are constantly transforming. The instance, above, is from Jacques Gaffarel, a Christian kabbalist of the 17th century, but the viability of the process is dependent on the Hebrew alphabet, where the absence of explicit vowels allows a wide range of meaningful readings.

(2)   "To the realm of practical Kabbalah . . . belong the many traditions concerning the existence of a special archangelic alphabet, the earliest of which was 'the alphabet of Metatron.' Other such alphabets of *kolmosin* ('[angelic] pens') were attributed to Michael, Gabriel, Raphael, etc. Several of these alphabets that have come down to us resemble cuneiform writing, while some clearly derive from early Hebrew or Samaritan script. In kabbalistic literature they are known as 'eye writing' (*ketav einayim*) because their letters are always composed of lines and small circles that resemble eyes." (G. Scholem, *Kabbalah,* page 186.)

Moses Cordovero (Hebrew, 1522–70)

THE 10 SEFIROT AS A LABYRINTH OF LETTERS

COMMENTARY

Depiction of the *sefirot* as stages of God's immanence (see above, page 11) has taken a variety of forms: e.g., as tree, as human body, as hand, as wheel of light, etc. Here Cordovero works off the initial letters of the *sefirot*, formalizing these into a maze pattern, with the initial letter of the tenth & closest *sefira—mem = malkhut* (= kingdom = shekinah)— in familiar form at center. The Hebrew letters throughout represent numbers as well as sounds (see below, page 431)—thus lead the way into a poetry of numbers, itself presented in a variety of modes.

Maria Hebrea (1st century B.C.)

THE NUMBERS

2 are 1
3 & 4 are 1
1 will become 2
2 will become 3

COMMENTARY

The entry through alchemy, in the figure of Mary the Jewess, said by some to be the mother of the art. Of her verbalizations only these formulas survive, reminiscent of E. E. Cummings' description of the poet's strategy: to hold that 2 times 2 *is 5*. Or Edmond Jabès of a *poesis* specifically Jewish: "The number '4,' he said, is the number of our ruin. Do not think I am mad. The number '4' equals 2 times 2. It is in the name of such obsolete logic that we are persecuted. For we hold that 2 times 2 equals also 5, or 7, or 9. You only need to consult the commentaries of our sages to verify. Not everything is simple in simplicity. We are hated because we do not enter into the simple calculations of mathematics." (*The Book of Questions,* page 92.)

It is at some such point that the equation "poet" & "Jew" (see above, page 141) reveals its meaning.

(Medieval, anonymous)
A TALISMAN FOR VENUS

22	47	16	41	10	35	4
5	23	48	17	42	11	29
30	6	24	49	18	36	12
13	21	7	25	43	19	37
38	14	32	1	26	44	30
21	39	8	33	2	27	45
46	15	40	9	34	3	28

COMMENTARY

(1)   "The total of the numbers is equal to the value—in letters—of the number [name] of the intelligence [guardian spirit] of Venus. The talisman is drawn on copper, the metal of the planet, and is used for operations in which spirits connected with this planet are invoked." (Idries Shah, *The Secret Lore of Magic.*) The columns & lines equal 175 in all directions.

(2)   Once viewed as aberrant, etc., forms like these can now be seen as more central, even centrally human. Writes Eric Mottram of "neo-Pythagorean arithmology" from Middle Ages to Mac Low: "Numerology assumes a universal unity, which can be drawn upon for limitations of nature; so that creation is a part of Creation, whether issued from an Author or made by an author in the image of universal authority. The poetry of numerology is part of the long dialectic of freedom and necessity, of the human search for a vocabulary and syntax through which to

explore and limit. . . . There is nothing slavish, degrading or anti-human in it, unless used as a limited imposition of geometry as the model of a State. Anarchism balances between chance and necessity, as nature does. The totalitarian state, simply, is not total but partial, an imposition of insane reason." (From "Compositions of the Magus: The Art of Jackson Mac Low," in *Vort* 8.) At least "numbers"—a traditional term for metrics, poetry, etc.—is seen in its full extent & tied at origin to an attempt to form a viable, transforming image of the real world.

(3) "THOU hast ordered all things in measure & number & weight." (Ecclesiasticus 11.21.)

Charlie Morrow (b. 1942)

A NUMBER BLESSING

1.	B	1.	B
2.	A	1.2.	BA
3.	R	1.2.3.	BAR
4.	U	1.2.3.4.	BARU
5.	CH	1.2.3.4.5.	BARUCH

12345 BARUCH
12345 BARUCH
12345 BARUCH
12345 BARUCH
12345 BARUCH

12341 BARU B
12341 BARU B
12341 BARU B
12341 BARU B
12341 BARU B

```
12311  BAR  BB
12311  BAR  BB
12311  BAR  BB
12311  BAR  BB
12311  BAR  BB

12111  BA   BBB
12111  BA   BBB
12111  BA   BBB
12111  BA   BBB
12111  BA   BBB

11111  BBBBB
11111  BBBBB
11111  BBBBB
11111  BBBBB
11111  BBBBB
```

1975

COMMENTARY

"Counting is a way of labeling pulses. Simple counting takes a calm, even tone of voice, a scientific tone—the cantillation of facts, facts by themselves—a list of the names of distances, a set of regular guideposts, equidistant.

"For a musician, counting is part of the job. Music is measured, and these measures are felt against a matrix of pulses.

". . . Hanging numbers like signposts on locations, as in the performance of my counts with complex sound systems or several counters, is a meditative geometry.

". . . The numbers may be read on one tone or associated with pitches, in scaleform or any form. They can be played on instruments.

"In the number blessing the word BARUCH (Hebrew: "blessed") is meant to be sung in the traditional ascending fourth.

". . . The space implied by the end of a line and the beginning of the next line should be dealt with consistently within any particular performance. It can be said of the number pieces, that it is the consistency of their realization that is special about them." (Charlie Morrow.)

(Yiddish, traditional)

A POEM WITH NUMBERS FOR THE DEAD

one

the heaviness of
death

two

knocks in the synagogue
the penalty
is paid in full

three

bitter drops fall
over a dead man's head

four

the weeks after
he died
(say) thirty days

five

mourners
mourning for
the dead

six

boards to lay
the dead on

seven

days spent mourning
mourn the dead

eight

grave clothes
wrapped around
the dead

nine

handbreaths
were deep enough
to dig a grave

ten

each one would read
a line

eleven

months remain
to say
the death chant

twelve

were 12 months later
candles lit
in service of the dead

J.R.

Rose Drachler (b. 1911)

THE COUNTING MADE THE CORNERS RIGHT

The counting made
The corners
Of the building
True

One
One and one
Two
Two and one

Four horns
Corners
One and seven he counted
One and six

The goat stayed fluid
It steamed
Yellow eyes, square pupils
Fringes of flesh at its throat

They beat him with sticks
They threw stones at him
They sent him away
The goats were a gift

One to die and one to drive away

One
One and one
Two
Two and one

The counting was washing
It was clean
It was for the building

25 GEMATRIA

Light
A mystery.

Eye
Silver.

The Upper World
Is all the chariot

He & He
This & this.

Metatron
The beard.
The beard.

Messenger
Five.

The Witness
A jewel.

The Body
The reward.

The World / The Year / The Soul
Evening.
Morning.
Noon.

First Adam
Hell is open.

Moses
I am.
I am.
I am.

The Garden
Shadow.
Stone.
The Brain.

The Soul of Adam
Lilith.

Israel
El Song.

Rebekka
This.
12.

The River
The prayerbook.

Incense
The ark.
613.

Wisdom
Is.
Was.
Will be.

Messiah
Snake.

The Devil
Fat-ash.

This Pope
This garbage.

Dominus
Demonus.

Money
The tree.

"& the king said

to Haman: the
money will be
yours"

Death
903.

Israel Alone
Therefore.

J.R./H.L.

COMMENTARY

Gematria is the general term for a variety of traditional coding practices used to establish correspondences between words or series of words based on the numerical equivalence of the sums of their letters or on the interchange of letters according to a set system. The numerical method— *gematria* per se—typically took *alef* as 1, *bet* as 2, *yod* as 10, *kuf* as 100, etc., through *tav* (last letter) as 400—although more complicated methods (e.g., reduction to single digits, etc.) were later introduced. Non-numerical methods included (1) anagrams, or rearrangements of the letters of a word to form a new word or word series, as "god" to "dog" in English; (2) *notarikon,* the derivation of a new word from the initial letters of several others & vice versa, as "god," say from "garden of delight"; & (3) *temura,* various systems of letter code, e.g., the common one in which the first half of the alphabet is placed over the second & letters are substituted between the resultant rows, etc., *in search of meaningful combinations.*

Processes of this kind go back to Greek, even Babylonian, practice, & early enter the rabbinic literature. But the greatest development was among kabbalists from the 12th century on, who used it both to discover divine & angelic names & to uncover correspondences between ideas & images by means free of subjective interference. When set out as poems, the resemblance of the *gematria* to a poetry of correspondences in our own time is evident, as also to instances of process poetry & art based on (more or less) mechanical formulas for the generation of both simple & extended series of permutations & combinations. Thus, Jackson Mac Low's "vocabularies," in which the text (or score) "is a drawing, painting or collage consisting of all the words I can think of (or fit on the paper or canvas) spelled solely with the letters of one person's name," is very close in method—even, ultimately, in intention—to the first non-numerical process described above.

While numerical *gematria* & coded *temura* come easily in a language like Hebrew which is written without vowels, the possibility of similar workings in English shouldn't be discounted. The *gematria*-generated poems, above, are, however, directly translated from traditional Hebrew sources—a fact which adds to the apparent "distance & power" of the combinations, a direct relationship that 20th-century poets like Reverdy saw as the basis of the poetic image.

Karen Shaw (b. 1942)

ADDITIONAL MEANINGS: 46 = Chaos

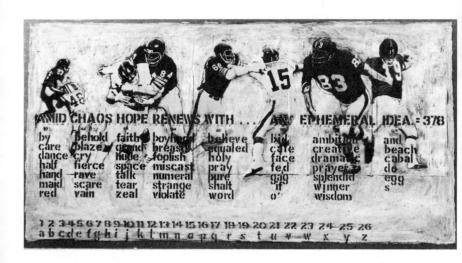

COMMENTARY

A gematria-derived performance by a contemporary artist, in which letters of the Latin alphabet are numbered A-1 to Z-26, & common situations using numbers (supermarket receipts, football jerseys, theater stubs, etc.) are read as any of a range of word equivalents, becoming messages or, even, poems. The key is given as part of the piece. In another context (fictional), she writes: "And so I spent all of February and March and April and 10 days of May of this leap year deprived of comfort, companionship and conversation. For 100 days and nights hurting and healing. All things being equal 100 equals USELESS (21 + 19 + 5 + 12 + 5 + 19 + 19), and so it was."

Charles Stein (b. 1944)
APPLE-LILITH-NIGHT

Let it happen at night
Let it happen at a gate
Let it happen

Let Lilith light at a gate
Let Lilith gape at an apple
Let an apple gape

Let pale pale Lilith gape at a pale pale nape
Let lithe apple Lilith gape at a pale pale nape
Let lithe apple Lilith leap at a gate
Let light leap at a gate

I light at a gate
I let light leap at a gate
I gape at a light pale apple Lilith let light at a gate
I leap at a gate
I let a light path leap at a night gate
I night gate

I let Lilith light at a high path
I let Lilith light at a thigh
I let Lilith light a high light thin pale nape

a pale pale thigh
a high thin nape
a lip
a nipple tip
a lap

a tight hip
a tap at a night tip
tap a tap at a tight tit
tip a tight hip
a hip tap at a tight lip
a night tip

Let a tight tip tap at a tight hip
Let a hip tap tip at a tight lip

Let it happen at night
Let it happen at a gate

a heat
a hat
a hit
a pit
     height
a tight hit
a tin hat
a hat tip

high heat at a hat tip
Let a high heat hit at a tall thin hat tip

Lilith
in heat
at a tall thin hat tip

Let it happen at night

Let a tin hat tip
Let a tin hat leap at a gate

a tall tin hat
a tall thin tail
a nape
a heat that let it happen at a tall tin gate

a night
in a hat
      that
Lilith
in a heat let
light at a gate

a light
a path
a hit
a hat
   that

Let it happen at night
Let it happen
Let it happen at a gate

COMMENTARY

From a series of "seed poems" built, like some of the work described above, on rearrangements of a restricted number of letters, of which he says: "All the words of the poem are generated from the letters of the seed words (i.e., title)." Among other contemporary examples are Emmett Williams' book-length *Sweethearts* & Otto Nebel's experiments with reduced alphabets.

An even larger area of "process poetry," etc., involves the transformation of traditional & found texts, in which the poet does not create the poem *ex nihilo* but, like the musician, orders & reassembles words already given. The play here may be for mind or mouth—or for both. But the reader would be well advised not to miss the possibility of sound in any instance: thus, the persistence of an oral poetry into an age of writing.

(Hebrew, medieval)

VARIATIONS ON A HEBREW AMULET

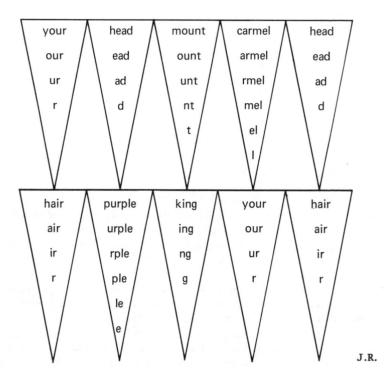

J.R.

COMMENTARY

Translation from a Hebrew amulet, in which words of a found text (Song of Songs 7.6) are reduced letter by letter, as sympathetic magic, to reduce the strength of forces in the outside world:

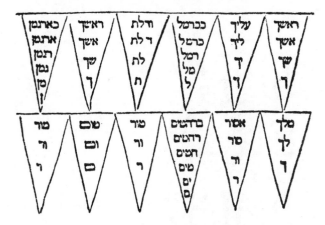

A traditional written form of poetic-magical structuring, it can be reversed for enhancement of the condition imaged—as here, the increase or decrease of sexual desire.

Jackson Mac Low (b. 1922)

KADDISH GATHA

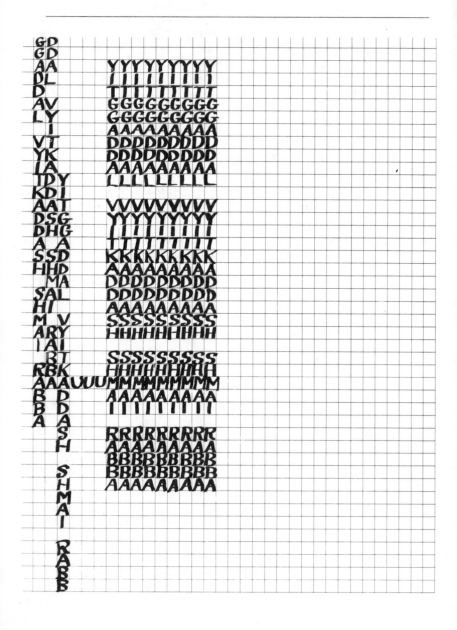

" 'Kaddish Gatha' (27 April 1975) is one of an open series of performance-poem notations lettered on quadrille paper, begun early in 1961. In each Gatha chance operations have helped arrange the letters of a mantram or mantramlike prayer (here the Aramaic 'kaddish': *yitggaddal v'yitkaddash shmai rabba,* 'magnified & sanctified be His Great Name')—often, as here, so that they cross an axis of A's, U's, & M's (letters of the seed syllable *AUM*). Performers (soloists or groups) begin at any square, reading or being silent for any duration (for empty squares), 'move' to any square adjacent to its sides or corners, & thus continue till the performance ends—by spontaneous agreement, a leader's signal, or arrival at a preselected time. Letters may be read as their English names, as any sound they can stand for in any language, or grouped as syllables, words, pseudowords, word-groups, &c., formed in any direction(s). Sounds, &c., may be repeated singly or in groups, & the basic mantram or prayer may be repeated *ad lib.* (any time—any number of repetitions). Prolongable sounds may be prolonged for any duration (producing 'chords' or 'organ points' in group performances). Rhythms, pitches, &c., are chosen freely but in relation to all other sounds heard (other performers, audience, ambient sounds). 'Listen' & 'Relate' are the most important rules. Performers, guided by awareness, sensitivity, tact, courtesy, & inspiration, produce sounds or observe attentive silence thru conscious choices to modify (or not) the total situation." (J.M.L.)

ZOHAR EVENT

A Simultaneity for 10 or More Readers

Cut up a chapter of the *Zohar* into as many segments as there are readers.

Distribute the cut pages, & have the readers sound their segments simultaneously.

From THE HAVDALA OF RABBI AKIBA

"A Realization"

Hear, he o that Israel, dwelleth the in Lord secret our place God, of the the Lord Most is High one. Shall hear, abide o under Israel, the the shadow Lord of our God, the the Almighty. Lord is one.

Hear, I o will Israel, say the of Lord the our Lord, God, He the is Lord my is refuge one. And hear, my o fortress: Israel, my the God; Lord in our Him God, will the I Lord trust. Is one.

Hear, surely o He Israel, shall the deliver Lord thee our from God, the the snare Lord of is the one. Fowler, hear, and o from Israel, the the noisome Lord pestilence. Our God, the Lord is one.

Hear, He o shall Israel, cover the thee Lord with our His God, feathers, the and Lord under is His one. Wings hear, shalt o thou Israel, trust: the His Lord truth our shall God, be the thy Lord shield is and one. Buckler.

Hear, thou o shalt Israel, not the be Lord afraid our for God the the terror Lord by is night; one. Nor hear, for o the Israel, arrow the that Lord flieth our by God, day; the Lord is one.

Hear, nor o for Israel, the pestilence Lord that our walketh God, in the darkness; Lord nor is for one. The hear destruction o that Israel, wasteth the at Lord noonday. Our God, the Lord is one.

Hear, a o thousand Israel, shall the fall Lord at our thy God, side, the and Lord ten is thousand one. At hear, thy o right Israel, hand; the but Lord it our shall God, not the come Lord nigh is thee. One.

Hear, only o with Israel, thine the eyes Lord shalt our thou God, behold the and Lord see is the one. Reward hear of o the Israel, wicked. The Lord our God, the Lord is one.

Hear, because o thou Israel hast the made Lord the our Lord, God, which the is Lord my is refuge, one. Even hear, the o Most Israel, High, the thy Lord habitation; our God, the Lord is one.

Hear, there o shall Israel, no the evil Lord befall our thee, God, neither the shall Lord any is plague one. Come hear, nigh o thy Israel, dwelling. The Lord our God, the Lord is one.

Hear, for o He Israel, shall the give Lord His our angels God, charge the over Lord thee, is to one. Keep hear, thee o in Israel, all the thy Lord ways. Our God, the Lord is one.

Hear, they o shall Israel, bear the thee Lord up our in God, their the hands, Lord lest one. Thou hear, dash o thy Israel, foot the against Lord a our stone. God, the Lord is one.

Hear, thou o shalt Israel, tread the upon Lord the our lion God, and the adder: Lord the is young one. Lion hear, and o the Israel, dragon the shalt Lord thou our trample God, under the feet. Lord is one.

Hear, because o he Israel, hath the set Lord his our love God, upon the me, Lord therefore is will one. I hear, deliver o him: Israel, I the will Lord set our him God, on the high, Lord because is he one. Hath hear, known o my Israel, name. The Lord our God, the Lord is one.

Hear, he o shall Israel, call the upon Lord me, our and God, I the will Lord answer is him: one. I hear, will o be Israel, with the him Lord our in God, trouble; the I Lord will is deliver one. Him, hear, and o honor Israel, him. The Lord our God, the Lord is one.

Hear, with o long Israel, life the will Lord I our satisfy God, him, the and Lord show is him one. My hear, salvation. O Israel, the Lord our God, the Lord is one.

J.R.

COMMENTARY

A realization of a simple collage event, in which the instructions were to alternate the words of the mantric *shema* prayer ("Hear, o Israel . . .") with those of Psalm 91. Writes Joshua Trachtenberg: "Already in the pages of the Talmud we read that 'the demons keep away from everyone who recites the *Shema* before retiring.' There grew up an increasingly elaborate scheme of prayer around this nocturnal recitation of the *Shema* . . . coupled with potent Biblical verses and psalms."

(*Jewish Magic & Superstition,* page 156.) While contemporary pieces of this sort are generally, but not invariably, more complex &/or randomized, the reader who sounds this aloud may still be aware of an intricate emergence, disappearing & interweaving of both texts.

(Hebrew, traditional)

From AN AMULET AGAINST THE EVIL EYE

Exodus 22.18

Thou shalt not suffer a witch to live
To live thou shalt not suffer a witch
To live a witch thou shalt not suffer

A witch to live thou shalt not suffer
A witch thou shalt not suffer to live
Not a witch shalt thou suffer to live

Jackson Mac Low (b. 1922)
4.5.10.11.2.8.4.2., the 2nd biblical poem

thither:/_____/to/_____/
not/_____//_____/tribe/_____/
every/_____/the not/_____//_____/the before lest/_____/
Arabah, a thy/_____/All/_____//_____//_____//_____/the
                                                                  /_____/
Get/_____/
/_____//_____/thy/_____/them,/_____/thy/_____/
/_____//_____/shalt/_____/
/_____/this

/_____//_____//_____//_____/
/_____//_____/of this/_____/
which round many slack/_____//_____/the might/_____/fathers
of is/_____/from/_____/the/_____/great Israel:/_____/you.
I/_____/
and ye shalt/_____/God there, and of
/_____/lent/_____//_____/
/_____//_____/

If the the/_____/
/_____/God to/_____//_____/
thou/_____//_____/chosen/_____//_____//_____/spoken.
                                          shall established.
/_____/not/_____//_____//_____//_____//_____/
                      /_____/Jebusite: neck/_____/
son/_____/
thou took/_____//_____//_____//_____//_____/die:
to/_____/be/_____/
house./_____/

/_____/ /_____/ /_____/ shall
/_____/ /_____/ the her and
/_____/ out/_____/ set/_____/ /_____/ a set thou/_____/
upon/_____/ thee with/_____/ /_____/ /_____/ /_____/
/_____/ /_____/ /_____/

thy thou
your nations;/_____/ it/_____/ /_____/ the/_____/
/_____/ /_____/ witness He
them,/_____/

/_____/ /_____/ be thy
And/_____/ /_____/ /_____/ with
Even will Me/_____/ /_____/ /_____/ the/_____/ /_____/ And
/_____/ /_____/ Naphtali/_____/ /_____/ /_____/ and
children/_____/ Moses/_____/

/_____/ /_____/
Have we/_____/ you./_____/ doors 'Sanctify/_____/
the cut And/_____/
the   of

/_____/ And/_____/ /_____/
/_____/ the/_____/ the/_____/
/_____/ us he/_____/ And/_____/ and out/_____/ /_____/
on the/_____/ and/_____/ /_____/ and against down be remaining.
/_____/ Israel
beforetime/_____/ that/_____/ /_____/ /_____/ /_____/
/_____/

/_____/ /_____/ the/_____/
the cities

/_____/ /_____/ the of
/_____/ this along Anak—/_____/
In the/_____/ /_____/ the/_____/ unto the/_____/ /_____/
/_____/ Moses the their their were city/_____/ in out families
/_____/ about
/_____/ /_____/ there/_____/ /_____/ /_____/ much that
/_____/ /_____/ /_____/ children,
/_____/ /_____/

not/_____/ /_____/of
the/_____/ /_____/them through
/_____/and/_____/ /_____/up after/_____/ /_____/Hebron
the
/_____/drove pass, as/_____/war,/_____/was/_____/
/_____/of
/_____/ /_____/
/_____/ /_____/ /_____/And Lord/_____/ /_____/ /_____/
And heart/_____/doth
/_____/her

Numbers 35:6–Judges 5:27

1st of January, 1955
New York City

COMMENTARY

(1) "It was just before New Year's 1955. I was thirty-two then. I started writing these 'biblical poems'—they were the first ones I wrote using systematic-chance operations, and I was fascinated by them. I thought, 'Well, I'll just see what happens.' The materials I used were one small die and a copy of the Hebrew Scriptures. Each time I had a decision to make, I threw the die first for the number of times to throw it. Then the first thing I did in writing each 'biblical poem' was to throw the die to get a certain structure of number of events. That's when I invented a kind of event structure, a kind of event metric, where the number of 'events' (words or silences) in each line and the number of lines in each stanza constitute a repeating structure. These numbers were determined by throws of the die. Then I filled out the structure with words taken from the Hebrew Scriptures and silences. The silences are equal in time to any word that you can think of, so they're indeterminate in length." (Jackson Mac Low, from interview in *The Craft of Poetry*, ed. William Packard.)

(2) "I'd been using the *I Ching* as both oracle and wisdom book since 1950 when the Wilhelm-Baynes translation was published by Pantheon. Also, I'd come across Gershom Scholem's *Major Trends in Jewish Mysticism* about 1950, and from it I'd learned about mystical methods such as *Gematria*, . . . *Notarikon* . . . and *Temurah*. . . . My own use of

similar methods is mediated by the Zen Buddhist teaching that close attention to any object or phenomenon can lead to enlightenment—that if we view *any*thing steadily with full attention, it can lead us to a realization of ultimate reality. Thus *any* words—any linguistic phenomena whatsoever, written or oral—can be treated as 'sacred texts' and subjected to Kabbalistic-like operations to lead us to basic insights." (Jackson Mac Low, from interview in *Vort* 8, ed. Barry Alpert. But see Scholem also, *re* Abulafia etc., in *Major Trends* . . . : "Every language, not only Hebrew, is transformed into a transcendental medium of the one and only language of God.")

(Greek, c. 1st century A.D.)

AN EPITAPH

E   S   T   E   R

A   S   T   E   R

A   S   T   A   R

COMMENTARY   .

From a Greco-Roman tombstone (Rome), in which a "single" word (Greek: ASTER) carries multiple meanings & sound echoes—thus foliating into three in the translation. Writes E. R. Goodenough: " 'Aster,' which may be a hellenization of Esther, as Frey suggests, and so a personal name, or may be an indication that the person buried has become a 'star.' It may indeed be both, since the name of the woman, if such it was, lent itself so well to such a pun. Cumont especially felt this conjunction, since immortality in the form of becoming one of the stars was an idea of such great importance at this time." (*Jewish Symbols in the Greco-Roman Period,* volume 2, page 9.) The word is surrounded by doves, menorah, grapes:

(Hebrew/Aramaic, c. 490 A.D.)

From THE BABYLONIAN TALMUD   "The Signs"

For Memory

1

like the sand of the purple blue scorpion stirring his basket

2

All time Jordan

3

Seas Gabriel Hungry

4

neither exact weight nor heaped up with market officers & with a
pound three & ten NEFESH   weighs a thick strike   you shall not
do   he shall not do

5

King Abraham the 10 years when he passed away he was exalted
lonely

6

he who does   Deadly Poison   Enthrusts   His fellow   Broken

7

& Rabbi Yose said: Your sign for memory is TABLE IN THE
NORTH & CANDELABRA IN THE SOUTH   the one increases
its own & the other increases its own   there is no difficulty   THIS
IS FOR US   & THAT IS FOR THEM

COMMENTARY

The Talmud, which incorporates a transcription of the older Mishna
as traditional oral discourse, still preserves occasional mnemonics
(*simanim* or signs): memory devices which sometimes take the form of a
recombination of key words from the interchanges that follow. The
results, as here, are a series of new utterances that both lead the mind
back to the sources in question &, like much contemporary collage poetry, open the possibility of new readings & combinations.

CHANCE COMPOSITION NO. 1

Stick a pin through the Talmud, take the different sentences pointed to by the pin, & make them into a single discourse.

CHANCE COMPOSITION NO. 2

Do the same for the *Zohar*.

Tristan Tzara (French, 1896–1963)

From MANIFESTO ON FEEBLE & BITTER LOVE

To make a dada poem
Take a newspaper.
Take a pair of scissors.
Choose an article as long as you are planning to make your poem.
Cut out the article.
Then cut out each of the words that make up this article & put them
    in a bag.
Shake it gently.
Then take out the scraps one after the other in the order in which
    they left the bag.
Copy conscientiously.
The poem will be like you.

(Aramaic, c. 210 A.D.)

From THE MISHNAH   "Clean & Unclean"

MISHNAH 1. IF IN A PUBLIC DOMAIN THERE WAS A DEAD CREEP-
ING THING & A FROG, & ALSO IF THERE WAS THERE AN OLIVE'S BULK
OF A CORPSE & AN OLIVE'S BULK OF CARRION, A BONE OF A CORPSE &
A BONE OF CARRION, A CLOD OF CLEAN EARTH & A CLOD FROM A
GRAVE AREA OR A CLOD OF CLEAN EARTH & A CLOD FROM THE LAND
OF THE GENTILES, OR IF THERE WERE TWO PATHS, THE ONE UN-

CLEAN & THE OTHER CLEAN, & A MAN WALKED THROUGH ONE OF THEM BUT IT IS NOT KNOWN WHICH, OR OVERSHADOWED ONE OF THEM BUT IT IS NOT KNOWN WHICH, OR HE ,SHIFTED ONE OF THEM BUT IT IS NOT KNOWN WHICH, RABBI AKIBA RULED THAT HE IS UNCLEAN, BUT THE SAGES RULE THAT HE IS CLEAN.

MISHNAH 2. WHETHER THE MAN SAID, "I TOUCHED AN OBJECT ON THIS SPOT BUT I DO NOT KNOW WHETHER IT WAS UNCLEAN OR CLEAN," OR "I TOUCHED ONE BUT I DO NOT KNOW WHICH OF THE TWO I TOUCHED," RABBI AKIBA RULES THAT HE IS UNCLEAN, BUT THE SAGES RULE THAT HE IS CLEAN. RABBI YOSE RULES THAT HE IS UNCLEAN IN EVERY CASE & CLEAN ONLY IN THAT OF THE PATH, SINCE IT IS THE USUAL PRACTICE FOR MEN TO GO BUT IT IS NOT THEIR USUAL PRACTICE TO TOUCH.

MISHNAH 3. IF THERE WERE TWO PATHS, THE ONE UNCLEAN & THE OTHER CLEAN, & IF A MAN WALKED BY ONE OF THEM & THEN PREPARED CLEAN FOODSTUFFS WHICH WERE SUBSEQUENTLY CONSUMED &, HAVING BEEN SPRINKLED UPON ONCE & A SECOND TIME & HAVING PERFORMED IMMERSION & ATTAINED CLEANNESS, HE WALKED BY THE SECOND PATH & THEN PREPARED CLEAN FOODSTUFFS, THE LATTER ARE DEEMED CLEAN. IF THE FIRST FOODSTUFFS WERE STILL IN EXISTENCE BOTH MUST BE HELD IN SUSPENSE. IF HE HAD NOT ATTAINED CLEANNESS IN THE MEANTIME, THE FIRST ARE HELD IN SUSPENSE & THE SECOND MUST BE BURNT.

MISHNAH 4. IF THERE WAS A DEAD CREEPING THING & A FROG IN A PUBLIC DOMAIN & A MAN TOUCHED ONE OF THEM & THEN PREPARED CLEAN FOODSTUFFS WHICH WERE SUBSEQUENTLY CONSUMED, & THEN HE PERFORMED IMMERSION, TOUCHED THE OTHER & THEN PREPARED CLEAN FOODSTUFFS, THE LATTER ARE DEEMED CLEAN. IF THE FIRST FOODSTUFFS WERE STILL IN EXISTENCE BOTH MUST BE HELD IN SUSPENSE. IF HE DID NOT PERFORM IMMERSION IN THE MEANTIME, THE FIRST ARE HELD IN SUSPENSE & THE SECOND MUST BE BURNT.

MISHNAH 5. IF THERE WERE TWO PATHS, THE ONE UNCLEAN & THE OTHER CLEAN, & A MAN WALKED BY ONE OF THEM & THEN PREPARED CLEAN FOODSTUFFS, & SUBSEQUENTLY ANOTHER MAN

CAME BY & WALKED BY THE SECOND PATH & THEN PREPARED CLEAN
FOODSTUFFS, RABBI JUDAH RULED: IF EACH BY HIMSELF ASKED FOR
A RULING THEY ARE BOTH TO BE DECLARED CLEAN, BUT IF THEY
ASKED FOR A RULING SIMULTANEOUSLY, BOTH ARE TO BE DECLARED
UNCLEAN. RABBI YOSE RULED: IN EITHER CASE THEY ARE BOTH UN-
CLEAN.

COMMENTARY

Babylonian Talmud, circa 5th century A.D., of which the Mishna (oral
discourse) goes back to the editing & transcription by Rabbi Jehudah the
Patriarch & his school, circa 200. An example of what David Antin,
in relation to the "prose" of Gertrude Stein, calls "phrasal poetry," but
also related to his own talking pieces, discourse out of Wittgenstein, etc.
The present passage is, of course, from a much longer series, an actual
discourse in which the process is one of testing, by recombinations from
a set series of situations, the possibility of deriving conclusions such as
x or not-x, "clean" or "not-clean," within the category of ritual purity &
contamination. Note, too, that the thrust is not toward closure but a
simultaneity of opposite conclusions, typified in the Talmud by the
"contradictory" propositions of the schools of Hillel & Shammai, etc.:
not to eliminate conflict but to recognize its presence at the heart of
discourse. And if one sounds the present text as a poem—even chants it
in recognition of the older practice—the sound itself assists in reconstruction of that ancient dialectic. (For more on contradictions, questions,
etc., see pages 60, 270–71, above.)

Addendum. "Thought is made in the mouth." (T. Tzara.)

Gertrude Stein (1874–1946)

From AN ELUCIDATION

I think I won't
I think I will
I think I will
I think I won't
I think I won't
I think I will
I think I will
I think I won't.
I think I won't
I think I will
I think I will
I think I won't
I think I will
I think I won't
I think I will
I think I won't.
I think I will
I think I won't
I think I won't
I think I won't
I think I won't
I think I will
I think I won't
Of course
I think I will
I think I won't
I think I won't
I think I will
This is a good example if you do not abuse it.

Where they like.

Can follow where they like.

I think this is a good example.

I think I will.

I am afraid I have been too careful.

I think I will.

Two examples and then an elucidation and a separation of one example from the other one.

I think I will.

Then very certainly we need not repeat.

Can there at this rate can there have been at this rate more and more.

Can at this rate can there have been at this rate can there have been more and more at this rate.

At this rate there can not have been there can not have been at this rate there can not have been more and more at this rate. At this rate there can not have been more and more. There can not have been at this rate, there can not have been more and more at this rate there can not have been more and more at this rate.

What did I say. Full of charms I said.

Full of what. Full of charms I said.

What did I say, full of charms I said.

If in order to see incidentally incidentally I request to see extraordinarily.

If in order to see incidentally I request to see.

I see you I see you too.

Ishmael ben Elisha (Hebrew, 2nd century A.D.)
A POEM OF THE MEASURES

Rabbi Ishamel says: By 13 measures you will draw out Torah.

1
from light
to heavy

2
the likeness
of the words

3
a father-form
in one writ
a father-form
in two writs

4
from a whole
& from a part

5
from a part
& from a whole

6
a wholeness & a part
a whole judged only
by its part

7
from a whole that needs
a part
& from a part that needs
a wholeness

8
every word
inside a wholeness
that left the wholeness
left to teach
but hasn't left to teach
about itself
but left to teach about
the wholeness
wholly

9
every word
inside a wholeness
that left the wholeness
to lodge a second claim
its content like the first
has left to lighten it
not make it heavy

10
every word
inside a wholeness
that left to lodge a second
claim
its content other than the first
has left to lighten it
& make it heavy

11
every word
inside a wholeness
that left to judge a new thing
you cannot then replace
within the wholeness
until the writ
replaces it within the wholeness
the way it is

12
a word that teaches
from its content
& a word that teaches
from where its content ends

13
& so two writings
that deny each other
until a third one comes
& splits the difference

J.R./H.L.

COMMENTARY

(1)   Included in his 2nd-century commentary on Leviticus (*Baraita de Rabbi Ishmael*), these thirteen principles for exegesis of the Bible (hermeneutics) were later inserted in the morning prayer service "to complete the daily minimum of Bible and Talmud study required of every Jew." (Philip Birnbaum, *Daily Prayer Book,* page 41.) Fixed & chanted, they are alive as long as they are sounded, but as they are now a written part of the service, they must also be resisted or read anew. Thus, the present translation departs from the usual "philosophical" terms ("inference is drawn from a minor premise to a major one," etc.) & returns to "literal" or "root" readings of the words.

(2)   "Philosophy, as we use the word, is a fight against the fascination which forms of expression exert upon us." (Ludwig Wittgenstein, *The Blue & Brown Books,* page 27.)

David Antin (b. 1932)

From MEDITATIONS

meditation 12

if we slowly approach a surface of water with our finger we often deceive ourselves about when we are wet   a patient may feel the surgeon's scalpel while it is still a slight distance away

"first we asked him"

first we asked him to think of birds   then we woke him and asked for their names   finally we requested him to give us without interruption the names of fish and trees   he said winter jackdaw sparrow eagle kite rooster nightingale wood blackbird falcon raven road siskin dove   he said forest wood bird goose duck sparrow crow jackdaw tomtit garden summer-sparrow   we said square   he said on the square they feed the doves   we said summer   he said gathering mushrooms raspberries darnel   it was pleasant to look at the sunset   to listen to the birds singing   to come back home and go to sleep   we said now   he said it was a winter evening   there was snow on the street   now i must go out today   it will be fine if it is snowing in the forest   a raven coughs   i remember something sad   we said factory   he said i dont know what to say   it seems strange today how the birds keep pursuing me   here in our town was a factory and it stood next to a house   we used to meet there and play   in the fields nearby we could hear the song of nightingales

meditation 15

a morsel of mashed potato on the tablecloth can be horrible if you pick it up thinking its a breadcrumb

COMMENTARY

". . . At some place or places, the world of human experience is intersected by the world of physics, and the intersection of these two language domains . . . is not only abrupt but somehow inevitable and maybe calamitous. . . . It took me to Wittgenstein, as later it took me to Chomsky and Quine and the later Carnap." (D.A.)

But note well, etc., his description of the making-of-the-poem as in itself an act of language, an event; thus: "In the first few [meditations] I was using in each case an arbitrary word set, like from a spelling list of difficult words for high school students. And I had these words and I had to use them to build all the lines of the poem with. . . . They were like obstacles, pebbles in my mouth that gave shape to what I had to say. . . . So the meditative act, as I was defining it in the work, was to respond to these givens, work with them, because the world is full of such givens and I was reenacting the sense of this givenness, my sense of something that would walk in on you while you were walking." (Interview in *Vort* 7, 1975.) And so points us back to the activating, reactivating stance of the poet/talker/thinker in search of meanings trapped in language. His most recent works have been "oral poetry" as pure discourse: a strategy of talking that moves us forward and returns us to "the infinitely moving, the constantly progressing and unfolding element" of Oral Torah (G. Scholem, above, page 381). Thus the *Zohar*—a source Antin is not too likely to invoke: "The Voice should never be separated from the Utterance, & he who separates them becomes dumb, &, being bereft of speech, returns to dust. Rabbi Simeon said: 'It is written: I was dumb with silence, I held my peace, having no good things to say, & my sorrow was stirred.'" (*Zohar* I.36a.)

SOUNDING EVENTS

Sound the words as quickly as possible
Sound the words as loudly as possible
Sound the words in a whisper

Sound the words while jumping in place
Sound the words while beating your chest
Sound the words while swaying sideways

Sound the words while clapping hands
Sound the words while turning somersaults
Sound the words while standing still

Sound the words a second time
Sound the words a third time
Sound the words a fourth time

Sound the words a fifth time
Sound the words a sixth time
Sound the words a seventh time

Sound the words an eighth time
Sound the words a ninth time
Sound the words a tenth time

Sound the words a hundred times
Sound the words a thousand times
Sound the words in silence

COMMENTARY

Examples of ways in which the written text (as prayer or meditation/mantra) was brought back to the world of sound & gesture.

(1)   "You will meet a company of seers coming down from the high place with a psaltery, a tambourine, a pipe, & a harp: & they will prophesy: & the spirit of Yahveh will come upon you, & you will prophesy with them, & will be turned into another man." (I Samuel 10.5–.6.)

(2)   "Prayer is copulation with the Shekinah. Just as there is swaying when copulation begins so, too, a man must sway at first & then he can remain immobile & attached to the Shekinah with great attachment. As a result of his swaying a man is able to attain a powerful stage of arousal. For he will ask himself: Why do I sway my body? Presumably it is because the Shekinah stands over against me. And as a result he will attain to a stage of great enthusiasm." (From *Tsava'at ha-Ribash,* quoted in L. Jacobs, *Hasidic Prayer.*)

(3)   "He who reads without melody & repeats without song, concerning him the Scripture says: Therefore I also gave them statutes which were not to their advantage." (Rabbi Yoḥanan, Talmud: *Megila* 32a.)

*

A series of events & happenings—for voice & body—follow, toward conclusion of the present "book."

WORD EVENTS

Read a verse.
Read each word backwards.
Read the entire verse backwards.

GOLEM MEDITATION EVENTS

1. Take pure earth from a mountain, strew some of it over your house, & wash it from your body. Knead the earth in running water & form a golem from it. Bury the golem in the ground, then walk around it in a circle & recite the 221 alphabets. Repeat the process 442 times, while concentrating on the Name of God.

2. Take a bowl full of water & a small spoon. Fill the spoon with earth & shake it: then slowly blow the earth across the water. While beginning to blow the first spoonful, utter a consonant of the Name in a loud voice & pronounce it in a single breath, until you can blow no longer. Keep your face turned downwards, & so begin to sound the combinations of consonants & vowels that will form the head, the limbs, & so on. This continues till a figure has emerged.

COMMENTARY

The "golem" as visual object-of-meditation, linked by Scholem to a series of "yoga practices that had been disseminated among the Jews chiefly by Abraham Abulafia." Part of that hidden, often fragmented tradition described by Gary Snyder as "the Great Subculture which goes back as far perhaps as the late Paleolithic," in which the Jews, like other peoples-of-the-book, continued to share long after the virtual disappearance of the shaman seers.

For more on the golem (as a humanoid creature created by magic), see above, page 98.

SOUND EVENT: THE SILENT ORCHESTRA

Construct an orchestra made up entirely of wooden "dummy" instruments: a violin, a double bass, a trumpet, saxophone, & drum, etc. Play music in silence, while others dance to it.

COMMENTARY

"As oil is soundless / so Israel is soundless in this world." (*Canticles Raba* I.21.)

Allan Kaprow (b. 1927)
WORDS: AN ENVIRONMENT

Two rooms, one 9′×9′, leading railroad style into another, 6′×6′, each 8′ high, constructed within a room. Doorways covered by white cloths.

Outside first room is a large electric sign saying "WORDS." Red and white lights blinking all around top of the walls. Inside, 4 lights hanging at eye level: a blue, a yellow, a green, and a white one, which alone blinks. Two vertical rows of lights, also not blinking,

from floor to ceiling, on opposite walls. On the other two walls are five continuous rolls of cloth, also floor to ceiling, on which are stenciled words. Operated manually, these rolls, containing fixed elements, can be aligned variously with each other to make sense-groups or non-sense, as one wishes. Governing the other two walls are word strips on paper (lettered by a group of friends and myself and derived at random from a number of poetry books, newspapers, comic magazines, the telephone book, popular love stories, etc.; these having been shuffled, I composed them into wall-sized poems). Overhead, are crudely-lettered signs urging the visitors to roll the rolls, to tear off more word strips from stacks nailed to a center-post, and to staple them over the ones already there; in addition,

they are exhorted to play the victrolas and listen to the records I had made, of talk, lectures, shouts, advertisements, ramblings of nonsense, etc.—either singly or all together.

In the smaller room, painted blue, illuminated by a single, weak light bulb and covered overhead by a plastic film, the atmosphere is very close and intimate (in contrast to the brash, open feeling of the first room). Many strips of cloth hang from the sheet of plastic filling the entire space; and above, through its filminess one can see crumpled newspapers scattered here and there on top. A visitor has to push through these hangings which brush his face like cobwebs. Clipped onto these hangings are many small pieces of paper with hand-written notes from, and to, different people. Near the doorway are a pencil, clips, and more paper for additional notes. Then, hanging all around the walls from strings are large colored chalks. (I and friends had written and drawn already on these walls to start things off and thereafter the visitors added whatever they wished.) Finally a record-player on the floor whispers when it is turned on.

This environment, therefore, is transformed every day.

BODY WORK

Yemen

1. Apply a thick paste of henna leaves to the hands & feet of the participants.

2. Wrap the painted parts in cloth.

3. After four or five hours, remove the bandages & watch the skin turn color. (This begins as a bright orange-red, then grows darker every day. In a few more days the skin color starts to fade, although the nails remain dark red until entirely grown out.)

4. [The words]: When the color is at its darkest, say: "Your grandmother is coming! Your grandmother is here!"

LEMON EVENT

Pelt a priest with sacred lemons.

Philip Corner (b. 1933)
POOR MAN MUSIC (1966)

"Simplify, simplify!" (Thoreau)   a sound which all may enter
—who will (willing. and a patience and desired restraint,
necessary   and not all that easy , as you discover. . . . what
not to do)

The simplest materials
and the things your own body is
and does
—claps, slaps, stamps.   rubbing and scratching : body—all
parts, and clothing if any
voices.   and all the sounds your voice and breath and throat
may make
/except words.   although a mightbe rare&special one-
sound deep word and meaning
/warning—affectations show up. If sincere, express.
Better a middle and easy utterance of like natural
soundings
& thus beyond outside things , but the matter might be the simple

sticks of every day life. The small stones and the fabrics
papers and textures, easily picked up.   rattle rattles; nuts
                                        little bells   seeds
                this is not quite the all of homemade noise
                                                        makers

The Rhythm
                        (how it sounds)

⎯⎯   ⎯⎯   ⎯⎯   ⎯⎯   ⎯⎯   ⎯⎯
  ·   ·   ·   ·   ·   ·   ·   ·   ·   ·   ·
                                        pulses
      ○   ○ ○   ○   ○   ○
─   ─   ─   ─   ─   ─   ─   ─   ─   beat beat beat beat beat

the drawing tendency   people & sounds silent and entering
the group cohesion   and reentering   and listen
                          ing   (ensemble sensitive)
    Out of a flux of differing individual tempi   to fuse into one
                                felt agreed beat
                    (this is easier, very easy, than it may seem)
    Or building up-on and out-from a single introduced beat by one
the group-beat may form at various tempos
    individual's accelerate and decelerate may lead to rest, or lead
            it back to-and-into the rest
        (or out, into silence)   always gradual , continuously,
                    never any sudden changes of tempo (or if
                        there is silence between, and then it is
                                        not sudden)
in periods of pulse   –   polyphony . . . . non-rationalizable multipl
                                        licity of the beats .
    (still feel the drawing, as a tendency, together,   , however long
                    ly   ,   coming back to group-in)
    When good togetherbeat strengths are going   individuals   as an
                            individual can a little vary
    by moving around it in miniscule irregularities   , before com
                                        ing back   .

    Watch out for 2 : 1 relations.   They are easy; only OK for short
        times. and when you fall into them , then tempo/change
                                                        rather-
        rapid to join the basic pulse.

Players may relate well by joining their sounds,   coming to gether
in types of material for use at one time, follow a principle of
    tone-color sequencing
(Pitch) :   will be the constant tone or some natural fluctuation
           with the beat but not a consciously melody
The openness of the sound and its making   will stimulate more
   joining-with : people's unprepared joinings.   Accept this—
   even when a dull self-expresser's wit fails to perceive the
   nature . and his comein is not "with".   As with random
     surrounding sounds, let your own involvements sensitivity
              just absorb that .

"Very much the feeling of what people —even every one—may be
              and do ,
even when some will have it not." (Nothing denied.   Richness
is of what we can choose of the ever-around and available)

And the whole at ease .   If ever at extremes, say of tempo, or
   of intensity, and moving towards their implication of passions,
   let it relax and tend intowards the mean, just the energy and
   the continuing which is devotion in every day life and works.

(Move with it too.   Make it moving and with movements)

RAIN EVENT ONE

Whisper until it rains.

COMMENTARY

(1)   The Hebrew word for magic—*kishuf*—literally "murmuring" or
"muttering."

(2) "If you see a generation over whom the heavens are rust-colored like copper so that neither rain nor dew falls, it is because that generation is wanting in whisperers. What then is the remedy? Let them go to someone who knows how to whisper." (Talmud: *Ta'anit* 8a.)

(3) "In oriental countries in general, the Jews have acquired, for one reason or another, a special reputation as rainmakers." (Raphael Patai, *The Hebrew Goddess*.)

RAIN EVENT TWO

---

1. Covering an altar with green willow branches
2. Walking around the altar with mixed branches
3. Beating the altar with palm or willow branches
4. The lighting of the lamps
5. The torch dance
6. Songs accompanied by numerous musical instruments: repeated blasts of trumpets
7. The procession to the well begins at cock-crow
8. The water-drawing: pouring water on the altar
9. Pouring out of wine
10. A tumult with palm branches on the Sabbath
11. Lightheadedness begins: the women watching from a separate place
12. Joy of the house of water-drawing

COMMENTARY

Part of the elaborated temple-events for rain, fertility, etc. (above, page 259), this one for the Feast of Tabernacles (*Sukot*) & onset of the rainy season. For more on Jewish rainmaking, see elsewhere in the present volume, pages 112, 236, 470, 537.

WOMEN'S FERTILITY EVENTS

(1)

A woman washes face & hands in water mixed with the sap of an apple tree.

(2)

At the foot of a fruit tree a woman buries a bowl filled with menstrual blood.

(3)

A woman crawls under the belly of a pregnant mare.

(4)

A woman strokes the limbs of a bride or bridegroom.

(5)

A woman drinks a mixture of wild tea leaves, or a woman eats a rooster complete with comb & gizzard, or a woman drinks water seeped in the ashes of a burnt male rabbit.

(6)

A woman swallows the foreskin of a newly circumcised infant.

COMMENTARY

"The line between art and life should be kept as fluid, and perhaps as indistinct, as possible. . . . Something will always happen at this juncture, which, if it is not revelatory, will not be merely bad art—for no one can easily compare it with this or that accepted masterpiece." (A. Kaprow, *Assemblages, Environments, & Happenings,* 1966.)

BREAD EVENT

Stab a wafer until it bleeds.

COMMENTARY

The so-called desecration of the Christian eucharist—though more likely a product of Christian than of Jewish imagination—may now be viewed as the central enactment in an ongoing Jewish "guerrilla theater." As with more contemporary instances, the danger to participants & bystanders is integral to the event itself.

The Living Theatre
per Judith Malina & Julian Beck
PARADISE NOW

"The Chart"

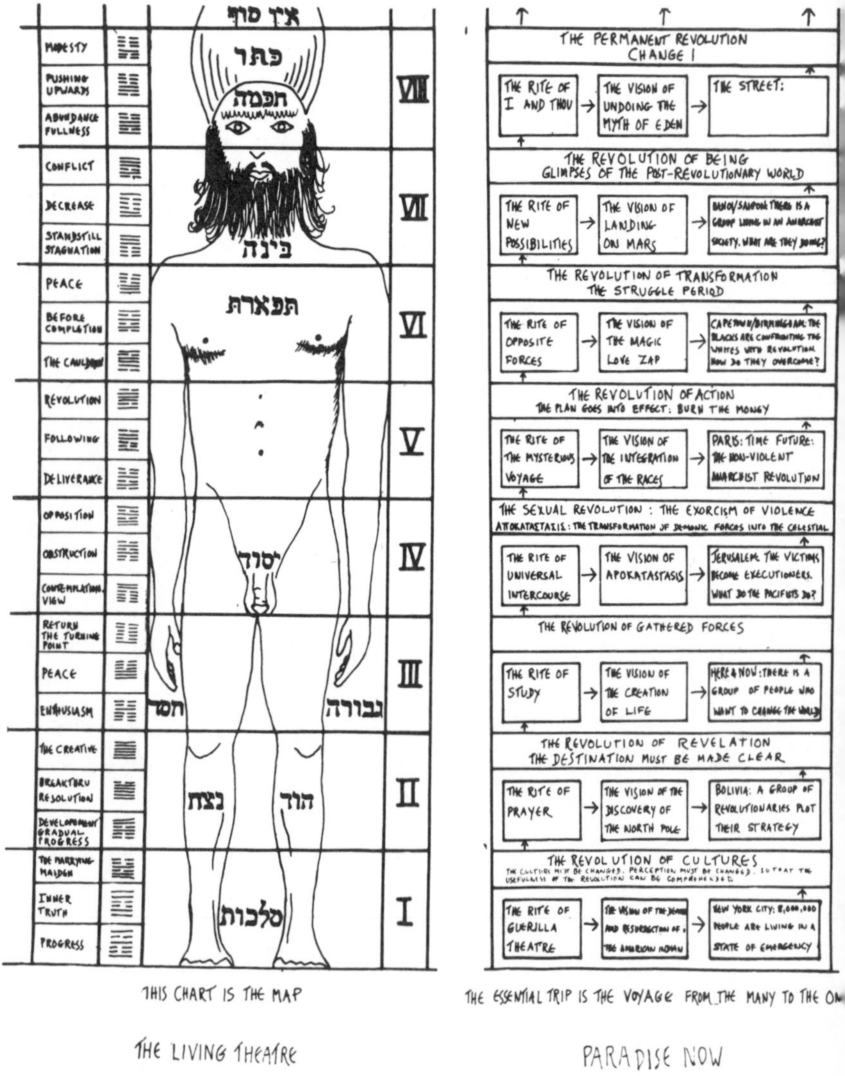

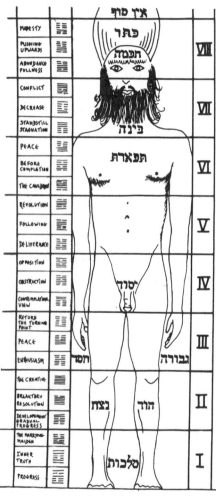

MODESTY	☷☶	
PUSHING UPWARDS	☷☴	VII
ABUNDANCE FULLNESS	☳☲	
CONFLICT	☰☵	
DECREASE	☶☱	VI
STANDSTILL STAGNATION	☰☷	
PEACE	☷☰	
BEFORE COMPLETION	☲☵	VI
THE CAULDRON	☲☴	
REVOLUTION	☱☲	
FOLLOWING	☱☳	V
DELIVERANCE	☳☵	
OPPOSITION	☲☱	
OBSTRUCTION	☵☶	IV
CONTEMPLATION VIEW	☴☷	
RETURN THE TURNING POINT	☷☳	
PEACE	☷☰	III
ENTHUSIASM	☳☷	
THE CREATIVE	☰☰	
BREAKTHRU RESOLUTION	☱☰	II
DEVELOPMENT GRADUAL PROGRESS	☴☶	
THE MARRYING MAIDEN	☳☱	
INNER TRUTH	☴☱	I
PROGRESS	☲☷	

Hebrew terms (top to bottom): אין סוף · כתר · חכמה · בינה · תפארת · יסוד · חסד · גבורה · נצח · הוד · מלכות

THE PERMANENT REVOLUTION
CHANGE I

THE RITE OF I AND THOU →	THE VISION OF UNDOING THE MYTH OF EDEN →	THE STREET:

VII

THE REVOLUTION OF BEING
GLIMPSES OF THE POST-REVOLUTIONARY WORLD

THE RITE OF NEW POSSIBILITIES →	THE VISION OF LANDING ON MARS →	RANGOON/SAIGON: THERE IS A GROUP LIVING IN AN ANARCHIST SOCIETY. WHAT ARE THEY DOING?

VI

THE REVOLUTION OF TRANSFORMATION
THE STRUGGLE PERIOD

THE RITE OF OPPOSITE FORCES →	THE VISION OF THE MAGIC LOVE ZAP →	CAPETOWN/BIRMINGHAM: THE BLACKS ARE CONFRONTING THE WHITES WITH REVOLUTION. HOW DO THEY OVERCOME?

VI

THE REVOLUTION OF ACTION
THE PLAN GOES INTO EFFECT; BURN THE MONEY

THE RITE OF THE MYSTERIOUS VOYAGE →	THE VISION OF THE INTEGRATION OF THE RACES →	PARIS: TIME FUTURE: THE NON-VIOLENT ANARCHIST REVOLUTION

V

THE SEXUAL REVOLUTION : THE EXORCISM OF VIOLENCE
APOKATASTASIS: THE TRANSFORMATION OF DEMONIC FORCES INTO THE CELESTIAL

THE RITE OF UNIVERSAL INTERCOURSE →	THE VISION OF APOKATASTASIS →	JERUSALEM THE VICTIMS BECOME EXECUTIONERS. WHAT DO THE PACIFISTS DO?

IV

THE REVOLUTION OF GATHERED FORCES

THE RITE OF STUDY →	THE VISION OF THE CREATION OF LIFE →	HERE & NOW: THERE IS A GROUP OF PEOPLE WHO WANT TO CHANGE THE WORLD

III

THE REVOLUTION OF REVELATION
THE DESTINATION MUST BE MADE CLEAR

THE RITE OF PRAYER →	THE VISION OF THE DISCOVERY OF THE NORTH POLE →	BOLIVIA: A GROUP OF REVOLUTIONARIES PLOT THEIR STRATEGY

II

THE REVOLUTION OF CULTURES
THE CULTURE MUST BE CHANGED. PERCEPTION MUST BE CHANGED. SO THAT THE USEFULNESS OF THE REVOLUTION CAN BE COMPREHENDED.

THE RITE OF GUERILLA THEATRE →	THE VISION OF THE DEATH AND RESURRECTION OF THE AMERICAN INDIAN →	NEW YORK CITY: 8,000,000 PEOPLE ARE LIVING IN A STATE OF EMERGENCY

I

THIS CHART IS THE MAP

THE ESSENTIAL TRIP IS THE VOYAGE FROM THE MANY TO THE ONE

THE LIVING THEATRE

PARADISE NOW

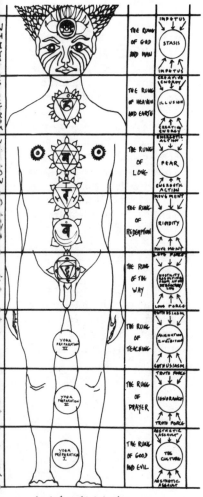

THE RUNG OF GOD AND MAN	IMPETUS — STASIS — IMPETUS
THE RUNG OF HEAVEN AND EARTH	CREATIVE ENERGY — ILLUSION — CREATIVE ENERGY
THE RUNG OF LOVE	ENERGETIC ACTION — FEAR — ENERGETIC ACTION
THE RUNG OF REDEMPTION	MOVEMENT — RIGIDITY — MOVEMENT
THE RUNG OF THE WAY	LOVE FORCE — HOSTILITY SEDUCTION FEAR OF THE ATTRACTION LOVE — LOVE FORCE
THE RUNG OF TEACHING	ENTHUSIASM — ANIMATION INHIBITION — ENTHUSIASM
THE RUNG OF PRAYER	TRUTH FORCE — IGNORANCE — TRUTH FORCE
THE RUNG OF GOOD AND EVIL	AESTHETIC ASSAULT — THE CULTURE — AESTHETIC ASSAULT

THE PLOT IS THE REVOLUTION

COLLECTIVE CREATION

COMMENTARY

"The play is a voyage from the many to the one and from the one to the many. It is a spiritual voyage and a political voyage. It is an interior voyage and an exterior voyage. It is a voyage for the actors and the spectators. It begins in the present and moves into the future and returns to the present. The plot is The Revolution.

"The voyage is a vertical ascent toward Permanent Revolution.

"The Revolution of which the play speaks is The Beautiful Non-Violent Anarchist Revolution.

"The voyage is charted. The Chart is the map. The Chart depicts a ladder of eight Rungs. Each Rung consists of a Rite, a Vision, and an Action which lead to the fulfillment of an aspect of The Revolution. The Rites are physical/spiritual rituals/ceremonies which culminate with a Flashout. The Visions are cerebral. They are images, symbols, dreams. The awareness which issues from the experience of the Rite and the awareness which issues from the experience of the Vision merge to precipitate the Action. The Actions are enactments of political conditions performed by the spectators and the actors. These conditions are specified as taking place in a particular city but lead to revolutionary action here and now. The Rites and Visions are performed by the actors, but the Actions are introduced by the actors and are performed by the public with the help of the actors. The Actions are introduced by a text spoken by the actors.

"The purpose of the play is to lead to a state of being in which non-violent revolutionary action is possible.

"The Chart contains information drawn from the Kabbalah, Tantric and Hasidic teaching, the I Ching, and other sources. The information on the Chart is arranged to aid the vertical ascent and to serve as a guide during the voyage. The Chart is designed so that it can be extended horizontally with any additional information that seems useful." (The Living Theatre, "Preparation" to *Paradise Now*.)

TREE SPIRIT EVENTS

Then sing the trees of the wood for joy
before the Lord.

One mounts to one side.
One descends on that side.
One enters between the two.
Two crown themselves with a third.
Three enter into one.
One produces various colors.
Six of them descend on one side & six of them on the other.
Six enter into twelve.
Twelve bestir themselves to form twenty-two.
Six are comprised in ten.
Ten are fixed in one.

COMMENTARY

". . . He had studied all manners of speech / even the utterance of mountains, hills & valleys / the utterance of trees & plants / the utterance of beasts & animals / He had learned them all": thus an earlier description of Hillel the Elder (first centuries B.C./A.D.), showing that reintegration with the natural world that characerizes the subterranean side of the western mystical tradition. But the obvious animism of the medieval "tree events" here given—identification of the trees of Eden with angels, etc.—combines as well with the numerology of Jewish mysticism & *poesis* (see above, pages 422ff). Also, since numbers & letters are here identical, the reader (if acquainted with such works as Graves' *White Goddess*) may recognize a resemblance to Celtic tree alphabets, etc.

Nachman of Bratzlav (Hebrew, 1772–1810)
VISION EVENT

Imagine that you could constantly recall all that we know about the future world.
There is an angel with a thousand heads.
Each head has a thousand tongues.
Each tongue has a thousand voices.
Each voice has a thousand melodies.
Imagine the beauty of this angel's song.

A SCENARIO FOR MIDNIGHT

1. God enters Paradise to rejoice with the righteous.

2. All the trees in Paradise burst into hymns.

3. A wind rises from the north, a spark flies from the power of the north, God's fire, & strikes Archangel Gabriel under his wings.

4. The cry of Gabriel awakens all the cocks at midnight.

THE END OF "A BOOK OF EXTENSIONS"

A Book of Writings

1

1

1

1

1

(Hebrew, 10th century B.C.)

THE GEZER CALENDAR

---

the moons of harvest
the moons of sowing
the moons of late planting
the moon of reaping flax
the moon of reaping barley
the moon of reaping & measuring
the moons of vine-tending
the moon of summer (-fruit)

a
b
g

YHVH'S BATTLE WITH THE SERPENT

1

Waken
Waken
Gird might of arm
YHVH
Waken as before endless generatings

Didn't you crush Rahab?
         hole Tannin?
Didn't you dry up Yam?
         mighty waters of Tehom?
        set the { YAM deeps a path for the saved to tread?
             sea

2

In his might he stirred the { sea
                         YAM
Then in his cunning crushed Rahab
By his wind set { YAM in net
           sea
His hand made holes in the twisty snake

3

You broke up { YAM in your might
          sea

You smashed Tanin-heads in the water
You crushed Leviatan heads
Made him food for desert folk
You split spring and creek
You dried up   mighty rivers
The ⌠ day is yours
    ⌡ yom
The night is yours
You set up light and sun
You determined earthbounds
Summer and winter
                you made them

                                                    H.L.

(Hebrew, Bible, 12th/11th century B.C.)
THE SONG OF DEBORAH

Deborah sang that day
with Barak son of Avino'am
"of warriors who let their hair grow long
"in Israel
"when armies went to war
                (bless Yahveh)
"would have kings hear it
"would have chiefs listen
"I who sing to Yahveh
"I to Yahveh
"who play the string for Yahveh
"elohim of Israel

"you Yahveh when you went from Se'ir
"when you marched from Edom's fields
"earth shook
"the sky rained loudly
"loudly the clouds rained water
"hills flowed in front of Yahveh
                                    you This-One-of-Sinai
            Yahveh elohim of Israel :
"in the days of Shamgar son of Anat
"days of Ya'el
                        roads were blocked
"travelers would go by winding roads
"arts of war were blocked in Israel
"blocked until you rose
"you Deborah you mother you in Israel
"when they took new gods
"war's meat hanging from the gates
            who saw a shield then
            or a spear?
"you 40 thousands in all Israel
"my heart is with the chiefs of Israel
"warriors in Israel
                        (bless Yahveh) :
"those who rode there on fine asses
"who sat on silks
"even those who walked the highways
                        hear me
            hear the cymbals' voices
"between water troughs
"where Yahveh's holy deeds dropped down
"deeds of the warriors in Israel
"who went up to the gates with Yahveh :
            o stand up stand up
                        Deborah
        stand up stand up o sing your song
"Barak step out & take your prisoners :
"when a handful went against great powers
"Yahveh's armies went with me

"against the warriors
                    some summoned from Efrayim
         roots in Amalek
"will be behind you Binyamin
"with all your troops
"from Makhir chieftains coming down
"others from Zevulun
"carried the warrior's club
"& princes of Issakhar were with Deborah
"were Barak's allies
"sent into the valley at his call :
"& Re'uven your divisions
"mighty heroes in their heads
"why did they sit it out between the sheepfolds
"why did they listen to the shepherds' flutes
"o Re'uven your divisions
"mighty talkers in their heads :
"while Gil'ad stayed put across the Jordan
"& Dan stuck to his ships
"& Asher kept beside the sea shore
"tight in his harbors
"only Zevulun mad to spill his life
"there with Naftali on the rises :
"kings came warring
"warring kings of Canaan
"in Ta'anakh by Megido's waters
"came but carried off no silver
"from the sky the stars fought
"fought with Sisra from their courses
"Kishon Brook has dragged them down
"a brook has mastered them
"you Kishon Brook that crushed strong spirits :
                    then a hammering
"of horses' hoofs in flight
"in galloping
"who galloped faster than his warriors :
"curse Meroz (Yahveh's angel says)
"curse those who live there

"who would not come to Yahveh's aid
"Yahveh's aid against the powers :
"but bless above all women
"Ya'el the wife of Kenite Heber
"more than the women in their tents
"her blessing   (sing)

> *when he asked for water*
> *she gave him milk*
> *she brought it in a deep cup*
> *brought him curds*
> *her hand was on the spike*
> *her right hand on the heavy hammer*
> *she brought it down on Sisra*
> *she smashed his head*
> *she crushed it*
> *struck the spike into his neck*
> *he bent down at her feet he fell*
> *he fell he lay down at her feet*
> *he bent down at her feet he fell*
> *fell where he bent*
> *he bent down at her feet he fell*
> *he lay there ruined*

                              (coda)

through her window Sisra's mother
looks & cries
& through her grill she asks
"why is his chariot
"so late coming
"why is the noise of chariots
"so late
her wisest princess tells her
is even echoing her words
"they must be
"splitting up the spoils
"one or two virgins
"for each man
"a spoil of colored cloth

"for Sisra
"embroidered colors for his spoil
"many cloths around my neck
"for spoil
O Yahveh Yahveh may your enemies
be lost
your lovers like the rising of the sun
in power

& so the land had rest
for forty years

J.R./H.L.

(Hebrew, Bible, c. 10th century B.C.)
From THE SONG OF SONGS

1

I came into my garden
saw my sister there
but saw her as my wife

I picked my sweet plant
ate my honeycomb with honey
drank my wine with milk

(I told them) eat, friends
drink & go on drinking
O sweet love

2

I slept
my heart was moving
heard her voice

a knocking at the door
(says) open for me
sister

love
my love
my dove
my head was wet
with dew   the night
bathed in my hair

3

he put his hand against
the keyhole

made me feel him
down my belly

4

I got up
I would let him in
my hands smelled sweet

my fingers
smelling sweet
against the lock

5

had opened for him
my sweet love
was gone   had left me

(says) he spoke
I felt my breath go
would look for him

but couldn't find him
& called to him
he didn't answer

6

is he more sweet
than others?
is she more beautiful?

is her sweet love
more beautiful?
has she told it to us right?

7

sometimes pale
he blushes
is better than 10,000 men

gold skin of forehead
bushy hair
& black   is like a crow

with dove's eyes
looking at a river
washed with milk
in perfect space

to hold his cheeks
a spice bed
his lips like lilies
breathing a sweet spice

through hands with gold rings
beryl at center
his belly is high ivory
& sapphire

marble legs
like columns into pure gold sockets
his face
a strength like cedar

sweetness at his mouth
"is altogether lovely
"is my sweet love
"is my friend

                                        J.R.

(Hebrew, 6th century B.C.)
PSALM 137

How can we sing King Alpha song
In a strange land

We sat & cried along Babylon rivers
remembering Zion.

We hung up our harps on Babylon trees
when our captors asked us for songs
when they mocked us calling for a happy tune:

"Sing us one of those Zion songs!"

If I forgot you Jerusalem
my right hand would wither
my tongue would stick to the roof of my mouth
if I didn't remember you
if I couldn't start up a tune with:
"Jerusalem . . ."

YaHVeH recall the Edomites
Jerusalem's day   when they said:
"Strip her   Strip her bottom bare!"

Now   thief Babylon   (a song for you):

"Happy He'll be to pay you
   the reward you've rewarded us
Happy He'll be to snatch your babies
   and smash them against a rock!"

H.L.

(Aramaic, 5th century B.C.)

From THE ELEPHANTINE FRAGMENTS

(1)

HAGGAI BAR NATHAN
HARMAN BAR OSHEA
OSHEA BAR YATHOM
OSHEA BAR HODAV
SHAMUA BAR HAGGAI
NATHAN BAR NERAIAH
MENAHEM BAR POSAI
YEOSH BAR AZANIAH
BETHEL'AKAB BAR ACHAR

TOTAL 9 MEN

NABU'AKAB BAR

(2)

THE KING, AND HE CRIED AND MEASURED

AND YOU SHALL HANG HIM

                              IT HAPPENS

LIKE THIS, LIKE YOU DID TO HIS SONS

UNLESS IN A PLACE BY THE SEA YOU HA
VE KILLED HIM

                    THIS, YOU SHALL GO DRINK

WITH THE GODS AND HE WHISPERED, HEL
P

WHICH HIS FATHER SHALL GIVE HIM
THE GODS OF EGYPT SHALL ASSEMBLE
EGYPT, AND THEY SHALL BE
AND RIGHTEOUSNESS SHALL PERISH

```
A   T        O        H        A        T  A
N   A        N        I        N        H  N
D   K                 S        D        E  D
    E        A                          Y
T   N        C        B                    H
H            C        O        A        S  E
E   O        C        D        N        H
    U        O        Y        D        A  S
M   T        U                          L  H
A            N        T                 L  A
N            T        O                 S  L
            O                           P  L
W            F        I                 E
A                     T                 A  A
S            H        S                 K  N
             I                             S
             S        G                 T  W
                      R                 O  E
             M        A                    R
             O        V
             N        E                 H
             E                          I
             Y                          M
```

KARL YOUNG

Ezekielos (Greek, c. 2nd century B.C.)

EISAGOGE, or THE TRAGEDY OF MOSES

he dwelt in the land of Midian: and sat down beside a well

MOSES:

    I see seven girls at the well.

he stood up, helped them, and watered their flock

ZIPPORAH:

    Stranger, they call this country Libya. ·
    Tribes from everywhere settled here—
    mostly Ethiopian blacks.
    One man rules, leads our wars,
    runs the town, takes care of God
    and judges us: my father.

content to dwell with the man: and he gave him Zipporah his
    daughter

MOSES:

    On Sinai I saw
    a throne on top of the mountain
    so big it swept heaven's fold.
    A prince of gentlest mien sat there
    crowned, sceptered.
    His hand ordered me to Him.

I stood before His face.
He held out the scepter:
I took it and sat down.
He got up. Told me:
"Sit where I sat."
I saw the world circling below.
I peered beneath that surface.
I looked up and saw myself
watching me.

he said, I have been a stranger in a strange land

MOSES:

Stars by thousands rained down
before my knees. I numbered each
until there were no more,
parading in lines and files
an army readying to fight,
startled me.
I leapt from sleep.

JETHRO:

God sent this lovely dream
to tell in sign
good things are coming your way.
I want to live
until it all comes true.
You are the one
will build that mighty throne
and sit on it,
giving us law,
laying out a road
others will follow.
Look everywhere
the Earth is home.
See below that place,

watch the sky
where stars hang.
Learn about time:
what it was and will be.

the children of Israel cried and their cry came up to God

MOSES:

Look—that bush burns:
it is speaking to me.
Others will call this a miracle
they can't believe.
Suddenly flaming, yet
those flames guard the leaves and flowers.
Must find out why,
this goes so far beyond
what people think can happen.

God called to him out of the midst of the bush

GOD:

Stay where you are,
hero among men,
and take off your shoes.
The ground you're walking on
belongs to me. Courage, child,
listen: since it leaves thought behind,
you who are born to die
should see what I look like.
Store in your heart
the words that compose Me.
I am God of your Fathers
whom you remember in prayer:
Yes, I am God,
God of Abraham,
God of Isaac,

third,
God of Jacob.
What I gave My people
still remains My thought.
I will save them,
I know the pain
of their present inheritance:
the slavedom
they were born to.
Go,
tell my Jews and then King Pharaoh
I have made and moved you
to take them from Egypt.

Who am I, that I should go to Pharaoh?

MOSES:

When I was born
I couldn't speak.
My tongue still has
a hard time:
spits
whistles.
Don't ask me
to talk to Pharaoh.
I can't.

the anger of the Lord burned against Moses

GOD:

Send Aaron, brother of your womb,
to Pharaoh. Teach him
what I have taught you.
You are My voice,
he yours.
What he learns
he shall instruct Pharaoh in.

by the way in the inn the Lord met him and sought to kill him

GOD:

What have you got in your hands there?
Don't wait. Tell me.

MOSES:

A cattle prod.
It also corrects
my enemies.

GOD:

Throw it down—
and run for your life.
The goad will be re-born
a dragon snake:
make you gasp,
sweat fear.

MOSES:

There!
God, stop—please stop!
I can't stop
shaking.

GOD:

Don't be such a baby.
Grab him by the tail,
he'll return your rod.
Now touch the womb in your chest,
watch it do
what I told it to.
Look at your hand—
white as leper's snow.
Put it back against your heart:
it will be renewed.

anyone who saw the serpent of brass lived

Let us go and sacrifice to our God

GOD:

Through the instrument of that rod
you will raise up plagues.
Blood will race through the Nile,
blood dye every spring and pool.
I will litter Egypt with frogs and fleas,
daub their flesh with furnace ash,
making them erupt and boil.
Dog-flies will root in their sex,
maddening them with shame.
Pest will strike to silence
the flint heart beating in them.
I will set heaven on them:
ice and fire to stone and stack their dead.
They will see their cattle
cough up life,
their bread wither and melt
before it leaves the field.
To darken them
I will enforce a shadow overhead.
Three-day locusts will cloud over
what they eat,
chew the green right off their wheat.
I will kill their first children,
every last one.
I will abate the pride of this nation
since it rises up in anger against Me.
Pharaoh will listen
once he holds the body of his oldest boy.
Then he will understand fear
and let My people go.
Tell them:
"now will be the first of the year,

the month starting months,
when I shall enroot you elsewhere,
as I promised the Patriarchs.
When the moon is full
give Me to eat
before sunset.
That will be Passover.
Smear your doors with blood
when the angel of My death
comes signifying.
That night eat baked meat.
Next day Pharaoh will be glad
to see you go.
But before you do—rob them.
Each of your women should take from theirs
pots, clothes, jewelry,
whatever they can load on their backs.
Don't forget back wages:
help yourselves to gold, silver, heavy robes.
When you reach the Promised Land,
upon the day's dawning of the day
you passed over,
eat bread without yeast seven days.
And give Me the oldest child
of everything that lives:
males, womb openers,
whose mothers deliver them
who have never borne before."

see, I have made you a god to Pharaoh

GOD:

Let the heads of My people
who are also householders,
on the tenth of this month,
from each family
draw out their wealth

perfect calves and lambs:
keep them safe
until the fourteenth has dawned.
Towards evening,
give them to Me for supper:
roast what remains,
meat and umbles,
and eat with your family.
Make sure your clothes
are tied up tight,
and staff in hand
that you wear boots up to the calf.
For that's when
Pharaoh will order you out.
So be ready to leave.
Every householder
will be called to account
for what he eats.
After dinner
take a bunch of hyssop by the leaves,
dip it in lamb's blood,
strike the top and sides
of your front doors
so that My Death will pass over
the homes of My Jews.
Keep this day to remember Me.
Use only bread made with no yeast:
where you live, you shall not eat yeast.
You will be delivered from this evil place;
this month will point you out of Egypt,
for it is the beginning of months,
the beginning of time.

when he saw no man, he slew the Egyptian and hid him in the sand

A SURVIVOR OF PHAROAH'S ARMY:

When King Pharaoh left the palace
he had a huge army,

all the cavalry and war chariots.
He put his best soldiers
up front and along side,
making us march
in a hard column: a phalanx.
The noise we made
would scatter heaven.
Infantry in the center,
guarded by flankers
who left alleys open
for the chariots to ride in and out of.
Horsemen on the right, the left.
I asked how many we were:
told ten thousand ten thousands,
each a hero.
We caught up with the Jews.
They'd thrown themselves down
by the Red Sea
where they all bunched up,
or else with their women
were feeding their children.
Beaten down, worn-out from walking.
They'd brought so many things from home.
When we marched into view,
the men who were unarmed
cried out their despair,
straining as if sharing
a single body
towards the sky,
up to the God of their Fathers.
We made camp,
our joy knew no limit.
The town of Beelzephron was nearby.
Titan Sun had almost set
behind West: `
we tried to control ourselves.
Cock crow tomorrow
we'd finish off the Jews,
six would get you one.
We had the numbers and means.

Then began the terrible witnesses
of divine wrath:
a pillar of smoke
rose up over Earth
between our lines and theirs.
Moses, their pioneer,
held up his pole
he'd used before against us,
struck the waves' broad back,
halving the Red Sea.
They ran away along this path
that just opened up,
down a road that never turned
but ran straight to the other side.
We chased them of course.
Suddenly our wheels locked tight,
wouldn't turn.
Blinding light,
angry fire
in front of us.
God was on their side.
From the far shore they watched
the water around us gurgle and swallow.
Someone screamed: "Home!
get away from the hands of their Most High:
He helps the Jews,
but us poor fools
he deals only death."
The sea recovered its road;
all our army sank.

they came to Elim where there were twelve wells

SOMEONE AT ELIM:

Lord of lords, Moses,
you already know

what we found here:
an oasis, grass, pools
spring watered.
Up there the pillar of fire burned.
A sign.
Dark meadows, a fountain
that brings up sweet water,
drawing twelve sources from a single rock.
Here the Earth deepens
and gives us all we need.
Look—date palms,
seventy of them,
strong, straight,
dressed in fruit.
Thick, flowing grass
feeds the stock.

the horse and rider he has thrown into the sea

SOMEONE AT ELIM:

We saw a bird,
a stranger a friend
one you won't see anywhere else:
twice the eagle's size,
wings of every shade and hue,
purple in his strength,
feet blush red,
gleaming, glowing
golden down filling his breast,
he made us feel good.
Face like a pet rooster's,
he looked out at the circling world
through apple yellow eyes.
He spoke: we thought
he must be king of the air.
Sure enough birds suddenly started showing up from everywhere,

hovering timidly behind his bulk.
Joy blew him out like a bull;
he strutted in front of his people
fast as you can see.

C.D.

(Greek, 3rd–1st century B.C.)

From THE SIBYLLINE ORACLES

1

watch out for the strong God's wrath
when plague slays
when all find just and terrible punishment
king seizing king and taking his land
nation against nation
rich against poor
lords fleeing their homes
their lands divided
an empire not of Greece assaults Greece
empties her wealth
people fighting for gold and silver
money love shepherding evil
their unburied
devoured by vultures by beasts
swallowed by great Earth
who will be left unsown unploughed her misery
betraying
the decadence of the age

2

a sign to know the end of all things
comes on Earth
see swords flashing among the stars
observe dust blown down from heaven
when the sun rises and sets
sunlight dark at noon the moon
bright at midday
blood dripping from rocks
in the clouds soldiers and horsemen
like a great cavalcade of hunters
bodies built of heavy mist
this is the execution of war
God who lives in heaven brings about

C.D.

(Syriac/Greek, c. 200 A.D.)

THE MAIDEN

                              I would sing of
who is daughter of light   on whom
brightness of kings does rest
I would delight in her image's rays
her beauty   whose garments
are flowers sweet odors rise from
a king looks out from her eyes
will feed those beneath him
in truth   truth covers her head
the tread of her feet brings pleasure
she spreads her lips open
for beauty   sings praise poems
32 singing her praises
tongue like a curtain the priest can raise up
& enter   her neck mounts high
like a staircase   first builder hung here
her hands that were speaking
in code   led the dance of the aeons
fingers that opened the gates
to the city   whose chamber
vibrates with light
the odor of sweet leaves & myrrh
strewn with branches of myrtle   sweet flowers
a door decked with reeds
stand the seven who guarded the groom
whom she chose   seven bridesmaids
who dance for her praise her
twelve more by her count who are servants
attend her   their gaze

toward the bridegroom
sighting of whom brings them light
of the joy of their entry
those who would be at that marriage
assemblage of princes   long feasting
long lives of those given to life
wore garments of light splendid raiment
would swoon in their joy in praise of
father of all   take his light down
exult in it   light of their vision
of godlight
sweet food now received
sweet perfection sweet drink
of his wine   ends thirst   desire
bursts into praises o breath
o father of truths o mother of knowing

J.R.

(Aramaic, c. 5th century A.D.)

AN INCANTATION BOWL AGAINST THE POWERS

(The words)   Tardi daughter of Oni o Hormisdar Tardi in the name
of AAAAAA be exorcised & sealed o Demon Devil Satan Ogres
Liliths that appear by night & that appear by day & that appear to
Tardi daughter of Oni in the name of Gabriel Michael Raphael
amen amen amen amen selah halleluia per AAAAAA

Eleazar ha-Kallir (Hebrew, 7th century A.D.)

A CALENDAR: THE YEAR OF THE MESSIAH

a

those days: that time:
the first month: NISAN

must surely be the 14th day
o day when Menaḥem ben Ami'el breaks
a path
a way
into Arvel Valley
where his favor burgeons
he will wear the robe of vengeance
as his cloak

b

those days: that time:
the second month: IYAR

hidden dead revealed
among the keepers of
the fallow year
here Korah's band arises
in sight of all the tribes
flies Asaf's banners
from desert sands in Moab
to Acacia's brook

c

those days: that time:
the third month: SIVAN

those who had died in desert
now wake up
great earthquakes overwhelm the walls
while on the mountain's top
corn grows in abundance
earth shaking
the hidden secret told

d

those days: that time:
the fourth month: TAMUZ

fury & rage in all
a king remote from heaven
enters
Old Brute our Enemy will tell him
YOU RIDE FORTH
(relief & rescue only for the few)

e

those days: that time:
the fifth month: AV

this perfect master
cloaked in the robes of vengeance
the Mount of Olives cracked by his rebuke
Messiah now climbs to his fullness
like the sun come forth in fierceness

f

those days: that time:
the sixth month: ELUL

when they see him
the son of Shalti'el
will blow the signal
Mikha'el & Gavri'el descending

the generals of El
propelling vengeance
not leaving life to one last
enemy of El

g

those days: that time:
the seventh month: TISHREI

riots & insurrections
every people
crying
GENOCIDE AGAINST THIS PEOPLE
whom the god of terrors forged
who pulled this people
from within a people
threats to the scorned soul
the hated people

h

those days: that time:
the eighth month: MARḤESHVAN

first exile & a storm
blows the Rose back into the desert
where
10,000 will appear
a re-enforcement
last exile how unlike the first

i

those days: that time:
the ninth month: KISLEV

sudden action
sword drops from the sky
blood of the uncircumcised now runs
like streams of water
THE TIME: from three to nine

the One-in-White cries louder
than the cry of water
& the dead rise up & live
"two days after"

j

those days: that time:
the tenth month: TEVET

those fervent each day
each day raise voices
oiiie (they cry) for the changed day
for a famine for 45 days
till they reach his town & praise Yah
each day
each day

k

those days: that time:
the eleventh month: SHEVAT

spasms for 90 thousand
a 100 thousand men in armor
fourth war on the tribal turf of Benjamin
& there
each one of you will chase
a thousand

l

those days: that time:
the twelfth month: ADAR

THREE will be ONE in its rebuilding
the Tishbite & Menaḥem
also Neḥemia
with lovely Tiferet like the priest beside them
& every soul will praise Yah there
AMEN

J.R./H.L.

Yosef ibn Abitur (Hebrew, mid-10th century–c. 1012)
THE "WHO?" OF IBN ABITUR OF CORDOBA

who
      ANCHORED the high skies
                set off the wheels for those who shine
who'd
      BE a god as great as El
                could tell El's greatness
who
      COMES to praise El Elohim
                with silence
who
      DID speak & speech became
                the day he pitched his skies
who
      EMITTED utterance & utterance remained
                the day he set his earths
who
      FIXED the ocean's depth
                the day he placed his lines
who
      GLUED earth's clods together
                the day he laid his valleys' floors
who
      HELD its measurements in place
                whose plumbline touched the earth
who's
      IN a king's robe
                fancy garments
who
      JUDGES righteousness
                on country roads

who's

KNOWN as strong Yah many-powered
all who stand up bow to him
who

LETS out secrets drop by drop
then names them speaking
who

MAKES speech bring to life without his word
but him
who

NARROWED the sea breakers
into sea deeps
who

OPENED 300 horses hoofs
between each wave
who

PRONOUNCED words
that broke a channel for the current
who

QUESTIONED the rain coming
two drops at a time to wash it out
who

ROUNDED up the winds in his cupped palm
trapped the waters in his robe
who

SIGNALS ninety-nine
birthshrieks for the mountain goat
who

TOLD the eagle she could grasp her children
in between her wings ascending
who

URGED the dragon
to bite the goat's womb
who

VISIONS to every thunderclap
a roadway of its own
who

BROKE a channel for the current
a road for his bolts of lightning

who

> YIELDED to every man
>> the number of hairs for his head

who

> YET made each hair unique
>> to keep from jamming together

who

> ORNAMENTED what man constructs
>> like the beauty of first-born Adam

who

> SAID that this should be like that
>> same form same speech same voice

who

> EXPRESSES commands to his face
>> & pays him when he obeys

whose

> FIVE fears were instilled
>> in the five great beasts of this world

who

> ORDAINED a fear of mosquitoes
>> beneath the elephant's thick hide

who

> FORCED the fear of the squirmer
>> on ancient Leviathan

who

> CALLED out loud to show them
>> that he rules over them all

who

> OPPOSES his ways
>> & can soften his heart to peace

who

> REVERSES oppressed & oppressor
>> so oppressor can't break loose

who

> DREW the sudden fear of the locust
>> over the lion's mind

who

> OVERCOMES the scorpion
>> with fear of the squirming spider

who
> BROUGHT the fear of the swallow
>> to the eagle up in the sky

who
> ANCHORED the ends of the earth

J.R./H.L.

Samuel ha-Nagid (Hebrew, 993–1056)

THREE LOVE POEMS

1

I'd sell my soul for that fawn
of a boy   night walker
to sound of the 'ud & flute playing
who saw the glass in my hand   said
"drink the wine from between my lips"
& the moon was a *yod* drawn on
the cover of dawn—in gold ink

2

take the blood of the grape from
her red jeweled glass like fire
in middle of hail
this lady with lips of scarlet
thread   roof of her mouth
like good wine
mouth like her body well perfumed:
from blood of corpses the tips
of her fingers are red   thus
half of her hand is like ruby
half quartz

3

that's it—I love that fawn
plucking roses from
your garden—
you can put the blame on me
but if you once looked at my lover
with your eyes
your lovers would be hunting you
& you'd be gone
that boy who told me: pass
some honey from your hive
I answered: give me some back
on your tongue
& he got angry, yelled:
shall we two sin against the living God?
I answered: let your sin,
sweet master, be with me

J.R./H.L.

Samuel ha-Nagid (Hebrew, 993–1056)

WAR POEM: when we conquered their land destroyed the fortresses & towers subjugated villages & towns & overwhelmed the capital with violence

1
field where the strong men lie
    puffed up like bellows
        like pregnant women
all together
    slave & noble
        prince & servant
with their king the new Agag they lie
    dung for the earth
        unburied
of a thousand only one was saved
    single grapes
        in a forsaken vineyard
Amalek's memory wiped out in Spain
    his army scattered
        kingdom destroyed

2
we left them to the jackals
    leopards & wild boars
        the flesh a gift to wolves
& birds of heaven
    tore at it
        so full so full
they dragged limbs across

        thorns & thistles
                lions would still their young with
& they tore at it
        so full
                so drunk with blood
hyenas made their rounds
        & night was deafened by
                the cries of ostriches

J.R.

Solomon ibn Gabirol (Hebrew, c. 1020–c. 1057)
THE 16-YEAR-OLD POET

I am the prince the song
's my slave   I am the
string all singers songmen
tune   my song's a crown for
kings for ministers a
little crown   am only
sixteen years old but my
heart holds wisdom like some
poet 80 year old man

J.R./H.L.

Solomon ibn Gabirol (Hebrew, c. 1020–c. 1057)

CONSTELLATIONS

. . . .

Who can know your ways
making houses for the seven planets within the twelve constellations?
Over Ram and Bull you flowed your strength joining them
the third Twins
two brothers in their unison
the face of them the face of man
and to the fourth the Crab
and to the Lion gave from your glory over
and his sister Virgin next to him
and to the Scales and the Scorpion set by its side
and the ninth made in the form of a hero his strength unfailing
a Bowshot
and so created the Goat and the Pail in your great strength
and by itself the last constellation
Adonai set a great Fish
These are the constellations high and raised in their rising
12 princes to the nations

H.L.

Moses ibn Ezra (Hebrew, c. 1055–c. 1135), per Carl Rakosi
TWO POEMS

1

Bring me that sickly looking wine glass.
See, when I fill it
it becomes as ardent as a lover's face
and chases off my beelzebubs.

Drink, my friend, and pass the beaker
So I may unburden myself
and if you see me going under
revive me with your minstrelsy.

2

Circumstance has estranged my friend.
He has bolted the door
but I will enter the portal
and knock
                despite my enemies.
I will shatter locks with words.
I will break bolts with my songs
and will persuade myself
that nettles are sprigs of balsam.
I will dance and shout to their bitter juice
as if I were drunk on wine
and humble myself
and pretend that hell stream is icy
if it will get me through darkness
                                into his light.

Go now, my song,
take this message to my beloved,
for song is a faithful messenger.

Judah ha-Levi (Hebrew, c. 1075–c. 1141)

THE GARDEN

1

You
    in Eden's trees:
a myrtle tree
& flowers
or among the stars:
Orion shining

God sent you myrrh
a cluster
            purely
his own work:
no perfume maker's
skill

The dove
day that she nested in the tree
the myrtle stole her scent
breathed out as perfume

While with her
do not ask the sun to rise
she does not ask
while with you
for risings of the moon

                                              J.R.

2

On the wind
in the cool of the evening
I send greetings to my friend
I ask him to remember the day
of our parting when we made a covenant
of love by an apple tree

CARL RAKOSI

Abraham ibn Ezra (Hebrew, 1089–1164)
"I HAVE A GARMENT"

I have a garment which is like a sieve
Through which girls sift barley and wheat.
In the dead of night I spread it out like a tent
And a thousand stars pierce it with their gleams.
Sitting inside, I see the moon and the Pleiades
And on a good night, the great Orion himself.
I get awfully tired of counting all the holes
Which seem to me like the teeth of many saws.
A piece of thread to sew up all the other threads
Would be, to say the least, superfluous.
If a fly landed on it with all his weight,
The little idiot would hang by his foot, cursing.
Dear God, do what you can to mend it.
Make me a mantle of praise from these poor rags.

ROBERT MEZEY

Isaac ben Abraham Gorni (Hebrew, 13th century)
PROENSA

In Provence Gorni's got a lot of enemies
who put down my songs as well.
Yet I know I am the poet,
the only one of my generation.
When I sing mountains dance
valleys & forests rejoice.
I take up my harp & happy
Zion's daughters form a circle.
If I want I can wake up bones
& make stones run like the Jordan.

. . . .

When I die girls will lament me everyday
& merchants make big deals in world-markets
for bags of dirt from my grave, out of my coffin's
planks others will carve amulets—special for barren women.
Someone will string harps & fiddles
with my hair & the tunes will come, O
lovely tunes sans strum or bow of human hand.
Even my clothes—revered—anything that's touched my skin.
    But grind my bones to dust,
    I won't promote idolatry.

GEORGE ECONOMOU

Immanuel ben Solomon of Rome (Italian, c. 1261–after 1328)
ITALIAN SONNET

Love knows neither law nor
rule, is deaf & blind to them,
admits no impediments. Love's
strength cannot be measured or
his will opposed. Love runs
the world, fills this earth and
neither *pater noster* nor any
other rite or charm will work.
Nobody puts down his pride
or turns off his power. Nobody slips out of Amor's
wide nets, and to all my
petitions the same old answer:
"That's the way I want it!"

GEORGE ECONOMOU

Kalonymos ben Kalonymos (Hebrew, 1286–after 1328)
From STONE OF CHOICE

Damn the one damn
Let his tongue split
Spit on the one
The onanist who gave
My father the "good" news:
You have a son!
Pity the fathers, yes,
And the mothers
Who have male children.
What a joke!
And what a terrible burden.
Armies, armies of prohibitions
And commandments lie in wait,
Positive, negative, and eternal
Who can fulfill these obligations?
No matter how responsible he is
Who can fulfill 613 commandments?
Who can do it?
It's impossible.
I'm a sinner and a lawbreaker.

It would have been wonderful
To have been born a girl—with flowing
Hair and green eyes
And be expert at a spinning wheel
Or crocheting with my friends.
During dusktime, the girls and I
Would drink coffee and
Eat cookies, telling stories,

Planning shopping trips to the city
Etc.
People would be impressed
At my talent for crocheting
I'd create the loveliest patterns!
Then at the appropriate time
I'd marry a beautiful youth
How he would adore me
We would touch each other everywhere.
His gifts, gold and diamonds,
Would adorn me
And he'd carry me around on his hands
Kissing and hugging me.

But my fate
The bitterness of it!
I was born a man
So God willed it.
I can't be changed.
I can't be changed
From a man into a woman.
I will accept it in love
And thank the Holy One, blessed be He,
With the words:
"Blessed art thou, Lord, who has
Not made me a woman."

ROCHELLE OWENS

Maulana Sahin (Judeo-Persian, 14th century)

THE CASTLE

high & green
was like the moon's face
he had placed
into the rose garden
4 gates opened on
its flowers
where the vizier stood
suddenly
the sky would strut up
to the king:
a circle
center of the castle
with a marble basin
held no pebbles
but rubies   jewels
& a hollow column
a golden peacock
stood on
spun around
poured water from its beak
the fountain filled
the king was like a rose
held wine in hand
or like narcissus drank

. . . .

& told the cup-bearer
to fill

the bowl with veils
the bearer (body
like a rose)
poured red into the bowl
a golden bird
at center
musk & ambergris
the king would raise it
to his mouth
(o roses)
& the bird called: drink
he kissed the earth
bowed down
the great king took
a hit of wine
drawn from the moon

J.R.

Israel ben Moses Najara (Hebrew, c. 1555–1628)
"CHILDREN OF THE TIMES"

Children of the times are vines
   Death the vintner gathers,
        as he pleases beneath the Creator's eyes—

        carefully gathers the grapes—
  bud and seed,
        old man, suckling infant,
  beggar, prince,
        the great and noble together with
          the despicable poor
and there's no one he misses.

  With a deaf ear for the cries of the transitory
      and a silver indifference
          that grinds ore back to dust.

And if the intelligent ones put in for their last supplies,
  he quashes that temporal lust,
        scythes through the sprouts,
        strives for perfection,
        finishes off the soul,
        for no Power, no Cunning,
        can defend against the Lord.

JACK HIRSCHMAN

3

3

3

3

3

(Hebrew, 14th century)

A CHARM AGAINST LILITH

"Black Striga
          black on black
"who eats black blood
                    & drinks it
"like an ox she bellows
"like a bear she growls
"like a wolf she crushes

J.R.

(Yiddish, 20th century)

THE EVIL EYE (THE GOOD EYE) EINEHORE

The child frets
yawns
or cringes a lot

The adult
yawns
"he just doesn't feel good"

or
they have a cold or a flu
"a light disease"

II DIAGNOSIS

The mother or the grandmother goes and
licks out the eyes

"the child has einehore   the eyes are salty"

"She takes a glass of water
and charcoal

She puts in three pieces of charcoal

If they fall down
If they sink . . ."

or
"You take a glass of water
You put three or four twigs on top of the glass
Crack an egg over the branches

If the egg sticks in them . . ."

or
"Hold a new knife at the head
If it turns black . . ."

By charm
 in silence
 in whispers
 facing east

Schneider:
 "I once asked
 'Tell me what it is woman
 what a good eye means

 How do you cast out a good eye?'

 She says
 'This is a secret'

 I say
 'Teach me the secret   I should know too'

 She says
 'I am only an old Jewish woman
 Should I teach you to cast out a good eye?
 It's nothing with nothing
 One time it may succeed
 and one time it may not succeed'

 She teaches me
 She says:
     'Woe is the child
     'So is the mama'

 She takes the corner of her dress or apron
 She chants

     'Orneh borneh
     dembeneh korneh
     buckwheat and beans
     dembeh korneh
     oaks and black beans:
     he who gave you the good eye
     from his head his own eyes fly'

or
'In the rafters two cracks lie

in wait to catch the evil eye
Cracks in all the corners lie
in wait to catch the evil eye'

or
'No evil no terror
no wheat and no bran
May Sarah abandon
her crying and pain
Not till the ceiling crops with rye
shall she receive an evil eye' "

H.L. & BARBARA KIRSHENBLATT-GIMBLETT

(German & Hebrew, 14th century)

A POEM TO EASE CHILDBIRTH

---

o bear mother lie down
   o you womb
o old as I am lie down
do not carry me into
the grave
to be buried inside me
   lie down
there's a book called the bible
   it says
o bear mother lie down
in your place
where God wills it
o holy this power of God

J.R.

(Hebrew, 17th century)

A SABBATEAN AMULET AGAINST ALL EVILS

     purified in the entire skull
the upright   guardian of love in brain's
track   splendor of the pupil of
that eye is fastened on my forehead
purely   in the trunk of love the lamp
of will of truth shines back across the node
of the closed brain   the brightness of
the sun inside her brain the root   of
mercy's plant fills up the skull
the brain   & in its sight are
life & peace in middle of cruel
whips of faith   & he
the prince of thoughts would tell me:
"your lips are into scarlet"   cure
& faithful guard to her who
wears this amulet against all
evil & misfortune & distress against all
troubles in the mind for now & always
eternally amen selah amen!
& may the strength of YHVH be greatly magnified!
o God I pray you cure her now!   Amen so
be thy will!   Amen amen

J.R.

(Ladino, 17th century)

SABBATAI ZEVI'S SONG FOR THE SHEKINAH OUR LADY OF THE TORAH

"From the mountain top
"Down to the river
"To meet the princess
"Our lady Meliselda

"Come up from bathing
"In the sweet waters
"Hair as dark as night
"Where the drops were falling

"Face a sword of light
"Eyebrows hard as steel
"Lips like blood or coral
"Body like white milk

J.R.

(Judeo-Arabic, Morocco)

CHILDREN'S RAIN SONGS

1

o the rain drop drop drop drop
o the farmers' little sons
o the landlord Bu-Sukri
o the trip down by the river
o his tumble down the well
o his mother's red tarboosh
o the one-eyed man one-eyed
down the silo in the dark

2

the wind the wind o the bellows
o my uncle o the bellows
it's the blacksmith's bellows
blacksmith gropes his way around
then calls out   children
o my children in the forest
they call   Papa
buy a shirt   or   Papa
buy a black shirt
shirt with carrot-colored sleeves
we eat it all up
whatever there is to eat

J.R.

(Arabic, Yemen)

BRIDE'S SONG AGAINST DEMONS

1
(scenario)

high on a pillow sits with bandaged hands & feet her double sits beside her dressed like her   large lighted candles   vessels with burning
oil   guard against the demons   on a table stands a basket filled with
eggs & flour   rue is fastened to her headdress

2
(the song)

is mercy's hour now
o devils fade
o devils in the hills of China
diving in its sea

green rue adorns her head
o moon   stretch out
your hands for baubles
for rejoicing   younger days

stretch out your hands for
coloring
the custom of the girls

J.R.

YOUNG WOMAN'S neo-aramaic jewish persian BLUES

would write a letter with
           my scissors mouth
                      (would say)
how you were once a big
           butter & egg man
                      just a beggar now
still would I kill
           myself for you
                      you in your soldier suit
be down to meet you
           in a taxi
                      honey
God's up in heaven
           he can get you
                      all that you need
the while your momma
           dies from it
                      because you wouldn't
let it just be

                                      J.R.

(Yiddish, traditional)
LULLABY A STORY

Once there was a story
The story wasn't feeling happy
The story started out by singing
About a Jewish king

Once there was a king
The king had a queen
The queen had a vineyard
Lullaby the vineyard

The vineyard had a tree
The tree had a branch
The branch had a nest
Lullaby the nest

The nest had a bird
The bird had a wing
The wing had a feather
Lullaby the feather

The king had to die
The queen had to fade away
The tree had a breakdown
The bird vanished from the nest

                                        J.R.

(Yiddish, traditional)

THE THIEF'S PLAY

ALL   open up   open up
              n lat us in
              we goink to make u heppy here
              if u wimminz shud remember
              what we done for u last year
              now dot it's dis year
              u shud lat us in again

JEW   go lookink around u
              fum all 4 sides
              pretty soon dot tief is
              comink ridink in

THIEF   yas   yas
              I am the thief
              & yer betcher I have cum here
              ter sharpen me old knife
                                (he stamps his foot)
              oh baby I yam one big thief

JEW   (he stamps his foot)
              oy meester u are vun big tief
                         (he pleads)
              so vhy u dunt take
              mine last piece bread
              u shudnt foist kill me
              tief tief tief

THIEF   I don't wantcher
last piece bread
but I do want to kill yer
Jew Jew Jew
                              (he stamps his foot)
oh baby I yam one big thief

JEW   (he stamps his foot)
oy meester u are vun big tief
                           (he pleads)
so vhy u dunt take
mine last piece cake
u shud lat me foist see
mine dotter married off

THIEF   I dont wantcher
last piece cake
& I couldn't care less
boutcher daughter married off
                              (he stamps his foot)
oh baby I yam one big thief

JEW   (he stamps his foot)
oy meester u are vun big tief
                           (he pleads)
so vhy u dunt take
mine last piece fish
u shud lat me foist give
to mine fambly ah kiss

THIEF   I dont wantcher
last piece fish
I dont wantcher ter give
yer famly a kiss
                              (he stamps his foot)
oh baby I yam one big thief

JEW   (he stamps his foot)
          oy meester u are vun big tief
                      (he pleads)
          so vhy u dunt take
          mine last liddle piece chicken
          u shud lat me foist be
          ah fodder by mine children

THIEF   I don't wantcher
          last little piece chicken
          I don't wantcher ter be
          a father to yer children
                      (he stamps his foot)
          oh baby I yam one big thief

JEW   (he stamps his foot)
          oy meester u are vun big tief
                      (he pleads)
          so vhy u dunt take
          mine last piece money
          u shud lat me foist live
          till ah handert mit twanty

THIEF   I dont wantcher
          last piece uh money
          I dont wantcher ter live
          till a hunnert n twunny
                      (he stamps his foot)
          oh baby I yam one big thief

JEW   (he stamps his foot)
          oy meester u are vun big tief
                  (the thief swats the Jew
                  with his sword & the Jew
                  falls down dead)

                                  J.R.

(Judeo-Arabic, Tunisia)

"O NIGHT LIGHTS OF JEW TOWN" A Song of the

Hara

o night lights of Jew Town
lift me up   carry me
to my grandfather's house
my grandfather o my sultan
took out his cash box & gave me
four coins that he gave me
to fix up my shoes
—my shoes are at the judge's
but the judge is unhappy
his wife screams all morning
at the roast meat   sausages—
o black maid o unwashed maid
lift your eyes to heaven
sky's dripping water
the married couples sitting
with apples in their hands
smells of acid & perfume
—o jews o jews
have you seen my uncle Moseud
playing the *gayta* & the lute
while the little dog bites at him
& I say "that's all right!"

J.R.

(Judeo-Arabic, Tunisia)

From THE ADVENTURES OF THE JEW

1 *The Bride Who Was Too Large*

One day a cry rose from the wedding house. Everything was ready, the guests were seated, the hors d'oeuvres were piled up in the kitchen, and the orchestra was waiting. Everybody's waiting for the bride. And where's the bride? Why, there she is! She's climbing up the stairs, she's starting to come through the door. My God, what agony! The door's a little low while she, the bride, the lovely woman, is too large, she's taller than the door. How will she get inside? What can we do for her? We waste ourselves in huddles and discussions. This is a disaster without end. Should we renounce the bride? Should we smash the door? While everyone is at it, someone says: "Call the Jew. Only the Jew can rescue us from this disaster."

Someone goes looking for the Jew. He arrives, looks at the bride, looks at the door, raises his clenched hands, and brings them crashing down on the bride's head. The bride says "ouch" while drawing in her head. He tells her: "Go and enter now."

People throw themselves upon his neck and hug him. Someone showers him with gold.

2 *The Tail of the Comet*

Once the Jew traveled into a country of yokels. He passed by an orchard where he spotted a stream of running water. The day was warm. He took his handkerchief, dipped it in the water, and stretched himself out in the shade of the tree. He stretched himself out for a siesta. He fell asleep. Evening came, but the Jew was so tired that he went on sleeping.

The people came out into the city for the evening, and the muezzin climbed the minaret of the mosque to call them to prayer.

He turned from side to side, and as he faced that tree (in the shadow of which the Jew was sleeping) he said: "My God, the tail of the comet!" And he began to cry: "The tail of the comet! The tail of the comet!"

When they heard him the people began to run in all directions, weeping, shouting: "It's the end of the world, the tail of the comet has appeared." The noise startled the Jew, who woke up astonished and said: "What's going on? They're saying that the world's in ruins!" He walked down to the city. Seeing the people in tears, he asked them: "What's wrong? Has some catastrophe befallen you?" They answered: "Don't you see? It's the end of the world, the tail of the comet has appeared." The Jew raised his head and saw that they were looking at his handkerchief (which he had hung up in the tree) and trembling. He told them: "That's it, huh? Tail of the comet, huh? What will you give me to get rid of it for you?"

"What will we give you? Why, what will we give you! We'll dress you up in gold: just lift this affliction from us, that's all we ask of you."

He told them: "Stay right here, don't budge."

The Jew went out of the city, came to the orchard, examined his handkerchief to make sure it was dry, folded it in four, put it in his pocket, and came back down.

He told them: "See, I've lifted this affliction from you." The women looked at each other and uttered cries of joy, the men embraced each other. And the Jew, loaded down with all his heart desired, made his way to Tunis.

They're out there, and we're back here.

J.R.

4

4

4

4

4

Heinrich Heine (German, 1797–1856)

MORPHINE

1

terrific resemblance between these two
young boys—real beauties—but the first one
paler, harder too
almost might say more fancy
than the other who would come up close,
lock me in his arms—loving, tender
like his smile, beatific look!
& the wreath of poppies on his head
sometimes would graze my forehead
smelling weird would drive all pain
out of my mind—sweet bliss
but too soon gone—can't get it all
together till that other brother
serious & white lowers his torch—
good sleeping, better dying—still
best never being born

2

o lamb lamb I was your shepherd once
guarded you against the world
I fed you with my bread
with water from this well—
o rage of winter storms
my breast was warm to you
I gripped you in tight love—
the rain had thickened
wolves & mountain rivers howled
from their stone beds
—o hard hard—you be not afraid
not trembling even when the bolt
cuts down the tallest pine
you in my lap you sleeping
carefree   carefree
                              but my arm
is getting weaker, death
is slinking past—the sheep's game,
shepherd's play runs out—
o God I'll shove the stick back
in your hand—you guard
this poor lamb when they lay me
down to rest—you keep
the thorns from cutting her—
o keep her fleece from brambles
& filthy sumps—her feet
surrounded by sweet grasses
let her sleep, be carefree
as she slept long days ago
against my lap

                                        J.R.

Sigmund Freud (German, 1856–1939)

From THE DREAM-WORK

Old Brücke must have set me some task. Strangely enough, it related to a dissection of the lower part of my own body, my pelvis
and legs, which I saw before me as though in the dissecting-room, but
without noticing their absence in myself and also without a trace of
any gruesome feeling. Louise N. was standing beside me and doing
the work with me. The pelvis had been eviscerated, and it was visible
now in its superior, now in its inferior, aspect, the two being mixed
together. Thick flesh-colored protuberances (which, in the dream itself, made me think of haemorrhoids) could be seen. Something
which lay over it and was like crumpled silver-paper had also to be
carefully fished out. I was then once more in possession of my legs
and was making my way through the town. But I was tired and I
took a cab. To my astonishment the cab drove in through the door of
a house, which opened and allowed it to pass along a passage that
turned a corner at its end and led into the open air again. Finally I
was making a journey through a changing landscape with an Alpine
guide who was carrying my belongings. Part of the way he carried me
too, out of consideration for my tired legs. The ground was boggy;
we went round the edge; people were sitting on the ground like Red
Indians or gypsies—among them a girl. Before this I had been making my own way forward over the slippery ground with a constant
feeling of surprise that I was able to do it so well after the dissection. At last we reached a small wooden house at the end of which
was an open window. There the guide set me down and laid two
wooden boards, which were standing ready, upon the window-sill, so
as to bridge the chasm which had to be crossed over from the
window. At that point I really became frightened about my legs,
but instead of the expected crossing, I saw two grown-up men lying

on wooden benches that were along the walls of the hut, and what seemed to be two children sleeping beside them. It was as though what was going to make the crossing possible was not the boards but the children. I awoke in terror.

JAMES STRACHEY

Gertrude Stein (1874–1946)

From A SONATINA FOLLOWED BY ANOTHER

---

[1]

The song of Alice B.

Little Alice B. is the wife for me. Little Alice B. so tenderly is born so long so she can be born along by a husband strong who has not his hair shorn. And what size is wise. The right size is nice. How can you credit me with wishes. I wish you a very happy birthday.

One two one two I come to you. Today there is nothing but the humble expression of a husband's love. Take it.

[2]

Willy nilly with a roasted kid, how you can you be so delicious and give it to the cat. I gave to the cat because we were uncomfortable. We are not naturally uncomfortable, we are a little nervous. I took a piece of pork and I stuck it on a fork and I gave it to a curly headed jew jew jew. I want my little jew to be round like a pork, a young round pork with a cork for his tail. A young round pork. I want my little jew to be round like a young round pork. I do.

I say it to you and I say it to you I say it to you how I love my little jew. I say it to you and I say it to you. I say it to you and I say it to you. I say it to you.

How I can I have the air of here and there and I say it to you I say it to you I love my own little jew. How can I have the air and I do care I care for her hair and there for the rest of her too my little jew. I love her too my little jew. And she will have endured the cold that is cured, it is cured it is cured and a cow how can a cow follow now a cow can follow now because I have a cow. I had a cow you have a cow, you have a cow now.

She is that kind of a wife. She can see.

And a credit to me.

And a credit to me she is sleepily a credit to me and what do I credit her with I credit her with a kiss.

      1. Always sweet.
      2. Always right.
      3. Always welcome.
      4. Always wife.
      5. Always blessed.
      6. Always a successful druggist of the second class and we know what that means. Who credits her with all this a husband with a kiss and what is he to be always more lovingly his missus' help and hero. And when is he heroic, well we know when.

Win on a foul pretty as an owl pretty as an owl win on a fowl. And the fowl is me and she is pretty as an owl. Battling Siki and Capridinks capridinks is pretty and winks, winks of sleep and winks of love. Capridinks. Capridinks is my love and my Coney.

Max Jacob (French, 1876–1944)
PROSE POEM   "1914"

Aren't lightning flashes the same shape in other countries too? At
my parents' house someone was disputing the color of the sky. Any
lightning? A rosy cloud was advancing. Oh, that everything would
change! My God! Is it possible for Your Reality to be so lifelike?
There is the paternal home. . . . The chestnut trees are glued to the
window, the Court House glued to the chestnut trees, Mt. Frugy
glued to the Court House: only summits, nothing but summits! A
voice announced, "God!" and he became a light in the darkness.
An enormous body hid half of the countryside. Was it He? Was it
Job?

He was poor; he bared his pierced flesh, his thighs hidden by a
loincloth: so many tears, Oh Lord! He climbed down . . . How?
Then some couples appeared, larger than nature, and they also
climbed down. They came from the air inside storage chests, inside Easter eggs: they were laughing, and thread black as dust
clogged the balcony of the paternal home. It was fearful. The couples
installed themselves in the paternal home and we watched them
through the window. Because they were wicked. Black threads
reached as far as the tablecloth in the dining room, where my
brothers were dismantling rifle cartridges. From then on, I was
watched by the police.

MICHAEL BROWNSTEIN

Franz Kafka (German, 1883–1924)

FRAGMENT

My longing was for the ancient times,
my longing was for the present,
my longing was for the future,
and with all this I am dying in a watchman's hut
    at the edge of the street,
an upright coffin that has always been
a piece of State property.
I have spent my life
restraining myself from smashing it to pieces.

I have spent my life resisting the desire to end it.

Osip Mandelstam (Russian, 1891–c. 1938)

THE CHARLIE CHAPLIN POEM

Charlie Chaplin
came out of the movies—
two soles and
a harelip,
two staring eyes
full of ink—
a fine
astonished strength.

O Charlie Chaplin,
a harelip
and two soles—
cruel fate,
as all of us live poorly—
strangers, strangers.

A tin
terror on his face,
his mind
barely can hold—
struts soot-black,
shoe-black, minces

gently
Chaplin says
For this I'm famous & beloved—
even a star
(the great road leads him on
to strangers, strangers.)

—Charlie Chaplin,
step on it.
O Chaplin, rabbit,
make a new role from it—
peel little oranges,
wear roller skates.
Your wife—
blind shadow—
weird stretch of distance that is
merely odd.

Where's
Chaplin's tulip from?
Why is the crowd
so loving?
—Could be that it's Moscow
Charlie, Charlie,
& we've got to risk it—

this would be the wrong time to go sour,
with your derby hat
—the same old ocean—
& Moscow now so close
you still could lose your heart
to that sweet road

BARBARA EINZIG & J.R.

Charles Reznikoff (1894–1976)

TWO POEMS

1

How difficult for me is Hebrew:
even the Hebrew for *mother,* for *bread,* for *sun*
is foreign.   How far have I been exiled, Zion.

2

What are you doing in our street among the automobiles,
horse?
How are your cousins, the centaur and the unicorn?

Jacob Glatstein (Yiddish, 1896–1971)

CADENZA & WHAT WE CAN LEARN FROM HIS
DEATH

He strolled up the steps,
four five six
and at the seventh a man confronted him.
Man: You must go back.
I have a whip, a pistol,
ammunition, power.
So he started to back down.

He thinks, When Cadenza
was hanged at the age of thirty
he already had a warm coat of his own,
a house, a wife, and would certainly have had an heir
who in time would have become the King of Marzeponia.
But they begrudged him such luck.
Who?
A man with ammunition, with power.
Before his death Cadenza reasoned—
not that he was innocent,
that was rubbish—
but he was convinced he died because
his mother had nice blue eyes.
Cadenza remembered very well
how he'd once stuck a piece of paper
in a fly's path.
The poor fly tried to retrace its steps
but probably never reached
its longed-for place.

He said to the man with power:
You're probably changing my whole biography.
Can you take such responsibility?
How can you come to me and say
Down, when I want to go up?
Who set you over me?
You, on the tenth stair of the cosmos?
Okay, I'll come down.
But you think it over a while longer.
I'll sit downstairs and wait.
And if I get tired,
I'll sleep in a cheap hotel;
very tired, in a hospital;
very very tired—
I'll die.
Come to me before I die
because you're very close to me.
You've directed my days,
man of pistols, ammunition and power.
Come to me. I'll kiss you before I die

and I'll say the same thing to you
that Cadenza said to his deathmakers:
Well, Marzeponia will have to get itself
another king.
But don't you boys forget to eat some lard
to keep your little hearts from growing weak.
Your work requires strong hearts
and a dexterous hand.
With these words on his lips,
Cadenza, you might say, passed out.

Perhaps you know the rest of the story:
his executioners each received three medals
which they kept cleaning and polishing all their lives
until that little bit of bronze glistened in the sun
like something real.
My god, life is such a complicated business.
Man's luck is so haphazard.
Whatever I want to do and should do
is in the sleepy brain of fate,
if that's what you want to call it.
A man with power (five-foot something)
sits over me
and is the mighty overseer
of my life.
How did this happen?
There's nothing easier
than to throw the entire guilt
on my mother and her nice blue eyes.

RUTH WHITMAN

Tristan Tzara (French, 1896–1963)
TRISTAN TZARA

Take a good look at me!
I am idiotic, I'm a joker, I'm a goof-off.
Take a good look at me!
I am ugly, my face is expressionless, I am short.
I'm just like all of you![1]
But before you look, ask yourself if the iris through which you shoot arrows of liquid sentiment is not fly-doody, if the eyes of your belly are not tumor sections whose glances will shoot out one day through some part of your body in the form of gonorrheal discharge. You see with your belly-button—so why are you hiding from it the ridiculous spectacle we are making of ourselves? And further down, toothed vaginas swallowing everything: the poetry of eternity, love —pure love, of course—rare steaks and oil painting. Everyone who sees and understands can easily be placed between poetry and love, between steak and painting. They will be digested, they will be digested. A little while ago I was accused of stealing furs. Probably because I was still classed among the poets. Among those poets who satisfy their legitimate needs for cold onanism in hot furs: *HahaHO,* I have other equally platonic pleasures. Call up your family on the phone and piss into the hole usually reserved for musical gastronomical and holy idiocies.
DADA suggests 2 solutions:

NO MORE LOOKING!
NO MORE WORDS![2]

[1] I wanted to do a little advertising for myself.
[2] No more manifestoes.

Don't look anymore!
Don't talk anymore!

For I, a chameleon change seepage with useful attitudes—multicolored opinions for all occasions dimensions and prices—I do the opposite of what I suggest to others.[3]

i have forgotten something:

where? why? how?
i.e.:
the fragile snake will use a fan of cold examples for a cavalcade and I have never had the pleasure of meeting you *mon cher,* the rigid ear will pop out of the envelope by itself like all naval supplies and products of the firm of Aa & Co. chewing gum for example and dogs have blue eyes, I drink the camomile tea, they drink the wind, DADA introduces new points of view, we now sit on corners of tables, in postures slipping a little to the left and right, that's why I'm angry at Dada, ask at all stores for the elimination of D's, eat Aa, rub yourself with Aa toothpaste, buy your clothes at Aa's. Aa is a handkerchief and the sex organ blowing its nose, rapid collapse—in rubber—noiseless, needs neither manifesto nor address book, he gives a 25% reduction buy your clothes at Aa's he has blue eyes.

DAVID BALL

[3] Sometimes.

Louis Zukofsky (b. 1904)

Her face the book of—love delights in—praises
                    —*Pericles* and *Two Gentlemen*

"will you give yourself airs
from that lute of Zukofsky?"

Praises Robert Duncan

"Yes, for I would have my share"

How will his praise sound back to him?
If I let it be
To confirm
One Henry Birnbaum
            and
                  quote
                        him

"I ought to thank
            Zukofsky,
a wonderful voice,
            Zukofsky."

No, my young-old well-wisher,
The second in less than six months,
That makes not you,
"That makes me eclectic"
As tho arm in arm with me
May I say your songs run up to me,
Unstring insensible judges
In their mid-century

With their Stock
Opera House of vocables—
None of us wants to sit in it—
Not I, 55, nor you, say, forward-looking
                                    back to me,
To Father Huc's tree
Of Tartary
On which we are each leaves' Poetry

Where She a breath
Comes out of drudgery
Notes a worked out knee deck her daisies
And apropos of nothing
'There are words that rhyme but
are never used together
You would never use *lute* with *boot*'—
So she has used them.

            Or again—
As where cheek touches forehead,
                        of face
      My father's *boot*
      by a *lute*
                  with eight courses—
                  I have rhymed
                        it:

To her face. Love delights, the book of praises.

Edmond Jabès (French, b. 1912)

From THE BOOK OF QUESTIONS

> *I sailed in my stones so long that I became the child of
> the five continents. And yet, I am only the son of the old
> wall at whose foot I lament with my brothers.*
> >   —Reb Angel

"The word of the voyage is subject to the wind."
>   —Reb Taleb

"Green, grey, black: the color of your words is that of the
road."
> >   —Reb Mahler

> *("God disdains memory. He travels."*
> >   —Reb Haim

> *"The journey refuses the word.
> One is silent in order to listen."*
> >   —Reb Accobas

> *"You travel to find the word of God. And until then
> you stifle your words."*
> >   —Reb Benlassin)

"You came, and our tree blossomed."
>   —Reb Hillel

> "I am no longer with myself.
> I am with all of you.
> With your foreheads. With your hands.
> For the same tomorrows.
> >   —Reb Avigdor

"Day is on your cheeks, night rings my eyes. I sleep against, drowned in my light."

—Reb Rami

"Unreason is the Jew's vocation. It means believing in his mission."

—Reb Doub

"The wind of freedom blows as hard as that of madness."

—Reb Houna

"In the hands of this man, there is a little soil of the country he comes from."

"Ask him to bury it in our soil."

"In the hands of this man, there are some seeds for the soil he comes from."

"Ask him to plant them in our soil."

"In the hands of this man, there is the silence of a child's prayer."

"Ask him to build his house here."

—Reb Oda

"We can only be saved by ourselves. Such is our luck."

—Reb Mires

ROSMARIE WALDROP

Nathaniel Tarn (b. 1928)
From LYRICS FOR THE BRIDE OF GOD   "Sparagmos"

> *"Almost as if I were coming back to myself*
> *lost for so long—*
> *the long vacation from wisdom . . ."*

Returning again and again
to the inescapable theme of our time: *SPARAGMOS,* explosion,
the quest and wandering: going out, coming in,
    the waiting to be fetched / that passively /
            ultimate loss of male identity
   if need be to the hilt,
         lashed at by Hera, the everlasting Mother:
Eli, Eli, Lama Sabachthani?
              As my blood returns into my mother's paps,
          my lymph into my father's testicles,
     as I drip with the juices of their copulation
  and the witch waits among linens at the left of their thighs
  at my conception to take the sparks—
as I hang here, tongue lolling,
   nails falling out,
     wooden splinters oozing out with body oil,
      beard-bristles dropping out one by one like thorns,
the heart panting out the great cry of wandering
          Eli, Eli, Lama Sabachthani?
       the eagle plucks out my heart through my mouth
         and he goes out from me who is to wander forever
          and stain the earth until my recognition—
I AM GOING, BUT YOU SHALL WAIT UNTIL
                 MY RETURN

Sparagmos: the falling to pieces
                the tearing to pieces
      of the world as body
                the humors falling / each cardinal a humor
the survival of a few shreds and patches / the tatters
            to evoke new worlds,
and, below,
                    the bodies of the women I've loved:
      arched: like white dolphins in the sea
            side by side like white rainbows
                        their fragrancies together . . .

No one,   ,under the appellation *"she,"*   ,reading,
will know whom I am calling anymore,
or praising, or disparaging—
                all these loves of my life
      I yearn for equally
        for all their qualities.
Can one believe in the one anymore, the one and only?
                      But / by same observation
I mean I marry but myself, and give whole time
            to my own claim and credence.
Relate to others, working full time:
            who will waste so
this universe and time when he has found the task
    of leaving it   out of the very core
            of staying within life
    O more exceedingly than anyone alive
yet dying all the same, from the center,
            as if the two were possible / in *single* breath
EXACTLY as they are!

  When young, and tall as a pine in my heart,
      I looked up at the planets, selecting the brightest,
          and I said: I want life like the Sun
                  that rises and dies and rises again forever,
  I want to shine during the day
                  and see all things of this world with my eye
          VIDERE ET SCIRE

and at night
                go down into the uncreated and sport in darkness
and in the depths of the sea, where Leviathan plays,
    I want the court of stars in my mirrors,
        the planets like eyes in my mirrors,
the great comets flashing through the deep, like bridal hair.
                        And so many years later
                            dropped in to talk with the Magus,
his dog, wary, one eye on him and one on me,
his fear at my black hair mixed with my silver hair
and the celestial fire in which I robed that day—
    and I said: show me in your mirror master, show me the sun,
        and behind the sun Rebekah
            bathing in Ramoth-Gilead, I knew as girl,
    I knew as enchantress on the banks of Kedron,
and he beat out
one thousand five hundred and ten years of my long life:
    I saw Rebekah and talked with her
                            then went my way

    And she wandered from that time on with me
but in opposite directions,
we would meet every hundred years in a passion of tears
but, as we met, sad parting was upon us immediately
and our caresses were spoiled with bitterness.
    She waxed and waned like the moon.
        I traveled with the sun, seductive to women,
        from time to time they took me for Elijah,
                            our male Persephone,
the wine quivered in glasses where I passed.
I was known as the green man,
being taken into heaven before my time
as the scarves of my years fell into the sea.

This ancient one,
    this unregenerate,
        so old time passes him by in the night sans recognition,
            so old his youth is as a caterpillar's
        thin trails of silk back in his memory,

so old his age is populous
with girls identical as day—
orgy of sexes thrown at his mouth, moon-gore of months,
odor di femina in nostrils, insatiable groans,
and I said
I shall be forgotten
she shall forget to come for me:
latter judgment and judgment after that
but my place will be forgotten among rocks
my cavern forgotten among waves
she shall be gathering up the sparks to take them home
who is last judgment herself, and how shall I be found
who must wander the earth always,
beyond all history? . . .

Confused in the minds of my people,
last of my race and first of another race as yet unborn,
they look up at my falling apart,
I fall upon the world with my arms outstretched,
I am staked out upon the lower world,
but this is not a passion of sadism and inquisition
with which to saddle a civilization for two thousand years:
it is the taking up of the vulture into the eagle
and the end of all wandering in the instant of now:

Rebekah bathing in Ramoth-Gilead.
"In the days of Abraham, she was called Sarah.
And in the days of Isaac, she was called Rebekah.
And in the days of Jacob, Rachel."
In the days of Adam, of course, she was called EVE,HEVAH,
HERA,
Royal Mother.
And in the days of my . . . (name) . . . , she was called . . .
(name) . . .

Moshe Sartel (Hebrew, contemporary)
PAPER KNIGHTS

Our great heads dulled and the skies grew too dull to let down
rain and dew and became iron.
And, inside our houses, we stopped seeing the outer walls. And we
did not see the outer walls.
And we did not see the inner walls. And we did not see the ceil-
ing. And not the floor.
We only see the streets running through our great heads.
And in the streets inside our heads a knight chases after a
knight.
And a knight smites a knight in the streets.

The skies grew too dull to let down rain and dew and our heads
dulled and went blind as rocks
and we sought ourselves in the streets and did not find ourselves
in the streets. And we cast
ourselves into the streets and dug our ten fingers into the streets
and we did not find ourselves
in the streets

Only a knight smiting the knight in the streets

And for this, for this and for this, for this pain we weep and are
not comforted. That this pain saws ribs like a man cutting cedars
with a saw and felling them, and are not comforted.
Precious stones from the North—there are none. Pearls from the
South—there are none. Only our heads
dulled like a basket of rotting grapes, or a basket of figs full of
flies. And we
mumble the words in pain . . . our heads are great and full our
heads are great . . .
our heads are great and rotting . . .

And paper men walk the streets in our heads, but these men bring
wood to kindle Gehenna and coals to kindle the fire that walks in
our corpses
And a paper knight smites a paper knight and a paper knight kills
the knight.
And this too will pass away from our streets, go farther and farther
away towards far places. It will go
far away will go on away—until knights die . . .
These knights we will never see at Kishon River.

And the streets are silent from loneliness and forgetting and only
paper men rustle quietly
in paper streets . . .

And a paper knight pursues a paper knight beats a paper knight
And there were wolves in our city, and the wolves wailed and
barked like dogs in our city
for rain and dew on our city. But the skies grew weak as a woman
and the soul suffers just
as the limbs of our bodies suffer, suffer and turn to paper. For the
skies dull and
our heads dull and become iron and stone and paper and paper
and iron.
And paper knight smites paper knight and strikes sparks of ink
like sparks
of blood on paper.

And a knight kills the knight.

And we hex the people walking the streets in our heads so the
women will not
be bearing, that they will not bear. And that the males will not be
siring, that they will not sire.
For all of them will be paper knights, all of them paper knights
rustling in the streets.

And all the birds fluttering in our city's skies, their bodies are
paper bodies but
beneath their wings—the knife . . .

And knight smites knight and a sword cuts their stems and we like golems of paper and rags
    answer after them—amen and amen. For everything comes from a paper and returns to paper in
    a black liquor of ink.

And they bury and we sing and they bury and we sing . . . none so beautiful as they
    none so pleasing as they . . . pleasure of colored papers.
    And the skies went dull and did not let the rain and dew come and the skies went dull and let down pieces
    of paper falling from the skies like manna from the skies.
    And our soul on account of this hope
    roars like lions for prey and does not weaken, roars for prey
    and devours the paper.

Dread outside and fear in the room and there are no inner walls and there are no outer walls for paper houses.
    Since the skies dulled like papers and our great heads dulled like iron
    on account of the papers.

H.L.

Paul Celan (German, 1920–70)
ZURICH, ZUM STORCHEN

For Nelly Sachs

The talk was of too much, too
little. Of Thou
and Thou again, of
the dimming through light, of
Jewishness, of
your God.

Of
that.
On the day of an ascension, the
cathedral stood on the other side, it passed
over the water with some gold.

The talk was of your God, I spoke
against Him, I
let the heart that I had,
hope:
for
His highest, His deathrattled, His
angry word—

Your eye looked at me, looked away,
your mouth
spoke to your eye, I heard:

We
simply do not know, you know,
we
simply do not know
what
counts.

JOACHIM NEUGROSCHEL

THE END OF "A BOOK OF WRITINGS"

SOURCES, &c.

A NOTE ON TRANSLITERATION

The editors' transliterations of Hebrew words have proceeded wherever possible or wherever advantageous—to produce new soundings & thereby new approaches—by the following system:

alef	' (or omitted if the *alef* is unsounded)
bet	b
vet	v
gimel	g (as in *g*olden)
dalet	d
hey	h (or omitted if the *hey* is unsounded)
vav	v (u or o when vocalic)
zayin	z
ḥet	ḥ (as in "yu*ccch*")
tet	t
yod	y (except vocalic *yod*)
kaf	k
khaf	kh (as in "yu*ccch*")
lamed	l
mem	m
nun	n
samekh	s
'ayin	'
pe	p
fe	f
tsadi	ts
kuf	k
resh	r

shin	sh
sin	s
tav	t

pataḥ/kamats	a (as in "father")
holam male',	
kamats katan	
& ḥataf kamats,	
ḥolam ḥaser	o (as in "cork")
tseyrey male'	ey (as in "baby")
tseyrey ḥaser	
& segol	e (as in "bet"
ḥirik	i (as in "feet")
kubuts, shuruk	u (as in "loose")
pataḥ-yod	ay (as in "buy")
ḥolam-yod	oy (as in "boy")
shuruk-yod	uy (as in "gooey")

We have, however, used traditional spellings of common terms & names (torah, Moses, Jerusalem, etc.) without regard to the systems of transcription that gave rise to them. We have also maintained to the letter any transcriptions occurring inside texts by other translators reproduced here.   (H.L./J.R.)

SOURCES, &c.

Page xv

"Rabbi Eliezer said." Translation by J.R. & H.L. from Babylonian Talmud: *Berakhot* 28b, 29b. Compare Ezra Pound (Canto 53):

> Tching prayed on the mountain and
> wrote MAKE IT NEW
> on his bath tub
> Day by day make it new

Page 1

"Question / Answer." From Irving A. Agus, *Rabbi Meir of Rothenburg* (Ktav Publishing House, New York, 1970), page 190. As when I asked my father: Do we have any illustrious ancestors? And he thought a while & said: Of course—Rabbi Meir of Rothenburg. (J.R.) Scholar, poet, martyr; born & buried in the town of Worms.

"I form the light." Isaiah 45.7.

Page 3

"The First, the Last." After translation of 4 Esdras in R. H. Charles, *Apocrypha & Pseudepigrapha of the Old Testament* (Clarendon Press, Oxford, 1913), volume 1, page 574. A Latin text, c. 3rd or 4th century A.D., from a Greek original, c. 2nd century A.D., & even earlier Hebrew. The original Ezra, "the scribe," led the return from Babylonia in 458 B.C.; this is Ezra "the apocalyptist."

Page 4

"The Greater Hekhalot." Adapted from the Hebrew & the English translation in Gershom Scholem, *Jewish Gnosticism, Merkabah Mysticism, & Talmudic Tradition* (Jewish Theological Seminary of America, New York, 1960), pages 59–60. *Hekhalot* = Palaces or Halls, referring to the Divine Throne, etc. For more on this, see throughout "A Book of Powers."

Page 5

"Elya." From E. Jabès, *Elya* (Tree Books, Berkeley, California, 1974), page 72. Born in Cairo, Jabès has lived in Paris since 1956.

Page 6

"The Great Holy Assembly." From Roy A. Rosenberg, *The Anatomy of God* (Ktav Publishing House, New York, 1973), pages 104–5. "The Great Holy Assembly" (*Idra Raba*) is a discrete section of the *Zohar* ([Book of] Splendor), a 13th-century assemblage by Moses de Leon but claiming to go back to the circle of Simeon bar Yoḥai (see page 274).

Page 8

"Sefer Raziel." From *The Book of Noah* (Tree Books, Berkeley, California, 1975), after Johann Maier's German version from the original Hebrew. "This is a Book out of the Books of Mystery given to Noah the son of Lamech . . . by the Angel Raziel in the Year of his entry into the Ark, at its doorway."

Page 9

"A Poem for the Sefirot as a Wheel of Light." Direct translation from *Sefer Emek ha-Melekh* [Book of the Valley of the King] (Amsterdam, 1648) & reprint in *Encyclopedia Judaica,* volume 10, pages 597–98.

Page 13

"1st Light Poem." From J. Mac Low, *22 Light Poems* (Black Sparrow Press, Los Angeles, 1968). Mac Low has been the principal proponent of chance (aleatory) methods in poetry. His "light poems" are composed from a chart of names for light subjected to a series of systematic chance procedures to determine order of occurrence; later interspersed with free choice methods for syntax & additional content. (See also pages 439, 445, above.)

Page 15

"Aether." From A. Ginsberg, *Reality Sandwiches* (City Lights Books, San Francisco, 1963), pages 89–90.

Page 16

"A Prologue to 'The Vision of the Chariot.'" Babylonian Talmud: *Ḥagiga* 11b.

Page 16

"The Vision of the Chariot." Direct translation from the Hebrew of Ezekiel, chapter 1. "Electrum" here is the traditional English Bible word for Hebrew *ḥashmal:* a mysterious substance or power, which led to intense, often dangerous speculations. Thus, elsewhere in *Ḥagiga* (13a): "There was once a child who was reading at his teacher's house the Book of Ezekiel, & he apprehended what *Ḥashmal* was, whereupon a fire went forth from *Ḥashmal* & consumed him." (N.B. *Ḥashmal* has since become the contemporary Hebrew word for "electricity.")

Page 22
"Shi'ur Koma." From *Merkava Shlema* (Jerusalem, 1921), a miscellany of texts from the manuscript collection of Solomon Musajoff.

Page 24
"Tablet V." From A. Schwerner, *The Tablets* (Grossman Publishers, New York, 1972). "The modern, accidental form of Sumero-Akkadian tablets provided me with a usable poetic structure. They offered, among other things, ways out of closures . . . made me feel comfortable in re-creating the animistic . . . & (enabled me) to put in holes where I wanted, or wherever they needed. . . ." (A.S.)

Page 25
"A Prologue to 'The Book of Concealment.'" Exodus 33.20–.23.

Page 26
"The Book of Concealment" (*Sifra de-Tsini'uta*). Collaged by J.R. from Roy A. Rosenberg, *The Anatomy of God* (Ktav Publishing House, New York, 1973), page 13.

Page 28
"For the Beard of the Great Face." Reprinted in *Encyclopedia Judaica,* volume 10, page 544.

Page 30
"A Poem for the Small Face." Translated with the assistance of Yerach-miel Weinstein from the Sefardic prayerbook. Luria—also known as *ha-Ari,* or "the lion"—was one of the pivotal kabbalist poets & myth-makers. Leader of an esoteric circle in Safed, his workings were oral, & the later writing down was by disciples such as Ḥayim Vital. "Before Luria's theoretical teachings became known, he won fame as a poet." (G. Scholem, *Kabbalah,* page 426.)

Page 32
"A Poem for the Shekinah on the Feast of the Sabbath." From J. Roth-enberg, *Poland/1931* (New Directions, New York, 1974), after a trans-

lation in Gershom Scholem's *On the Kabbalah & Its Symbolism*. A companion piece to the preceding.

Page 37

"There Is a Beautiful Maiden Who Has No Eyes." From *Tree* 3, ed. David Meltzer (Bolinas, California, 1972), page 145. "The maiden who has no eyes" was a traditional image for Shekinah in exile. Cp. the blindfolded statue of "The Synagogue" in Strasbourg Cathedral, per Nathaniel Tarn:

> How poor yet how beautiful you are
> madonna in your snows condemned to childlessness
> blindfold   broken-staffed   with a young girl's figure
>
> . . . .
>
> one suspects more and more that a Jew broke the rule
> to make you synogogue of Strasbourg beside the smirking church
> (From The Beautiful Contradictions, 1970.)

Page 39

"Lyrics for the Bride of God." Opening of the Kitchen section from N. Tarn, *Lyrics for the Bride of God* (New Directions, New York, 1975), pages 3–4. "The poems you are about to hear belong to the time of wandering. . . ."

Page 42

"The Revelation of Moses." J.R.'s working after translation in Moses Gaster, *Studies & Texts in Folklore, Magic, Medieval Romance, Hebrew Apocrypha, & Samaritan Archaeology* (Ktav Publishing House, New York, 1928, 1971), volume 1, pages 127–30. Original Hebrew (no date, probably "medieval") published as *Gedulat Moshe* in Jellinek, *Bet-hamidrash,* volume 2 (1854).

Page 46

"The Apocalypse of Gorgorios." J.R.'s working after translation in Wolf Leslau, *Falasha Anthology* (Schocken Books, New York, 1951), pages 84–85. Falashas are Ethiopian black Jews of ancient origin, isolated, often highly particularized in customs, literature, etc. The Apocalypse of Gorgorios probably derives from a Christian source but stripped down to Jewish essentials. Of Gorgorios, one tradition has him as "founder of an order of ascetics of the region of Wolqait in the fourteenth century." According to another: "Gorgorios was a native of Jerusalem. After his marriage he was separated from his wife and went to the desert where he lived an ascetic life. After a time his wife found him in the desert and brought him food. They agreed between them that his wife would approach his cavern only when the light that he kept burning there disappeared. One day the light was extinguished and they found him dead. He had written on the rock of the cavern: 'I am Gorgorios.'" (Leslau, page 77.)

Page 49

"The Primordial Torah as the Cloak of God." From S. Eliashov, *Sefer Hakdamot ve-Sha'arim* (1908), pages 140–41.

Page 52

"The Greater Hekhalot." J.R.'s working from Hebrew & translation in Gershom Scholem, *Jewish Gnosticism, Merkabah Mysticism, & Talmudic Tradition* (Jewish Theological Seminary of America, New York, 1960), page 32. Scholem points to the "non-literary" character of the imagery, e.g. the reference to the Hippodrome in Caesarea, waterworks in Kidron, etc., "based on a . . . concrete Palestinian reality known to the writer."

Page 53

"Before the Law." From F. Kafka, *The Penal Colony* (Schocken Books, New York, 1948), page 148.

Page 56

"The Book of Enoch." J.R.'s working after translation in R. H. Charles, *Apocrypha & Pseudepigrapha of the Old Testament* (Clarendon Press, Oxford, 1913), volume 2, pages 235–36.

Page 58

"Angel." Translation from text in T. Tzara, *Oeuvres Complètes* (Flammarion, Paris, 1975), page 198. Tzara, born Samuel Rosenstock in Moinesti, Rumania, came to Zurich, circa 1916, to found Dada. From Paris & elsewhere thereafter, he was a key figure in the Surrealist revolution, etc. "between the wars." Another version of "Angel" appears in his *Poèmes Nègres,* an early attempt (largely by translation) to explore the human bases of poetry beyond the European nexus.

Page 59

"The Book of the Left Pillar." Direct translation from the text of *Sefer Amud ha-Smoli* in Gershom Scholem, "Le-Ḥeker Kabbalat R. Yitsḥak ben R. Ya'akov Ha-Kohen," *Tarbiz* IV (1933).

Page 62

"Hero/Lil." From D. Meltzer, *Hero/Lil* (Black Sparrow Press, Los Angeles, 1973).

Page 68

"The 3 of Beginning." Translation from Hippolytos's account (*Refutatio*, c. 3rd century A.D.) in C. Doria & H. Lenowitz (eds.), *Origins* (Anchor Books, New York, 1976), page 322. The Sethians were a Jewish gnostic sect active in the 1st century B.C.–1st century A.D. "The cosmogony of some of the most important Gnostic groups, even those of an antinomian character, depends not only on biblical, but to a very large measure also on aggadic and esoteric Jewish elements." (Scholem, *Kabbalah,* page 22.)

Page 70

"The Crown of Kingdom." Translation from Gabirol's long poem, *Keter Malkhut*. The title names the first & last of the *sefirot* (see above, page 11), indicating a possible kabbalistic reading of the work. Related as well to his philosophical treatise, *Mekor Ḥayim* (The Source of Life). His country: Spain.

Page 75

"The Hidden Sacred Book of Moses." Translation in Doria & Lenowitz (eds.), *Origins* (Anchor Books, New York, 1976), page 18, from Papyrus XIII in Preisedanz (ed.), *Papyri Graecae Magicae* (Leipzig/Berlin, 1931). "A Greek text written in Egypt probably by a heterodox Jew."

Page 77

"Elya." From E. Jabès, *Elya* (Tree Books, Berkeley, California, 1974), page 30. (See note, page 580, above.)

Page 78

"The Withdrawal, the Exile." From J. Gikatilla, *Ginat Egoz* (1274): an introduction to alphabet & number mysticism, etc., his earliest surviving work. Born in Castile, lived many years in Segovia; a student of Abraham Abulafia & acquaintance, circa 1280, of Moses de Leon, author of the *Zohar*.

Page 79

"The *Yod* of Creation." Working after a translation in M. Simon & H. Sperling (eds.), *The Zohar* (The Soncino Press, London, 1934), volume 5, pages 87–88. A major work of the *nous poetikos* (creative mind), the *Zohar* was written &/or assembled in Aramaic by Moses de Leon, who attributed it to Simeon bar Yoḥai (see above, page 274). Starting as exegesis of the Bible, the books joined under its title (*Zohar* = brightness, splendor) exude a sense of *logopoeia* ("dance of the intellect among words"—E. Pound) turned to the service of "vision." Too extravagant for some, as when Rabbi Yishai mocked Simeon bar Yoḥai's image of the "egg of truth," the latter answered: "Before the egg breaks open, you shall depart this world." And so, the *Zohar* adds, it came to pass.

Page 80
"Livingdying." From C. Corman, *Livingdying* (New Directions, New York, 1970).

Page 81
"A Prologue to 'The Torah of the Void.'" In Martin Buber, *Tales of the Hasidim* (Schocken Books, New York, 1947), volume 1, page 270.

Page 82
"The Torah of the Void." Translation from *Likutei Maharan* 1.64, in *Tree* 4 (Berkeley, California, 1974), condensed by present editor. A great-grandson of the Baal Shem Tov (see below, page 607), Nachman's brand of hasidism involved a system of solitary meditation called *hisbodidus* (*hitbodedut*)—practiced at times as a virtual return to forest & wilderness. (". . . You know the story about the rebbe who walked over a cliff while he was in *hisbodidus* & then walked back without even noticing." —Weiner, *9½ Mystics*.) In addition, a stress on story-telling (see below, page 607) &, as here, music as means to enlightenment; thus "in the high spheres there exist temples that can be opened through song only."

Page 89
"Nothing." For Gikatilla, see above, page 584.

Page 90
"The Vertical Inscriptions." From W. C. White, *Chinese Jews* (University of Toronto Press, 1942), page 140. The Jewish community in K'ai-fêng, capital of Honan Province, went back to the 9th or 10th century A.D. It originally consisted of some thousand people from Persia or India, invited into China by the Emperor, and survived to the 20th century. The inscriptions in Chinese are from the pillars of the Chinese-style synagogue—a fusion of torah & tao (see above, page 76).

Page 92

"Fragment." From "Fragments" in F. Kafka, *Dearest Father* (Schocken Books, New York, 1954), page 303.

Page 92

"The Book of Formation." From Lenowitz's translation of *Sefer Yetsira* in Doria & Lenowitz (eds.), *Origins* (Anchor Books, New York, 1976), pages 57–62. The foundation work of Jewish kabbala, alphabetic *poesis,* etc. "The Hebrew letters are the living elements of the Qabala, or rather, the Qabala brings them to life, revealing the code in which the living meaning of the Bible is written. It is a code which uses these equations and not ordinary words as we are accustomed to use them. It trains the mind to hold together, *all at once,* a complex structure each part of which is relevant to every other part." (Carlos Suarès, *The Cipher of Genesis.*)

Page 100

"Glowing Enigmas." From N. Sachs, *The Seeker & Other Poems* (Farrar, Straus & Giroux, New York, 1970), page 393. "Death was my teacher . . . my metaphors are my sounds."

Page 101

"The Mind of Genesis." From D. Slabotsky, *The Mind of Genesis* (Valley Editions, Ottawa, Canada, 1975).

Page 103

"Time." From H. Shapiro, *This World* (Wesleyan University Press, Middletown, Connecticut, 1971), page 57.

Page 104

"A Prologue to Genesis." Genesis 1.1.

Page 104

"The Ten Words of Creation." From James A. Montgomery, *The Samaritans: The Earliest Jewish Sect* (1907), pages 272, 274. Reputed survivors of the Northern Kingdom (Israel/Samaria) & clearly within that configuration, the Samaritans are, according to their own chronicles, "the direct descendants of the Joseph tribes, Ephraim and Manasseh" (*Encyclopedia Judaica*). Further: "It is too often and too easily forgotten . . . that in speaking of Samaritans we are speaking of heretical Judaism." (G. Scholem, *Jewish Gnosticism*, etc., page 4.) The original is presented here in Samaritan Hebrew script.

Page 105

"Variations on Genesis." (1) From *The Baraita of the Work of Creation*, translation by Jack Hirschman in *Tree* 2 (Bolinas, California, 1971), page 54. (2) J.R.'s working after translation in M. Simon & H. Sperling (eds.), *The Zohar* (The Soncino Press, London, 1934), volume 1, page 63. (3) Translation of Genesis 1.1–.5, in Doria & Lenowitz, *Origins* (Anchor Books, New York, 1976), page 37.

Page 107

"The Pirke de Rabbi Eliezer." From J. Rothenberg, *The Pirke & the Pearl* (Tree Books, Berkeley, 1974), after a translation in Gerald Friedlander, *The Pirke de Rabbi Eliezer* (London, 1916; Benjamin Blom, New York, 1971), pages 15–16. The *pirke* (i.e. "chapters") go back, by way of reputation, to Eliezer-the-Great ben Hyrkanos, who lived circa A.D. 150, "was known for his great erudition . . . but was ultimately excommunicated." For the events that led up to his banishment, see "Torah on Earth" (above, page 270). The story continues: "Great was his anger on that day, for everything at which he cast his eyes was burned. Rabban Gamaliel, too, was traveling in a ship when a huge wave rose to drown him." (*Encyclopedia Judaica*, volume 6, page 622.)

Page 108

"The End." From A. Ginsberg, *Kaddish* (City Lights Books, San Francisco, 1961), page 99. ". . . *The End* records a vision experienced after drinking Ayahuasca, an Amazon spiritual potion. The message is: Widen the area of consciousness." (A.G.)

Page 109

"The Joe 82 Creation Poems." From R. Owens, *The Joe 82 Creation Poems* (Black Sparrow Press, Los Angeles, 1974), page 44. This one is called "Wild-Man & the Temptation in the Forest."

Page 110

"A Prologue to the Elements of Creation." From M. Simon & H. Sperling (eds.), *The Zohar* (Soncino Press, London, 1934), volume 3, page 80.

Page 111

"Fire-Poem." Direct translation from M. Zulay (ed.), *Piyutei Yannai* (1938). Yannai was one of the first known *paytanim* (from the Greek, *poētēs*), makers of a kind of poetry called *piyut:* "compositions added to . . . the ancient prayers [of the synagogue] . . . to constitute—in contrast to the stable and stationary standard prayers—an ever-changing and restless element within the Jewish liturgy . . . that was responsible for the development within medieval Judaism of about half a hundred different rites" (Shalom Spiegel). His work was rediscovered in the 20th century, largely through fragments in the *geniza* (storeroom) of the Cairo Synagogue.

Page 112

"Water-Poem." Direct translation from the Hebrew prayer book of the rain prayer (*piyut*) chanted on the eighth day of *Sukot* (Tabernacles) for the *musaf* service. Like Yannai (see preceding), Kallir was an early *paytan* & a greatly prolific poet. "Many of Kallir's *piyutim* are interlaced with Hebrew folk language. Like the Palestinian *piyut,* Kallir's works are an organic continuation of ancient Hebrew, while the Hebrew poetry of Spain is a revival of the Biblical language." (*Encyclopedia Judaica,* volume 10, page 715.) For this & the expansiveness of their language, the eastern *paytanim* were targets for medieval classicists like Abraham ibn Ezra, later Enlightenment types, etc.—though by our time the balance may be shifting. (See also page 625, below.)

Page 117

"Air-Poem." J.R.'s working after translation in Hugo Odeberg, *3 Enoch or The Hebrew Book of Enoch* (Cambridge University Press, 1928; Ktav Publishing House, New York, 1973), pages 81–83. Mistitled "Hebrew Book of Enoch" (in sequence with other "Enoch" books), it is more the spirit-journey of Ishmael ben Elisha (2nd century A.D.) led by Enoch transformed to angel Metatron. "A late *Hekhalot* compilation . . . previously known as *Sefer ha-Hekhalot* [The Book of Palaces]" (Jonas C. Greenfield, Prolegomenon to Odeberg's edition). Names of the winds are drawn from biblical quotations.

Page 120

"The Domesday Dictionary." From A. Schwerner & D. Kaplan, *The Domesday Dictionary* (Simon & Schuster, New York, 1963), pages 85–87.

Page 122

"Double Memory." Original appearance in Alternative Press "postcard series" (Grindstone City, Michigan, 1976).

Page 123

"Psalm 19." From D. Rosenberg, *Blues of the Sky* (Harper & Row, New York, 1976). "I wanted to translate the form of the literal psalm—not the precise words, but the original atmosphere. . . . Still, they are *attempts* at literal translation, from the lost archaic originals into the form of a psalm or hymn, a poem of 'public meditation.' . . . Modern . . . An immediacy of author's presence in the process of listening to himself speaking." (D.R.)

Page 127

"The Book of Mysteries." Direct translation from Mordecai Margalioth (ed.), *Sefer ha-Razim* (American Academy for Jewish Research, Jerusalem, 1966), pages 96–100. "A newly recovered book of magic from the Talmudic period . . . collected from *geniza* fragments & other sources."

Page 132

"The Code of Day & Night." Working after J. M. Allegro, "An Astrological Cryptic Document from Qumran," *Journal of Semitic Studies,* volume 9 (1964), pages 291–94.

Page 133

"Talismans: Star Magic." From R. Grossinger (ed.), *Io* 6 (Summer 1969), pages 197–98.

Page 135

"The Zohar." From translation in M. Simon & H. Sperling (eds.), *The Zohar* (The Soncino Press, London, 1934), volume 2, page 317. For more on *Zohar,* see above, page 580.

Page 136

"Three Poems." New version by Kevin Power after Ladino original in *Trece de Nieve,* Madrid, December 1976—an issue devoted to Lorca.

Page 137

"The Black Plague." From D. Antin, *Definitions* (Caterpillar Books, New York / Los Angeles, 1967).

Page 140

"Poem with Sky & Earth." George Economou's working after David Goldstein, *The Jewish Poets of Spain* (Penguin Books, Harmondsworth, England, 1965). Ha-Nagid (i.e., "the prince") was, with Gabirol, ha-

Levi, and the ibn Ezras, one of the prolific Hebrew poets of medieval Spain. (See above, pages 513–23.)

Page 141

"And with the Book from Tarussa." From P. Celan, *Speech-Grille & Selected Poems* (E. P. Dutton, New York, 1971), page 207. (See below, page 633.)

Page 144

"Menorah." Arranged by J.R. from E. R. Goodenough, *Jewish Symbols in the Greco-Roman Period* (Pantheon Books, New York, 1953), volume 4, pages 92ff: a discussion of menorah / tree of life in the *Zohar,* etc.

Page 146

"The Great Sentence." Translated from Hippolytos, *Refutatio* [Refutation of all Heresies] (ed. Wendland), VI 9. The work is the *Megale Apophasis,* here attributed to Simon the Magus of Gitta, Samaria, reputed "first gnostic" & "messiah" ("son of God"), contemporary of Jesus. (See below, page 601.)

Page 149

"The Inner Trees." From Y. Goll, *Poems* (Kayak Books, Santa Cruz, California, 1968), page 19.

Page 150

"A Poem & a Commentary." Previously unpublished materials, from a letter to J.R., August 13, 1974.

Page 152

"A Prologue to the Works of Adam." Genesis 5.1–.2.

Page 153

"The Fathers According to Rabbi Nathan." J.R.'s working after translation in Judah Goldin, *The Fathers According to Rabbi Nathan* (Yale University Press, New Haven, 1955), pages 127–28. Ascribed to Natan ha-Bavli ("the Babylonian," mid-2nd century A.D.) as his commentary on the *Pirke Avot* (Chapters of the Fathers) section of the Mishna, or as someone else's commentary on his version of the *Pirke Avot.*

Page 155

"The Book *Baruch*." Translation from Hippolytos's 3rd-century text ("The Refutation of All Heresies"), in Doria & Lenowitz (eds.), *Origins* (Anchor Books, New York, 1976), page 169. "This Greek text is probably a condensed translation of Justin's Hebrew or Aramaic original, c. A.D. 40–70." (C.D.) Of the identification of the Supreme God with Priapos—a high sexuality in common with eastern Tantrism, etc.— Hippolytos writes: "I have seen a great many heresies, my well-beloved; I never met with any, however, that was worse than this. Truly we must imitate the Hercules of Justin in cleaning out these Augean stables—or rather sewers." A process set in motion almost to the present.

Page 159

"Green." From *Tree* 5 (Berkeley, California, 1975), page 201.

Page 160

"The Naasene Cosmology." Translation from Hippolytos's 3rd-century account (see above), in Doria & Lenowitz (eds.), *Origins*, pages 327, 333–34. "This is a cosmology from the Ophites (Naasenes), a Jewish gnostic sect of snake-worshippers active from the first century B.C. through the second century A.D." (C.D.) The antiquity of the idea can be seen in the following Ugaritic temple poem (circa 1000 B.C.), which shows the other face of the Edenic snake, etc.; tied in as well to alternative Jewish cult practices:

When the king offers slain offerings
to *Ušḫr,* the serpent,
in the inner sanctum of the god of the temple (?)
A male head of small cattle for the serpent,
and a dove for *Qlḥ.*
A male head of small cattle for the *ḫll ydm* rite
in the sanctuary of the god of the temple (?)
The woman (= the queen) partakes.
A male head of small cattle for the god of the temple (?) as the
    šlmm offered in connection with
the *kalil.* He (= the king) partakes of it.
And in the inner sanctum, a libation
A male head of small cattle for *Ušḫr,* the serpent,
and a dove for *Qlḥ.*
Day: One.

(From Baruch A. Levine: previously unpublished translation based on Text 611 in C. Gordon, *Ugaritic Textbook*.)

Page 162

"Serpent." For more on Nathan of Gaza, the prophet of the "heretical" 17th-century messiah Sabbatai Zevi, see below, pages 605–6. The poem as *gematria* (page 431, above) turns up in Scholem's biography of Sabbatai & many other sources.

Page 163

"Anatomy of a War." Previously unpublished translation, from T. Carmi, *Hitnatslut ha-Meḥaber* (1973).

Page 164

"The Wind   Two Trees   Men and Women." From *Tree* 5 (Berkeley, California, 1975), pages 8–9. "The form is modelled on the standard presentation of text and commentary in Hebrew religious books."

Page 167

"The Iyyob Translation." From Zukofsky's contemporary masterpiece, *A* (Grossman, New York, 1964)—the opening of the 15th section a translation-by-sound from the Hebrew Book of Job," principally the whirlwind sections of Chapter 38. Z.'s major working in this manner is his translation from Latin of complete *Catullus* (Cape Goliard–Grossman): a counterpointing & close imitation of the source language, or post-Joycean attempt to deliver meaning by pun & rhythm.

Page 169

"The Book of Job." Translation of Job 40.8–41.34.

Page 173

"Nothing, only an image." From F. Kafka, *Dearest Father* (Schocken Books, New York, 1954), pages 313, 261.

Page 173

"If you are 'my witnesses.'" As quoted in *Pesikta de Rav Kahana* 102b. With which, compare Don Juan Matus to Carlos Castaneda: "There is no way to refer to the unknown. One can only witness it." (*Tales of Power*, page 266.)

Page 175

"Patriarchal Poetry." From G. Stein, *Bee Time Vine* (Yale University Press, New Haven, 1953), page 263. ". . . There are all these emotions lying around; no reason why we shouldn't use them."

Page 176

"The Book of Genesis: Begettings." Genesis 5.1–.32; through the P document, from an earlier oral tradition.

Page 179

"The Song of Lilith." Previously unpublished translation from R. Ombres, *Love Bestiary* (original Italian: 1974). "In the poems in which she appears in this Book, Lilith is a sorceress, but above all a 'different' woman: she gives birth by parthenogenesis and is certainly not seducing men. She is accompanied by a unicorn that, as everybody knows, is a very submissive animal, and often even affectionate, but only with virgins." (R. Ombres.)

Page 183

"The Genesis Apocryphon: The Mystery." From Joseph A. Fitzmyer, *The Genesis Apocryphon of Qumran Cave I* (Biblical Institute Press, Rome, 1971), page 51. "One of the seven major scrolls which were found in Qumran Cave I in 1947," it forms in effect a kind of "Little Genesis" or "Book of the Patriarchs" freely reworked.

Page 184

"The Book of Enoch: The Animal Visions." J.R.'s working after translation in R. H. Charles, *Apocrypha & Pseudepigrapha of the Old Testament* (Clarendon Press, Oxford, 1913), volume 2, page 250. "In the *Book of Enoch* the scribe says that the first two-legged creatures had the private parts of great studs, and it may well be that Methuselah and Jared and Mahalalel were mountains and that from their middle hung hills which were their organs of generation. Otherwise, it is impossible for one to imagine how they could live for nine hundred years without wearing out their genitals. It is known that Og, King of Bashan, had an iron bedstead seven cubits long, and that the giants of Anak had six fingers." (Edward Dahlberg, *The Sorrows of Priapus.*)

Page 187

"The Genesis Apocryphon: After the Flood." From J. A. Fitzmyer, *The Genesis Apocryphon* (Biblical Institute Press, Rome, 1971), page 57.

Page 188

"Bottom: On Shakespeare." From L. Zukofsky, *Bottom: On Shakespeare* (University of Texas Press, Austin, 1963), pages 103–4.

Page 190

"The Book of Formation." J.R.'s working, after various translations, of the traditional ending of the *Sefer Yetsira* (see above, page 586), attributing the "authorship" (authority) to Abraham. "This means that in order to receive the revelation Abraham had to use his intelligence, had to learn to make and do something with it first. It was a matter of *understanding*." (C. Suarès, *The Cipher of Genesis*.)

Page 191

"The Genesis Apocryphon: Of Sarah." Modified from J. A. Fitzmyer, *The Genesis Apocryphon* (Biblical Institute Press, Rome, 1971), page 63. The quote from the *Pesikta Rabati* uses the translation of William G. Braude (Yale University Press, New Haven, 1968).

Page 193

"The Book of Genesis: The Offering." Translation of Genesis 22.1–.14, in E. Fox, *In the Beginning* (*Response,* Waltham, Massachusetts, 1972), pages 54–56. Fox's version of Genesis is based on an earlier German working by Martin Buber & Franz Rosenzweig, who sought to reclaim the "spokenness" of the original as against the "writtenness" of "Old Testament" scripture: "a reading and translation of the Bible which center on sounds." They proceeded by a recasting into verse lines corresponding to their sense of oral pattern, by attention to etymology (root-meanings) & to "concrete" over "abstract" language, & by a sensitivity to turns of sound & image (puns, homophonies, etc.) not normally within the scheme of theological translation. Wrote Buber: "As if the spirit of a speech were to be sought out anywhere other than in its linguistic form."

Page 196

"The Sacrifice." From H. Schwartz, *Lilith's Cave* (Shambhala Publications, San Francisco, 1975).

Page 197

"The Book of Genesis: Jacob & the Angel." Translation of Genesis (J Document) 32.21–.30, in E. Fox, *In the Beginning* (*Response,* Waltham, Massachusetts, 1972), page 90.

Page 200

"The Testaments of the 12 Patriarchs." Working after translation in M. Gaster, *Studies & Texts* (Ktav Publishing House, New York, 1928, 1971), volume 1, page 81. "This is the will (testament) of Naphtali, son of Jacob."

Page 204

"Exodus." From G. Oppen, *Collected Poems* (New Directions, New York, 1975), page 229.

Page 205

"A Prologue to the Works of Moses." From "The Revelation of Moses" in M. Gaster, *Studies & Texts* (Ktav Publishing House, New York, 1928, 1971), volume 1, page 126. "There has never yet risen in Israel a prophet like Moses, whom the Lord knew face to face." (Deuteronomy 34.10.)

Page 205

"Molad Mosheh." Modified from Selig J. Miller, *The Samaritan Molad Mosheh* (Philosophical Library, New York, 1949), pages 136–38. The exaltation of Moses is central to Samaritan theology: the single prophet acknowledged before the future coming of the Taheb as the messianic prophet. (See John MacDonald, *The Theology of the Samaritans,* 1964.) But the commentaries, above, show related ideas of transformation elsewhere in the Jewish enterprise.

Page 208

"The Image of Speech at Sinai." From Eleazar ben Judah of Worms, *Sodei Razaya* [Secrets of Secrets] (ed. Kamelhar, Bilgoraj, Poland, 1936), page 43. *"I have seen the eternal* interior, not ocular vision. . . . *I have spoken to the prophets; I have multiplied the visions & through the intermediation of prophets, I have pointed out appearances."* (Eleazar of Worms, "The Book of Prophecy.") A mystic, theologian, & poet, Eleazar endured the murders of wife, daughter, & son in persecutions following the fall of Jerusalem to Saladin, then gave it testimony in a long & detailed poem. He became a legendary hero after death, said to travel like Elijah from place to place in a cloud—especially to distant circumcision ceremonies. A master of the "secrets," many works were attributed to him by later generations.

Page 209

"The Book of Exodus." Direct translation from Exodus 15.1–.21, one of the oldest documents in the Bible, from the very beginnings of the Yahvist cult in Israel. "We have been taught that every one who sings this hymn daily with true devotion will be worthy to sing it at the Redemption that is to be, for it refers both to the past world & to the future world. . . . The Shekinah will sing this song to the Lord, because the King will receive Her with a radiant countenance." (*Zohar: Exodus* 54b)

Page 213

"A Dialogue. The Death of Moses." J.R.'s working, after prose translation by T. Carmi in *Present Tense,* volume 2, number 2, pages 48–49. The full sequence of death poems—by various hands—appears "in several synagogue rites printed in Italy (as) part of the Simhat Torah ritual."

Page 213

"The Book of Psalms: 12 for Yahveh." A translation of sections from Psalm 68, "to the chief Musician, a Psalm or Song of David." The present translation follows the suggestion of W. F. Albright that the 68th Psalm is in fact "a catalogue of hymns" consisting of first lines or first strophes, or that of T. H. Robinson: "Not strictly a single poem at all, but . . . a collection of sequences & phrases taken from a number of different poems, & strung together haphazard." A more contemporary view—in light of both current poetics & discussions of formulaic models in traditional oral poetry—would view the resultant work as "collage" or (re)-"assemblage," a serial poetry open to a shifting (indeterminate) order of presentation. The translators have selected 12 of the 30 poems isolated by Albright & have presented them as a numbered sequence of hymns to Yahveh.

Page 217

"The First Book of Samuel." Translation & working from I Samuel 28.3–.14 (the "Samuel strain"), with assistance on the varieties of Jewish shamanism from Arvid S. Kapelrud, "Shamanistic Features in the Old Testament," in Carl-Martin Edsman (ed.), *Studies in Shamanism* (Scripta Instituti Donneriani Aboensis, 1967). An Israelite judge & prophet, Samuel lived in the 10th century B.C. & was involved with Saul & David in the "transition from a loose confederation of Hebrew tribes to a centralized monarchy" (*Encyclopedia Judaica*)—hence the elimination of the more free-wheeling shamanistic practices. (N.B. The "shaman" [*mekhashefa*] of the third commentary, above, is feminine, a word usually translated as "witch" or "sorceress," but clearly tied to the aboriginal religion; *c.f.* Babylonian *kassapu* = darkness, privacy, cutting [of the self, of the entrails].)

Page 219
"Tohu." From D. Meltzer, *Tens* (McGraw-Hill Book Company, New York, 1973), pages 124–25.

Page 221
"The Dead Sea Psalms." From J. A. Sanders (ed.), *The Dead Sea Psalms Scroll* (Cornell University Press, Ithaca, New York, 1967), page 87.

Page 222
"The Davithea Incantation." Translation from Coptic text in A. M. Kropp, *Ausgewählte koptische Zaubertexte* (Brussels, 1930–31), volume 1, pages 29–31; "image" from Kropp, volume 3, plate viii. The "image" in fact is a "calligram," composed entirely of letters from the Greek, Coptic, & celestial alphabets; for which see also pages 414, 419, above.

Page 227
"If the Prophets Broke In." From N. Sachs, *O the Chimneys* (Farrar, Straus & Giroux, New York, 1967), pages 59–61.

Page 229
"A Vision in the Voice of Yahveh." Direct translation from Amos 8.1–.12. "I am no prophet, nor a prophet's son; but I am a herdsman & a dresser of sycamore trees, & the Lord took me from following the flock, & the Lord said to me, Go, prophesy to my people Israel." (Amos 7.14–.15.) Circa 8th century B.C., Amos was the first of the "latter prophets" & probably the first to write things down.

Page 232
"The Book of Daniel." Direct translation from Daniel 7.1–.15. Traditional dates for the book are circa 545–535 B.C., though probably the work of various authors in the 3rd & 2nd centuries. The name is likely that of an earlier regional hero ("an obviously pre-Mosaic saint"— *Encyclopedia Judaica*), who also turns up among Phoenicians & Canaanites, etc.

"A Dream Service." Direct translation from Hebrew text in Philip Birnbaum (ed.), *Ha-Siddur ha-Shalem* (The Daily Prayer Book); derived from Talmud: *Berakhot.*

"Elijah & the Priests of Baal." Direct translation from I Kings 18. An extreme Yahvist of the 9th century B.C. & later legendary hero, central to the messianic myths, etc.

"A Poem About Ashera." Translation based on C. Gordon, *Ugaritic Textbook* (Ventnor Publications, Ventnor, N.J., 1965), Text 51, in H. Lenowitz, *A Reasonable Proposal for the Translation of Ugaritic Mythopoetry* (dissertation, University of Texas, 1971), pages 52–54.

"In the Mountain of the Song That Shows." From G. Quasha (ed.), *Active Anthology* (The Sumac Press, Fremont, Michigan, 1974), page 254.

"The Alphabet of Ben Sira." From *Alfabeta de-ben Sira* (Warsaw, 1927), Version One. The actual Ben Sira, author of Ecclesiasticus (The Wisdom of Ben Sira), goes back to the 2nd century B.C.; the connection with the earlier Jeremiah relates to the numerical equivalence of their names, etc. The *Alphabet* itself is a much later (medieval) work: a series of epigrams & stories arranged alphabetically. Satirical, pornographic, "heretical" in its thrusts "not only," as here, "[at] Jeremiah . . . & all the institutions of established religion . . . but God . . . as well." (Joseph Dan, in *Encyclopedia Judaica,* volume 4, page 549.)

"A Poem for the High Priest." Direct translation from the Yom Kippur prayer book, with the assistance of Yerachmiel Weinstein. The poem occurs in the Yom Kippur service at the time of the priestly benediction. Related to descriptions of the High Priest Simon in the Wisdom of Ben Sira (c. 170 B.C.). The hereditary priesthood is itself an ongoing tradition for purposes of ritual.

"Travels of a Latter-Day Benjamin of Tudela." From *Exile* (Toronto, Canada, 1975), volume 3, number 1. "Benjamin of Tudela was an exploring Rabbi in medieval Spain who travelled widely throughout the Levant in search of lost or unknown Jewish communities." (Yehuda Amichai.) Urim & Thummim: the precious stones on the breastplate of the High Priest.

Page 257

"Children of the Flowers of the Priesthood." Arrangement of materials from Raphael Patai, *Man & Temple* (Ktav Publishing House, New York, 1947). *Teki'ah / teru'ah / teki'ah* = traditional sounds of *shofar* (ram's horn) in the temple service.

Page 260

"The Acts of Saint John." J.R.'s redaction &/or working, based on versions by Edgar Hennecke, Max Pulver, & G. R. S. Mead from the gnostic Acts of Saint John. "After a while the Christ rose & said he was very glad to see his children. . . . 'My children, I want you to listen to all I have to say to you. I will teach you, too, how to dance a dance, & I want you to dance it.' . . . Then he commenced our dance, everybody joining in, the Christ singing while we dance." (Description—by Porcupine, circa 1890—of Wovoka, the Christ of the American Indian "ghost dance" religion.)

Page 266

"Prologue in Six Parts." From A. Schwerner, *Seaweed* (Black Sparrow Press, Los Angeles, 1969), pages 53–56.

Page 270

"The Babylonian Talmud: Torah on Earth." Translation from Babylonian Talmud: *Baba Metzia* 59b, in N. Glatzer, *Hammer on the Rock* (Schocken Books, New York, 1948), pages 96–97. For the banishment of Eliezer the Great that follows thereon, see above, page 587. The date of the oral narrative is obviously older than that for the first publication of the Talmud given above.

Page 272

"A Poem for Bar Yoḥai." Direct translation from the *Tikum Shabat* ceremony of the Sephardic rite. "When they took up his bier, it rose in the air & fire burned around about it. They heard a voice, 'Come one & all to participate in the wedding feast of Rabbi Simeon. *He comes in peace; they shall rest upon their beds.* [Isaiah 57.2.]'" (From "The Lesser Holy Assembly" [*Zohar*], in Roy A. Rosenberg, *The Anatomy of God,* page 181.)

"The Babylonian Talmud: Beauty That Withers." Translation from Babylonian Talmud: *Berakhot* 5b, in N. Glatzer, *Hammer on the Rock* (Schocken Books, New York, 1948), page 20. "Rabbi Yohanan lost ten sons; he carried a bone (according to the Arukh, a tooth) of the tenth son with him."

"The Great Lament." From the Talmud: *Mo'ed Katan* 25b, as cited in Emanuel Feldman, "The Rabbinic Lament," in *Jewish Quarterly Review,* volume 63, number 1 (July 1972), page 72.

"I Am the Babe of Joseph Stalin's Daughter." From R. Owens, *I Am the Babe of Joseph Stalin's Daughter* (The Kulchur Foundation, New York, 1972). *Din* ("judgment") is an alternative term for the sefira *gevura* (see above, page 11). "In her book . . . one aspect of the kabbalistic system dominates: the sefira called DIN; more generally, the left side of God." (H. Lenowitz, "Din & Razel," in *Margins,* number 24, page 84.)

"Palestine Under the Romans." From C. Reznikoff, *By the Waters of Manhattan* (New Directions, New York, 1962), pages 51–52. "Based on the Mishna as translated by Herbert Danby."

"A Poem for the Masters." Based on translations from the Babylonian Talmud: *Pesaḥim* 57a in Meyer J. Perath, *Rabbinical Devotions* (Koninklijke van Gorcum, Netherlands, 1964) & Hugh J. Schonfield, *The Jesus Party*. "Street-ballad on extortions and nepotism on the part of . . . the here-mentioned priestly families . . . to all intents and purposes the rulers of the theocratic Jewish State during the first half of the first century C.E." (M. J. Perath.)

"Apocalypse." Direct translation of Revelation 12 (New Testament), with special reference to J. Massyngberde Ford, *Revelation: A New Translation* (The Anchor Bible, Doubleday & Company, New York 1975). Prophetic writings but "clearly . . . more akin to Jewish apocalyptic literature than to Christian. . . . *Revelation* is a composite work from the 'Baptist School' who represented a primitive form of Christianity and inherited the Baptist's prophetic, apocalyptic and 'fiery' (boanergic) tendencies. . . . The [Jewish author] who seems most suitable is John the Baptist" (J. M. Ford)—although the attribution of the twelfth chapter is to "a disciple of John the Baptist . . . between A.D. 60 and 70 when the war between the Romans and the Jews in Palestine was gathering momentum." From a lost Hebrew & Aramaic original.

Page 282

"The Prophecy of Jesus ben Hananiah." From Flavius Josephus, *The Wars of the Jews*, 6.301. A 1st-century prophet & messiah, Jesus ben Hananiah repeated this oracle for years prior to the city's fall & again at his death in the siege of Jerusalem. Other 1st-century "messiahs" included Jesus of Nazareth, Simon Magus, Judah the Galilean, the Pharisee Saddok, Theudas, Menahem ben Judah, & Simeon bar Giora; thereafter: Simeon bar Kokhba, Abu Isa, Yudqhan, Mushka, Ibn Aryeh, Solomon ha-Kohen, Moses Al-Dari, David Alroy, Abraham Abulafia, the Prophet of Avila, Hasdai Crescas, Asher Lemlein, David Reuveni, Solomon Molcho, Sabbatai Zevi, & Jacob Frank. The list of claimants, mystical & revolutionary by turns, is far from complete.

Page 283

"Toldot Yeshu." Translation & working after Hugh J. Schonfield, *According to the Hebrews* (Duckworth, London, 1937), with additions from the Strasburg manuscript (*Ma'ase Yeshu ha-Notsri*) in Samuel Krauss, *Das Leben Jesu nach jüdischen Quellen* (Berlin, 1902). A Jewish "life of Jesus," or counter-gospel, many versions of which were compiled & written from the Geonic period on, though obviously relying on earlier sources. Similar magical abuses were attributed by the early Christians to other messiahs like Simon Magus or to the Jews in general: "And what are the wonders that he works? . . . . Sometimes he flies." (*The Clementine Homilies*, II.32.) In Jewish folklore Jesus remains a "magician" or latterday (dark) shaman—as here, with Judas, in a struggle of shamanic forces.

Page 285

"Corpus Christi Play." From John Cohen (ed.), *The Essential Lenny Bruce* (Random House, New York, 1967), pages 68–70.

Page 287

"The Story of Simon & Helen." Translation from Irenaeus, *Against Heretics*, I, 23, 1–4. Simon Magus (above, page 590) was the 1st-century Samaritan messiah & reputed originator of Gnosticism, of whom the Book of Acts: ". . . used sorcery . . . bewitched the people . . . to whom they all gave heed . . . they said, This man is the great power of God." (8.9–.10.) The pattern, as here, of a "Son of God" accompanied by the exiled, often prostituted female presence (Shekinah, Sophia, Ennoia, etc.) returns in Sabbatai Zevi's Sarah, Jacob Frank's daughter Eve (pages 321, 606), as in the Magdalene of the Egyptian gnostics: "A revelation . . . on the mountain . . . Jesus started to unite with her, then took his seed in his own hand, & showed her, said, We must do so that we may live." (From *The Great Questions of Mary,* an early gospel, whose revelation of a sexual gnosis, etc., met with later fierce repression.)

Page 290

"A Spell for a Blaspheming Woman." J.R.'s working, after translation in E. R. Goodenough, *Jewish Symbols in the Greco-Roman Period* (Pantheon Books, New York, 1953), volume 2, page 107.

Page 291

"Jerusalem the Golden." From C. Reznikoff, *By the Waters of Manhattan* (New Directions, New York, 1962), page 19.

Page 292

"A Karaite Dirge." Modified from L. Nemoy, *Karaite Anthology* (Yale University Press, New Haven, 1952), pages 318–19. A fundamentalist sect, founded by Anan ben David in the 8th century, the Karaites went back to Scripture in denial of the talmudic (rabbinic) tradition: "God forbid that I should join a wicked people to walk along their path / or that I should give heed to their lying jeers or to their scoffing / or that I should turn to the false claims of their books or to their vanity / or that I should study the ordinances of their Mishna invented by themselves / Rather do I deny that it is a tradition and a secret commanded by the Rock to His congregation on Mount Sinai to cherish these false things / and I believe only in the written Law given by God to His own people / : One Law to which I add nothing, one rule to which I assign no second." (From Moses ben Abraham Dar'i, *The Alexandrian Notebook.*) The dirge, above, was adapted from the non-Karaite poet, Eleazar ha-Kallir & recited by Karaite pilgrims in Jerusalem.

Page 293

"The Withdrawal of the Shekinah." From Raphael Patai, *The Hebrew Goddess* (Ktav Publishing House, New York, 1967), page 143. "A new chapter in the life of the Matronit [Shekinah as divine daughter & bride of God] opened when her bedchamber, the Temple of Jerusalem, was destroyed. Since her husband, the King, was wont to copulate with her only in the Temple, its destruction meant the sudden disruption of the intensely pursued love-relationship between the two. . . . The Matronit was banished from her holy abode and from the Land of Israel. . . . The King . . . lost stature and power, was no longer King, nor great, nor potent. . . . [Unable] to endure the misery of solitude, he let a slave-goddess take the place of his true queen . . . [:] none other than Lilith, [who] now assumed the rule over the Holy Land. . . . This act, more than anything else, caused the King to lose his honor." (*Hebrew Goddess*, pages 196–97.) But the exile of the Shekinah (= Israel) is also the "separation of the masculine and feminine principles in God" (G. Scholem): the exile of God from God, etc. The restoration may then be seen—in Blake's sense or in Reich's—as a "heightening of sensual pleasure," God & his Shekinah mating, says the *Zohar,* "face to face." (For more on the Shekinah, etc., see pages 32–41, above.)

Page 294

"A Song of the Mourners of Zion." Translation (1) from Babylonian Talmud: *Baba Batra* 60, & (2) from *Ḥazon Barukh* 1.6 [1st-century apocalypse], using texts in Yehuda Even-Shmuel (ed.), *Midreshei Ge'ula* (Mosad Bialik, Jerusalem / Tel Aviv, 1968), page 35. "Those who mourn for Zion . . . trees of righteousness . . . the planting of the Lord." (Isaiah 61.3.)

Page 295

"The Shule of Jehovah." From A. Stone, *The Shule of Jehovah* (previously unpublished manuscript).

Page 298

"The War of the Sons of Light . . ." From A. Dupont-Sommer, *The Essene Writings from Qumran* (Basil Blackwell & Mott, Oxford, 1961), page 169. Introduction to "a collection of military regulations [for] 'The War of the Sons of Light against the Sons of Darkness.'. . . This warlike aspect of Essenism is closely bound to the eschatological perspectives of the Bible" (A. D.-S.): a messianic impulse in common with Zoroastrians, gnostics, & other Eastern religious groups in face of domination by Rome (= Kittim, "Army of Belial," etc.). The work is also called "The Scroll of the War Rule."

Page 299

"A Letter & a Dirge." Fragment discovered circa 1960 in the "Cave of Letters" in Judaea; from Yigael Yadin, *Bar Kokhba* (Weidenfeld & Nicolson, London, 1971), page 139. "When Akiva saw Bar Kokhba, he exclaimed: 'This is the king Messiah,' but Yoḥanan ben Torta answered: 'Akiva, grass will grow in your cheeks & the Son of David will not have come.' " (Jerusalem Talmud: *Ta'anit* 4.8.) The revolt led by Simeon bar Koseva (called Bar Kokhba, "son of a star") began in 132 A.D., lasted under four years, left 580,000 Jewish dead.

Page 299
"A Curse & Angry Poem Against the Nations." From the Passover Hagada; the "poem" here is the opening of Psalm 115.

Page 301
"Midrash of the Absent" (*Midrash ha-Ne'elam*). Translation of "The Palace of Splendor & the Bird's Nest" from "The Book of the Ways of Life, called The Testimony of Rabbi Eliezer the Great," in Yehuda Even-Shmuel (ed.), *Midreshei Ge'ula* (Mosad Bialik, Jerusalem / Tel Aviv, 1968), pages 309–10. "This section of the Testimony of Eliezer the Great is in fact a portion of the *Midrash ha-Ne'elam*" (esoteric or concealed commentary), a series of writings that forms the earliest layer of the *Zohar*.

Page 303
"Piyut: 'A Great Music.' " Direct translation from text in Ḥayim Schirman, *Shirim Ḥadashim min ha-Geniza* (Jerusalem, 1966), page 57. The *piyut* (see above, pages 588, 625) works off a single end rhyme & an acrostic, *Alvan Ḥazan Ḥazak* (= Alvan, the singer, be strong).

Page 304
"From Jehuda Halevi's Songs to Zion." From C. Reznikoff, *By the Waters of Manhattan* (New Directions, New York, 1962), pages 92–93. Ha-Levi left Spain en route to the Holy Land & likely died in Egypt. But legend has it "that he managed to reach the city of Jerusalem, &, as he kissed its stones, a passing Arab horseman . . . trampled on him just as he was reciting his elegy, 'Zion, do you ask if the captives are at peace.' " (*Encyclopedia Judaica.*)

Page 305
"How He Went as Messiah." Translation from A. Abulafia, *Sefer ha-Eydut* from text in G. Scholem, *Ha-Kabala shel Sefer ha-Tmuna v'shel Avraham Abulafia* (Akademon, Jerusalem, 1968), page 197. Accused of charlatanism & messianic claims, Abulafia fled to the desolate island of Comino (near Malta), developed a system of lettristic meditation ("Path of the Names") toward prophecy & communion with God. (See above, page 405.)

Page 307

"The Muslim." Translation from German in Chajim Bloch, *Lebenserin-
nerungen des Kabbalisten Vital* (Vernay-Verlag, Vienna, 1927), page 75.
Vital was the principal disciple & interpreter of Isaac Luria (see above,
page 581). The "Rabbi Ashkenazi" of this piece is Luria himself, the name
deriving from his father's birth in central Europe (*Ashkenaz*). Of Prophet
Elijah as a Moslem, a Sephardic folksong says: "Heart's joy / the god /
gave him the right to / come & go / among the angels // When needed /
turned up as an Arab" (per Alan D. Corré). He was also identified with
the Moslem Alḥidr, the Green Man.

Page 308

"The Rainbow Calendar of Isaac Luria." Direct translation from *Sefer
Simanei Ra'ashim ve-Ra'amim ve-Likui ha-Me'orot* [Book of the Signs of
Earthquakes, Thunders, & Eclipses] (Lemburg, 1848). While the calendar
is obviously pseudepigraphic, it relates to the sense of catastrophe, etc. in
Luria's great myth of exile (the "breaking of the vessels," for which see
page 88, above). "From a historical point of view, Luria's myth constitutes a response to the expulsion of the Jews from Spain, an event which
more than any other in Jewish history down to the catastrophe of our
time gave urgency to the question: why the exile of the Jews and what is
their vocation in the world? This question, the question of the meaning of
the Jews' experience in exile, . . . lies indeed at the heart of the new con-
ceptions which are the essence of Luria's system." (G. Scholem, *On the
Kabbalah & Its Symbolism,* page 110.)

Page 310

" '1648': For Cossacks." Translation from Yiddish text in Ruth Rubin,
Voices of a People: The Story of Yiddish Folk Song (McGraw-Hill, New
York, 1973), pages 200–2. The source of the song was the peasant &
Cossack uprising led by Bogdan Chmielnicki against Polish rule in the
Ukraine. Allied with the Polish nobility, the Jews suffered greatly in the
attendant massacres—a trauma which influenced the messianism of
Sabbatai Zevi & Jacob Frank, the emergence of Hasidism, etc.

Page 311

"The Vision of Rabbi Abraham." Adapted from a translation in Gershom
Scholem, *Sabbatai Ṣevi* (Princeton University Press, Princeton, New
Jersey, 1973), pages 224–26. Nathan of Gaza—here working under the
pseudonym of a 13th-century sage named Rabbi Abraham—was the
prophet ("holy lamp") of the 17th-century messiah Sabbatai Zevi. The
sabbatean movement itself survived Sabbatai's "fall" & conversion to
Islam, reinterpreting it as a step toward that liberation from the "cruel

commands," etc. to which it was germinal & which it helped bring about in later centuries. The Serpent, here & in the songs that follow, is a symbol both of the Messiah's enemy & of Sabbatai himself as Liberator. A development of Luria's kabbala, its relation to "the central symbol of the first- and second-century gnostic sect known as Ophites, or Naasenes" is also inescapable. (See above, page 162; also Nathan's "Treatise on the Dragons" in Scholem's *Sabbatai Ṣevi,* pages 297–325.)

Page 312
"Satan in Goray." From Isaac Bashevis Singer, *Satan in Goray* (The Noonday Press, New York, 1955), pages 200–2.

Page 314
"4 Poems for Sabbatai Zevi." Translations from Ladino & Hebrew in M. Attias & G. Scholem, *Songs & Hymns of the Sabbateans* (Tel Aviv, 1948), pages 136, 172, 123, 180, & 88. Songs largely of the Dönmeh sect, i.e. of the Sephardic "believers" who followed Sabbatai Zevi into Islam & a life as covert Jews. The Shekinah (Matronita)—as God's (mythically female) presence on earth—was given concrete form in the person of Sabbatai's third wife, Sarah ("prostitute" & "convert," in fulfillment of Hosea: "Take a wife of whoredoms"), but later identified with Sabbatai himself. (Compare Eve, the daughter of Jacob Frank, below, & Helen, the companion of Simon Magus, page 601, above.) For the account of Sabbatai's battle with the serpent, loss & recovery of clothes, etc. (an event celebrated as a new Purim), see Scholem, *Sabbatai Ṣevi,* pages 145–46.

Page 317
"The Song of the Sexton." Cited also in Abraham J. Heschel, *The Earth Is the Lord's* (Henry Schuman, New York, 1950), page 48.

Page 317
"The Golem Wheel." From D. Meltzer, *Tens* (McGraw-Hill Book Company, New York, 1973), page 30. Legend of the "golem" (magically created human) as a force of liberation, etc. For other aspects of golem-making, see pages 98, 462, above.

Page 321
"The Book of the Sayings of the Lord." Previously unpublished translations from Frank's *Księga Słów Pańskich* (Book of the Sayings of the Lord), based on texts in the Hebrew edition of A. Kraushar's *Frank & His Following* ("original" in Polish; Hebrew translation by N. Sokolow).

Of Frank's relation to Sabbatai Zevi (page 311, above & notes), etc., Harris Lenowitz writes: "Frank kept Sabbateanism alive and ended its tribalism, opening its adherents to the world outside Judaism. Sabbateanism become Frankism was one of the most important of the 18th-century movements which freed man. The great revolution in consideration, and the French and American revolutions, sprang from his loins. He was the father of Adam Mickiewicz. Yankiel. The Jew spreading thought, and liberty to Jews." A greatly threatening figure, Frank has been written about at length, never translated.

Page 328

"Drypoints of the Hasidim." From F. T. Prince, *Drypoints of the Hasidim* (The Menard Press, London, 1975), pages 6–9. Israel ben Eliezer, the Baal Shem Tov (or "Master of the Good Name"), was the founder in the 18th-century of "hasidism," an ecstatic form of orthodox Judaism. The movement, which formed communities around charismatic *rebbes* or *tsadikim* (= "saints"), is commonly viewed as a response within Judaism to the Sabbateans, etc.

Page 332

"Rabbi Nachman's Dream." From H. Schwartz, *Lilith's Cave* (Isthmus Press, San Francisco, 1975). The hasidism of Nachman of Bratzlav emphasized music & story-telling (here dream-telling as well) as religious modes. "All of life is a dream from which a person can be awakened by the stories of the tsaddik." (Rabbi Nachman, quoted in H. Weiner, *9½ Mystics*.) For more on Nachman, etc., see page 585, above.

Page 333

"Illustrious Ancestors." From D. Levertov, *The Jacob's Ladder* (New Directions, New York, 1961), page 87.

Page 334

"Five for the Rebbe." From Ruth Rubin, *Voices of a People* (McGraw-Hill, New York, 1973). Songs by proponents & enemies of hasidism; the line between reverence & scorn is at this point very thin.

Page 336

"The Cemetery at Kozin." From I. Babel, *The Collected Stories* (World Publishing Company, Cleveland, 1960), page 107. Translation by Nadia Helstein (1929).

Page 337

"Poor People." From Irving Howe & Eliezer Greenberg (eds.), *A Treasury of Yiddish Poetry* (Holt, Rinehart & Winston, New York, 1969), page 230.

Page 337

"Two Poems." From Howe & Greenberg (eds.), *A Treasury of Yiddish Poetry* (Holt, Rinehart & Winston, 1969), pages 180–82. Born in Volhynia & later resident in Paris, Markish returned to the U.S.S.R. in 1926. Arrested in 1948, executed 1952.

Page 339

"Zaritsky's Children." Translations from Yiddish texts in Ruth Rubin, *Voices of a People* (McGraw-Hill, New York 1973). Zaritsky's cigarette factory was in Cherkassy, near Kiev. The quote at the end is from *Talmud: Ḥagiga* 9b.

Page 341

"The Voluminous Agony of Karl Marx." From R. Owens, *I Am the Babe of Joseph Stalin's Daughter* (Kulchur Foundation, New York, 1972), pages 89–90. Ambitious for poetry as a young man ("he could no more think of living without poetry than living without his vision of a Communist world"—R. Payne), Marx wrote a Faustian tragedy called *Oulanem,* the central soliloquy of which might be compared to Owens' piece:

> Ruined! Ruined! My time has clean run out!
> The clock has stopped, the pygmy house has crumbled,
> Soon I shall embrace Eternity to my breast, and soon
> I shall howl gigantic curses on mankind.
> Ha! Eternity! She is our eternal grief,
> An indescribable and immeasurable Death,
> Vile artificiality conceived to scorn us,
> Our selves being clockwork, blindly mechanical,
> Made to be the fool-calendars of Time and Space,
> Having no purpose save to happen, to be ruined,
> So that there shall be something to ruin.
> There had to be some fault in the universe,
> The dumb agony of pain wrapped all around her,
> A giant's mighty soul waltzing through the air;
> So Death becomes alive, wears shoes and hose,
> Suffering of plants, the stifling death of stones,
> Birds vainly seeking their songs, bemoaning

The sickness of their airy lives, wars and dissensions
In blind assemblage shuddering, exterminating
Itself from its very self in violent clashes.
Now there emerges a man, two legs and a heart,
Who has the power to utter living curses.
Ha, I must bind myself to a wheel of flame
And dance with joy in the circle of eternity!
If there is a Something which devours,
I'll leap within it, though I bring the world to ruins—
The world which bulks between me and the Abyss
I will smash to pieces with my enduring curses.
I'll throw my arms around its harsh reality:
Embracing me, the world will dumbly pass away,
And then sink down to utter nothingness,
Perished, with no existence—that would be really living!
While swinging high within the stream of eternity,
We roar our melancholy hymns to the Creator
With scorn on our brows! Shall the sun ever burn it away?
Presumptuous curses from excommunicate souls!
Eyes that annihilate with poisoned glances
Gleam exultantly, the leaden world holds us fast.
And we are chained, shattered, empty, frightened,
Eternally chained to this marble block of Being,
Chained, eternally chained, eternally.
And the worlds drag us with them in their rounds,
Howling their songs of death, and we—
We are the apes of a cold God.
And yet we keep the viper beautifully warm
With foolish toil at the full breast of love
Which reaches up to the Universal Image
And sneers at us from the heights!
And the interminable angry waves keep roaring
To drain away the nausea from our ears.
Now quick—the die is cast—all is prepared,
And what the lying poem dreamed is utterly ruined,
And what began with curses the curses have fulfilled!

(From Robert Payne, *The Unknown Karl Marx*)

Of Jews specifically (his parents had converted to Protestantism the year before his birth) Marx wrote: "Money is the jealous God of Israel, by the side of which no other god may exist. . . . The God of the Jews has secularized himself and become the universal God. Exchange is the Jew's real God. . . . The social emancipation of the Jew is the emancipation of society from Judaism." (*On the Jewish Question*, 1843.)

Page 343

"A Lullaby for Tsars." Adapted from a translation of "Shlof, Alexey" in R. Rubin, *Voices of a People* (McGraw-Hill, New York, 1973), page 304.

Page 344

"Ginivishov, Poland—1885." Documentary & interview from *Big Deal*, ed. Barbara Barracks (New York, 1975), number 3, pages 84–87. Documentation & mapping as an aspect of "conceptual art."

Page 349

"The East Village 1970–1971." From R. Kostelanetz, *I Articulations* (Kulchur Foundation, New York, 1974). A center of early 20th-century New York Jewish culture (Yiddish theater, Café Royale, etc.) seen here in its transformations circa 1970. Of that former East Village Harry Roskolenko writes: "At the Café Royale one saw every actor, playwright, poet, and revolutionary; every name from Second Avenue's massive Yiddish drama of a street. Every sitter talked with a majestic pause, acting around some pickled herring, black bread and tea. But the Royale would close up one day after another war. . . . One of the oldest sitters would attempt suicide—for he had no other home. A second would die in his apartment amid ten thousand books on Americana—the specialty of a man whose real language was Russian-Yiddish. The café itself would become a cleaning store, an American-enough symbol of sanitation, if without the glass of tea and the lemon." (*The Time That Was Then*, pages 193–94.) For more on mapping, etc., see the preceding note & text.

Page 350

"A-12." From L. Zukofsky, *A 1–12* (Doubleday & Company, New York, 1967). "In a sense the poem is an autobiography: the words are my life. The form of the poem is organic—that is, involved in history and a life that has found by contrast to history something like perfection in the music of J. S. Bach (a theme threaded through the entire poem). Or to put it in other words, the poet's form is never an imposition of history but the desirability of projecting some order out of history as it is felt and conceived." (L.Z.)

Page 355

"Bowery Motifs." From I. Howe & E. Greenberg, (eds.), *A Treasury of*

Yiddish Poetry (Holt, Rinehart & Winston, New York, 1969), pages 294–95. Born in Volhynia, immigrated to U.S.A. at age fifteen.

Page 356

"The Last Words of Dutch Schultz." An excerpt from the *New York Times* (October 25, 1935) of death-bed statements transcribed by J. F. Long, a Newark Police Department clerk-stenographer. Schultz had been gunned down in the men's room of the Palace Chop House.

Page 358

"The Murder Inc. Sutra." From J. Rothenberg, *Poland / 1931* (New Directions, New York, 1974), page 114. The enforcement arm of the New York rackets in the 1920s/30s, Murder Incorporated was a Brooklyn-centered, largely Jewish operation. The Isaac Babel references are to his *Tales of Odessa,* focusing on Benya Krik as fictional "king" of the Odessa Jewish underworld: " 'Reb Arye-Leib,' I said to the old man, 'let us talk of Benya Krik. Let us talk of his thunderclap beginning & his terrible end. Three black shadows block up the paths of my imagination.' "

Page 361

"Poem." From B. Raffel & A. Burago (eds.), *Complete Poetry of Osip Emilevich Mandelstam* (State University of New York Press, Albany, 1973), pages 92–93. "All the elegant mirage of Petersburg was merely a dream, a brilliant covering thrown over the abyss, while round about there sprawled the chaos of Judaism—not a motherland, not a house, not a hearth but precisely a chaos, the unknown womb world whence I had issued, which I feared, about which I made vague conjectures and fled, always fled." (Osip Mandelstam, *Selected Poems,* translated by Clarence Brown & W. S. Merwin.)

Page 362

"The Flea of Sodom." From E. Dahlberg, *The Flea of Sodom* (New Directions, New York, 1950), pages 56–57.

Page 363

"Good Night, World." From Ruth Whitman (ed.), *The Selected Poems of Jacob Glatstein* (October House, New York, 1972), pages 59–60. Born in Lublin, Poland, Glatstein emigrated to the U.S.A. in 1914: American & Yiddish.

Page 365

"A Death Fugue." From J. Rothenberg (ed.), *New Young German Poets*

(City Lights Books, San Francisco, 1959), pages 16–17. For more on Celan, see below, page 633.

Page 366

"God in Europe." From R. Mezey (ed.), *Poems from the Hebrew* (Thomas Y. Crowell, New York, 1973), pages 98–99. Born in eastern Galicia & resident since 1924 in Israel, Greenberg's poetry touches the old "moral madness" of the Prophets (see above, page 231). "Our body is very wild. It is a wandering body of symbols. And is our nervous system in any way like that of the Gentiles? The Hebrew mouth is more like a wound; behind the Hebrew forehead an eagle screams."

Page 368

"The Stranger." From D. Ignatow, *Poems 1934–1969* (Wesleyan University Press, Middletown, Connecticut, 1970), page 90.

Page 369

"El Topo." From film script in A. Jodorowsky, *El Topo* (Douglas Book Corporation, New York, 1971), pages 48–52. "The mole is an animal that digs tunnels underground searching for the sun. Sometimes his journey leads him to the surface. When he looks at the sun, he is blinded."

Page 372

"Liner Notes to *Highway 61 Revisited*." From B. Dylan, *Writings & Drawings by Bob Dylan* (Alfred A. Knopf, New York, 1973), page 181.

Page 373

"National Thoughts." From Y. Amichai, *Selected Poems* (Penguin Books, Middlesex, England, 1971), page 64.

Page 374

"Jaweh and Allah Battle." From *The Holy Beggars' Gazette* (San Francisco, 1975), Winter–Spring issue, pages 22–27.

Page 377

"The Conspiracy." Sections II & III of "The Conspiracy" in E. Roditi, *Emperor of Midnight* (Black Sparrow Press, Los Angeles, 1974), pages 88–89.

Page 378

"Semite." From G. Oppen, *Collected Poems* (New Directions, New York, 1974), pages 246–47.

Page 381

"Tradition, according to its mystical sense . . ." From G. Scholem, *The Messianic Idea in Judaism* (Schocken Books, New York, 1971), page 296.

Page 383

"The Book of the Letter." Translation from *Sefer ha-Ot* in *Tree* 1 (Bolinas, California, 1970), pages 145–46. For more on Abulafia, see pages 405, 604.

Page 384

"The Hidden Sacred Book of Moses." From Ludwig Blau, *Das Alt-jüdische Zauberwesen* (Budapest, 1897–98), page 142. "Nothing is more excellent than the mysteries which ye seek after, saving only the mystery of the Seven Vowels & their forty-nine Powers, & the numbers thereof. And no name is more excellent than all these vowels, a Name in which are contained all Names & all Lights & all Powers." (*Pistis Sophia,* c. 3rd century A.D.)

Page 385

"A Performance from 'The Secret Book of Moses.'" Translation from a text in K. Preisedanz (ed.), *Papyri Graecae Magicae* (Leipzig/Berlin, 1931).

Page 387

"The Young Girl's Tears." From Jean-Paul Curtay (ed.), *La Poésie Lettriste* (Editions Seghers, Paris, 1974), page 195.

Page 389

"The Hebrew Book of Enoch." From Hugo Odeberg (ed.), *3 Enoch or the Hebrew Book of Enoch* (Cambridge University Press, 1928; Ktav Publishing House, New York, 1973), Part II, pages 128–29. "The Holy One Be Blest said: 'I require workers.' The Torah told Him: 'I will put 22 workers at your disposal—the 22 letters that are in the Torah—& to each I will give his own work.'" (*Midrash Tanḥuma.*) For more on letter & number in creation, see the section beginning on page 92, above.

Page 390

"Life of the World to Come: The Permutations." Transliterations from manuscript editions of the *Ḥayei ha-Olam ha-Ba* (also called "Book of the Name" & "Book of Circles") in the British Museum: 12 groupings of 12 permutations of the tetragrammaton.

Page 392

"The Garden of Pomegranates." From Moses Cordovero's *Pardes Rimonim,* the work of the outstanding kabbalist of Safed before Isaac Luria.

Page 393

"Amulet on the Tetragrammaton." From manuscript folder 467, number 9, in the Hebrew Union College Library, Cincinnati, Ohio.

Page 395

"Concrete Poem." Translation from "Samaritan Phylacteries & Amulets" (Hebrew text) in Moses Gaster, *Studies & Texts* (Ktav Publishing House, New York, 1928, 1971), volume 3, page 128.

Page 396

"Le Coeur à Gaz." From T. Tzara, *Oeuvres Complètes* (Flammarion, Paris, 1975), volume 1, page 180. For more on Tzara, see page 583, above.

Page 397

"Composition Around the Ineffable Name." From manuscript of Moses Cordovero, *Pardes Rimonim* ("The Garden of Pomegranates") in the Bibliothèque National, Paris. (See note to page 392, above.)

Page 398

"Name Event One." From description in R. Patai, F. L. Utley, & D. Noy (eds.), "Two Remedy Books in Yiddish from 1474 & 1508" in *Studies in Biblical & Jewish Folklore* (Indiana University Press, Bloomington, 1960), pages 294–95.

Page 399

"Name Event Two." From description in Joshua Trachtenberg, *Jewish Magic & Superstition* (Atheneum, New York, 1939, 1970), page 83.

Page 399

"Name Event Three." From Gershom Scholem, *On the Kabbalah & Its Symbolism* (Schocken Books, New York, 1965), page 136. "We possess numerous manuscripts of a 'Book of the Putting on and Fashioning of the Mantle of Righteousness,' in which the ancient Jewish conception that names can be 'put on' is taken very concretely. . . . I doubt whether this initiation in water was practiced after the fourteenth century." (G. Scholem.)

"Life of the World to Come: Circles." From one of several manuscripts of *Ḥayei ha-Olam ha-Ba* in the British Museum; the work is sometimes called *Sefer ha-Igulim,* "The Book of Circles."

"On the Hebrew Letters." From *Tree* 2 (Bolinas, California, 1971), pages 43–44. Description of an attempt to make "splash prints" with Hebrew letter-blocks within a roughly abstract-expressionist perspective: "I dip the block into the paint (which is thinned to the tone of black ink itself) and 'come-at' the paper as though I held a fist. . . . When I smash the letters on paper, they spatter and there is a jolt of freedom in the act."

"Image of the Wall." From *Tree* 5 (Berkeley, California, 1975), page 210. "In Wallace Berman's shack in Beverly Glen, I first encountered a then 'hip' american work combining a turned-on sensibility with Hebrew letters. Berman later was to develop this through collagic-dada sensibilities and make use of Hebrew letters within the photoplay submissive to the 'earth' of southern california, i.e. Mother Nature dedoubled via the lens. Berman and others within the scope of using kabbalistic signs in works continued that early Head tradition already preparing for the big Rock epoch up ahead." (Jack Hirschman.)

"Clairvoyant Journal." Previously unpublished, from a portion of her manuscript subtitled "The Retreat 1974." The part "that begins 'MY POEM . . .' was written at the initiation and discovers a *hidden* mantra." Joseph Caro, mentioned in the commentary, was author of the *Shulḥan Arukh* (great "code" of rabbinic Jewish law) but also a kabbalist & teacher of Moses Cordovero, etc. His experience of the *maggid*—i.e. of "automatic speech" unmediated by a condition such as trance & audible to others—is the subject of his mystical diary, *Maggid Mesharim* ("The Teller of Truths").

"The Masora Calligrams." From various medieval manuscripts, as reproduced in Berjouhi Bowler, "The Word As Ikon," *Typographica* 8 (London, 1968).

Page 415

"A Prayer for the King." Same as the preceding; also in B. Bowler, *The Word as Image* (publisher unlisted, London, c. 1970), page 45.

Page 417

"Calligram." From T. Tzara, *Oeuvres Complètes* (Flammarion, Paris, 1975), volume 1, page 522.

Page 418

"The Scroll of Esther as a Bear." From the library of the Jewish Theological Seminary, New York, as reprinted in the *Encyclopedia Judaica*, volume 14, pages 1055–56.

Page 419

"Celestial Alphabet Event." From J. Gaffarel, *Curiosités innoviés* (1637), in Kurt Seligmann, *The Mirror of Magic* (Pantheon Books, New York, 1948), page 330. Says the *Zohar:* "He who travels in the early morning shall look carefully to the east. He will see there something like letters marching in the sky, some rising, others descending. These brilliant characters are the letters with which God has formed heaven & earth." Read alternatively as numbers, they recall the Pythagoreans' vision of the sky set down by Aristotle: "They supposed the elements of number to be the elements of all things, & the whole heaven to be a musical scale [harmonia] & number." (*Metaphysics* 985b.)

Page 421

"The 10 Sefirot as a Labyrinth of Letters." From Moses Cordovero, *Pardes Rimonim* ("The Garden of Pomegranates"), in the Bibliothèque National, Paris.

Page 422

"The Numbers." From *Encyclopedia Judaica*, volume 2, page 546. As an early Jewish claim to alchemy, she was said to have written: "Do not touch [the philosopher's stone] with your hands: you are not of our stock, you are not of Abraham's bosom." But otherwise the Jewish contribution to alchemy seems minimal.

Page 423

"A Talisman for Venus." From Idries Shah, *The Secret Lore of Magic* (The Citadel Press, New York, 1958), page 293. An extensive Jewish presence behind medieval magic, often invoked in texts like these by names like Moses, Solomon, etc. Part of the image of the Jew as magician *par excellence,* the dangerous possessor of occulted powers.

Page 424
"A Number Blessing." From C. Morrow, *A Book of Numbers,* unpublished manuscript of compositions based on simple counting.

Page 426
"A Poem with Numbers for the Dead." Translation from a Yiddish text in R. Rubin, *Voices of a People* (McGraw-Hill, New York, 1973), page 143. Traditional Jewish counting songs.

Page 428
"The Counting Made the Corners Right." From R. Drachler, *Burrowing In, Digging Out* (Tree Books, Berkeley, California, 1974), page 40.

Page 429
"25 Gematria." Mostly traditional examples of gematria, from J. Rothenberg & H. Lenowitz, *Gematria 27* (Membrane Press, Milwaukee, Wisconsin, 1977). "Jewish merchants, and others, often used a ten-letter word combination in order to record the price paid for an item alongside the selling price, which was written for the customer's benefit in numbers. My parents, for example, still use the code

1 2 3 4 5   6 7 8 9 0
B L A C K   H O R S E .

There is a long history of such usages, possibly even the origins of gematria and alphabet itself in Phoenician sailor-trader invoices." (H. Lenowitz.)

Page 432
"Additional Meanings: 46 = Chaos." From the collection of Seth Kahn, New York City, as originally exhibited at the Bertha Urdang Gallery, New York, October 1976. Magazine photographs, crayon, pencil on paper, $19\frac{1}{2} \times 36$ inches. "It is all in shades of gray except the statement: Amid chaos . . . which is in red."

Page 433
"Apple-Lilith-Night." From G. Quasha (ed.), *Active Anthology* (The Sumac Press, Fremont, Michigan, 1974), page 138.

Page 436

"Variations on a Hebrew Amulet." Previously unpublished translation from *Sefer Raziel* 40b.

Page 438

"Kaddish Gatha." Previously unpublished poem. Commissioned for the present volume.

Page 439

"Zohar Event." From a discussion with Alan D. Corré concerning some Sephardic Jewish prayer practices & the simultaneities of Jackson Mac Low.

Page 440

"The Havdala of Rabbi Akiba." The poem, previously unpublished, follows instructions in the medieval text (see Commentary), which does not include a realization *per se*. The 91st Psalm, used here, was particularly effective against demons.

Page 442

"Amulet Against the Evil Eye." A wide-spread amuletic formula. For more on the "evil eye," etc., see page 532 & the note, below, to page 532.

Page 443

"4.5.10.11.2.8.4.2., the 2nd biblical poem." From G. Quasha & R. Gross (eds.), *Open Poetry* (Simon & Schuster, New York, 1973), pages 491–92.

Page 446

"An Epitaph." From a description in E. R. Goodenough, *Jewish Symbols in the Greco-Roman Period* (Pantheon Books, New York, 1953), volume 2, page 9.

Page 447

"The Babylonian Talmud." From I. Epstein (ed.), *The Babylonian Talmud* (Soncino Press, London), especially volume 4, part 2: *Baba Batra*. The reader may note the recent re-attention to the ancient "art of memory," etc. in writers like Frances Yates; but the point of the present viewing is to force attention on the language of the "signs" themselves rather than on their referential function.

Page 449

"Chance Compositions." From a description in Herbert Weiner, *9½ Mystics: The Kabbala Today* (The Macmillan Company, New York, 1969), page 80. Here the use of "chance" is limited to opening up new channels of association—as Mac Low ("The Friendship Poems"): "O blessèd chance continue to happen to me! / For I wd never plan so well— I wd have died of my planning. . . ." In a related, if trivial, process, talmudic scholars showed their erudition by sticking a pin through a volume of the Talmud, taking note only of the top word punctured, then calling out the sequence of the punctured words below.

Page 450

"Manifesto on Feeble & Bitter Love." From *Dada manifeste sur l'amour faible et l'amour amer*, read at the Galerie Povolozky, Paris, December 9, 1920, & reprinted many times elsewhere. For more on Tzara, see above, page 583.

Page 450

"The Mishnah." From I. Epstein (ed.), *The Babylonian Talmud: Tohorot* (Soncino Press, London), volume 5, pages 385–87.

Page 453

"An Elucidation." From G. Stein, *A Primer for the Gradual Understanding of Gertrude Stein* (Black Sparrow Press, Los Angeles, 1971), pages 97–99. "It is impossible to put words together without sense. I made innumerable efforts to make words write without sense and found it impossible. Any human being putting down words has to make sense out of them."

Page 455

"A Poem of the Measures." Direct translation from Hebrew text in P. Birnbaum (ed.), *Ha-Siddur ha-Shalem* [Daily Prayer Book] (Hebrew Publishing Company, New York, 1949), pages 41–45.

Page 458

"Meditations." From D. Antin, *Meditations* (Black Sparrow Press, Los Angeles, 1971).

Page 460

"Sounding Events." Multiple sources & observations—& the suggestion per Harris Lenowitz that the fast reading of prayers in synagogues etc. is in fact a kind of speed mantra.

Page 461

"Word Events." From description in J. Trachtenberg, *Jewish Magic & Superstition* (Atheneum, New York, 1939, 1970), page 111.

Page 462

"Golem Meditation Events." Condensed from descriptions in G. Scholem, *On the Kabbalah & Its Symbolism* (Schocken Books, New York, 1965), pages 187–88.

Page 463

"Sound Event: The Silent Orchestra." From description in Herbert Weiner, *9½ Mystics* (The Macmillan Company, New York, 1969), page 151.

Page 463

"Words." Photos from A. Kaprow, *Assemblages, Environments, & Happenings* (Harry Abrams, New York, 1966), from an environmental happening at the Smolin Gallery, New York, 1962. Word events ("language happenings"—E. Williams) are increasingly part of the work of visual artists, musicians, etc.: an old ground regained. The term "happenings" itself—with or without language—originated with Kaprow, an early & major proponent.

Page 467

"Body Work." Condensed from Johanna Spector, "Bridal Songs & Ceremonies from San‘a, Yemen," in R. Patai, F. L. Utley, & D. Noy (eds.), *Studies in Biblical & Jewish Folklore* (University of Indiana Press, Bloomington, 1960), pages 256–57.

Page 468

"Lemon Event." Condensed from Raphael Patai, *Man & Temple* (Ktav Publishing House, New York, 1947), page 37: as part of the old Temple rituals.

Page 468

"Poor Man Music (1966)." From *some/thing* 4–5 (New York, 1970), pages 118–19. The music was used in conjunction with J.R.'s *Gift*

Event III (Technicians of the Sacred, pages 378–82). *"I too am a Technician of the Sacred.* Jerry Rothenberg says on page 425 that *Anything can deliver a song.* (Can any song deliver a thing?)"

Page 470
"Rain Event One." From multiple sources, e.g., those in the commentary; the connection to "murmuring, muttering" from *The Friday Night Book* (Soncino Press, London, 1933). "Said Rabbi Eleazar ben Perata: Ever since the Temple was destroyed, rain is diminishing in the world." (Talmud: *Ta'anit* 19b.)

Page 471
"Rain Event Two." From R. Patai, *Man & Temple* (Ktav Publishing House, New York, 1947), page 32.

Page 472
"Women's Fertility Events." From Jerome Rothenberg, *Poland/1931* (New Directions, New York, 1974), after sources in J. Trachtenberg, *Jewish Magic & Superstition.*

Page 474
"Paradise Now." From *Paradise Now: Collective Creation of the Living Theatre,* written down by J. Malina & J. Beck (Random House, New York, 1971). The depiction on the left of the *sefirot* as *adam kadmon* ("primordial man") comes from tradition (*kabbala*); for other images, etc., see above, pages 11–12, & elsewhere in the present gathering.

Page 477
"Tree Spirit Events." From H. Sperling & M. Simon (eds.), *The Zohar* (Soncino Press, London, 1934), volume 1, page 261. "Once, when Rabbi Yoḥanan ben Zakai & Rabbi Lazar ben Arakh were discussing the Vision of the Chariot, they sat down under a tree. The fire descended from heaven & surrounded them. The ministering angels danced before them as members of a wedding dance before a bridegroom. . . . Forthwith all the trees opened their mouths & sang a song, *then shall all the trees of the forest sing for joy* [Psalm 96.12]." (From Talmud: *Ḥagiga* 2.1.)

Page 478
"Vision Event." From Nathan of Nemirov, *Rabbi Nachman's Wisdom* [*Shevachay Ha-Ran*] (Leonard M. Kaplan, Brooklyn, 1973), page 222. But, adds Nachman, ". . . if you could imagine such things without

forgetting, . . . comparing your own limited abilities to the immensity of such a being . . . it would be utterly impossible for you to endure life. . . . You would die before your time."

Page 478

"A Scenario for Midnight." From description in Gershom Scholem, *On the Kabbalah & Its Symbolism* (Schocken Books, New York, 1965), page 147. A mythologized version of a midnight ritual (*tikun hatsot*) "in which the exile of the *Shekhina* is dramatized & lamented. . . . At midnight the *Shekhina* . . . sings songs & hymns to her spouse . . . & a dialogue or even a *hieros gamos* is enacted between God & the *Shekhina*." (See above, pages 36, 38.)

Page 479

"The Gezer Calendar." From *Inscriptions Reveal: Documents from the Time of the Bible, the Mishna & the Talmud* (Israel Museum, Jerusalem, 1973), page 8. One of the earliest surviving Hebrew inscriptions, it was engraved on a limestone tablet in ancient Hebrew script. Among other possibilities the content is described as "a popular folk song, listing the months of the year according to the agricultural seasons." (*Encyclopedia Judaica*.) Such functional lunar namings are widespread among American Indians, others.

Page 480

"YHVH's Battle with the Serpent." From H. Lenowitz & C. Doria (eds.), *Origins* (Anchor Books, New York, 1975), pages 289–90: Lenowitz's translations of Isaiah 51.9–.10, Job 26.12–.13, and Psalm 74.13–.17. "These Canaanite-Hebrew texts are remnants of a Canaanite myth contained within the Hebrew Bible." For which, see also "The Battle between Yam & Baal" (*ibid.*, pages 273–75).

Page 481

"The Song of Deborah." Direct translation from Judges 5. A judge & prophetess in Israel circa 1200–1125 B.C., Deborah promoted a "war of liberation" against Jabin, king of Canaan. Her military commander, Barak, attacked the army of Sisra, a Canaanite general, & sank his chariots in the mire caused by Kishon's flooding. This led to Sisra's flight & murder at the hands of Ya'el, wife of an allied Kenite chieftain. From an actual oral tradition, the song was "probably sung antiphonally" or as a kind of (bardic) re-enactment. There is some possibility that the poet was a woman.

"The Song of Songs." J.R.'s working after various translations of verses from the Song of Solomon 5. The gathering is itself an anthology of erotic poem-songs, later allegorized but clearly related to the religio-sexual practices of the "alternative" Jewish cults, neighboring religions, etc. Compare, e.g., Sumerian & Egyptian love poetry recently recovered:

> When I leave you, my Brother, and feel your love,
>   my heart stalls within me.
> When I see sweet cakes, they turn to salt.
> Pomegranate-wine, once so delicious, is like bird's gall.
> The breath of your nostrils, nothing else frees my body.
> What I have found, may Amen grant me forever.

(Thus: Milton Kessler & Gerald E. Kadish, in "Love Songs & Tomb Songs of Ancient Egypt," *Alcheringa* 5, 1973.)

"Psalm 137." Translation from the Hebrew text: this one a virtual song-of-protest made *in situ* at the time of the Babylon "captivity." Lenowitz's epigraph is from a Jamaican reggae (Rastafarian) version by B. Dowe & F. McNaughton, reflecting "another movement-in-exile in which the leaders are singers" (H. Lenowitz). The reader can also compare the refusal to sing with, e.g., the Acoma Indian: "long ago her mother / had to sing this song and so / she had to grind along with it / the corn people have a song too / it is very good / I refuse to tell it." (Translation by A. Schwerner.)

"The Elephantine Fragments." Typographic workings after texts in A. Cowley, *Aramaic Papyri of the Fifth Century* B.C. (Clarendon Press, Oxford, 1923). From a military colony at Elephantine, Egypt, run by Jewish mercenaries, who spoke Aramaic, had a temple of Yaho (Yahveh), & "practiced"—with Egyptian admixture—"the popular religion as described & denounced by Jeremiah & Ezekiel." (Roland de Vaux, *Ancient Israel,* page 341.) See also pages 36, 241, above.

"Eisagoge." Translation of a text (about a third of the original play) in Eusebius's *Praeparatio Evangelica* 9.28. The only surviving Jewish drama from antiquity, the *Eisagoge* ("induction") comes from Alexandria—by Ezekielos's time a city two-fifths Jewish. Beyond the biblical source, it conveys (like Philo, etc.) a sense of the prevailing "mysteries." Writes E. R. Goodenough: "[Ezekielos] has indeed shown us a mystic origin for Philo's kingship of Moses. The conception of God has come directly from Orphic sources, and the conception is . . . that of the astral mystery of Egypt. . . . It is quite to be expected that the symbolic representation of Moses with the heavenly bodies should reappear in the iconography." (*Jewish Symbols in the Greco-Roman Period*, ix, 101; see also pages 205–8, above.) The italicized quotations from the biblical Exodus were designed by the translator to fill in numerous gaps in the narrative & action of the play.

Page 504
"The Sibylline Oracles." C.D.'s working, after English translation in R. H. Charles, *Apocrypha & Pseudepigrapha of the Old Testament*, volume 2 (Clarendon Press, Oxford, 1913). A Greek prophetess-figure—spontaneous & ecstatic—the Sibyl came to be identified with the Jews & other groups under imperial domination. "A combination of Babylonian astrology & Persian millenarian speculations . . . (later) evolved into virulent anti-Roman propaganda." (Yehoshua Amir, *Encyclopedia Judaica*.)

Page 506
"The Maiden." J.R.'s working, after various English versions, but especially that of R. McL. Wilson in Edgar Hennecke, *New Testament Apocrypha* (The Westminster Press, Philadelphia, 1964), volume 2, pages 445–46. In other texts, "the maiden" is already allegorized into Church, etc.; here she retains the presence of Shekinah, Sophia, etc., or simply "maiden."

Page 508

"An Incantation Bowl Against the Powers." From J. A. Montgomery, *Aramaic Incantation Texts from Nippur* (University of Pennsylvania Museum, Philadelphia, 1913), page 201, plate 20. The inscriptions followed the contour of the bowls

& were inscribed on the inside, sometimes the outside as well. A survival beyond proscriptions against same, they may have been used for divination or, when turned upside-down, as "prison houses for demons." The inscriptions on the arms of the manacled figure in the text read "prohibition" & "permission"; on the lower parts of the body are the names of the sorcerer's client.

Page 509

"A Calendar: The Year of the Messiah." Translation of text in Yehuda Even-Shmuel (ed.), *Midreshei Ge'ula* (Mosad Bialik, Jerusalem / Tel Aviv, 1968), pages 113–16. The translation tries to suggest the twists of *piyut* verse-making, while omitting the usual acrostic & end rhyme. An example of high rhyming—sometimes despised by "classicists," etc., but not distant from the "internal" rhyme structurings of Stein, Zukofsky, Duncan, others in our time—is the following *piyut* by Ḥedvata bar Avraham, circa 10th century, here given as a sound-poem:

A KROVA FOR THE FEAST OF WEEKS

harim alfu zalfu ḥalfu ke-azlu
ba'u meratsdim merakdim mekadedim ve-yagolu
gedura gezura gemura sha'alu
dagar dahar da . . . hallalu
ke-ḥarazta *anokhi* magen—nasim nazolu

nazlu ve-tsiot getsiyot detsiyot nedoney
gavnunim dinunim rinunim megizim mediney
dila gila ila feniney
hushpal hutpal hu'pal ke-meytim ba-anyinei
ke-dibarta matlil *lo yihye nihya mi-pney*

(For more on this in Yannai, ha-Kallir, etc., see above, page 588.) Menaḥem was a common name for the Messiah; the Tishbite is the prophet Elijah.

Page 513

"The 'Who?' of ibn Abitur." Translation from Hebrew text in Hayim Schirmann (ed.), *Ha-Shira ha-Ivrit bi-Sfarad u-vi-Frovence* (Jerusalem / Tel Aviv, 1954), page 56. First of the "new poets" of medieval Spain but still heavily into *piyut* practice—as in the acrostic (alphabet & poet's name) translated here as such. The pronoun "who," like other pronouns (see above, page 89), was itself thought of as a name of God.

Page 516

"Three Love Poems." Translation from text in H. Schirmann (ed.), *Ha-Shira ha-Ivrit,* etc. (Jerusalem / Tel Aviv, 1954), pages 168, 167, 154. Ha-Nagid—Isma'il ibn Nagrela in Arabic—was vizier to the King of Granada & for 18 years commander of his armies. He was one of the first in whom a strong influence of Arabic "literary" modalities opened up new possibilities of form & content, though such Arab influence is hardly needed to explain the homosexual presence, etc., here & elsewhere.

Page 518

"War Poem." J.R.'s working after an unidentified prose paraphrase in Israel Zinberg, *A History of Jewish Literature* (Case Western Reserve University, Cleveland, 1972), volume 1, page 29. (See preceding note.)

Page 519

"The 16-Year-Old Poet." Translation from H. Schirmann, (ed.), *Ha-Shira ha-Ivrit,* etc. (Jerusalem / Tel Aviv, 1954), volume 1, page 192. For more on Gabirol, see above, page 584.

Page 520

"Constellations." The 22nd section of Gabirol's long poem *Keter Malkhut,* for which see pages 70–74, above.

Page 521

"Two Poems." From C. Rakosi, *Ere-Voice* (New Directions, New York, 1971), pages 68, 71. Moses ben Jacob ibn Ezra (Abu Harun in Arabic) was a Hebrew poet & philosopher from Granada; the author as well of *Kitab al-Muḥadara wa al-Mudhakara,* a treatise on Hebrew poetics but written in Arabic.

Page 522

"The Garden." (1) Previously unpublished working. (2) From C. Rakosi, *Ere-Voice* (New Directions, New York, 1971), page 70. For more on ha-Levi, see page 604, above.

Page 523

"I Have a Garment." From R. Mezey (ed.), *Poems from the Hebrew* (Thomas Y. Crowell Company, New York, 1973), page 65. A poet, grammarian, biblical commentator, philosopher, astronomer, physician, Abraham ibn Ezra was probably the most innovative of the Spanish Hebrew poets, working at times with shaped poems, mixed languages, letters, riddles, epigrams, etc.

Page 524

"Proensa." G.E.'s working based on a translation in Israel Zinberg, *A History of Jewish Literature* (Case Western Reserve University, Cleveland, 1972), volume 2, pages 99–100. Touched by the surrounding *poesis* of Provence, he was "a kind of Jewish troubador who made the rounds of the communities with his musical instruments, as he himself states in some of his poems." (Don Pagis, *Encyclopedia Judaica,* volume 13, page 689.)

Page 525

"Italian Sonnet." G.E.'s working based on a translation in I. Zinberg, *A History of Jewish Literature* (Case Western Reserve University, Cleveland, 1972), volume 2, page 209. Manoello Giudeo in Italian, he wrote a long visionary poem, *Maḥberet ha-Tofet ve-ha-Eden,* a journey to Hell & Paradise modeled on that of Dante. He also worked, as here, in Italian; introduced the Petrarchan sonnet into Hebrew.

Page 526

"Stone of Choice." R.O.'s working based on a translation in I. Zinberg, *A History of Jewish Literature* (Case Western Reserve University, Cleveland, 1972), volume 2, page 224. Born in Provence, Kalonymos (called Maestro Calo) was active mostly in Italy as a poet & parodist. The quote that ends this poem is from the morning prayer service.

Page 528

"The Castle." J.R.'s working based on a translation in Jes P. Asmussen, *Studies in Judeo-Persian Literature* (E. J. Brill, Leiden, 1973) of Sahin's "Epic of King Kishvar." The name Kishvar (literally "region" or "country") is probably made up, & the work shares the fantastic side of Persian *poesis,* of which it is in fact a part. Sahin's own name means "the falcon."

Page 530

"Children of the Times." Previously unpublished working based on an earlier translation into German. Najara was born in Damascus & was associated with Luria's kabbalists in Safed; the Sabbateans later took him as a messianic-prophet.

Page 531

"A Charm Against Lilith." From the Hebrew text in G. Scholem, *Jewish Gnosticism, Merkabah Mysticism, & Talmudic Tradition* (Jewish Theological Seminary of America, New York, 1960), page 73. "She told him she was Lilith & that if he let her go she would teach him all her names. The names she wrote down were

LILITH	ABITR	ABITO	AMORFO
KKODS	IKPODO	AYYLO	PTROTA
ABNUKTA	STRIGA	KALI	PTUZA
	TLTOI-PRITSA.		

He told her he was Elijah." (Traditional amulet.) For more on Lilith as a "child-devouring female demon," etc., see pages 62, 182, above.

Page 532

"The Evil Eye (The Good Eye) Einehore." From *Alcheringa,* old series

(New York, 1973), number 5, pages 71–76; based on interviews with ten Yiddish-speaking informants in Toronto & Regina Lilienthal's "classic article" in *Yidishe Filologye* (1924). "To the magic of the Evil Eye that is black, we oppose one that is blue, not white. For the Eye that is good is of the color of the sky and watches over us with a mother's protective love." (E. Roditi.)

Page 534

"A Poem to Ease Childbirth." J.R.'s working after prose translation in J. Trachtenberg, *Jewish Magic & Superstition* (reprint by Atheneum, New York, 1970), page 200. "Rhymed charm against colic and labor pains, in which the bowels and the womb are directly apostrophized. . . . A contemporaneous Christian version conjures the *bermuoter* [= womb] by 'the sacred blood, the sacred day, the very sacred grave, the five holy wounds, and the three holy nails which were driven through the hands and feet of our lord Jesus Christ.'" (J.T.)

Page 535

"A Sabbatean Amulet." From French translation in M. Danon, *Amulettes Sabbatiennes* (Paris, 1910).

Page 536

"Sabbatai Zevi's Song for the Shekinah." Spanish text in M. Attias, *Romancero Sefaradi* (Jerusalem, 1961), pages 82–83. Part of an old ballad (*romance*) that Sabbatai Zevi had turned to his own purposes, singing it while dancing with the Torah in his arms. "Having invited the most prominent rabbis to a banquet, he erected a bridal canopy, had a Torah scroll brought in, and performed the marriage ceremony between himself and the Torah." (G. Scholem, *Sabbatai Ṣevi,* page 159.) See also above, page 606.

Page 537

"Children's Rain Songs." From French translation in Louis Brunot & Elie Malka, *Textes Judéo-Arabes de Fès* (Institute des Hautes Études Marocaines, Rabat, 1939), page 305. A series of songs sung by children in times of drought. Of other instances of same, Raphael Patai writes, in *Man & Temple:* "In Morocco the Jews send four children to the streets to march about holding the four edges of a white linen sheet. The children sing: 'The sheaf is thirsty / water it, O Lord!' & the people whom they pass pour water on the sheet." Similar events are recorded in the Babylonian Talmud, etc. (For more on Jewish rain-making, see pages 112, 470, above.)

Page 538

"Bride's Song Against Demons." J.R.'s working, after translation in Johanna Spector, "Bridal Songs & Ceremonies from San'a, Yemen," from R. Patai, F .L. Utley, & D. Noy (eds.), *Studies in Biblical & Jewish Folklore* (Indiana University Press, Bloomington, 1960), page 257. The "coloring" (henna) & bandages refer to the "Body Work" event on page 467, above. "Almost everywhere in the Muslim world, one of the feast days preceding the consummation of a marriage is set aside for the ritual dyeing of the bride's hands & feet with henna. . . . The true aim of the dyeing is probably . . . to protect against the evil eye." (*Encyclopedia of Islam.*)

Page 539

"Young Woman's Blues." J.R.'s working, after translation in Irene Garbell, *The Jewish Neo-Aramaic Dialect of Persian Azerbaijan* (Mouton & Company, The Hague, 1965), page 273.

Page 540

"Lullaby a Story." J.R.'s translation from the oral tradition.

Page 541

"The Thief's Play." Translation from Yiddish text in Noah Priluzky & Samuel Lehman, *Studies in Yiddish Philology, Literature & Ethnology* (Warsaw, 1926–33), volume 1, pages 287–90. An example of the non-biblical side of the folk theater (i.e., *Purim-shpil*) connected with the Purim holiday as Jewish equivalent to Carnival, etc.

Page 544

"O Night Lights of Jew Town." From David Cohen, *Le Parler Arabe des Juifs de Tunis* (Mouton & Company, The Hague, 1964), page 138. The *hara* was the Jewish quarter of Tunis, founded in the 10th century by the Muslim mystic Sidi Mahrez.

Page 545

"The Adventures of the Jew." From French translation in D. Cohen, *Le Parler Arabe des Juifs de Tunis* (Mouton & Company, The Hague, 1964), pages 141, 140. A similar culture hero turns up elsewhere as the Prophet Elijah, sometimes called "Der Yid."

Page 547

"Morphine." Direct translation from the German of Heine's poem. Born

Ḥayim or Harry, he became Heinrich & a Lutheran in 1825 as "an admission ticket to European culture." Lived in Paris after 1831, still moving as a "Jew" & outsider in the center & margins of post-Romantic Europe.

Page 549
"The Dream-Work." From S. Freud, *The Interpretation of Dreams* (Basic Books, New York, 1965), pages 489–90. The "dream-work" was Freud's own term for the process of dreaming & its resultant structure: a recovery of old lore but a model also for the dream poems of the Surrealists & others. His own take on the prose accounts he wrote & published ("the words which are put together in this way are no longer nonsensical but may form a poetical phrase of the greatest beauty & significance") was often aesthetic: a sense of form & a tendency to titles like "A Beautiful Dream," etc., but with awareness always of what Robert Duncan calls "the lowness of the story," not "theosophical" or "high-minded" as with Jung but truly "mythic." The commentaries in *The Interpretation of Dreams* do in fact read like a text on poetics (condensation, contraries, etc.) not unlike that projected in the present volume.

Page 550
"A Sonatina Followed by Another." From G. Stein, *Bee Time Vine* (Yale University Press, New Haven, 1953), pages 12–32, *passim.*

Page 552
"Prose Poem." From *The World,* special translation issue (The Poetry Project, New York, 1973), page 43. A major poet among the Cubists, etc., Jacob saw visions of Jesus & converted, 1915, to Catholicism. He retired to the monastery of Saint-Benoît-sur-Loire in 1921 & died (1944) in the Drancy concentration camp after four years in prison. "His conversion," writes Andrei Codrescu, "became, in retrospective, another illumination." (For more on the "prose poem" qua dream, etc., see the note on Freud, above.)

Page 553
"Fragment." From F. Kafka, *Dearest Father* (Schocken Books, New York, 1954), page 303. "What have I in common with Jews? I have hardly anything in common with myself & should stand very quietly in a corner content that I can breathe."

Page 554

"The Charlie Chaplin Poem." Direct translation from Russian, circa 1937. Mandelstam was exiled in 1934 for satirizing Stalin, thus: "the ten thick worms his fingers, / his words like measures of weight, / the huge laughing cockroaches on his top lip, / the glitter of his boot-rims // Ringed with a scum of chicken-necked bosses / he toys with the tributes of half-men / . . . he rolls the executions on his tongue like berries / wishes he could hug them like big friends from home." (Translation by Clarence Brown & W. S. Merwin.) Arrested a second time "for counter-revolutionary activities," he died in transit to an eastern prison.

Page 556

"Two Poems." From C. Reznikoff, *By the Waters of Manhattan* (New Directions, New York, 1962), pages 14, 25. " 'Objectivist.' images clear but the meaning not stated but suggested by the objective details and the music of the verse; words pithy and plain; without the artifice of regular meters; themes, chiefly Jewish, American, urban."

Page 556

"Cadenza & What We Can Learn from His Death." From J. Glatstein, *The Selected Poems* (October House, New York, 1972), pages 54–56.

Page 559

"Tristan Tzara." Translation of one of Tzara's "dada" manifestoes, from *The World,* special translation issue (The Poetry Project, New York, 1973), pages 52–53. "If words weren't anything but signs / postage stamps for all things / what would it all come out to / dust / empty gestures / waste of time / no agony no joy / in that odd world."

Page 561

"Her face the book of." From L. Zukofsky, *All: The Collected Short Poems 1956–1964* (W. W. Norton, New York, 1966), pages 63–64. The opening from Duncan goes on: "Yes, for I would have my share / in the discretion I read from certain jews, / not ἰδιώτης but standing apart . . ." & again of said "discretion": "separate, distinct, peculiar."

Page 563

"The Book of Questions." From E. Jabès, *The Book of Questions* (Wesleyan University Press, Middletown, Connecticut, 1976), pages 124–25. "So, with God dead, I found my Jewishness confirmed in the book, at the predestined spot where it came upon its face, the most grieved, the most unconsoled that man can have. / Because being Jewish means exiling yourself in the word and, at the same time, weeping for your exile." (E.J., *Elya*.)

Page 565

"Lyrics for the Bride of God." Poem 7 from the Invisible Bride section in N. Tarn, *Lyrics for the Bride of God* (New Directions, New York, 1975), pages 65–68. Long resident in Belgium, France, & Britain, Tarn came to the U.S.A. in 1968 & makes his home here. Of *sparagmos* he writes: "A Greek expression for rendering, tearing into pieces, mangling, applicable to the dismemberment of fertility gods (Dionysos, Orpheus) and, by extension, to the Crucifixion. In directions indicated by Northrop Frye, it extends, in my own work, to breaking or falling apart, to de-totalization: that is, any fragmentation of a whole into parts, of a structure into process(es) working towards the construction of new structures. Sparagmos, then, also as: the original form of exile, constitutive exile, exile in the world's bones (the breaking up of the primal skeleton) before there is any talk of persons, or the retrenchment of a part of the godhead so that room is left for creation. In this poem [above], exile is: whole/part; others/self; he/she; age/youth; original sin / last judgment; as well as a range of transexual voicings involving the Shekinah as x, y or z anywhere, anytime for anyone conscious of her. More precisely: the girl whom the Wandering Jew remembers distantly, he spanning all time in all directions to such an extent that his greatest fear is of being the one forgotten element in the ultimate re-structuration." (See also, above, pages 36, 38, 602.)

Page 569

"Paper Knights." Previously unpublished translation from Hebrew text in *Ma'ariv*, literary supplement for Rosh ha-shana 5736 (viz. 1975).

Page 572

"Zurich, zum Storchen." From P. Celan, *Speech-Grille & Selected Poems* (E. P. Dutton, New York, 1971), page 179. Celan's parents were killed in a German death camp, which he survived to become the first great postwar poet in the German language; later an exile & a suicide:

> We were, we are, we shall remain
> a Nothing,
> blooming:
> the Nothing-, the
> No-man's-Rose.

Would to God that all the Lords people
were Prophets
Numbers XI. ch 29 v.

חזק חזק ונתחזק
ḤAZAK ḤAZAK VENITḤAZEK
Strong Strong we make ourselves Strong

14 Sivan 5736
the day called "hand"

THIS IS THE END OF *A Big Jewish Book*